Action and Its Environments

Action and Its Environments

Toward a New Synthesis

Jeffrey C. Alexander

Columbia University Press

NEW YORK 1988

Library of Congress Cataloging-in-Publication Data

Alexander, Jeffrey C.
Action and its environments.

Bibliography: p.
Includes index.
1. Social structure. 2. Social action. 3. Social
structure—United States. I. Title.
HM24.A4647 1988   305   87–23910
ISBN 0–231–06208–7

Columbia University Press
New York   Guildford, Surrey
Copyright © 1988 Columbia University Press
All rights reserved

Printed in the United States of America

Clothbound Columbia University Press editions are Smyth-
sewn and printed on permanent and durable acid-free paper

Book design by Ken Venezio

*To my mother and father, Esther and Fred Alexander,
who balanced the internal and external
environments of action*

Contents

Preface

These essays have been prepared over the last eight years. They were produced occasionally, as the opportunity presented itself and the situation demanded. Like all contingent activity, however, these essays are specifications of broader commitments, not completely independent statements. That, at least, is the case I make in the introductory statement that follows.

Years ago Warren Hagstrom wrote that the scientific community rests upon the exchange of information for recognition. This still seems to me entirely apt. Every piece collected here was, at one time or another, presented in spoken form. From the direct responses of colleagues on these occasions I have greatly benefited. Because their number is great and because many were unknown to me, I can extend my gratitude only indirectly. Those who read and commented on these papers in draft form are directly acknowledged in the essays themselves.

It is customary when introducing collections of this sort for authors to say that, while various changes could have been made, they have preferred to reproduce them in their original form. My preference is much the same, but I must admit that, where alterations and additions have clearly been called for, I have made them. In only a few cases has this involved substantial change. For aesthetic purposes the system of annotations has been slightly altered. Most of the notes appear as footnotes, on the bottoms of pages. A few longer ones have been moved to the ends of the chapters.

During the period these essays were written I received substantial assistance from various scholarly agencies. To the Ford Foundation, John Simon Guggenheim Memorial Foundation, The Markle Foundation, and the UCLA Faculty Senate I would like, therefore, to record my gratitude.

I prepared the final versions of these essays as a member of The School of Social Science at the Institute for Advanced Study in Princeton, New

Jersey. The combination of bucolic repose and collegial riposte proved particularly stimulating.

With the exception of the paper on social structure, most of which was prepared in 1978, the publication dates of these papers reflect the approximate time of their actual composition.

Acknowledgments

"Social-Structural Analysis" (chapter 1) first appeared in *Sociological Quarterly* (1985) 25: 5–26 and is reprinted here by permission of the Midwestern Sociological Society.

"Core Solidarity, Ethnic Outgroup, and Social Differentiation" (chapter 3) first appeared in Jacques Dofny and Akinsola Akiwowo, eds., *National and Ethnic Movements* (1980), and is reprinted here by permission of Sage Publications.

"The Mass News Media in Systemic, Historical, and Comparative Perspective" (chapter 4) first appeared in Elihu Katz and Thomas Szecsko, eds., *Mass Media and Social Change* (1981) and is reprinted here by permission of Sage Publications.

"Three Models of Culture and Society Relations: Toward an Analysis of Watergate" (chapter 5) first appeared in *Sociological Theory* (1984) 3: 290–314 and is reprinted here with permission from the American Sociological Association.

"The University and Morality" (chapter 6) first appeared in *The Journal of Higher Education* (1986) 57: 463–476, and is reprinted here by permission of Ohio State University Press.

"Social Differentiation and Collective Behavior" (chapter 7) first appeared in *Sociological Theory* (1985) 3: 11–23, and is reprinted here by permission of the American Sociological Association.

"The Individualist Dilemma in Phenomenology and Interactionism" (chapter 8) first appeared in S. N. Eisenstadt and H. J. Helle, eds., *Macrosociological Theory* (1985) and is reprinted here by permission of Sage Publications.

"From Reduction to Linkage" and "Action and Its Environments" (chapters 9 and 10) first appeared in Alexander, Bernhard Giesen, Richard Munch, and Neil J. Smelser, eds., *The Macro-Micro Link* (1987) and is reprinted here by permission of University of California Press.

None of these essays have been republished in precisely their original form.

Action and Its Environments

Introduction

When social scientists look at society they are confronted with questions that seem vaguely familiar. They should be, since these are the questions that they themselves have asked. No doubt there is solipsism here. But society cannot tell itself. It is human beings who pose the questions. We establish the value commitments that make inquiry worth the trouble. We create the frameworks from which empirical studies are designed and on the basis of which we interpret our results.

What makes theorists different from other social scientists is their explicit attention to this question-asking process. If values and frameworks are essential, it would seem plausible that they become objects of reflection in their own right. This is one thing that theorists do. They also, of course, address themselves directly to society. When they do, they are particularly concerned with developing a general explanatory framework.

Although these essays clearly build upon foundations established in my earlier *Theoretical Logic in Sociology,* their focus differs in some important ways. First, they address themselves more to contemporary debates than to classical theorists. Second, while several essays remain primarily interpretive in intent, my efforts here are more directly empirical. I develop classifications, make definitions, build models, and offer explanations. Third, there is a more explicit ideological and political dimension to these essays. Finally, on questions that directly overlap with my earlier work I open up here some new theoretical ground.

My arguments in these essays revolve around the nature of social structures and social actions and their possible interrelation. These issues have a venerable history in the annals of social thought. In recent debates, they have become crystallized in a particularly vivid way. Vis-à-vis structure, the essays that follow criticize normative and materialist formulations; they redefine social structure in a multidimensional manner; and they illustrate how this dynamic and synthetic approach can illuminate a range of empirical problems. Vis-à-vis the problem of action, these essays criticize both exclusively micro and exclusively macro approaches. I argue that the centrality of contingency and historical specificity must be recognized but that the socially structured nature of action can never be overlooked. I develop a systematic model for integrating contingency and structure and, once again, apply this model to empirical concerns.

Why have the issues of structure and action become so central in recent debate? The answer, I think, is a historical one. Parsons, of course, tried to develop a synthesis that went beyond the action-structure split. Despite their fecundity and sophistication, however, his functionalist formulations were attacked and eventually defeated. Parsons' synthesis had serious weaknesses, to be sure; in my view, however, they had more to do with failure to meet his synthetic goal than with the nature of the goal itself. The problem is that in the course of the battle against functionalism, the very commitment to theoretical synthesis was thrown into doubt. In the wake of Parsons' decline, traditions that emphasized action and structure in one-sided ways assumed center stage.*

There are clear indications throughout Western sociology, however, that this protracted period of theoretical bifurcation may be coming to an end. A number of ambitious works have appeared, all of which aim at producing some form of theoretical reintegration. The recent writings of Giddens, Collins, and Habermas exemplify this new movement. My *Theoretical Logic in Sociology* had a similar goal. In the essays that follow, my focus is a bit different but my intent remains the same. My aim is to bring action theory and structure theory back together, in a postParsonian way.

I turn now to a brief consideration of these essays themselves. "Social-Structural Analysis: Presuppositions, Ideologies, Empirical Debates" was written before the others (although not published until 1984) and appears first in this book. In the course of surveying the most important classical and contemporary contributions to the structural debate, a general framework is established for thinking about the issues taken up in the essays that follow. I restate the case for a collectivist treatment of voluntary action. First, I contend that individual freedom—whether conceived of

---

*For this relationship between Parsons and his critics, see my *Twenty Lectures: Sociological Theory since World War II* (New York: Columbia University Press, 1987).

in epistemological, ideological, or empirical terms—cannot be opposed to the social structures that supposedly encumber it. The problem with arguments that insist on this opposition is that they ignore the role that social forces play in creating the capacity to be free. The actor's experience with his or her society actually forms the self. If freedom is to be conceptualized in a sociologically relevant way, therefore, it is the historically variable nature of this social experience, not the historically constant fact of individual contingency, that should become the object of study. It follows from this argument that social structures, the "forces outside" the contingent actor, must be understood as not only material but also moral and symbolic phenomena. How else could they be conceived of as having the capacity to form the interior self?

In the final part of this introductory essay I argue that, despite these limitations in the individualistic approach to freedom, there are real achievements to such theorizing that cannot be ignored. These achievements present a challenge to collectivist theory that must be pursued. "The conceptualization of these symbolic and material structures," I suggest in conclusion, "must be historically specific and, equally important, must be conceived in a manner that recognizes the continual possibility for their fundamental reformulation."

Articulation of a multidimensional theory of social structure and an approach to contingent action constitute two of the major preoccupations in the remaining essays that constitute this book. My opening essay introduces a third focus as well, for it pays special attention to the conditions for a democratic society. By democratic I mean to imply both Tocquevillian standards, liberty and equality. I discuss classical and contemporary arguments, then, not only as theories about structure and action but also as conceptions of modern social development. My concern here is empirical and ideological rather than analytical. Democratic societies can be sustained only in a pluralistic environment. What are the processes that allow a society's resources to be pluralized and what processes prevent this? In later essays I call this the problem of social differentiation.

There are, then, three central questions around which this collection of essays revolves: multidimensional social structure, contingent action, and democratic society. The major sections of this book parse these three questions in different ways. In the first group of essays I pursue the action-structure issue in the context of work primarily devoted to the conditions of social and cultural differentiation. In the section's first essay,

"Durkheim's Problem and Differentiation Theory Today," I lay out the rationale for what has become an extensive research program on social differentiation, defining the critical problems that this program must face. The four essays that follow—on ethnic domination, mass communications, the Watergate crisis, and university responsibility—reflect these concerns. They suggest that plural democracy is a highly uneven accomplishment and that even in the best of societies the resources for sustaining it are difficult to obtain. In "Three Models of Culture and Society Relations: Toward an Analysis of Watergate," I suggest, for example, that "progressive" and modernizing struggles often have unintended consequences. They polarize even democratic societies, and in doing so create forces that can undermine them in a variety of ways. The paradox is that differentiated institutions can sustain themselves only by continually creating such conflicts between values and groups. I document this necessity and develop a framework not only for explaining but also for evaluating it in my analysis of the university's collegial and corporate structures in "The University and Morality."

This empirical and ideological research program is permeated by my more general commitment to synthesizing material and ideal approaches to social structure.* In discussing media and ethnicity, for example, I place special emphasis on social solidarity, a realm that mediates between values and organizational power in distinctive ways. I am careful, however, not to allow this recognition of solidarity to obscure the role of self-interested conflict groups. In "Core Solidarity, Ethnic Outgroup, and Social Differentiation," I suggest that societies are founded by solidary core groups that try to maintain their power by defining the wider solidary community in their own ethnic terms. Because of this initial interpenetration of power and meaning, shifting ethnic hierarchies must be related both to the subjective responsiveness of core to outgroup and to the nature of the environment within which core and outgroup interact. In the companion essay, "The Mass News Media in Systemic, Historical, and Com-

---

*That differentiation theory need not always be associated with such theoretical commitments is well illustrated by the insightful work of Dietrich Rueschemeyer, whose *Power and the Division of Labor* (Stanford: Stanford University Press, 1986) filters what are basically similar empirical and ideological interests through a more traditionally materialist theory. For a volume of essays that exemplify the approach recommended here, see the articles collected in Alexander and Colomy, *Differentiation Theory and Social Change: Comparative and Historical Approaches* (New York: Columbia University Press, forthcoming).

parative Perspective," I argue that the media have an interpretive and solidarizing function but, at the same time, that media institutions are initiated by groups struggling to assert over other community members their singular interpretations. While I elaborate the often complex interchanges between solidarizing news media and institutions in other subsystems, I suggest that the media often remain fused with ambitious social groups in their struggle for domination. Even when relatively autonomous media emerge, moreover, their autonomy is continually threatened. Powerful institutions try to blackmail the media by withdrawing critical symbolic and material support, and they often succeed.

Alongside this multidimensional theory of structure there emerges in these essays an emphasis on contingency and action. In contrast to some vaguely evolutionary or purely functional argument, my approach here is historically specific. My focus is on social groups and real events. I talk about the actual foundings of ethnic societies, the interpretative ambitions of reporters, the indeterminate and ramifying outcomes of political crises, and the value interests that sustain university autonomy. A phenomenological subtext can also be seen. I emphasize the internal environment of ethnic relations, the typifying capacities of reporters, the ritualistic resourcefulness of senators, and the experience of moral violation of professors.

The second group of essays takes up the questions of structure, action, and differentiation in quite a different way. My focus here is much more metatheoretical. Political and empirical concerns about differentiation now take a back seat, entering the discussion only in the context of broader analytic, or "presuppositional," concerns. In the essay I prepared on social structure in 1978, I was pessimistic about the possibility for a new effort at theoretical synthesis. By the early 1980s it seemed to me that just such a new theoretical movement might well be underway.* If my treatment of differentiation can be seen as one reflection of this development, the essays in this second section just as clearly constitute a manifestation of another kind.

In this work I open an area that I left as a black box in my earlier *Theoretical Logic*. There my effort had been devoted to establishing the possibility for a social individualism. I argued that in order to do so

---

*I discuss this development in "The New Theoretical Movement," in Neil Smelser, ed., *Handbook of Sociology* (Los Angeles: Sage Publications, 1988).

individualistic theory was insufficient; instead, collectivist theories must be enlarged to include meaning and volition. In the wake of recent discussions about action and structure, however, it became apparent to me that a more appreciative response to individualistic theory must also be made. Contingent action itself must be theorized and related to cultural and material constraints. The challenge is to do this without resorting to the atomism and mechanism that often detracts from the synthetic efforts of theorists like Giddens and Collins or to the residues of romanticism and rationalism that affect Habermas' quite different synthetic attempts.*

In chapter 7, "Social Differentiation and Collective Behavior," Paul Colomy and I outline how the positive contributions of individualistic theory can, in fact, be brought directly into a systematic theory of social differentiation. In making explicit Eisenstadt's revisionist challenge to Parsons, we show that any satisfactory approach to differentiation must theorize contingent phenomena like social movements, leadership, and historical events. Just such theorizing can be found in the collective behavior tradition of symbolic interactionism. Building on a synthesis of collective behavior and differentiation theory, we go on to develop a series of propositions about the relationship between social movements, public opinion formation, and social change.

In the chapter that follows, "The Individualist Dilemma in Phenomenology and Interactionism," my argument becomes more exclusively concerned with presuppositions. I isolate what I take to be the critical differences between classical macro theorizing and the micro traditions of interactionism and phenomenology. While criticizing their reductionism, I reconstruct from the major pragmatist and phenomenological works the elements they contribute to a more balanced, synthetic approach. Contingent individual action must be seen, I argue, as an attempt to specify collective order in situations that cannot be predicted by broader patterns.

In the long essay that follows, "From Reduction to Linkage: The Long View of the Micro-Macro Debate," Bernhard Giesen and I generalize this

---

*See Alexander, "Habermas' New Critical Theory: Its Promise and Problems," *American Journal of Sociology* 91 (1985): 400–24. As Margaret Archer ("Structuration Versus Morphogenesis," in S. N. Eisenstadt and H. J. Helle, eds., *Macro Sociological Theory* [London: Sage Publications, 1985], pp. 58–88) has observed, Giddens' exaggerated separation of individuals from their environments is the other side of his frequent overemphasis on the coercive materiality of social structure.

discussion. Tracing the argument about contingency versus structure back to the historical situation in medieval times, we link it analytically to ontological and moral concerns. In the course of this extended theoretical discussion, five ideal-typical approaches to the micro-macro link have emerged. Once again, this exercise in interpretation serves theoretical ends. Our intent is to demonstrate the need for a model that can encompass each of these five emphases without endorsing the selectivity that follows when they are polemically embodied in one-sided general theories. "This can be achieved," we suggest in our conclusion, "on the basis of an emergentist, or collective, understanding of order, a multidimensional understanding of action, and an analytic understanding of the relations among different levels of empirical organization." In one sense this statement reiterates the conclusion I had reached in my essay on structure written some years before. What differs this time around is my understanding of how microtheorizing helps to explain the relationship between different levels.

My intent in the concluding essay, "Action and Its Environments," is to develop the model for which Giesen and I asserted the need. I argue that the contrasting concrete, empirical types of action envisioned by competing individualistic traditions can be reduced to analytic components of action as such. Conceptualizing contingent action as simultaneously strategic and interpretative, I differentiate the latter into typifying and inventive components. However, even when it is so reconceptualized in a multidimensional form, contingent action can never be equated with the behavior of the individual in an empirical sense. It, too, must be viewed analytically. Contingent action can be conceived, I believe, as occurring within collectively structured environments. Because two of these, the psychological and the cultural, constitute internal environments, they are rarely experienced by the actor as collective constraints. Indeed, they form the very self that experiences action as contingent. It is only the third, external environment—the social system—that readily appears to be outside the actor. For this reason, social systems have become, quite wrongly in my view, the main object of explanation in social science. Against this tendency, I would argue that because contingent action is meaningful, a more complex understanding of the nature and dimensions of meaning becomes central to any micro-macro link. This renewed attention to culture and meaning is also, of course, vital to the program for transcending reductionistic conceptions of social structure. For these reasons, a large part of this concluding is devoted to developing a new model of the structures and dynamics of cultural systems.*

The essays that follow speak for themselves or not at all. My aim in this introduction has simply been to suggest a broader context within which they may be read. Social theory is not, after all, entirely solipsistic. It cannot be, since the questions theorists ask are not entirely of their own making. They are variations on questions posed to them by their intellectual disciplines and communities. When theorists answer, they try for originality. But it is with the community's voice that they answer back as much as it is with their own.

---

*Indeed, there has recently emerged a series of programmatic calls for reinstating the centrality of culture in sociology. For two of the most far-reaching efforts, see Margaret Archer: *Culture and Agency* (London: Cambridge University Press, forthcoming), and Robert Wuthnow, *Meaning and Moral Order: Explorations in Cultural Analysis* (Berkeley and Los Angeles: University of California Press, 1987). Such work gives further evidence that a new theoretical movement is underway that seeks to go beyond the one-sided micro and macro theorizing of recent years. My own perspective on what the new cultural sociology should look like is further elaborated in Alexander, ed., *Durkheimian Sociology: Cultural Studies* (New York: Cambridge University Press, 1987) and Alexander and Steven Seidman, eds., *Culture and Society: Contemporary Debates* (New York: Cambridge University Press, 1988).

PART I

The Problem Stated

Social Structural Analysis: Presuppositions, Ideologies, Empirical Debates

Social scientists have begun to move away from the positivist and empiricist models within which they have traditionally conducted their behavioral studies. The change has been effected by the impact of historians of science like Koyré and Kuhn, and philosophers of science like Polanyi and Lakatos, and by the impact, as well, of the disruptive social developments that destroyed the ideological consensus of the postwar period. In the United States, however, this movement toward a postpositivist perspective is still very much confined to a small minority of social science practitioners. Indeed, it has been paralleled by a strong movement in an opposite direction, an increasingly self-confident scientism among the positivists and empiricists themselves. Thus, while postpositivist sensitivity has been increasing, we are still living with the fact that important disciplinary journals, like the *American Sociological Review,* have been transformed from broad intellectual organs into specialized outlets for a "scientific sociology" that is more concerned with verification, falsification, and deductive precision than with theory in a truly substantive sense. Nonetheless, the minority who now rejects positivism and empiricism is a vocal one, and it has an increasing impact on the various disciplines. This impact has coalesced around the idea of "paradigm," the concept Kuhn (1962) introduced to indicate the strong effect that nonempirical assumptions have on the very perception of empirical variables.

This essay investigates the impact of certain kinds of paradigmatic, or framing, elements on social science, specifically, the understanding that action is organized by structural constraints that are, in some sense, external to any particular actor. In order to place this discussion in its proper perspective, however, I must deal briefly with certain analytic problems in the term *paradigm* itself. There is, of course, an enormous literature on this issue; in the present context, I deal with it only as it relates to the particular problem at hand.

In his initial formulation, Kuhn defined a paradigm as a framework that provided scientists with preprogrammed information that reduced the normal task of empirical investigation to mundane acts of atheoretical problem solving. The "paradigm" is a jigsaw puzzle in which most of the pieces are already in place; the scientist examines reality only to find out how the three or four remaining pieces should be arranged. Yet, while apparently straightforward, this formulation actually obscured some important problems, problems that relate to Kuhn's tendency to exaggerate the unity of science. For while insisting that paradigms provide ready-made frameworks for research, Kuhn also identified paradigms with general metaphysical assumptions, like atomism or holism, and with particular kinds of models, like equilibrium or dynamic models. He associated paradigms, in other words, with both very general and very specific kinds of commitments, with philosophical orientations, and with complex propositions attached to strongly developed research strategies. Now if paradigms refer only to generalized orientations, they will not produce the scientific consensus that Kuhn assumed, for there is a great range of variation in the way general philosophical orientations can be specified. On the other hand, if paradigms refer only to agreement on propositions and research strategies—what Kuhn later called "exemplars"—then much of the richness of the original formulation is lost (Alexander 1982b); the excitement this seminal idea created was due, in large part, to the way it linked the metaphysical environment of science to changes in mundane research.

Kuhn's original formulation of paradigm, then, was undifferentiated. I am suggesting, by contrast, that paradigms contain a range of elements of different levels of generality. These elements, moreover, are not necessarily tied closely together. This issue is directly relevant to the task at hand. When we speak, for example, of rational choice theory, we are actually referring to a number of different levels of analysis. On the one hand, we are speaking of general assumptions about actors—that they are efficient and rational. On the other, we are talking about concrete theories within which these assumptions are made operational, theories associated with particular carrier groups rather than with diffuse traditions—"the British Utilitarians," "Simon's shop," Skinner's research team," "Tilly's group," "resource mobilization theory." Paradigms in social science operate forcefully at both general and specific levels of orientation. "Rational action," "normative action," and "social structure" function as philosophical orientations and as broad traditions that create the most general lines of division between different kinds of social scientific work. These traditions cross disciplinary lines, for their assumptions refer to presuppositional, analytical problems rather than to the empirical and ideological concerns that differentiate, for example, political science and sociology. At the same time, these three orientations are embodied, or made operational in "research programs" (for this term, see Lakatos 1969), in theories that have highly elaborated, empirically specified world views: for example, neoclassical economics, organization theory, symbolic interactionism, Marxism, and structural functionalism. For a discussion of structural analysis to be accurate and revealing it must address itself to both the general and specific dimensions of this term.[1]

The Problems of Action and Order

The most fundamental assumptions that inform any social scientific theory concern the nature of action and order (Alexander 1982a:62–112). Every theory of society assumes an image of man as an actor, assumes an answer to the question, "What is action?" Every theory contains an implicit understanding of motivation. Is it efficient and rational, concerned primarily with objective calculation? Or is it nonrational and subjective, oriented toward moral concerns or altruism, strongly affected, perhaps, by internal emotional concerns? The problem of action is concerned, in other words, with epistemology, with the relative materialism and idealism of action. Action has vexed and divided classical thinkers from Plato and Aristotle to Augustine and Hobbes, and it continues to do so today. Modern social science was born from the eighteenth- and nineteenth-century struggles between Enlightenment rationalists and traditionalists, and later between romantics and utilitarians. This struggle was, to an important degree, a fight about whether—and how—action was "rational."

No intellectual tradition, however, can be grounded in conceptions of action alone. We are concerned here with *social* theories, and every social theory must also be concerned about the problem of order. How is action arranged to form the patterns and institutions of everyday life? There have been two prototypical answers to this problem of order, the individualistic and the collectivistic. Society may be viewed as the product of negotiation freely entered into, as the result of individual decisions, feelings, and wants. On the other hand, we can view society as constituting, in Emile Durkheim's famous phrase, a reality sui generis, a reality "in itself." Such a collectivist view does not have to posit society as a metaphysical entity that has an ontological status. It can simply see individual decisions as aggregated through a long historical process: the decisions of those who came before us have become sedimented into institutions. When we make decisions today, we can do so only within the context of this social environment.

Every conception of order is necessarily informed by assumptions about action. If we adopt an individualistic approach, we must know whether these negotiating actors will evaluate one another in an objective or subjective way. If by contrast, we conceive of order as rooted in the collectivity, we shall want to know whether it asserts itself by appealing to rational interest or by promoting feelings of altruistic obligation. It is, of course, logically possible for theories to combine rational and nonrational modes of action; in practice, it is rare for them to do so.

Individualistic theories have exercised a powerful attraction on modern social science because they emphasize a quality at the heart of modernity itself: voluntarism. Modern social thought emerged out of the long process of secularization and rebellion against the hierarchical institutions of traditional society. In the Renaissance, Machiavelli emphasized the autonomy of the rational prince to remake his world. English contract theorists, like Hobbes and Locke, from whom so much of contemporary thought derives, also broke free from traditional restraints by emphasizing the individual bargaining upon which social order must depend. The same kind of path was followed by some of the principal thinkers of the French Enlightenment, who were the first to transform this new secular social thought into an attempt at empirically oriented science. Each of these individualistic traditions was strongly rationalistic. In different ways and with an emphasis on different kinds of individual needs—power, happiness, pleasure, security—each portrayed society as emanating from the choices of rational actors. Today these classical traditions have many progeny. The crucial conceptual bridge was Utilitarianism, particularly classical economics, for its theory of markets and resources provided an empirically elegant explanation of how individual decisions can be aggregated to form "societies." There is but a short step from the early Bentham to the organization theories of Simon (1964), the exchange theories of Homans (1961), the collective decision-making theories of Coleman (1966), and the political theories of Downes (1957).

Yet despite their origins in the secular rebellion against traditional thought, individualistic theories have also assumed a nonrational form. In its inversion of the Enlightenment and its revulsion against Utilitarianism, nineteenth-century Romanticism inspired theories about the passionate actor, for example, Wundt's social-psychological writing on the central role of emotional needs. Freud is the most famous modern exemplar of such Romantic theorizing, and the psychoanalytic perspective continues to supply one of the fundamental strands of individualistic thinking about society. Another, less scientistic branch of this antirationalistic movement issued is phenomenology, a movement that can be traced from Hegel, Schleiermacher, and Dilthey through Husserl to modern movements like existentialism. In terms of the social scientific paradigms that have concretized this kind of individualistic approach, one thinks of symbolic interactionism, the tradition rooted in the American pragmatism of Dewey, Mead, and Blumer, and in more recent years, of the theoretical developments of ethnomethodology, which takes its immediate intellectual roots from Husserl, Schutz and Heidegger.

But if individualistic theories have the great advantage of embodying the freedom we associate with the modern age, this is also their great weakness, for it seems that they have achieved voluntarism much too easily. Do actors really create social order by a process of purely individual negotiation? This, indeed, seems like an extremely unlikely proposition. Let us consider, for a moment, the problem of order and the rational actor. Are we really so rational that we can be aware of all the influences and constraints that enter into our decisions? We might think, perhaps, that we are simply trying to drive the best bargain with a salesperson for a new car, but is this negotiation completely unaffected by external factors, for example, by the size and variety of the particular dealership, the oligopolistic structure of the automobile market, or the government's regulation of production? These external factors, in turn, can be seen as the outcome of a vast range of other extraindividual facts, from the speed of technological innovation to domestic political struggles over ecology and revolutionary upheavals in the Middle East. Our individual negotiation, then, may appear to be confined to two parties, but it actually is constrained by a whole host of factors, which we, as individuals, have not negotiated at all. Our decision to buy an automobile will, moreover, create constraints for future actors: could any actor ever be so omnisciently rational as to follow out all the ramifications of this individual choice?

Thus far, I have confined my illustrations to individualistic approaches within the rationalistic tradition, but the same arguments can be made against individualism that takes a more nonrational form. Consider the actor as an emotional being who is conceived as dealing with the outside world in terms of personality needs. Are the personalities of actors their own, which they have developed purely as the result of their individual acts? Or is personality not itself the product of a lifetime of interaction, something in which the needs, wishes, and intentions of significant others have become synthesized and internalized to form a self? Emotionally sensitive actors, therefore, while appearing to respond to one another merely as individuals, actually are responding as two separate lines of social development. The same might be said for interactionist theories, like those of Goffman (1959), that stress the moral sensitivity of individuals to questions of face, propriety, and taste. These concerns, after all, are forcefully embodied in standards. Certainly individuals may negotiate in relationship to them, yet the standards themselves are never established by the individual interaction.

When we closely examine the most conscientious individualistic theories, we see, in fact, that they make assumptions about social structure that they do not actually theorize about: they leave them, rather, as unthought-out residual categories. Rational choice theories, for example, often assume a certain distribution of resources and a certain relationship of bargainers to one another; they assume, in other words, important facts about economic and political *structure*. Homans' writings on exchange admit that standards of distributive justice are critical, but he never explains how they come about. Coleman (1966) argues that collective structures can be seen as products of rational cost accounting, but he acknowledges that the conflict so produced must be regulated by certain givens like constitutions. Nonrational individualistic theories place similar brackets around the structuring of the symbolic world. They assume—without explaining—the aftereffects of socialization, the resources of cultural symbolization, the norms that define the nature of social solidarity.

Goffman (1961), for example, explains insanity as the product of the self-conceptions of the professionals who manage asylums, yet the sources of professionalization, and the reasons for the existence of asylums, are never discussed. In Garfinkel's (1981) later search for the ethnomethodology of individual orientation to the collectivity, he also leaves the normative order of the collectivity unexamined.*

The realization that individualistic theories cannot and do not stand without some reference to a collective order has always been the stimulus for social theory to move toward the perspective of social structure itself. Such a movement has occurred within both the orientations to action I have described. Hobbes [1982 (1651):98] was the first great theorist of social structure within the rationalist tradition, for he recognized that if society were actually composed only of rational and completely selfish individuals it would soon be destroyed.

And therefore if any two men desire the same thing, which nevertheless they cannot both enjoy, they become enemies; and in the way to their end, which is principally their own conservation, and sometimes their delectation only, endeavor to destroy, or subdue one another.

Hobbes formulated a conception of an all-powerful sovereign, the Leviathan, which would counteract this imminent chaos of individualism through intimidation and hierarchical control. The parallel for this breakthrough in the normative tradition can be found in Durkheim's critique of Spencer, the nineteenth-century individualistic social scientist par excellence. Durkheim argued against Spencer's contract theory in terms that strongly recalled Hobbes. "If interest relates men," Durkheim [1938 (1893):203] wrote, "it is never for more than some few moments . . . [and] each individual finds himself in a state of war with every other." It was to counter such "provisory and precarious" contractual relations that Durkheim created his conception of the "collective conscience," the normative center of society that controlled individualism by penetrating and socializing individual consciences. From Hobbes' Leviathan and from Durkheim's collective conscience every modern theory of social structure can be logically derived.

*For an analysis of the persistence of striking residual categories in individualistic non-rational theories, see chapters 8 and 9, below.

Social Structural Theory in
Its Instrumental Form

The revolt against individualistic instrumental explanation in the nineteenth century always occurred for ideological, as well as for analytic, reasons. The first great theories that placed rational action within a collective context were those of Bentham and his Utilitarian followers. Bentham (see Halévy 1972 [(1901–04)]) saw through the facile assumption of the "natural identity of interest" by which classical political economy justified its purely individualist argument. Realizing that economic and political actors actually possessed unequal power and wealth—and that, consequently, no "invisible hand" would ever produce consensus and equilibrium—Bentham argued that government must act to reformulate the social context in which such action occurs. The identity of interests, if it were ever to be achieved, must be one that is artificially constructed by such external force. Bentham used this theoretical argument to suggest aggressive reforms of criminal law and state bureaucracy, and there is a direct link between his structural orientation and the social and historical theorizing about the effects of the capitalist social structure that Fabian writers produced at the end of the century.

The greatest theorist of social structure in the instrumentalist tradition, however, was Marx. If his critique followed the general lines of Bentham's, it carried the logic much further; indeed, it translated the general social structural argument into an empirically specific theory, or exemplar, which in one form or another would dominate this strand of structural thinking throughout the twentieth century. Marx refuted the argument that society is the product of individual exchange. It is not simply a bargain between two individuals that determines the contract of labor, he wrote, or even the aggregation of individual decisions through an impersonal market. The labor contract, he insisted, was determined by a peculiarly coercive kind of social structure that issues from the concentration of private wealth: capital. "Capital," Marx wrote (1963 [1844]:85), "is the power of command over labor and its products."

The capitalist possesses this power, not on account of his personal or human qualities, but as the owner of his capital. His power is the purchasing power of his capital, which nothing can withstand [ibid].

Social structure, in Marx's view, affected action by fixing in advance its material environment. Since actors are rational, their behavior will follow the structure of this external environment just as response follows stimulus. Marx's capitalism is a tightly interdependent system within which economic exigencies set the pace. He specified the function of the economy as ever more efficient production, and these productive demands established the individual role structure of capitalist society. The other institutions in his system were the bourgeois state and ideology, yet as "superstructures" they performed tasks that were subordinated in complex ways to the demands of capital. Human beings entered this social structure in their role as members of classes, groups of like-minded individuals who performed the same general kind of economic tasks. Role relations reflected this systemic hierarchy: capitalists dominated proletarians as the economic base dominated the superstructure. Yet although Marx emphasized social structure over voluntary negotiation, he did not view his system in a static way. To the contrary, capitalism was driven by contradictory functional requirements, contradictions that produced a struggle for existence between workers and capitalists and, eventually, the transformation of the capitalist system itself.

Marx set the tone for subsequent rationalist theorizing about social structure. Even those who "secularized" his work by neutralizing its revolutionary, chiliastic spirit followed closely his general logic. The greatest among these ambivalent secularizers, the man who has been called the "Marx of the bourgeoisie" and the only twentieth-century thinker whose contributions to the rationalist tradition rank with Marx's own, was Max Weber. Although we will see in a following section that Weber also made an effort to criticize instrumentalist thinking, his contributions are as much to the Marxian tradition as to any other.

Weber carried Marx's approach to social structure from the economic into the political realm and carved out independent structures of stratification and conflict that Marx had never imagined. Weber (1946:196–244) insisted that bureaucracy is a coercive structure every bit as powerful as economic systems. Bureaucracy responded to demands for administrative efficiency much as economic structures like markets, factories, and contracts respond to needs for productive efficiency. Bureaucratic roles, like economic ones, follow from those external demands: if capitalism demanded competition and exploitation, bureaucracy demanded impersonality and rationality. Bureaucracy created order through political domination from above and passive subordination from below, a structure, once again, that followed the logic if not the empirical content of Marx's earlier model. If Weber gave any functional system dominance, it was the political sphere within which he discovered this bureaucratic force, and where Marx analyzed precapitalist societies in terms of their economic arrangements, Weber (1968:1006–1111) defined feudalism as a system that created certain distinctive political conflicts. Yet he emphasized that social systems, particularly modern ones, are never ruled by one form of external sanction alone. Weber (1946:180–95) described three hierarchical domains, those of class, status, and power. Each hierarchy of control structured instrumental rewards in a distinctive way, and each was the scene of struggles for different kinds of power. People could use a surplus in one kind of goods, moreover, to increase their power by exchanging this surplus for goods of another type. They could trade money for prestige, as the nouveau riche do when they train their offspring to enter the professions or the arts. They could, on the other hand, exchange power for money, as corrupt politicians and bureaucrats do when they enrich themselves through political office. In each case, the motivation is instrumental, but the bargaining proceeds within highly structured systems of stratification (for a good empirical application, see Azarya [1978]).

The theoretical legacies of Weber and Marx have framed modern instrumentalist explanations of social structure. Although each theory retains its orthodox adherents, more often there has been a more or less conscious melding of the two. The most important contributions have followed Marx and Weber in their concentration on economic and political systems and these systems' effects on role stratification and conflict. Arguments about the economy have focused on whether the functional exigencies of capitalism have changed, and if they have, what new role structures and social conflicts result. There has been general agreement that in its late stage capitalism has shifted toward capital-intensive production that involves more mental than physical labor, labor that relies, in turn, increasingly upon education. On more specific levels, however, there has been vast disagreement about the shape that these new external conditions take: (1) Is "capitalism" still a relevant way of describing these conditions? (2) If so, does property ownership continue to be decisive in structuring role position and conflict? (3) If not, what structures and forces remain?

Because Goldthorpe and Lockwood (1963) argue that property ownership is still primary for structuring economic roles, they can argue that the new privatism and individualism of ideological *embourgeoisment* is braced by an ideological collectivism. This collectivism, they argue, becomes more widespread as the newly created classes are forced—because of their propertylessness—to enter the trade union movement. Baran and Sweezy (1966) agree that economic production in Western societies is "capitalist," and they link this capitalist character to the external exigencies of private property. For them, however, ownership and, indeed, wealth distribution become largely irrelevant; profit maximization and wasteful surplus are the primary "structures" of later capitalist society, and they produce social conflict on qualitative rather than quantitative grounds. Braverman (1974) elaborates these qualitative consequences, arguing that capitalism's destruction of worker's skills constitutes the "objective" conditions within which any working class action must be understood. Wright (1978) continues the movement away from property ownership as such; he articulates the structural, antisubjective constraints of capitalist society in a differentiated and specific way, emphasizing the contradictory, ambiguous character of various class positions. These contradictions are, however, thoroughly "external." They are the product of advanced economic development, and the class conflict they produce is structured by changes in differential interest in turn.

"Critical theorists" and other structuralists have articulated these economic changes in a less orthodox way. Marcuse (1964) views the productive power of late industrial capitalism as bursting the economic barriers of private property itself; he sees its unlimited affluence and technical control as blurring the capitalist/socialist distinction and as anesthetizing potential conflict over economic roles. Other theorists, like Bell (1973), have deemphasized the significance of the "capitalist" element in a more liberal direction, describing recent economic development as a movement toward a postindustrial society that will have the same basic structural characteristics whether capitalist or socialist: the decline of manual labor as a volatile force, the growth of work that centers on abstract knowledge, and the growing centrality of political decisions in a society whose security and progress depend more on the quality of the public ethic than on economic organization. Lipset and Bendix (1959) contributed to this anti-Marxist theory of economic structure by suggesting that economic mobility depends simply upon the complexity of the economic division of labor rather than upon the capitalist or socialist framework within which this division occurs. Treiman (1977) makes this argument much more elaborate and precise, producing a "structural theory of prestige" that aggressively denies any independent role to cultural causation.

Modern debates over the state have taken economic development as a parameter, focusing instead on the possibility for democratic participation in a capitalist system whose unequal economic opportunities are taken as given. The theoretical assumptions are, however, the same: first, the objective resources available to actors will determine the course of political events; second, the course this particular social structure—the state—sets will determine the course of the rest of society. Empirical argument centers around the tightness of the link between economics and politics, whether and how political actors are subordinated to the needs of dominant economic classes. Within the Marxist camp, Domhoff (1967) has taken the orthodox view that capitalists reproduce themselves directly in the corridors of power; there is one homogeneous "ruling class," which has an economic and a political branch. By contrast, while Miliband (1969) sees the state as completely devoted to capitalist needs, he emphasizes the relative indirection of this process: the importance of factors like differential educational opportunities to bureaucratic recruitment and the inevitable dependence of the state on corporate funds. O'Connor (1973) takes this argument further, suggesting that the contradictions of modern capitalism will take the form of the fiscal crisis of the state.

Another tradition of contemporary political theorizing, less directly Marxist, comes out of Mills' argument that the coercive power over society is really a "power elite" that fuses military, political, and economic power. This elite, in Mills' (1959) view, is composed of those who control the functional exigencies of these different sectors rather than of members of a hereditary upper class. Yet the actors who fill these functional directorships are subsequently interrelated through a complicated system of revolving directorships, intermarriages, and social clubs. Mills' argument has been challenged, or at least empirically specified, by sociologists, like Bottomore (1974: 132–43), who make the issue of elite recruitment into the government bureaucracy an issue that varies in different capitalist countries. Lindbloom (1977), by contrast, has recently argued that the structural independence of different elites is partly neutralized by the necessary reliance of the state on financial resources in private, corporate hands. Skocpol (1979) has made a broadly similar argument for the "relative" autonomy of state and economy in revolutions. But this institutional autonomy, she makes clear, has nothing at all to do with the autonomy of individual actors in a presuppositional sense. Describing her theory as a "nonvoluntarist, structural perspective," she links her explicit exclusion of individual effort and goals to the elimination of ideology as a cultural force.

The line of thought that actually led to a more exclusively political view of state control began with Michels' (1949 [1911]) argument—strongly influenced by Weber—that political power had to be sharply differentiated from the economic. Michels insisted, nonetheless, that any organizational elite was bound to monopolize political resources to ensure its continued domination. While Selznick (1957) agreed that fragmented patterns of participation often allowed organizational elites to rule unopposed, he expressed confidence that certain kinds of organizational resources, like leadership, could encourage more effective participation and more responsive power. Lipset and his colleagues (1956) argued that norms assuring the opportunity for electoral challenge would structure the self-interest of outgroups in a manner that would lead them to challenge entrenched elites. And Bendix (1964) and Lipset (1963) both emphasized that the effect of constitutional government in Western nations was to produce a "democratic class struggle" in which the formerly oppressed masses could now participate strongly in their own government. Aron (1960) took the argument for a pluralist political structure to its most extreme form, suggesting that far from enslaving modern society to the exploitation of a primordial ruling class, the extraordinary differentiation of modern society has produced a situation in which functional exigencies cannot be coordinated by any overarching group. The result, he believed, is a dangerous stalemate between different elites of roughly equal power.

The instrumental version of the social structural paradigm has, then, taken a number of different concrete forms, shaped by different kinds of successful research strategies and by different political ideologies. It has, of course, been applied to a wide range of subjects that I do not have space to mention—to education, to race relations, to mass communication, to law—but the basic theoretical logic informing such various efforts is the same. The great accomplishment of instrumental structuralism is to demonstrate that individual action is strongly affected by the material context within which it occurs, but this very achievement points also to the tradition's great weakness. For by assuming that actors are efficient calculators of their own material environment, the instrumental approach to social structure makes action largely subservient to external control.

Now, the antivoluntaristic implications of this general position can be modified by certain empirical propositions. For example, while theorists may assume that actors are rational and directed by external constraints, they can describe these constraints in a way that makes them extremely pluralistic (e.g., Aron). Actors in such a pluralistic society will then have a relatively wide choice among different material options. Thus, although any specific actor will be described in a way that eliminates reference to internal volition and will, the situation of modern society as a whole can be described in a voluntaristic way.*

On the whole, however, the social structural paradigm in its instrumental form denies the possibility of individual control. While it has clearly articulated the darker side of modernity, it has obliterated another side that can scarcely be ignored—the feeling that modernity has opened up a vast, almost uncontrollable range of individual freedom and responsibility at the very center of society. After all, we may agree with Hobbes that individualistic approaches to order are figments of the analytical imagination without deferring to his belief that the alternative to individualism must assume a purely material form. There is a different way of conceptualizing the action that informs collective order, one that avoids this difficulty. I now turn to this normative approach.

Social Structural Theory in
Its Normative Form

The aim of the normative approach to social structure has been to allow for collective order without eliminating the consideration of individual control. This can be accomplished, however, only if the individual is viewed in a manner that is not rationalistic. Only if theorists are sensitive to the internal components of action, to the actor's emotions and moral sensibilities, can they recognize that social structure is located as much

---

*This is precisely the option that Blau's (1977) social structural theory allows. On the one hand, the structures Blau identifies—the inequality of power and the size and heterogeneity of groups—are conceived to be physically external to the individual actor. On the other hand, Blau suggests that under certain empirical conditions these structures allow the individual—indeed, to be more precise, they force him or her—to make choices among a wide variety of options. The fact that this possibility exists within an instrumentally structuralist theory illustrates, once again, the need for a conception of paradigm in which specific research programs and ideologies are given autonomy vis-à-vis more general philosophical assumptions.

within the actor as without. Only with this recognition can social theory make the individual a fundamental reference point without, at the same time, placing him outside his social context.

Although we can go back to earlier nineteenth-century theorists, it was Durkheim who translated the logic of anti-Utilitarian Romanticism—and the antimechanistic strand of Enlightenment thought—into its modern sociological form. For Durkheim, the emotional bonds of social solidarity and the symbolic codes of social morality were the fundamental social structures from which all others emerged. These structures, moreover (1973 [1898]), protected the independence of the individual rather than eliminated it. On the one hand, Durkheim insisted on the collective status of moral facts as "things" external to isolated individuals. At the same time, he argued that individuals themselves were social beings, and these "moral things" were precisely what gave him his very sense of individuality (see, e.g., Durkheim 1951 [1897], 1958 [1896], 1961 [1903], 1915 [1912], 1957 [1900]).

Durkheim developed an intricate theory of social structure that inverted the base-superstructure of Marx and challenged the belief that a theoretical emphasis on social morality had to share the conservative ideology of traditional society. At the heart of society Durkheim found a system of beliefs, symbols representing collective moral commitments. This symbol system had a distinctive kind of organization, for it articulated and, indeed, enforced morality by dividing symbols into contradictory patterns of sacred and profane and by encasing sacred symbols in rituals that made violation sacrilegious. Despite its clear reliance on the forms taken by traditional and primitive religion, Durkheim believed that his theory of the symbolic core of society applied equally to secular modernity. The content of symbolic systems can change, but the form does not.

Modern society, Durkheim believed, is centered around a diffuse civic morality that emphasizes the rights of individuals in a highly abstract, generalized way. This "religion of individualism," Durkheim insisted, permeates modern life. Particular social roles evolve when different institutions "specify" this moral individualism. Schools, for example, inculcate rationality, individualism, and discipline through the powerful pedagogy of the dedicated teacher. The state also reinforces individualism, for its differentiated institutional status vis-à-vis general morality allows "representation" to focus public opinion, to define different perspectives more sharply, and to develop a morality that can be rationally related to specific situations. Other secondary groups produce different morally regulated roles. Occupational associations, like the professions, translate the abstract obligations of individual rights into economically appropriate forms, and the legal system develops an elaborate system of justice to articulate such rights in every possible situation. In times of crisis, Durkheim believed, consciousness would withdraw from these restricted roles and embrace the social, i.e., moral, whole. In such periods, society would be reintegrated through ritualistic ceremonies like rallies, speeches, and marches. Such periods of "collective effervescence" would revivify the moral structure.

Durkheim's work, then, formulated a complex economy of moral obligations. Much as Marx had viewed morality as a superstructure irrelevant to the material base, Durkheim relegated economic factors and the political struggle for material rewards to an equally inconspicuous position. He was not conservative. He too perceived a "crisis of modernity" (see Seidman 1983), but it was a crisis of moral rather than material scope. He recognized the often destructive egoism and conflict in modern life but insisted they could be counteracted only by a moral regeneration that could restructure the internal environment of action.

Although Durkheim created a powerful school before the First World War, his legacy to contemporary social science has been more indirect than Marx's. In the interwar years Durkheim's impact was limited to anthropology. British functional anthropologists like Radcliffe-Brown (1952) studied morality in its complicated interaction with specific institutions, but the more recent movement of French "Structuralist" thought centered around Lévi-Strauss (1966) has concentrated on the internal patterns that Durkheim described in the symbolic order itself. This symbolic Structuralism, indeed, provides the best possible illustration that the social structural paradigm can assume a subjective, as well as objective, form (see, e.g., Sahlins 1976). In most Structuralist analysis, movement and change is considered to be generated by the internal contradictions of the symbolic system itself. In Douglas' (1966) reformulation of Durkheimian theory, however, the binary polarities of culture take on a more specifically moral tone, and the opposition between pure and impure is related to group conflicts in the social system itself. Turner (1969, 1974; cf. Moore and Meyeroff 1975), in turn, has pushed the anti-Structuralist revival of such Durkheimian theory more toward a renewed consideration of solidarity and ritual process, and Shils' (1975) post-Parsonian writings on sacred charisma as the source of social structure revises Durkheim in much the same way. Sewell's (1980) work, on the centrality of ideas about, and forms of, fraternal solidarity to the working class struggles of postrevolutionary France, continues this return to a more socially sensitive Durkheimianism, posing an illuminating contrast to "structural" analyses of revolution of the more instrumental type (e.g., Skocpol 1979).

Despite this recent revival, however, the fundamental reference point for the Durkheimian tradition in contemporary sociology and political science remains the work of Talcott Parsons. Later we will see that Parsons offered a significant synthesis of the idealist-materialist traditions, but his thinking contained a strong strand of idealist theorizing as well. In terms of this dimension of his work, Parsons' theory (Parsons 1964, Parsons and Bales 1955) functioned to specify and elaborate normative structure in a manner that Durkheim himself never approached. Where Durkheim had merely asserted the complementarity of individual consciousness and cultural order, Parsons developed a philosophically sophisticated and empirically specific analysis of the "socialization" of the individual. The process centered on the internalization of moral symbols in a wide range of learning situations, in families, in early schooling, in higher education, in work, and in play. To accomplish this analysis, Parsons performed the critical integration of Freud's personality theory with the Durkheimian theory of morality and demonstrated that the individuating process that Freud called ego development could also be seen as the inclusion of the individual into the system of moral regulation. Yet the other side of this symbiosis was just as crucial, for Parsons insisted that in modern society moral integration itself depends on individuation, on the progressive differentiation of the individual person from authoritarian controls, either moral or material.

From the Parsonian perspective, therefore, social structure marked the intersection between culture and socialization, and differentiated roles were created by understanding how socialization and culture came to be particularized in different situations. Parsons (e.g., in Parsons and Shils 1951: part 2) defined five different dimensions along which cultural definitions could vary, which he called the "patttern variables." The pattern variables structured situations in terms of the emotional control and symbolic universalism they demanded, and although the particular pattern-variable combination responded to the functional exigencies of particular institutions, it was responsive also, and independently of any practical consequences, to the religious and cultural history of the nation within which these institutions were embedded. Levy (1949) used the pattern variables to describe the conservative impact of the Chinese familial values on economic development, and Lipset (1963) employed them to argue that the traditionalism and particularism of French and German cultural structures explained the difficulty of their political development and class relations. Barber (1952) and Merton (1973 [1942]) talked about the cultural regulation of science through universalistic norms, and Pitts (1974) described the hippie movement as an emotional, particularistic cultural reaction against the universalistic, antiaffective cultural norms of the meritocracy. Almond and Verba (1963) used Parsons' cultural theory to explain the degrees of democratic activism in different Western political systems. Bellah (1970:168–89) linked the relative solidarity and progressiveness of American politics to the intensely universalistic American "civil religion." Deutsch (1963) elaborated the Parsonian theory of culture to outline the delicate cybernetic "communication" between morality and government.

The empirical foci of normative structuralism demonstrate how different assumptions about action create their own distinctive questions about social development, even if these theoretical orientations take an equally collectivist approach and are equally committed to a humanistic and liberal order. Since the instrumental structuralists give to the economy a determinate power, they have devoted considerable energy to the internal evolution of industrial economies in the twentieth century. Normative structuralists, in their turn, have focused on recent cultural changes, particularly on whether the process of secularization—which deprives institutions of a common religious base—must necessarily create a society without any moral coordination or solidarity at all. This transition toward a morally disciplined secularism is accomplished, they argue, if moral codes become abstract and generalized and if their substantive focus shifts to the "individual" and away from any particular group. In this way, the rationality of secular thinking can be achieved without sacrificing meaning or soliarity (e.g., Parsons 1969:439–73). Yet this achievement is not only cultural, these thinkers have discovered; it depends also on a vast network of internal psychological controls that can be established only through an excruciatingly long process of socialization. Because this process makes heavy demands on the individual for ego autonomy and self-denial, alienation is always a possibility, and with it a return to the security of group-oriented, particularistic morality (Weinstein and Platt 1969: chapter 7; Parsons 1954:298–322).

Instrumental structuralists link economic freedom to separating economic modernization from private property; for normative thinkers, freedom depends on separating cultural modernization from the debilitating effects of particularistic morality and psychological regression, from structural constraints that produce the in-group/out-group morality of ethnic and religious war. Instrumental structuralists study the processes by which the democratic state gains autonomy from the economy and the uneven relationships between political and economic sectors. Normative theorists study how "rational" or cognitive codes become differentiated from moral and expressive ones (Geertz 1973:193–233), and they try to understand what the optimum balance should be between each kind of cultural thinking. Should law, for example, be completely independent of religion? Should the cognitive science of the university be radically separated from other cultural concerns like morality and art (Parsons and Platt 1973:304–45)? Do professional ethics have to be oriented more to technical, cognitive questions than moral ones; do they have to conflict, in other words, with civic morals (Durkheim 1957 [1900])? Instrumental thinkers study how the material aspects of social structure can overcome the invidious aspects of stratification by promoting economic mobility and political pluralism. Normative structuralists, by contrast, locate the sources of equality in the interface between culture and socialization. Equality depends, in their view, on the degree to which the universalistic and rational codes of education can penetrate the traditionalism and passivity of "family values," shifting the course of socialization to a path emphasizing independence rather than deference. The new emphasis on universalistic knowledge also creates the possibility for more collegial and egalitarian relationships within organizations (Parsons 1971:86–121), since professional relationships based on achievement and skill increasingly supersede authority based on inherited wealth or arbitrary power. This increased equality depends, in their view, on the continuing vitality of a solidarity that institutionalizes feelings of civil obligation (Alexander 1980, Prager 1982).

If instrumental structuralists demonstrate the impact of the material environment on individuals, normative thinkers just as forcefully indicate that action is regulated by moral structures internalized in the personalities of individuals. Normative structuralism demonstrates, moreover, that a "social" approach to action does not necessarily have to neglect the contributions of the individual, the nature of his or her inner emotion and the extent to which collective order depends upon his or her voluntary participation. Yet this very attention to voluntarism also reveals the weaknesses in a purely normative view. If structure is taken only as a normative, the impression is created that society depends entirely upon the voluntary acquiescence of its members, even if this acquiescence itself is informed by internalized symbols. It ignores, in other words, the very real possibility that material structures can enforce an order whether or not individuals participate or morally approve. Further progress in structural analysis depends upon the successful integration of these antithetical theoretical traditions and the various research programs they have informed.

The Social Structural Theory in
Its Multidimensional Form

Weber and Parsons both produced conceptualization of social structure that moved beyond the dichotomous traditions to which they also contributed. Weber's best known multidimensional theory focused on the notion of "legitimation" (1968:212–301). Weber described political power as involved in a constant dialectic of belief and effectiveness. If power is accepted as subjectively legitimate, it has authority, not just strength. Since authority is a matter of belief, it must be linked to cultural codes, so there must be a relationship between the history of a political development and religious evolution (ibid:399–634). The universalistic theology of monotheistic religions, for example, contributed to the emergence of impersonal, "rational-legal" norms of political legitimacy, and the rise of bureaucratic political structures contributed to the evolution of more universalistic religions in turn. Although Weber himself rarely made these explicit connections between religion and politics (see, e.g., Alexander 1982c), his formal definitions pointed in this direction and the extraordinary catholicity of his historical investigations certainly supplied the material.[2]

Where Weber did make the link between material and normative structure clear and explicit was in his discussion of social class. Weber

(1968:468–599; 1946:267–301) accepted Marx's argument that the labor performed by different classes made them more or less susceptible to different ideological orientations, but he insisted that any particular orientation must be viewed as the product of specific religious and cultural factors in the class' environment. He demonstrated, for example, that the political and economic ethics of urban strata have varied greatly in different civilizations and that the revolutionary ideology of the Western bourgeoisie was as much a product of Judeo-Christian eschatology as of economic rationalization. It was just this multidimensional intention that inspired Weber's famous investigation into the relation between the Protestant ethic and the "spirit of capitalism." Walzer's (1965) more recent illumination of the symbiotic relationship between the rising English gentry and the alienated Puritan clergy that helped to trigger the English Civil War continues this multidimensional approach to structure, as does Bendix's (1964) discussion of the interrelationship of economic and religious factors in the modern proletariat's struggles for citizenship. Eisenstadt's studies (1978) examine how revolutionary transformation depends on certain unique conjunctures of cultural development and political-economic conditions.

Parsons' multidimensional theorizing was inspired by Webeis, and in the most successful strand of his work he combines Durkheim's with Weber's insights to produce a fundamental revision of social theory. Idealist and materialist thinking can be transformed, Parsons understood, only if social structures are viewed in an analytic rather than a concrete way. Every structure, no matter how apparently material or ideal, is actually a product of forces representing both kinds of pressures. For the social system, Parsons (see Parsons and Smelser 1956) identified four primordial dimensions: the economic, concerned with maximizing efficiency and "means"; the political, focused on organization and "goals"; the solidary, representing direct emotional bonds and "norms"; and the pattern-maintenance, oriented to stable symbolic patterns and "values." Parsons called these four dimensions subsystems, arguing that each is in a continuous interchange with the other three. The state, for example, needs economic resources, but it also needs the legal legitimation and cultural meaning provided by norms and values. If the state is to receive these "inputs," however, it must produce the kinds of "outputs"—the kinds of political decisions—that the other systems need in turn. From this perspective, the state can be seen as the single, concrete product of a number of different analytic dimensions, although it combines these dimensions with its own particular goal.

By conceptualizing reciprocity and conflict between the ideal and material dimensions of society—indeed, their symbiosis and fundamental interpenetration (cf. Münch 1981)—Parsons transformed the dichotomous orientation that has polarized and diminished the social structural approach. Smelser (1959) used the interchange model, for example, to show how factory reorganization in the early phases of industrialization created social crisis because of the way it affected family relations and how this disruption, in turn, was resolved by political developments, as well as by changes in solidary groups. Eisenstadt (1963) used interchange, on a more informal level, to formulate the complex interrelationship of religious rationalization, economic development, normative evolution, and political leadership that created the first great bureaucratic empires. Easton (1965) used interchange in an implicit way in his effort to build a systematic portrait of political life interweaving material demands and cultural support.

Although Parsons did not always do so, it is clear that this interchange model can subsume his insights that normative structure represents the interpenetration of culture and personality. The most important product of this synthesis is his conception of the "generalized media" of exchange, which represents his most direct response to the bargaining model of instrumental individualism (cf. Münch 1983). When people confront each other in interaction, Parsons asks, what kind of sanctions do they have at their disposal? He identifies four "media" of exchange—money, power, influence, and value commitments—each of which can be seen as a product of one of the four subsystems of society. On the one hand, individuals manipulate these sanctions in an instrumental and self-interested way to gain their ends; on the other hand, each of these sanctions is a complex product of the larger exchange between institutions within which interaction is embedded. Chalmers Johnson (1966) has demonstrated that revolutionary change is always preceded by a gross deflation of the value of legitimate power sanctions, so that political leaders can no longer bargain effectively for their ends. Smelser (1971) has also focused on power, showing how political corruption represents the degeneration of the power sanction created by an overreliance on money in relationship to influence, value commitments, and political power in the interchange process.

The Mertonian tradition of postwar functional theory also elaborated a multidimensional conception of social structure that tried to incorporate the warring schools. While Merton (e.g., 1968:86–88) tried to define structure in an empirical and agnostic way without reference to paradigmatic schools, he was clearly inspired in this synthetic effort by Weber and Parsons. His work on the origins of science (Merton 1970 [1938]) stressed structural context rather than individual invention and carefully included in this context military, technological, and religious forces. The sociology of science that emerged from this early effort stressed that the structural basis of science was political and normative, that the relative weight of either factor was a matter only of empirical variation (see Barber 1952 and, e.g., Merton 1968 [1939]: 591–603 and 1968 [1942]:604–15). In Merton's (1968 [1938]:185–214) early and extraordinarily influential essay, "Social Structure and Anomie," he moved from the tension between means and ends to the uneven interpenetration of cultural norms about success and the economic resources to achieve it, and the tradition this essay inspired continued to see deviance as produced by the strain between cultural and economic systems (e.g., Hyman 1953 and Cohen 1955). Similarly, Merton's reference group theory (1968 [1957]:279–334 and 1968:335–440) moves back and forth between the notion of role sets as structures that exist in institutionalized subjective expectations and the insistence that such sets must be rooted in stratification systems and the concrete constraints of social groups. Goode (1960) elaborated this multidimensional, structural theory in his concept of role strain.

The Prospects and Problems
of the Social Structural Approach

I began this chapter by arguing for the significance of nonempirical assumptions in social science and by suggesting that "paradigms" combine general philosophical assumptions with a variety of more concrete research programs. By differentiating the problems of action and order I defined four fundamental general orientations. After discussing the advantages of the individualistic models, namely, their recognition of the centrality of individual volition in modern societies, it was suggested that structural approaches were more realistic, if often more complicated, ways of conceptualizing the sources and consequences of individual acts. I then discussed a number of different research programs that have been undertaken from within each of the structuralist traditions—the instrumental and normative—focusing particularly on their investigations of the scope of freedom in modern society. Although the clear advantages of an instrumental approach to collective order were recognized, it was argued that normative structuralism could more effectively incorporate the important voluntaristic emphasis of individualistic theory. Yet if instrumental structuralism is too deterministic, normative structuralism is too voluntarist. I suggested, in conclusion, that a more successful approach to social structure would combine elements of these dichotomous traditions into a multidimensional whole. This, it seems to me, is the principal challenge for structural analysis in sociology.

It would be satisfying to report that a movement toward such an analytically sophisticated model of structure is underway. Yet, while there are, indeed, certain indications of movement in this direction, a widespread commitment to such theorizing has not occurred.[3] As for the positive developments, I have mentioned already the work of Eisenstadt (1963) and Smelser (1959, 1971) within the Parsonian tradition (cf. Barber 1979 and Zelizer 1979, 1985). Geertz's (e.g., 1973) writings have promised an even greater extension of Parsons' advance, for they are more closely in touch with the newest developments in cultural theory without in any way sacrificing a social system base. Yet Geertz's (1980) most recent monograph falls far short of this promise; it reintroduces the dichotomy of structure and meaning even while it claims to transcend it. Within contemporary Weberian sociology, only Schluchter (1981) has systematically pursued the multidimensional course that Bendix (1964) earlier laid out. Despite the great turn toward subjectivity in contemporary Marxism, only Habermas (e.g., 1975) has seriously begun the dismantling task that a noninstrumental critical theory would presume (though see also, in this regard, Gouldner 1976).

There is no necessary historical progress toward more multidimensional forms of theorizing. The two great progenitors of this approach, Weber and Parsons, both produced highly ambivalent work: their theories were subject to internal pressures that produced strains of purely mechanical and purely voluntaristic theory respectively. Indeed, after Parsons' relatively brief period of dominance in the postwar period, critics seized on the weaker points in his synthetic efforts to propose Parsonian idealism and Weberian materialism, either as models for new forms of one-dimensional theorizing or as justification for continuing standard reductionistic practices. Much of the revival of Durkheimianism follows a similar reductionist path.

It is evident from my earlier reconstruction of the opposing currents in recent structural work that the last decade has witnessed a return to more exclusively instrumental and normative work.* This can be seen in the reinvigoration of orthodox Marxism and in the prestige of cultural structuralism and hermeneutics. There has also, in the name of greater "specificity" and "realism," been a return to more purely individualistic models. Collins' work (1975, 1981) paradoxically exemplifies these recent trends. On the one hand, actors confront each other as mechanical exchangists, struggling against one another within highly structured situations of unequal material resources. On the other hand, Collins acknowledges that these structures rely on voluntary behavior that is nonrational. To reconcile these pressures, he describes actors as motivated by emotional profit-seeking undeterred by normative conditions as such; the external environments of polity and economy create cathartic needs that ritualize social relations in mechanical, almost ethological ways.

Yet even if the structural paradigm were much more consistently multidimensional, certain theoretical problems would remain unsolved. These problems refer, once again, to the real achievements of individualistic theorizing that the collectivist has not yet fully addressed. Despite the progress that normative theory made by incorporating personalities into its notion of the social, the problem of "voluntarism" remains partly unresolved.

Collectivist theories have not found ways to successfully incorporate historical specificity and temporal contingency. The first problem occurs because structuralist theory, both in its instrumental and normative form, tends to focus on the systemic qualities of different kinds of social roles: "lawyers" have certain kinds of ethics, "workers" engage in expected patterns of conflict, the "middle class" is conservative (or liberal), "intellectuals" are always radical. Indeed, the very notion of "class" carries with

---

*It is precisely here that the dated element in this essay becomes evident. As I mentioned in my introduction, this essay was composed in 1978 and only revised slightly before its publication in 1984. Since 1978, the modes of one-sided structural theorizing I describe here have—at the very height of their disciplinary power—begun to be undercut by a broad new movement toward theoretical synthesis. The intellectual reasons for this movement can be found, in part, in the weakness of the structural positions I have described here. See chapter 9, "From Reduction to Linkage: The Long View of the Micro-Macro Link," below, for a more optimistic scenario about the future of sociological theory.

it the quintessential properties of this generalizing, systemic analysis; whether applied to material structure, as in Marxist or Weberian studies of the middle class, or to normative structures, as in the study of intellectuals, "class analysis" implies a transhistorical and cross-cultural similitude that often camouflages the true empirical situation.

When we look at actual history, to the contrary, we see, for example, that depending on the particular development patterns of each nation, middle classes and intellectuals have behaved in highly variable ways: both have been conservative and both have been radical. This historical specificity in the discussion of economic classes is the whole point of Weber's work (1968:1212–1374; 1946:267–301) on urban strata, yet it has been only fitfully absorbed by later Weberians (for an important exception, see Lacroix and Dobry [1977]) and hardly recognized by Marxists. This anti-Weberian rigidity is equally apparent in the "new class" studies by normative structuralists, for example, the analysis of intellectuals by Parsons and Platt (1973:267–302). Gouldner's work (1979) combines instrumental and normative forms of such "class analysis," insisting that intellectuals—because of structural circumstances that are both normative and material—have a uniformly critical ideology and will, inevitably, be the basis for progressive historical change. Yet numerous historical studies have shown this is hardly the case (for Germany, see, e.g., Ringer 1969 and Herf 1981; for England, see, e.g., Wiener 1981). The point is not that the individual members of economic or cultural "classes" are not subject to social structural constraint but that the particular structures must be understood in historically specific and contingent, as well as in systemic, ways.

The second problem refers to the promise of the future rather than to the effect of the past. The virtue of structural theories is that they illuminate the constraints that limit individual action, and the better the structural theory the more effectively it organizes these external constraints in a systematic way that makes empirical sense. The problem is, however, that the more a structure appears coherent the more it appears to be ruled by reified naturalistic laws that are self-contained and inviolable, and while the former property is desirable and true, the latter is not. The continuity of social systems is at every moment dependent upon human action: this is the seminal insight of the individualistic tradition. The imperatives of social structure are probabilistic; they are always open to the possibility, no matter how remote, of reversal or revision.

The most widely discussed implication of this obdurate fact is a renewed concern with incorporating aspects of individualistic theory into collectivist work, the so-called micro/macro connection (see, e.g., Knorr-Cetina and Cicourel 1981; Collins 1981; Giddens 1976, 1979; Alexander 1985; chapter 8, below). But another implication has not had nearly as much attention. This concern with contingency returns, once again, to the significance of history, for it opens the analysis of social structure to the importance of critical events.

The analysis of critical events, like the attention to historical specificity, must balance attention to contingency with an appreciation for social context. This challenge has, in fact, recently drawn the attention of theorists in different structural traditions, though it has hardly ever been the object of continuous concern. Thompson (1966) criticized orthodox Marxism for its mechanistic and unhistorical approach to revolutionary class consciousness, arguing that classes should be seen as "made" by actors through a process of ongoing social interaction rather than as the mechanical reflection of economic development. In the Parsonian tradition, Eisenstadt (1978) has tried to utilize notions of individual negotiation to study periods of social creativity, developing the idea of "institutional entrepreneurs" (see Alexander and Colomy 1985 [chapter 7, below]). But the most fertile work done on such social creativity is Turner's symbolic anthropology. Drawing on the theory of *rites de passage*, Turner (e.g., 1974) argues that social crisis often creates liminal periods of "anti-structure," periods during which role differentiation gives way to expressive community, and societies reformulate, or reinforce, their fundamental orientations through more or less open-ended rituals. Turner's approach to contingent ritualization must be refined and systematically related to the more traditional concerns of structural analysis (see, e.g., Katz et al. 1981; Alexander 1984, 1986; chapter 5, below).

In an ironic way, therefore, social structural theory continues to be bound by the issues that individualistic theory has raised. Structural analysis must evolve so that its emphasis on constraint will reformulate the conditions of voluntarism rather than completely eliminate it. This involves two different tasks. First, externality and constraint must be defined symbolically, as well as materially, for only in this way can the actor be viewed as producing social order and not just as responding to it. Second, the conceptualization of these symbolic and material structures must be historically specific and, equally important, must be conceived in a manner that recognizes the continual possibility for their fundamental reformulation. These tasks should set the research program for structural analysis for years to come.

NOTES

1. The inability to incorporate systematically the general constraints that paradigms exert on structural analysis is, I believe, responsible for the relatively unsatisfactory quality of Mertonian investigations into the broad theme of structural analysis in sociology (e.g., Merton 1981 and Blau 1981)—this, despite the significant substantial contributions Merton has made to the formulation of social structure (see below). The empiricist, or "pre-Kuhnian" status of Merton's understanding of theoretical conflict in social science—which is in keeping with his belief that sociology can be conducted entirely within the "middle range"— is revealed by his attempt to explain different approaches to social structure as problem-generated rather than theory-generated. Thus, rather than genuine theoretical *antagonism* in sociological writing about social structure—an antagonism involving the attempt to explain the same phenomenon from incompatible points of view—Merton insists that there is primarily theoretical *pluralism,* i.e., the invocation of different frameworks to explain different aspects of reality. "Diverse theoretical orientations," he writes (Merton 1981:i) in an introduction to a book he co-edited, *Continuities in Structural Inquiry* (Blau and Merton 1981), "are variously effective for dealing with diverse kinds, and aspects, of sociological and social problems." The commitment to empirical description, not to a priori paradigms, induces theoretical disagreement.

With the institutionalization of science, the behavior of scientists oriented toward norms of organized skepticism and mutual criticism works to bring about such theoretical pluralism. As particular theoretical orientations come to be at the focus of attention . . . they give rise to a variety of new key questions requiring investigation [and] to the extent that current theoretical frameworks prove unequal to the task of dealing with some of the newly emerging key questions, there develops a composite social-and-cognitive pressure within the discipline for developing new and revised frameworks (ibid., v–vi).

Peter Blau, in a companion essay, makes much the same kind of point. Referring to the incredible disagreement that exists in the volume, Blau (1981:1) suggests that "such diversity and pluralism of approaches in a discipline tend to be the main source of advances in systematic knowledge."

This chapter takes a postempiricist (e.g., "Kuhnian") position in the sense that I view conflict in social science as much more deeply rooted, as deriving in many instances from preempirical commitments. Major theorists of social structure, it seems to me, usually conceive of themselves as trying to explain the same thing with different concepts, and it is precisely this confrontation that explains the fundamental and ongoing character of theoretical and empirical conflict in social science. That they cannot, in fact, really explain the same thing in different ways—a fact to which Merton points to sustain his pluralism thesis— shows how competing, widely accepted theoretical concepts can make some "empirical facts" seem inviolate.

2. Weber also pointed the way toward an integration of the methodology of cultural investigation with the methodology of more instrumentally structural analysis. Although I am not focusing on methodological issues in this essay but rather on presuppositional, ideological, and empirical disputes, some implications for methodological controversies

might be mentioned. The theoretical position I have suggested here implies the methodological injunction that the cultural environment of action must become an object of systematic empirical study. One barrier to this, however, has always been the difficulties presented by cultural methodology for the positivist persuasion in social sciences. Instrumentally structural environments, like economic and political position, wealth and socioeconomic status, are not particularly hard to find or to measure, especially with the advances in statistical techniques. Either they themselves are visible in a material sense, or they can be tied to indicators that are. By contrast, the variables that compose cultural structures are harder to find and much more difficult to measure, let alone to understand.

Weber (1968:5) put the methodological contrast well when he contrasted "observational explanation" with "empathic understanding." When sociologists engage in observational explanation, they must assume that people are acting rationally according to the observer's own commonsense standards of rational action. The observer can "see" only the external structures of action—those that are external to the actor in a material sense. The tradition of instrumental structuralism, then, implies the methodology of observational explanation in Weber's sense, for the focus is on what might be called the opportunity structures of action. Economic and political organizations are conceived of as offering opportunities with which to act, and it is assumed that people will so act according to the observer's own notions of strategic self-interest.

But Weber warns us that if the actor's motives are not rational according to our own commonsense standards, then we cannot be content with merely observational explanation. We must, instead, get inside other people's heads through the exercise of *Verstehen,* or understanding. To gain such empathic understanding, the method of interpretation must be employed. It was Dilthey (1976), of course, an older contemporary of Weber's, who investigated the interpretative, or hermeneutical, method in the most extensive and systematic way. Dilthey insisted that the subjectivity of interpretation ensured a circular quality and that the inherent relativity of hermeneutics meant that a culturally sensitive social science must be limited to normative as opposed to what I have called instrumental structures. Weber differed from this methodological version of German idealism by arguing that interpretation could, and must, be combined with observational explanation and the investigation of materially constraining structures it subsumed. Indeed, Weber defined sociology as a science that attempts the interpretative understanding of social action in order thereby to arrive at a causal explanation of its causes and effects. Just as in his more substantive writings, then, Weber pointed to a multidimensional approach in his methodological ones. In this respect he goes well beyond the celebration of subjectivity that continues to define the hermeneutic method that Gadamer (1975) has laid out.

3. This last observation indicates, once again, the gulf that divides the empiricism of Merton's analysis of "structure perspectives in sociology" from the postempiricism that informs my own. In many respects, my theoretical purpose is similar to his. Both of us argue for a more integrative framework that can incorporate divergent points of view. We differ in how this can be obtained. Merton (see note 1, above) argues for incorporating different approaches as they are, on the grounds that each truly reflects the nature of a different kind of empirical phenomenon—hence Merton's theoretical "pluralism." Given my concern with nonempirical commitments, by contrast, I search for this integrative perspective by deconstructing the confrontation between incompatible fundamental assumptions. Only after such a deconstruction, I believe, can empirical pluralism actually emerge, for what follows is an effort to produce a new general framework that can incorporate complementary empirical insights.

Even as I formulate the beginnings of a more integrative framework, however, I am under no illusion that this "progressive" theory will, in fact, fundamentally defuse theoretical conflict and fragmentation. Merton's empiricist framework considers theoretical conflict and fragmentation to be pathological anomalies, whereas the postempiricist framework offered here takes them as normal expectancies. Thus, Merton (1981:i) speaks of "the notorious tendency for theoretical pluralism to degenerate into theoretical fragmentation" and suggests (ibid., iv) that failure to recognize pluralism results in "mock controversies" that "recurrently pepper the history of the sciences." From my point of view, however, there is no initial agreement from which degeneration can occur, and the controversies that ensue from paradigm divergence are not mockeries of serious theorizing but the stuff of serious science itself. Blau (1981:9, italics added), for his part, while insisting that "one can discern a common denominator underneath all these different views of social structure," acknowledges that "conceptions of social structure . . . differ greatly and *even* contain contradictory elements." My contention in this essay, by contrast, is that agreement about the existence of emergent properties is where theorizing about social structure begins, not ends, and that if we are to understand the stakes such theorizing involves we must face as directly as possible the conflicting presuppositional, ideological, and empirical implications that follow.

REFERENCES

Alexander, Jeffrey C. 1980. "Core Solidarity, Ethnic Outgroup, and Social Differentiation: A Multidimensional Model of Inclusion in Modern Societies." In Jacques Dofny and Akinsola Akiwowo, eds., *National and Ethnic Movements*. Los Angeles and London: Sage.

—— 1982a. *Positivism, Presuppositions, and Current Controversies*. Vol. 1 of *Theoretical Logic in Sociology*. Berkeley and Los Angeles: University of California Press (1982–83).

—— 1982b. "Kuhn's Unsuccessful Revisionism: A Rejoinder to Selby." *Canadian Journal of Sociology* 7(2):66–71.

—— 1982c. "Max Weber, La théorie de la rationalisation et le marxisme," *Sociologie et Sociétés* (9):33–43.

—— 1984. "Three Models of Culture and Society Relations: Toward an Analysis of Watergate." *Sociological Theory* 2:290–314.

—— 1985. "The Individualist Dilemma in Phenomenology and Interactionalism: Toward a Synthesis with the Classical Tradition." In S. N. Eisenstadt and H. J. Helle, eds., *Perspective on Sociological Theory*, vol. 1, pp. 25–57. Beverly Hills and London: Sage.

—— 1986. "The 'Form' of Substance: The Senate Watergate Hearings as Ritual." In S. J. Ball-Rokeach and Muriel G. Cantor, eds., *Media, Audience, and Social Structure*, pp. 243–51. Beverly Hills and London: Sage.

Alexander, Jeffrey C. and Paul Colomy. 1985. "Toward Neofunctionalism," *Sociological Theory* 3(2):11–23.

Almond, Gabriel and Sydney Verba. 1963. *The Civic Culture*. Princeton: Princeton University Press.

Aron, Raymond. 1969. "Social Class, Political Class, Ruling Class." *European Journal of Sociology* 1(2):260–81.

Azarya, Victor. 1978. *Aristocrats Facing Change: The Falbe in Guinea, Nigeria, and Cameron.* Chicago: University of Chicago Press.

Baran, Paul A. and Paul M. Sweezy. 1966. *Monopoly Capital.* New York: Monthly Review.

Barber, Bernard. 1952. *Science and the Social Order.* New York: Free Press.

—— 1979. *Informed Consent in Medical Therapy and Research.* New Brunswick, N.J.: Rutgers University Press.

Bell, Daniel. 1973. *The Coming of Post-Industrial Society.* New York: Basic Books.

Bellah, Robert M. 1970. *Beyond Belief.* New York: Harper and Row.

Bendix, Reinhard. 1964. *Nation-Building and Citizenship.* New York: Doubleday.

Blau, Peter M. 1977. *Inequality and Heterogeneity.* New York: Free Press.

—— 1981. "Diverse Views of Social Structure and Their Common Denominator." In Blau and Merton, eds., *Continuities in Structural Inquiry,* pp. 1–27.

Blau, Peter M. and Robert K. Merton, eds. 1981. *Continuities in Structural Inquiry.* Beverly Hills and London: Sage.

Braverman, Harry. 1974. *Labor and Monopoly Capital.* New York: Monthly Review Press.

Bottomore, T. B. 1974. *Sociology as Social Criticism.* New York: Pantheon.

Cohen, Albert K. 1955. *Delinquent Boys.* New York: Free Press.

Coleman, James. 1966. "Foundation for a Theory of Collective Decisions." *American Journal of Sociology* 71:615–27.

Collins, Randall. 1975. *Conflict Sociology.* New York: Academic Press.

—— 1981. "On the Microfoundations of Macrosociology." *American Journal of Sociology* 86:984–1014.

Deutsch, Karl. 1963. *The Nerves of Government.* New York: Free Press.

Dilthey, Wilhelm. 1976. *Dilthey: Selected Writings,* H. P. Rickman, ed. Cambridge, England: Cambridge University Press.

Domhoff, William. 1967. *Who Rules America?* Englewood Cliffs, N.J.: Prentice-Hall.

Douglas, Mary. 1966. *Purity and Danger.* London: Penguin Books.

Downes, Anthony. 1957. *An Economic Theory of Democracy.* New York: Harper and Row.

Durkheim, Emile. 1938 [1893]. *The Division of Labor in Society.* New York: Free Press.

—— 1958 [1896]. *Socialism.* Silver Springs, Colorado: Antioch University.

—— 1951 [1897]. *Suicide.* New York: Free Press.

—— 1973 [1898]. "Individualism and the Intellectuals." In Robert N. Bellah, ed., *Emile Durkheim on Morality and Society.* Place: Publisher.

—— 1957 [1900]. *Professional Ethics and Civil Morals.* New York: Free Press.

—— 1961 [1903]. *Moral Education.* New York: Free Press.

—— 1915 [1912]. *Elementary Forms of Religious Life.* New York: Free Press.

Easton, David. 1965. *A Systems Analysis of Political Life.* New York: Wiley.

Eisenstadt, S. N. 1963. *The Political System of Empires.* New York: Free Press.
—— 1978. *Revolution and the Transformation of Society.* New York: Free Press.
Gadamer, Hans-Georg. 1975. *Truth and Method.* New York: Crossword.
Garfinkel, Harold, et al. 1981. "The Work of a Discovering Science Construed with Materials from the Optically Discovered Pulsar." *Philosophy of Social Science* 11:131–58.
Geertz, Clifford. 1973. *The Interpretation of Cultures.* New York: Basic Books.
—— 1980. *Negara: The Theatre State in Nineteenth Century Bali.* Princeton, N.J.: Princeton University Press.
Giddens, Anthony. 1976. *New Rules of Sociological Method.* New York: Basic Books.
—— 1979. *Central Problems in Social Theory.* Berkeley and Los Angeles: University of California.
Goffman, Erving. 1959. *Presentation of Self in Everyday Life.* New York: Doubleday.
—— 1961. *Asylums.* New York: Doubleday.
Goldthorpe, John H. and Lockwood, David. 1963. "Affluence and the British Class Structure." *The Sociological Review* 11:133–63.
Goode, William J. 1960. "A Theory of Role Strain." *American Sociological Review* 25:483–96.
Gouldner, Alvin W. 1976. *The Dialectic of Ideology and Technology.* New York: Seabury.
—— 1979. *The Future of Intellectuals and the Rise of the New Class.* New York: Seabury.
Habermas, Jürgen. 1975. *Legitimation Crisis.* Boston: Beacon.
Halévy, Elie. 1972 [1901–04]. *The Growth of Philosophic Radicalism.* City, N.J.: Kelley.
Herf, Jeffrey. 1981. "Reactionary Modernism." *Theory and Society* 10:805–32.
Hobbes, Thomas. 1962 [1651]. *The Leviathan.* New York: Colliers.
Homans, George C. 1961. *Social Behavior: Its Elementary Forms.* New York: Harcourt, Brace, and World.
Hyman, Herbert H. 1953. "The Values Systems of Different Classes." In R. Bendix and S. M. Lipset, eds., *Class, Status, and Power,* pp. 426–42. New York: Free Press.
Johnson, Chalmers. 1966. *Revolutionary Change.* Boston: Little Brown.
Katz, Elihu, Daniel Dayan, and Pierre Motyl. 1981. "In Defense of Media Events." *Communications in the 21st Century.* New York: Wiley and Sons.
Knorr-Cetina and Aron V. Circourel, eds. 1981. *Advances in Social Theory and Methodology: Toward an Integration of Micro- and Macrosociology.* London: Routledge.
Kuhn, Thomas. 1962. *The Structure of Scientific Revolution.* Chicago: University of Chicago.
Lacroix, Bernard and Michael Dobry. 1977. "A la recherche d'un cadre théorique pour l'analyse political des classes moyennes," Extrait des Annales de la Faculté de Droit et de Sciences Politique, vol. 14.

Lakatos, Imre. 1969. "Falsification and the Methodology of Scientific Research Programmes." In Lakatos and Alan Musgrave, eds. *Criticism and the Growth of Knowledge*, pp. 91–196. London: Cambridge University Press.

Lévi-Strauss, Claude. 1966. *The Savage Mind*. Chicago: University of Chicago Press.

Levy, Marion J. 1949. *The Family Revolution in China*. Cambridge, Mass.: Harvard University Press.

Lindbloom, Charles E. 1977. *Politics and Markets: The World's Political-Economic Systems*. New York: Basic Books.

Lipset, Seymour. 1963. *The First New Nation*. New York: Doubleday.

Lipset, Seymour, Martin Trow, and James Coleman. 1956. *Union Democracy.*, New York: Free Press.

Lipset, Seymour and Reinhard Bendix. 1959. *Social Mobility in Industrial Society*. Berkeley and Los Angeles: University of California Press.

Marcuse, Herbert. 1964. *One Dimensional Man*. Boston: Beacon.

Marx, Karl. 1963 [1844]. "Economic and Philosophic Manuscripts." In T. B. Bottomore, ed., *Karl Marx: Early Writings*. New York: Doubleday Anchor.

Merton, Robert K. 1968. *Social Theory and Social Structure*. New York: Free Press.

—— 1970 [1938]. *Science, Technology and Society in 17th-Century England*. New York: Harper and Row.

—— 1973 [1942]. "The Normative Structure of Science." In Merton, *The Sociology of Science*, Norman W. Storer, ed. Chicago: University of Chicago Press.

—— 1981. "Remarks on Theoretical Pluralism." In P. M. Blau and Merton, eds., *Continuities in Structural Inquiry*. London: Sage.

Michels, Robert. 1949 [1911]. *Political Parties*. Glencoe, Ill.: Free Press.

Miliband, Ralph. 1969. *The State in Capitalist Society*. New York: Basic Books.

Mills, C. Wright. 1959. *The Power Elite*. New York: Oxford University Press.

Moore, Sally and Barbara Meyeroff, eds. 1975. *Symbol and Politics in Communal Ideology*. Ithaca, N.J.: Cornell University Press.

Münch, Richard, 1981. "Talcott Parsons and the Theory of Action. I. The Kantian Core." *American Journal of Sociology* 8:45–76.

—— 1983. "From Pure Methodological Individualism to Poor Sociological Utilitarianism: A Critique of an Avoidable Alliance." *Canadian Journal of Sociology* 8:45–76.

O'Connor, James. 1973. *The Fiscal Crisis of the State*. New York: St. Martins Press.

Parsons, Talcott. 1954. *Essays in Sociological Theory*. New York: Free Press.

—— 1964. *Social Structure and Personality*. New York: Free Press.

—— 1969. *Politics and Social Structure*. New York: Free Press.

—— 1973. *The System of Modern Societies*. Englewood Cliffs, N.J.: Prentice-Hall.

Parsons, Talcott and Edward A. Shils, eds. 1951. *Towards a General Theory of Action*. New York: Harper and Row.

Parsons, Talcott and Robert F. Bales, eds. 1955. *Family, Socialization, and Interaction Process*. New York: Free Press.

Parsons, Talcott and Gerald M. Platt. 1973. *The American University*. Cambridge, Mass.: Harvard University Press.

Pitts, Jesse. 1974. "The Hippies as a Counter-Meritocracy." *Dissent* 21:304–16.

Prager, Jeffrey. 1982. "Equal Opportunity and Affirmation Action: The Rise of New Social Understandings." *Research in Law, Deviance, and Social Control* 4:191–218.

Radcliffe-Brown, R. R. 1952. *Structure and Function in Primitive Society*. New York: Free Press.

Ringer, Fritz. 1969. *The Decline of the German Mandarins: The German Academic Community 1890–1933*. Cambridge, Mass.: Harvard University Press.

Sahlins, Marshall. 1976. *Culture and Practical Reason*. Chicago: University of Chicago Press.

Schluchter, Wolfgang. 1981. *The Rise of Western Rationalism*. Berkeley and Los Angeles: University of California Press.

Seidman, Steven. 1983. *Liberalism and the Origins of European Social Theory*. Berkeley and Los Angeles: University of California Press.

Selznick, Phillip. 1957. *Leadership and Administration*. New York: Harper and Row.

Sewell, William H., Jr. 1980. *Work and Revolution in France*. London and New York: Cambridge University Press.

Shils, Edward A. 1975. *Center and Periphery: Essays in Macrosociology*. Chicago: University of Chicago Press.

Simon, Herbert A. 1964. *Administrative Behavior: A Study of Decision-making Processes in Administrative Organizations*. New York: Macmillan.

Skocpol, Theda. 1979. *States and Social Revolutions*. London and New York: Cambridge University Press.

Smelser, Neil J. 1959. *Social Change in the Industrial Revolution*. Chicago: University of Chicago.

—— 1971. "Stability, Instability, and the Analyses of Political Corruption." In Alex Inkeles and Bernard Barber, eds., *Stability and Change*. Boston: Little-Brown.

Thompson, E. P. 1966. *The Making of the English Working Class*. New York: Vintage.

Treiman, Donald. 1977. *Occupational Prestige in Comparative Perspective*. New York: Wiley and Sons.

Turner, Victor. 1969. *The Ritual Process*. Chicago: Aldine.

—— 1974. *Dramas, Fields, and Metaphors*. Ithaca, N.Y.: Cornell University Press.

Walzer, Michael. 1965. *Revolution of the Saints*. Cambridge, Mass.: Harvard University Press.

Weber, Max. 1946. *From Max Weber*. New York: Oxford University Press.

—— 1968. *Economy and Society*. Berkeley and Los Angeles: University of California.

Weinstein, Fred and Gerald M. Platt. 1969. *The Wish To Be Free*. Berkeley and Los Angeles: University of California.

Wiener, Martin. 1981. *English Culture and the Decline of the Industrial Spirit: 1850–1980*. London and New York: Cambridge University Press.

Wright, Erik Olin. 1978. *Class, Crisis, and the State*. London: New Left Books.

Zelizer, Viviana. 1979. *Morals and Markets*. New York: Columbia University Press.

—— 1985. *Pricing the Priceless Child*. New York: Basic Books.

PART II

Structure, Action, and Differentiation

TWO

Durkheim's Problem and Differentiation Theory Today

Differentiation comes closer than any other contemporary conception to identifying the overall contours of civilizational change, and the texture, immanent dangers, and real promises of modern life. As a general process, differentiation is fairly well understood, and it is this general outline that provides the backdrop for making sense of everyday life today. Institutions gradually become more specialized. Familial control over social organization decreases. Political processes become less directed by the obligations and rewards of patriarchy, and the division of labor is organized more according to economic criteria than by reference simply to age and sex. Community membership can reach beyond ethnicity to territorial and political criteria. Religion becomes more generalized and abstract, more institutionally separated from and in tension with other spheres. Eventually, cultural generalization breaks the bonds of religion altogether. Natural laws are recognized in the moral and physical worlds, and in the process, religion surrenders not only its hierarchical control over cultural life but also its institutional prominence.

In terms of these general contours of world history, and the intuitive representation of modernity they provide, the immanent dangers and promises of modernity can be understood. Thus, because of the need to develop flexible and independent control over social complexity, large-scale bureaucratic and impersonal organizations emerge (Eisenstadt

Prepared for the second German-American Theory Conference, Theories of Social Change and Modernity, Berkeley, California, August 26–28, 1986, sponsored by the National Science Foundation. I acknowledge my colleagues in the School of Social Sciences at the Institute for Advanced Study in Princeton, New Jersey, whose member I was when this essay was composed, and particularly the stimulation of Michael Walzer.

1963). Such centralization—political, economic, informational—provides an ever present resource for the exercise of organized cruelty and domination. Yet precisely because it is impersonal and bureaucratic rather than primordial and diffuse—because it is differentiated—this centralization is experienced, even in totalitarian societies, in importantly new ways. Rarely is it experienced as an all-powerful and archetypical reality: more typically, it is experienced as a development that challenges the existence of deeply entrenched institutions of private and public life (e.g., Touraine et al. 1983). These countercenters are not confined to the primary groups, or lifeworlds, which Habermas (1984) presents as the last bastion against colonization by rational systems. It is not one-dimensional colonization but uneven differentiation that characterizes the modern world. Indeed, as Walzer (1983) has shown, the very existence of social and cultural differentiation—not colonization—allows social critics dedicated to justice in modern societies to demand for the spheres of public and private life ever greater autonomy and self-control.

But knowing the outlines of differentiation and its problems and possibilities in general terms is not enough. If the perspective of differentiation is going to produce a theory of social change, it must be brought down to earth. Obviously, not all societies and institutions differentiate. Sometimes they stagnate. Often they become brittle and reactionary, concentrated and inflexible. Why do these responses happen? Why, by contrast, is differentiation sometimes able to proceed?

Merely to describe differentiation as a general process, moreover, makes it appear to be automatic, an equilibrating mechanism that occurs whenever adjustments must be made to conflict and strain. This is not the case. The social processes that produce differentiation must be described in specific, concrete terms. When they are, the contingency of differentiation will be more clearly understood and its responsiveness to historical variation more easily seen as well. Is a certain orienting ideology necessary for differentiation to occur? Are particular kinds of interest group formations? If so, in what societies and historical conjunctures are such requirements likely to occur?

Finally, what is the relation between differentiation and the historical formations that are the traditional objects of classical theories of social change? Do feudalism, fascism, capitalism, and socialism represent a continuum of differentiation, or do they represent amalgamations of institutions that are differentiated in varying degrees? Does thinking of change as differentiation allow us to conceptualize the strains and conflicts in these formations more effectively than traditional theories do?

These questions mark the frontier of differentiation theory. They arise not just from scientific curiosity but also out of theoretical competition (Wagner and Berger 1984). They are the questions that other theories put to theorists who think they see differentiation in social change. If the theory is to be maintained, it must be improved, and these questions must be answered.

In this chapter I formulate what some answers might be. I do this, in part, by suggesting that in the theoretical community today there is already an upsurge of investigation (see e.g., the essays in Alexander, ed. 1985, and in Alexander and Colomy forthcoming) directed precisely to these ends. In larger part, however, I provide some answers to these questions myself or at least produce a framework within which such answers can be more readily conceived. I begin by suggesting that the questions I have enumerated can be viewed not simply as parochial preoccupations of recent neofunctionalist work but also as issues that go back to the classical foundations of sociology itself. Indeed, I argue that, properly understood, they are generic questions that must be faced by every effort to understand social change in a serious way. I show how these questions define the achievements and limitations of Durkheim's theory of change. By examining Parsons' later theorizing in these terms, I argue, we gain a new handle not only on the criticisms of the functionalist theory of change but also on the efforts that have been made to improve it. These considerations inform my suggestions, offered in the conclusion, about what future efforts at understanding differentiation might be.

"Durkheim's Problem"

Although the notion that society changes through a process of institutional specialization can be traced back to ancient times, the modern theory of social change as differentiation may be seen as beginning with Durkheim.*

---

*This even though Spencer articulated a wide-ranging historical classification of history as differentiation well before Durkheim's work appeared. Although Spencer had a significant influence on Durkheim, it was from Durkheim, not from Spencer, that subsequent thinking about differentiation in the social sciences has drawn. Moreover, in ways that are very significant for the problems and prospects of differentiation theory today (see not only the

In *The Division of Labor in Society,* Durkheim (1933 [1893]) put Spencer's earlier theory in a new form and began a research program that extends to the present day. Although Durkheim's first great work has, of course, become one of the classics of Western social science, its association with this program has not usually been made. In the context of the present discussion, therefore, *Division* is of particular interest. Whereas each of the problems I find in this classical work have been noted before, they have never been understood by reference to differentiation theory. Because they have not, their theoretical interrelation has been impossible to see.

Durkheim's first great work serves as an exemplar of differentiation theory in several different ways. It can be considered the first and still one of the most powerful applications of the theory itself. It can also be seen as embodying some of this traditions' most typical and debilitating weaknesses. Durkheim's early work presents in a nutshell, in other words, the achievements of differentiation theory and the difficulties it often creates.

In book one of *Division,* entitled "The Function of the Division of Labor," Durkheim outlines a general portrait of social change as differentiation. Societies were once mechanically organized. They had repressive laws and were dominated by a particularistic and omnipresent collective conscience. Gradually they have moved toward organic solidarity, where laws are restitutive and collective morality is generalized and abstract. In terms of institutional references, Durkheim focuses here primarily on economic change, on the one hand, and on the separation of religion from political and legal functions on the other. There is also a brief but important discussion of cultural generalization as indicating the increasingly person-centered character of the collective conscience.

This initial discussion is, however, of a particularly sweeping kind. While conferring power and scope, this sweep makes it difficult to incorporate any real discussion of particulars—specific historical phases through which differentiation proceeds, particular institutions and sectors upon which distinct periods of differentiation depend, historically specific social problems that differentiation systematically might generate. Durkheim's argument in book one is evolutionary rather than developmental

---

discussion of Durkheim that immediately follows above but also my treatment of Parsons' neglect of war below), Spencer's approach to differentiation contrasted in various ways with that which Durkheim developed.

in the sense that no phase-specific strains are outlined. It is functional in the sense that there is no theory of how particular structures are involved. It is ideal-typical in the sense that there is no account of the processes of change by which an episode of actual social differentiation actually occurs.*

What is fascinating about this work, however, and what makes it so paradigmatic of differentiation theory as such, is that Durkheim goes on to supply such particulars in books two and three. Book two, entitled "Causes and Conditions," is his effort to supply a theory of social process. Durkheim argues that population growth leads to greater density and that greater specialization is a quasi-Malthusian response to the need for more adaptive and efficient distribution of resources. Durkheim's third book, "Abnormal Forms," is an effort to discuss a particular historical phase of differentiation and the problems it typically engenders. He suggests that because industrial society is not yet fully differentiated, the division of labor is coercive and disruptive. When birth is further separated from wealth, and political from economic organization, industrial relations will be mature and society less conflictual.

The fatal weakness of *The Division of Labor* is that its three books cannot be related to one another in a systematic way. That demographic pressure is the principal process through which differentiation proceeds, as Durkheim asserts in book two, is in itself open to doubt. More significant from a theoretical point of view is that this emphasis seems to directly contradict the notion that differentiation involves cultural and political phenomena, which Durkheim argued in book one. What either demographics or systemic differentiation more generally understood have to do with the forced division of labor—Durkheim's topic in book three—is problematic as well. For if, indeed, the division of labor is anomic and coercive in 1890, there is nothing in Durkheim's general theory, or in his specific account of social process, to supply an explanation. What is necessary is a more phase-specific model of general differentiation and of social process alike. Only with such a theory would it be possible to stipulate criteria for predicting "normal" and "pathological" outcomes of a particular social formation.

To establish links between the three parts of Durkheim's work, in other

*In developing these distinctions, I am reworking and extending some of my earlier ideas (Alexander, 1983:128–44, 259–72) about the different levels of change theory. In doing so, I draw upon the important arguments by Gould (1985) and Colomy (1985).

words, would require a detailed account of structures and processes and a systematic effort to link these theories to the general theory of differentiation. This is precisely the goal, I argue, for which contemporary differentiation theory must strive.

Social Change Theory and Durkheim's Problem

In order to relate this agenda for a particular research program to issues about social change more generally, one must recognize that "Durkheim's problem" was not simply his own. Through the lens of differentiation theory he was groping with issues that are generic to the study of social change as such. Each of *Division*'s three parts represents one important way in which social change has been conceptualized—through the construction of general models, through the development of accounts of social process, and through historically specific analyses of tensions and strains. Durkheim's problem, in other words, is an enduring one, one with which every perspective on change must come to grips.

In these terms, I briefly examine the principal classical theories of change with which Durkheim's must compete. Although Weber certainly defines a general theme, "rationalization," he does not emphasize this level of his analysis in anything like a comparable way. His only effort to produce a general account of rationalization is the "Author's Preface" (Weber 1958 [1920]: 13–31) to his collected essays in the sociology of religion, which was written only at the end of his career and was much more an afterthought than the basis for his theoretical program. The minimalist character of the rationalization theme can also be seen from the fact that a debate is still raging about the simple definition of rationalization itself.* I am not suggesting that this general conception was not important for guiding Weber's thinking, for most certainly it was. But to conceptualize and elaborate it was not something with which Weber was centrally concerned.

---

*Here is how one of the most interesting recent contributions to this debate begins: "The idea of rationality is a great unifying theme in Max Weber's work . . . an idee-maitresse . . . that links his empirical and methodological investigations with his political and moral reflections. [Yet] Weber frequently uses the term 'rational' without qualification or explanation. . . . No fewer than sixteen apparent meanings of 'rational' can be culled [from his writings]. The reader may well be perplexed by what appears to be a baffling multiplicity of denotations and connotations" (Brubaker 1984:1–2).

The heart of Weber's work is his theorizing about processes of change, the role in it of institutions and groups, and the historically specific strains involved. The Protestant ethic creates capitalism in the West, patrimonialism overwhelms autonomous urban centers in the East, charismatic leadership becomes routinized and bureaucratic, priests and later legal notables have an interest in producing formally rational law—these are the middle-range propositions with which Weber is concerned. How and why these are connected to historical rationalization is implicit but never clearly spelled out. One result is that the relation between Weber's various middle-range theories of change is never easy to see. Bendix (1961) devoted one very ambitious book to spelling out these connections, and Schluchter (1981) has devoted another. But though presented as commentaries on Weber's theories, these works must actually be seen as theoretical constructions that try to fill this gap. Another result of this disarticulation of Weber's specific theories from one another and from his general perspective is that the relevance of these historical accounts for explaining other episodes of change, and for thinking about the future course of change, is far from clear.

Moreover, whereas Weber's historical explanations of traditional society often involve phase-specific accounts of conflict and strain—his theory of the patrimonialism-feudalism dilemma must be seen as a prototype in this regard—this genetic, or developmental, quality disappears from his treatment of the capitalist and modern periods. Again, this disarticulation between the strands of Weber's change theory leaves fundamental questions unanswered. Will bureaucratization dominate party politics in the modern era, or will it be continuously challenged by charismatic politicians? Will formal law reign indefinitely, or will there be challenges to such formulations from different kinds of social groups, whose demands can be formulated in a substantive and historically specific way? Does the otherworldly character of Puritanism eventually lead to cultural universalism or to secularism in a purely political sense? At the back of these problems are Weber's historicist difficulties with the concept of capitalism. Does late capitalism vitiate the processes that Weber has identified with its earlier creation? What can distinctively define late capitalism, if, indeed, a new postcapitalist historical phase will have to be introduced? Will this phase differ at all from the socialist form of industrial society, which at one point Weber (1971 [1918]) suggested must be seen merely as capitalism in another form, or from communist industrialism, which at another point (Beetham 1974: 46ff) Weber believed to differ fatefully from capitalism not only in economic but also in political and moral terms? Once again, my point is not that Weber has nothing to say about these issues; obviously, he did. My point is, rather, that the failure to articulate the different levels, or forms, of his theorizing makes his contributions in these regards fragmentary and ad hoc. To suggest that there are paradoxes created by the rationalization of culture (Schluchter 1979) is suggestive but does not go nearly far enough, nor is it sufficient to translate Weberian political theory into a story of the production of citizenship (Bendix 1964), though such an effort is certainly valuable in its own right. Weber's theory remains the most perceptive theory of institutional change ever written, and it continues to inspire the most searching writing on the processes of change today (e.g., Collins 1986a). Even for Weberian theory, however, Durkheim's problem remains.

It has been Marxists, of course, who have pointed most forcefully to these weaknesses in Weber's change theory, and when we look at Marx's approach to change, by contrast, we cannot help but admire its beauty and theoretical power. Marx coherently and compellingly united the different kinds of theorizing about social change. His general theme describes a dialectical movement—thesis, antithesis, synthesis—that occurs within each historical period and over the course of human history as a whole. His institutional theorizing neatly translates this dialectic by defining thesis as class domination in the service of economic production, antithesis as the struggle by classes who are exploited in production, and synthesis as the revolutionized social formation that ensues. Phase-specific strains are handled in an equally elegant and interconnected way, at least for the capitalist period. Production processes rest on the forces of production; classes are established by property rights, which define their relations to production; as the relations of production begin to strangle the forces of production, class conflict begins; equilibrium can be restored only if the revolutionary transformation of property relationships is achieved.

It is, at least in part, because Marx seems to provide the solution to Durkheim's problem that his change theory has had such wide appeal. In times of great conflict and anxiety, it supplies a coherent interpretation of events. It has also clearly identified some of the most specific and obvious features of contemporary social life. That there is capitalism and class conflict cannot be denied. It is also clear that the redistribution of property continues to preoccupy capitalist welfare states and that the twentieth century has been transformed by a series of communist revolutions. Despite its intellectual power, however, Marxist change theory has, in my view, been refuted time and time again, perhaps, indeed, first and still most powerfully by Max Weber himself. Only when domination is experienced as intensive and relatively monolithic do Marxist theories become plausible. Insofar as social life returns to its more typically fragmented and pluralized shape, Marxism loses its attraction. We are living in such a period today. The social convulsions of the 1960s produced a renewal of Marxism, but in the contemporary period Marxism is in distinctive decline. The centrality to change of relatively autonomous noneconomic institutions has come to be emphasized once again (e.g., Sewell 1980 and Evans at al. 1985), and against sweeping dialectical theories, temporal and spatial specificity has been emphasized (Giddens 1981, 1986).

As this consideration of Marxism indicates, there is more to the development of social change theories than Durkheim's problem alone. In every mode of theorizing specific commitments must be made, empirical processes described, conflicts predicted, and moral possibilities prescribed. Indeed, the more explicit a theory becomes at each of the different levels of theoretical work, and the more tightly knit the interrelation it can propose, the more contestable its substantive empirical and moral commitments become. As an advocate of more pluralistic theorizing, it should not be surprising that I find Marxism's substantive formulations implausible, even while I admire its theoretical scope. It is one thing to solve Durkheim's problem; it is quite another to solve it empirically and reasonably in moral terms. It seems to me that Weber's change theory is much closer to empirical reality than Marx's. The moral possibilities Weber implies, though flawed in many ways, are more liberal and emancipating as well.

The challenge is to solve Durkheim's problem without giving up Weber's institutional work, which is to suggest that differentiation theory must be pushed in a Weberian direction. This was Parsons' intention. Let us see the kinds of advances he made over Durkheim's earlier theorizing before we insist, once again, that he did not really solve Durkheim's problem at all.

Parsons' Change Theory and Durkheim's Problem

Whereas Parsons is generally considered, by himself (Parsons 1967 [1960], 1971:74, 78) and others (Smith 1973), to have taken up differentiation theory where Durkheim left off, it is worth noting that Parsons saw himself to be carrying out Weber's perspective on social change as well. While I argue that Parsons' theory is Durkheimian in its most fundamental thrust, there is a certan sense in which Parsons' self-perception must be credited. The substantive formulations in Parsons' evolutionary writings cannibalize Weber's change theory in an extraordinary way. No one, indeed, has ever taken Weber's institutional theorizing as seriously; no one has pursued the implications as strenuously or tried as hard to find a model within which they could be interrelated and explained. It is here that the paradox of Parsons' differentiation theory lies. For while Parsons finds his critical evidence and illustrations in Weber's institutional work, he never theorizes from within the institutional and processual level itself.* Weber's work is grist for the mill of Parsons' improved differentiation theory; it never threatens to displace Durkheim's approach as such.

It is good grist, to be sure. Parsons' account of change is vastly superior to Durkheim's because it can be couched in the terms that Weber provides. In Durkheim there is sketchy generalization, and even in the most historical of his works (e.g., Durkheim 1977 [1938]), shifts from one historical phase to another are described in schematic terms. In Parsons' theory (1966, 1971), by contrast, differentiation is mapped in terms of actors, groups, institutions, social movements, civilizations, and states. As a result, Parsons is able to provide a much more intuitively compelling reconstruction of the modern world than Durkheim was able to do. He can succeed in demonstrating what Durkheim merely suggested—the extraordinary distance that has been traveled from band societies to the societies of the present day. In doing so, Parsons succeeds in legitimating the meaningful foundations of modern life.

*The indexes to the major works that Parsons (1966, 1971) devoted to history as differentiation include many more references to Weber than to Durkheim, and in the introduction to the second he emphasizes (1971:2) that it "is written in the spirit of Weber's work." Yet he immediately qualifies this in a telling way—"one important difference in perspective has been dictated by the link between organic evolution and that of human society and culture." Parsons refers here to the evolutionary theory of adaptation and differentiation he drew in the most immediate sense from Durkheimian work.

It would be impossible here to communicate the nuance and complexity of this Parsonian account, but some indication of the scope and coherence of his generalized scheme can be made. For Parsons, historical evolution involves what might be called the de-familialization of the world. In band societies, kinship ties define important social, cultural, and even psychological activity. Totemism is a good example. An animal or vegetable symbol of ethnic identity and "religion," it fuses the band's existence with the natural world and with human kinship as well. It is no wonder, according to Parsons, that prohibitions like the incest taboo play such a socially decisive role, for the intermixing of kinship and social criteria makes behavior diffuse, particularistic, affective, and, above all, prescriptive and ascribed. If societies are to become more flexible and individualized, they must make such "blood-related" qualities a much smaller part of social life. In order to do so, the significance of kinship must be drastically reduced.

This fused situation changes when one of the two lineages that usually form a band society seeks to improve its status. The equality of marriage exchange is altered; restricted intralineage marriage emerges, and other resources are controlled as well. On the one hand, it is here that stratification and inequality arise. On the other, because power has itself become the basis for defining the extension of kinship ties, it marks the beginning of the possibility for more powerful and adaptive forms of social direction and control. Property comes into being, and kinship begins to be strategically subordinated to it. States are developed to protect the surplus wealth of the dominant lineage, but, Parsons emphasizes, this is differentiation too, for from this point on the institutional structure of politics cannot be deduced from the nature of kinship itself. These economic and political developments, moreover, cannot be sustained for any length of time without a religion that is far more elaborate and independent of kinship than totemism. This new religion must stretch over nonmarrying lineages and must explain and justify social hierarchy and inequality. It does so not only by formulating a broader and more differentiated conception of the supernatural realm but also by developing a more generalized conception of "the people." Another result of the initial creation of stratification is the emergence, for the first time, of some nonfamilial conception of the societal community. There emerges a territorial referent for human community that strongly emphasizes group as distinguished from lineage boundaries.

These processes continue in archaic and historic societies. Religion becomes more formalized and abstract. Cults emerge, as do other groups with specifically religious ambitions. Eventually churches develop, institutions with highly specialized religious personnel. Politics continues to differentiate as well. It becomes more impersonal and bureaucratic, both in order to gain control for the privileged class—which involves placating lower class groups by developing primitive welfare functions—and in order to ensure the safety of larger territories and the continuous productivity of economic life. Economic life becomes more functionally divided and stratification increases. Within the now established range of "national" solidarity, heterogeneous groupings develop that are arranged in horizontally, as well as in vertically, segmented ways. While these developments ensure a more flexible and productive social organization, they also ensure new levels of hierarchy and inequality. Aristocracies represent continued linkage of function to kinship, and new forms of domination emerge, like kingship and church, which fuse the control of various goods.

In the early modern and modern periods, primarily in the West, these intermediate levels of social development are pushed much further still. The Reformation moves religion toward a more abstract and less institutionally fused position. The emergence of parliaments and common law makes government more independent of social groups and economic position. With citizenship, social solidarity eventually becomes more independent of actual position in various social spheres. The advance of universal education makes culture still more generalized and accessible regardless of particular group and origin. Competence, rather than traditional connection or personal charisma, becomes the arbiter of authority. The organization of technical knowledge through professional authority provides a systematic counterbalance to the hierarchical power derived from bureaucracies and the money power derived from markets.

Because he has one hand resting on Weber's shoulders, Parsons is able to describe the stages of differentiation with much more precision and concreteness than Durkheim himself. Even so, Durkheim's problem remains. Parsons has taken his general bearings from Durkheim, and primarily from *The Division of Labor,* book one. Like Durkheim's before him, Parsons' general theory does not provide an account of how change occurs. To suggest that, because a differentiated institution is more effective and flexible, it will eventually develop to cope with problems posed by other spheres says little about the actual processes by which that new and more differentiated institution actually came about. Parsons acknowledges the imbalance. He is concerned with "the structural ordering of social data," he argues (1966:112), not in the first instance with "the analysis of process and change." He does not seem aware, however, of the intellectual difficulties that such a position presents. His insistence (1966:111) that "structural analysis must take a certain priority over the analysis of process and change" recalls his troubling assertion in *The Social System* that the analysis of stability must precede the analysis of change. It was in response to the manifest inadequacy of that earlier claim that Parsons moved to the differentiation theory I have just described. The problem now seems to have reappeared in a new form. Even when he is committed to a theory of social change, it is the morphology of change, not its dynamics, that must come first.

But whatever Parsons' personal inclinations, this separation is actually impossible to make. Book one of *Division* was followed by book two, even though Durkheim could never connect them in an intelligible way. There is no second book for Parsons, but there is, in fact, an implicit strain of theorizing about what some of the actual processes of change might be. Unfortunately, the tone of this unwritten second book is Darwinian in a rather vulgar sense. Parsons himself has a more sophisticated parallel to Darwin in mind. He suggests that, like Darwin, he is justified in setting out a structural morphology of evolution without an explanation of just how evolution occurs. Now this was certainly true of Darwin's work. Because he did not have access to Mendel's theory of genetic mutation, he could only outline the macro constraints within which species changed. But surely this situation does not apply to Parsons. Darwin *could* not set out a theory of evolutionary process; the knowledge simply was not there. When Parsons is writing, by contrast, a great deal of knowledge about the processes of social evolution already exists. Parsons *chooses* not to discuss it. The real parallel between Parsons and Darwin is a less ennobling one. In Parsons' implicit theorizing about social change processes, he tries to make do with Darwin's theory of macro constraints alone. He takes over Darwin's theory of species competition and adaptation, which Spencer called the survival of the fittest. Even while eschewing an institutional understanding of process, therefore, there are suggestions in Parsons of how and why transitions from one form to another take place. This latent perspective, we will discover, allows Parsons to overlook knowledge about change processes that he prefers not to see.

For Parsons the world is an evolutionary field. Societies are species. They may die out, but innovations—breakthroughs to more differentiated phases—eventually occur. As a general theory of evolutionary change, there is nothing to fault this. The problem is that Parsons implies that it is a specific theory as well, that it is in order to adapt to an environment that breakthroughs in evolution actually occur. In presenting institutions and societies as problem solvers, Parsons' implicit second book takes a dangerous turn. In the long run, adaptation may be the result of a given institutional innovation, but it is rarely its efficient cause (see Alexander and Colomy 1985). Because Parsons incorporated so many of Weber's specific and antiteleological explanations, this confusion could often be avoided. That adaptation and problem solving are everywhere at work, however, is an implication of his work that cannot be denied (cf., Smelser 1985).

The results for his change theory are often disastrous. Thinking that adaptation is both cause and result provides an ideological patina for thinking about the moral implications of rationalizing change. It also hides from Parsons' understanding the full theoretical implications of his decision to ignore real processes. These ideological and theoretical difficulties come together in Parsons' sotto voce dialogue with war.

At several critical points in his evolutionary work, Parsons seems to acknowledge that the transitions between phases of differentiation may be carried out by war. In his discussion of early societies, I suggested earlier, Parsons emphasizes that upper class lineages typically depended on religious legitimation to maintain their domination, making use of this fact to explain the beginnings of religious generalization. He acknowledges, however (Parsons 1966:44), that an exception to this dependence on legitimation exists in cases "in which a group subordinates another group by military conquest." He tries to mitigate this fact in a revealing way. Whereas domination through conquest may have "played an important part in *processes* of social change," he insists, military conquest cannot be considered "*differentiation* in the present sense" (italics added). The conquerors in such situations are "a foreign group, not a structural segment of the original society." Moreover, it is "a rare, limiting case when such a group altogether eschews claims to religious legitimation and operates in terms of its naked self-interest alone." But Parsons' efforts to avoid the implications of his insight into the significance of war are beside the point. Of course, domination through conquest is not differentiation;

of course, these conquerors are not part of domestic society but a foreign group; of course, this conquering group will at some point need religious legitimation itself. None of this, however, denies the crucial fact that the transition toward a more complex society is often the result of war.

What if we knew that the transition from band to stratified societies often involved political repression and ferocious violence? This would do nothing to negate the fact that as the result of this transition more differentiation and flexibility occur. Nonetheless, this knowledge would certainly change our understanding of the meaning and implications of differentiation itself.

By underplaying process in his change theory, Parsons is able to deny the centrality (e.g., MacNeill 1982) of war in human history. Military conquest is not, of course, practiced only by conquering bands. Differentiated societies have experienced dark ages and the massive destruction of their civilizations as well. No matter what the innovations of a group, its survival is not assured. Even if a society is significantly more differentiated than those around it, one of its neighbors may be developed in a direction that is, at that historical moment, much more strategically significant in military terms. Parsons cannot see this, because he confuses differentiation with adaptive success. When he cannot avoid historical disasters, he becomes whiggish in a truly embarrassing way. He writes (1966:130), for example, that "the Nazi movement, even with its immense mobilization of power, seems to have been an acute sociopolitical disturbance, but not a source of major future structural patterns." But what does "seems to have been" mean? If a repressive system is defeated on the field of battle, this does not mean that its features were less adaptive in any short-run sense. If certain contingencies were different, some historians of the Second World War suggest, the Nazis could well have emerged victorious. Its vicious and reactionary structures would, then, certainly have established dominant social patterns throughout Europe, for an uncertain period of time.

It is because he has ignored processes like war that Parsons' differentiation theory cannot understand the fundamental role of backwardness and structural fusion in creating the history of the modern world. Sandwiched between his elegiac accounts of the Renaissance and Reformation, on the one hand, and his laudatory analysis of the industrial and democratic revolutions, on the other, one finds scarcely four pages in Parsons' book (1971:50–54) about the Counter-Reformation and its enormous repercussions for social and cultural life. Indeed, after his analysis of the democratic revolution in France, Parsons moves directly to his analysis of how high levels of social and cultural differentiation have stabilized American and Western European nations in our time. The clear implication is that steady progress was made, that "problems" like the Counter-Reformation came up and that were solved by cultural and institutional adaptation.

It might well be argued, however, that quite the reverse is true. It took hundreds of years to destroy the effects of the Counter-Reformation, which was itself a response to differentiation in the early modern period. Divisions were created throughout Europe, murderous and long-lived conflicts broke out between nations, and basic patterns of cultural particularism and social authoritarianism emerged. The massive wars of the twentieth century must be seen in this context. It was not adaptation through differentiation that ended the authoritarian systems whose roots lay in the reaction to the Renaissance and Reformation; it was more or less continuous war and revolution (Maier 1975). In the twentieth century, moreover, war has created not just the restabilized democratic systems Parsons extols but totalitarian and repressive states as well.

By ignoring process and war, however, Parsons did not simply commit the sin of sanguinity. He has also failed to generate a powerful and coherent theory of social change. In the conclusion to his work on modern societies, he acknowledges (1971:140–41) that "there has, of course, been a great deal of conflict, 'frontier' primitivism, and lag in some of the older parts of the system relative to the more progressive parts." He even allows that "certainly the history of modern systems has been one of frequent, if not continual, warfare." The conclusion that follows has about it a stunning incongruity. "The striking point," Parsons writes, "is that the *same* system of societies within which the evolutionary process that we have traced has occurred has been subject to a high incidence of violence, most conspicuously in war but also internally, including revolutions" (original italics). Indeed! As I have just suggested, this striking point is exactly what Parsons' history of the modern world does not explain.

I have spent a great deal of time on the unwritten second book of Parsons' change theory. One reason is that it spells out so clearly the problems with Parsons' unwritten third. In his own third book, Durkheim developed a compelling if theoretically contradictory account of the strains that threatened the social and moral equipoise of his time. Because Parsons emphasizes adaptation through differentiation, however, he himself can do nothing of the kind. It is worth noting, I think, that this was not always the case. In the middle period of his work, which extended from the late 1930s to the late 1940s and resulted (Parsons 1954a) in a series of essays on modern society, Parsons' writing about social change had a sharply critical edge (cf., Alexander 1981b, 1983:61–71). He did not talk about differentiation as such, but in the light of his later work it was clearly differentiation that he had in mind. The tensions between home and office, the discontinuous and sex-linked socialization processes that this separation implied, the abstraction and rationalization of modern culture, the discipline and market orientation of labor—these were institutional developments, which Parsons would later call differentiation, that he viewed as creating enormous problems for the modern world. They led to the distortion of gender identities and relationships, to alienation and interpersonal aggression, to harsh ethnic and racial conflicts, and, indeed, also to war (see, e.g., Parsons 1954b). In the midst of the period that extended from the Great Depression to Fascism and world war, Parsons saw differentiation as a cause of social problems and upheavals. In the period of postwar equipoise, by contrast, he saw differentiation as a problem-solving solution.

Because the tensions of the past are underplayed in Parsons' differentiation theory, the strains of the present cannot be displayed. In Parsons' later account, the anxiety and pathos that continue to mark the twentieth century simply fail to exist. It is not that, like Durkheim, Parsons recognizes these problems but fails to integrate his account with his general theory. It is that Parsons cannot write Durkheim's third book at all. His theory lacks a developmental notion of historically specific strains and conflicts. Thus, while he plausibly argues against the feudalism-capitalism-socialism trichotomy of Marx, he does not distinguish coherent phases of his own. References are made (Parsons 1971:141–43) to "coming phases" of modernization and to "major changes . . . in process," but, aside from vague reminders about the dangers of excessive rationality and impersonality, Parsons never tells us what these phases and changes might be.

In regard to the contemporary period, it appears, Parsons is not as interested in explaining changes as in changing explanations. In the closing pages of his studies on evolution, he attacks the "widespread pessimism over the survival of modern societies . . . especially among intellectuals," and he suggests that the goal of his work should be understood in these terms—"to establish sufficient doubt of the validity of such views." Once again, there is a furtive backward glance at the tabooed subject of war. Parsons acknowledges "the undeniable possibility of overwhelming destruction." But the possibility of war in the future will not be pursued any more than its reality was pursued in the past.

Parsons sees the twentieth century as a period of opportunity and achievement, virtually ignoring the periods of massive destruction and the phenomenon of total war. In the last phase of his life he has become the can-do American pragmatist, the irrepressible evangelical who is utterly confident that the future will be shaped in a human way. "Our view is relatively optimistic," Parsons concludes. The problem is that he cannot identify exactly the historical period he is optimistic about. His general theory certainly established the meaningful validity of "modern society." His inability to explain institutional process and to engage in genetic explanation has made it impossible, however, to know whether this meaningful social framework will be able to survive.

In the midst of the Great Depression, classical economists predicted that Say's Law remained valid. In the long run, they continued to maintain, demand would come back into equilibrium with supply and the slumping capitalist economies would revive. Keynes responded that in the long run we are all dead. The problem is the short run. In our own lifetimes, Keynes demonstrated, there is only partial equilibrium and Say's law does not everywhere apply. Without confronting pathologies in the short run, even the most meaningful civilizations may not survive. Durkheim's second and third books must be written, and they must be systematically integrated with the first.

Theoretical Revision and
Durkheim's Problem

In the polarized political climate of the 1960s and early 1970s, Parsons' version of differentiation theory became increasingly hard to sustain. It was challenged in the name of more historically specific and processual theorizing (e.g., Nisbet 1969, Smith 1973). Theorists wanted to speak of specific events, like the French Revolution (Tilly 1967) and of precise variations in national outcomes (Moore 1966). They wanted to explain specific phases and uneven development, for example, the emergence of the world capitalist system in early modern Europe (Wallerstein 1974) and the monopoly phase of capitalism (Baran and Sweezy 1966). They wanted to be able to talk about how modernization creates systemic conflicts and strains (Gusfield 1963, Gouldner 1979). Interactionists and resource mobilization theorists (Turner 1964, Gamson 1968) made claims for the centrality of social movements, and on this basis they developed explanations about the scope of change that went far beyond anything in Parsons' work. Conflict theorists (Collins 1975, Skocpol 1979) developed theories of state building and revolution that were much more historically specific and comparatively precise. There was, moreover, a pervasive shift in ideological tone. Theories became more critical and sober about the possibility that change would take a satisfactory course. These challenges insisted that Durkheim's second and third books must be written. Eventually, Marxism drew up many of these particular theories and challenged Parsons' first book as well. As I suggested above, Marxism is remarkably successful in interrelating general and specific theories of change. In that earlier period of turbulent movements for social liberation, the elegance of Marxist theory seemed empirically compelling as well.

Empiricist philosophy of science, which continues to legitimate most social science today, holds that theories live and die through falsification. As Kuhn (1969), Lakatos (1969), and other postpositivist philosophers and historians of science have shown, however, falsification cannot—or, at least, in practice usually does not—disprove a general theory, even in the natural sciences. Lakatos (cf. Wagner and Berger 1984) has developed the most plausible account of how the resistance to falsification occurs. Theories differentiate between core notions, which are positions considered essential to the theory's identity, and other commitments, which are more peripheral. Faced with studies that throw some of their important commitments into doubt, general theories can sustain their vivacity by discarding peripherals and defending their core. They seek to incorporate challenges by reworking and elaborating their new peripheral points. Of course, this kind of vivacious defense is no more than a possibility. Whether an effective shoring up process actually occurs depends on the empirical actors and the social and intellectual conditions at a particular time.

When differentiation theory first encountered the challenges to its predictions and its mode of explanation, it seemed as if no successful defense would be made. Parsons himself was never able to throw the weaker points of his general change theory overboard or to expand it in an ambitious way. Faced with the choice of abandoning the theory or changing it, many functionalists simply left it behind. A theory can be abandoned even if it is not refuted, and the effect on the course of scientific development is much the same.

Some of the most important early works of Parsons' students can be seen as attempts to set the theory right by elaborating what should have been Parsons' second book. Smelser (1959) and Eisenstadt (1963) discussed differentiation in terms of distinctive historical phases and elaborated specific processes of change; Bellah (1969) and Smelser (1963) tackled the problems of specific institutional spheres. However, while important examinations of change in their own right, as theoretical revisions these studies did not go far enough. Eventually Smelser and Eisenstadt separated the core from the periphery of differentiation theory in a much more radical way. Eisenstadt (1964) insisted that theorizing about general differentiation and specific social process was impossible to conceive in isolation. He showed (cf. Alexander and Colomy 1985 [chapter 7, below] that there are particular carrier groups for particular kinds of differentiation and that their interest structures and ideological visions determine the actual course differentiation will take. He insisted on the historical and comparative specificity of differentiation and gave to civilizational factors like culture a permanently arbitrating role (see Eisenstadt 1982, 1986). Smelser also initiated a fundamental critique from within. In his work on higher education in California, he insisted that differentiation might be seen as a self-limiting process. He insisted on the resistances to differentiation and outlined a theory of the symbiotic relationship between differentiation and self-interested elites. Eventually, he (Smelser 1985) attacked the very problem-solving framework of Parsons' differentiation theory itself.

These revisions were intellectually powerful, but they did not, at first at least, have a significant impact on debate in the field of social change. By the late 1970s this situation began to change. Several factors were involved: (1) The glow began to fade from the more institutional and phase-oriented theories that had initiated the response to Parsons' work. Neomarxist theories of the world capitalist system were challenged, for example, by rising economic growth in some third-world nations and by the fact that the threat of imminent world economic crisis began to recede. For their part, conflict perspectives appeared to have underestimated the resilience of capitalist and democratic institutions. Weber's approach to institutional process and social strain began to seem plausible once again. (2) These developments created strain between Marxism's general theory and its more specific predictions and explanations. Ideological events, moreover, lessened the political attractiveness not only of Marxism's more sweeping conclusions but also of its phase-specific theory of strains as well. (3) A new generation of theorists emerged who had not personally been involved in the revolt against differentiation and, more generally, modernization theory and did not, therefore, have a personal stake in continuing the controversy.*

By the late 1970s and early 1980s the revision of differentiation theory, which had been signaled by Smelser's and Eisenstadt's work, became both more pronounced and more widespread.† This work emerged both in Germany (Schluchter 1979; Luhmann 1981, 1987; Münch 1982, forthcoming) and the United States (Rueschemeyer 1977, Robertson 1978, Alexander 1978). These revisions proceed from the common assumption that differentiation does, indeed, provide an intuitively meaningful framework for understanding the nature of the modern world. But an effort to interrelate this general model to institutions, processes, and phase-specific strains preoccupies most differentiation theorists in the present day.‡ One group of efforts has been particularly directed to the issue of phase-specific conflicts and strains. Indeed, Gould (1985) first formulated the distinctiveness of this theoretical task in his prologemona to a theory of social

---

*It is revealing of the generic qualities shared by different approaches to change that important writers in this newer generation have criticized Marxism on the same grounds as I have criticized Parsons himself. Giddens (1986) argues, for example, that Marxism is too evolutionary in its history and that it ignores the centrality of war. Indeed, that Marx and even Weber (but see Alexander forthcoming a) ignored the centrality of war to social change indicates that the problem goes beyond difficulties with "Durkheim's problem" to very deeply routed blinders of an ideological kind. For other parallels between the recent criticism of Marxist change theory and the critique of Parsons', see my discussion of Marx's change theory earlier in this chapter.

†Colomy (forthcoming b) has provided the most extensive examination of these new developments in differentiation theory and of the criticisms to which they are a response.

‡This does not seem to apply to Luhmann's program, however. Luhmann certainly differs from Parsons in the intensity with which he has elaborated the effects of differentiation in various institutional spheres, e.g., in law, religion, family, and political life. He has not, however, succeeded in linking his general theory more firmly to institutional processes or phase-specific strains. Although any detailed consideration of Luhmann's imposing corpus cannot be given here, it is my belief that the framework suggested in this chapter can be used to critically examine his work as well.

crisis, and he has concretized it (Gould 1987) in a study of the capitalist and patrimonal origins of the English Revolution. Lechner (1985, forthcoming) has used differentiation theory to find indicators for contemporary fundamentalist movements and for structural reactions against modernity more generally. Mayhew (1984, forthcoming) had developed a notion of the differentiated public as corresponding to the early modern origins of capitalist society.

Other developments have been directed more to Durkheim's second book, to linking differentiation to specific theories of institutional behavior and processes of change. Champaigne (1983, forthcoming) has formulated a complex model for explaining the failure and success of differentiation, in particular American Indian societies, and Rhoades (forthcoming) has explained why the differentiation of higher education systems has been blocked by the nationally specific organization of professional and governmental spheres. Colomy (1982, 1985, forthcoming a) has developed the most ambitious program in this regard. Elaborating a theory of "uneven structural differentiation," he has explained the actual paths differentiation has taken in terms of the "institutional projects" developed by strategic social groups. Explaining the forces that form these projects in a systematic way, he distinguishes among institutional entrepreneurs, conservatives, and accommodationists.

Between this new wave of differentiation theory and the actual strains and conflicts that characterize change in the contemporary world there still remains too large a gap. Obviously, social science must separate itself from the direct preoccupation of everyday life. But, especially in theorizing about social change, a clear and identifiable linkage must be made. Only this connection anchors theorizing in the effervescence of everyday life, and only this value relevance makes such theorizing compelling, as well as true. I close with some illustrations of the linkages I have in mind.

Even in relatively developed countries, the autonomy of the societal community—its differentiation from religious, primordial, political, and economic spheres—is tentative. In liberal capitalist nations, for example, the media of mass communication (Alexander 1980 [chapter 4, below]) are often still partly fused with political, economic, and ethnic groupings. Even when a certain autonomy is achieved, moreover, short-term stability is far from the result. Similarly, even in societal communities that are relatively differentiated, particularistically defined core groups continue to occupy privileged positions (Alexander 1981a [chapter 3, below]). Because exclusion from this core on religious, ethnic, and social class grounds remains, struggles for inclusion are not bounded episodes but permanent and inescapable features of modern life.

It is possible to argue, in other words, that in contemporary "modern" societies differentiation still has a very long way to go. Contemporary activities in virtually every social sphere can be understood in this way. Thus, while there is no doubt that kinship and blood have vastly receded in civilizational terms, the significance of gender in virtually every area of modern society demonstrates that much fusion remains. Feminist movements can be seen, in these terms, as efforts to differentiate kinship and biology from evaluations of competence and, hence, from the distribution of economic, political, and cultural goods (cf. Walzer 1983:227–42). Current struggles for workers' control and participation can be seen in much the same way. While in democratic societies public governments have been separated from immediate economic criteria and constraints, private government—for example the organizatiaon of power in factories and organizations—remains dominated by market criteria in corporate economic life (Walzer 1983:281–312). How sharply it can be differentiated remains to be seen, but an autonomous political and participatory sphere can certainly be extended (Siriani 1981).

To recognize that differentiation is a process carried by contemporary movements of social change suggests that differentiation theory needs to elaborate a conception of social polarization. Differentiation is demanded by coalitions of elites and masses, and it is opposed by similar coalitions who benefit from less differentiated structural and cultural arrangements. Depending on the historical setting, this polarization will issue in revolution, reform, or reaction (Alexander 1981b); in the course of polarization, crises emerge (Alexander 1984 [chapter 5, below]) whose resolution is critical in determining which structural arrangement may result.

This refusal to identify differentiation with the Western status quo today, and the access to a more systematic understanding of conflict that this refusal opens up, is demonstrated in the most dramatic manner when attention is shifted from the domestic to the international plane. As I have intimated above, the emergence of more powerful and adaptive social systems not only has been stimulated by war-making but also has laid the basis for much more continuous, widely diffused, and deadly warfare in turn (cf. Collins 1986b). Not only the intranational causes of war but also the international social control of war can become an object of differentiation theory. The world system is not only an economic order but also a social one. Differentiation theory suggests that social systems can control conflict only through the creation of relatively autonomous regulatory mechanisms. From this perspective, the contemporary world system remains in a primitive and archaic form. Primordial solidarities are dominant and the possibilities for intrasystemic regulation are only regionally conceived. The relationship between this deficient regulatory system and war constitutes a vital but virtually unexplored topic for differentiation theory. War will be eliminated only to the degree that the world system replicates the processes of differentiation—incomplete as they are—that have transformed the framework of national societies.

Contemporary struggles and strains need not be conceived only in terms of the structural and cultural fusions that remain. The achievement of differentiation does not do away with social problems but, rather, shifts them to a different plane. Even when news media are independent, for example, they are subject to dramatic fluctuations in their trustworthiness (Alexander 1981a [chapter 4, below]), and they can magnify and distort contemporary information as a result. The competition that ensues between autonomous media and other powerful institutions, moreover, generates manifold possibilities for corruption. Similar strains affect the relationship between autonomous universities and their host societies. Once the university has become committed to defending the autonomy of scientific or cognitive rationality, conflicts about the university's moral obligations to society can take on new and extraordinarily vexing forms (Alexander 1986 [chapter 6, below]).

In social science, general theories are never disproved. Rather, like the proverbial soldiers of old, they simply fade away. For quite a few years it looked as if this would be the fate of differentiation theory. In this chapter I have argued that it is not. I have suggested that the difficulties faced by this approach are the same as those encountered by every ambitious theory of social change, and after examining Durkheim's classic work *The Division of Labour in Society,* I have called these difficulties "Durkheim's problem." Parsons' revisions of Durkheim's original contribution went beyond the substance of Durkheim's theorizing but did not overcome Durkheim's problem in a more generic sense. Indeed, in critical respects Parsons did not face this problem nearly as well. Weberian ideas have addressed this problem in important ways, but they neglected other aspects at the same time. Marxism addresses Durkheim's problem most successfully of all, but its empirical implausibility, I have suggested, undermines its considerable theoretical power. In response to these difficulties, and to internally generated revisions as well, a new round of differentiation theory has begun. That it addresses Durkheim's problem more effectively is certain. Whether it can solve his problem and retain its verisimilitude remains to be seen.

REFERENCES

Alexander, Jeffrey C. 1978. "Formal and Substantive Voluntarism in the Work of Talcott Parsons." *American Sociological Review* 43:177–98.
—— 1980. "Core Solidarity, Ethnic Outgroup and Structural Differentiation: Toward a Multidimensional Model of Inclusion in Modern Societies." In Jacques Dofny and Akinsola Akiwowo, eds., *National and Ethnic Movements,* pp. 5–28. Beverly Hills: Sage.
—— 1981a. "The Mass News Media in Systemic, Historical, and Comparative Perspective." In Elihu Katz and Thomas Szecsko, eds., *Mass Media and Social Change,* pp. 17–52. Beverly Hills: Sage.
—— 1981b. "Revolution, Reaction, and Reform: The Change Theory of Parsons' Middle Period," *Sociological Inquiry* 51:267–80.
—— 1983. *The Modern Reconstruction of Classical Thought: Talcott Parsons.* Vol. 4 of *Theoretical Logic in Sociology.* Berkeley and Los Angeles: University of California Press.
—— 1984. "Three Models of Culture/Society Relations: Toward an Analysis of the Watergate Crisis." *Sociological Theory* 2:290–314.
—— 1986. "The University and Morality: A Revised Approach to University Autonomy and Its Limits." *Journal of Higher Education* 57(5):463–76.
—— 1987. "The Dialectic of Individuation and Domination: Max Weber's Rationalization Theory and Beyond." In Sam Whimpster and Scott Lash, eds., *Max Weber, Rationality and Modernity.* London: Allen and Unwin, pp. 185–206.
—— forthcoming. "Introduction: Differentiation Theory, Problems and Prospects." In Alexander and Colomy, eds., *Differentiation Theory.*
Alexander, Jeffrey, ed. 1985. *Neofunctionalism.* Beverly Hills: Sage.
Alexander, Jeffrey C. and Paul Colomy. 1985. "Towards Neofunctionalism: Eisenstadt's Change Theory and Symbolic Interactionism," in *Sociological Theory* (Fall), 3: 11–23.
Alexander, Jeffrey, and Paul Colomy, eds., forthcoming. *Differentiation Theory: Problems and Prospects.* New York: Columbia University Press.
Baran, Paul and Paul Sweezy. 1966. *Monopoly Capital.* New York: Monthly Review.

Beetham, David. 1974. *Max Weber and the Theory of Modern Politics.* London: Allen and Unwin.

Bellah, Robert N. 1969. *Beyond Belief.* New York: Random House.

Bendix, Reinhard. 1961. *Max Weber: An Intellectual Portrait.* New York: Doubleday Anchor.

—— 1964. *Nation-Building and Citizenship.* New York: Doubleday Anchor.

Brubaker, Rogers. 1984. *The Limits of Rationality. An Essay on the Social and Moral Thought of Max Weber.* London: Allen and Unwin.

Champagne, Duane. 1983. "Social Structure, Revitalization Movements and State Building." *American Sociological Review* 48:754–63.

—— forthcoming. "Culture, Differentiation, and Environment." In Alexander and Colomy, eds. *Differentiation Theory.*

Colomy, Paul. 1982. "Stunted Differentiation: A Sociological Examination of Political Elites in Virginia, 1720–1850." Ph.D. dissertation, UCLA.

—— 1985. "Uneven Differentiation." In Alexander, ed. *Neofunctionalism,* pp. 131–56. Beverly Hills and London: Sage.

—— forthcoming a. "Strategic Groups and Political Differentiation in the Antebellum United States." In Alexander and Colomy, eds., *Differentiation Theory.*

—— forthcoming b. "Revision and Progress in Differentiation Theory." In Alexander and Colomy, eds., *Differentiation Theory.*

Collins, Randall. 1975. *Conflict Sociology.* New York: Academic Press.

—— 1986a. *Weberian Sociological Theory.* Cambridge, England: Cambridge University Press.

—— 1986b. "Sociological Theory, Disaster Research, and War." Paper delivered at Symposium on Social Structure and Disaster, College of William and Mary, May 15–16, 1986.

Durkheim, Emile. 1933 [1893]. *The Division of Labor in Society.* New York: Free Press.

—— 1977 [1938]. *The Evolution of Educational Thought.* London: Routledge and Kegan Paul.

Eisenstadt, S. N. 1963. *The Political System of Empires.* New York: Free Press.

—— 1964. "Institutionalization and Social Change." *American Sociological Review* 29:235–47.

—— 1982. "The Axial Age: The Emergence of Transcendental Visions and the Rise of Clerics." *European Journal of Sociology* 23:294–314.

—— 1986. *A Sociological Approach to Comparative Civilizations: The Development and Directions of a Research Program.* Jerusalem: Hebrew University.

Evans, Peter B., Dietrich Rueschemeyer, and Theda Skocpol, eds. 1985. *Bringing the State Back In.* Cambridge, England: Cambridge University Press.

Gamson, William. 1968. *Power and Discontent.* Homewood, Ill.: Dorsey Press.

Giddens, Anthony. 1981. *A Contemporary Critique of Historical Materialism.* Vol. 1: *Power, Property, and the State.* Berkeley and Los Angeles: University of California Press.

—— 1986. *The Nation-State and Violence.* Vol. 2 of *Contemporary Critique of Historical Materialism.* London: Macmillan.

Gould, Mark. 1985. "Prologomena to Future Theories of Societal Crisis." In Alexander, Jeffrey, ed., *Neofunctionalism,* pp. 57–71. Beverly Hills and London: Sage.

—— 1987. *Revolution in the Development of Capitalism.* Berkeley and Los Angeles: University of California Press.

Gouldner, Alvin W. 1979. *The New Class.* New York: Seabury.

Gusfield, Joseph. 1963. *Symbolic Crusade.* Urbana-Champagne: University of Illinois Press.

Habermas, Jürgen. 1984. *The Theory of Communicative Action,* vol. 1. Boston: Beacon.

Kuhn, Thomas. 1969. *The Structure of Scientific Revolutions.* Chicago: University of Chicago Press.

Lakatos, Imre. 1969. "Criticism and the Methodology of Scientific Research Programmes." *Proceedings of the Aristotelian Society* 69:149–86.

Lechner, Frank. 1985. "Modernity and Its Discontents." In Alexander, ed., *Neofunctionalism,* pp. 151–76. Beverly Hills: Sage.

—— forthcoming. "Fundamentalism and Sociocultural Revitalization: On the Logic of Dedifferentiation." In Alexander and Colomy, eds., *Differentiation Theory.*

Luhmann, Niklas. 1981. *The Differentiation of Society.* New York: Columbia University Press.

—— 1987. "The Evolutionary Differentiation Between Society and Interaction." In J. Alexander, B. Giesen, R. Munch, and N. Smelser, eds., *The Micro-Macro Link.* Berkeley and Los Angeles: University of California Press.

MacNeill, William H. 1982. *The Pursuit of Power: Technology, Armed Force, and Society since A.D. 1000.* Chicago: University of Chicago Press.

Maier, Charles. 1975. *Recasting Bourgeois Europe.* Princeton: Princeton University Press.

Mayhew, Leon. 1984. "In Defense of Modernity: Talcott Parsons and the Utilitarian Tradition." *American Journal of Sociology* 89:1273–1305.

—— forthcoming. "The Differentiation of the Solidary Public." In Alexander and Colomy, eds., *Differentiation Theory.*

Moore, Barrington. 1966. *The Social Origins of Dictatorship and Democracy.* Boston: Beacon.

Münch, Richard. 1982. "Talcott Parsons and the Theory of Action," pt. 2, *American Journal of Sociology* 87:771–826.

—— forthcoming. "Differentiation, Rationalization, and Interpenetration: Three Basic Features of the Emergence of Modern Societies." In Alexander and Colomy, eds., *Differentiation Theory.*

Nisbet, Robert. 1969. *Social Change and History.* London: Oxford University Press.

Parsons, Talcott. 1954a. *Essays in Sociological Theory.* New York: Free Press.

—— 1954b. "Certain Primary Sources and Patterns of Aggression in the Social Structure of the Western World." In Parsons, *Essays in Sociological Theory,* pp. 298–322. New York: Free Press.

—— 1966. *Societies: Evolutionary and Comparative Perspectives.* Englewood Cliffs, N.J.: Prentice-Hall.

—— 1967. [1960]. "Durkheim's Contribution to the Theory of Integration of Social Systems." In Parsons, *Sociological Theory and Modern Society.* New York: Free Press.

—— 1971. *The System of Modern Societies.* Englewood Cliffs, N.J.: Prentice-Hall.

Rhoades, Gary. Forthcoming. "Political Competition and Differentiation in Higher Education." In Alexander and Colomy, eds., *Differentiation Theory.*

Robertson, Roland. 1978. *Meaning and Change: Explorations in the Cultural Sociology of Modern Societies.* New York: Oxford University Press.

Rueschemeyer, Dietrich. 1977. "Structural Differentiation, Efficiency, and Power." *American Journal of Sociology* 83:1–25.

Schluchter, Wolfgang. 1979. "The Paradoxes of Rationalization." In Guenther Roth and Schluchter, *Max Weber's Vision of History,* pp. 11–64. Los Angeles and Berkeley: University of California Press.

—— 1981. *The Rise of Western Rationalism: Max Weber's Developmental History.* Berkeley and Los Angeles: University of California Press.

Sewell, William H., Jr. 1980. *Work and Revolution in France: The Language of Labor from the Old Regime to 1848.* Cambridge, England: Cambridge University Press.

Siriani, Carmen. 1981. "Production and Power in a Classless Society: A Critical Analysis of the Utopian Dimensions of Marxist Theory." *Socialist Review* 59:33–82.

Skocpol, Theda. 1979. *States and Social Revolutions.* New York: Cambridge University Press.

Smelser, Neil J. 1959. *Social Change in the Industrial Revolution.* Chicago: University of Chicago Press.

—— 1963. *The Sociology of Economic Life.* Englewood Cliffs, N.J.: Prentice-Hall.

—— 1973. "Epilogue: Social Structural Dimensions of Higher Education." In Parsons and Platt, *The American University,* pp. 389–422. Cambridge, Mass.: Harvard University Press.

—— 1974. "Growth, Structural Change, and Conflict in California Higher Education, 1950–1970." In Smelser and Gabriel Almond, eds., *Public Higher Education in California,* pp. 9–141. Berkeley and Los Angeles: University of California Press.

—— 1985. "Evaluating the Model of Structural Differentiation in Relation to Educational Change in the Nineteenth Century." In Alexander, ed., *Neofunctionalism,* pp. 113–130. Beverly Hills and London: Sage.

Smith, Anthony. 1973. *The Concept of Social Change: A Critique of the Functionalist Theory of Change.* London: Routledge and Kegan Paul.

Tilly, Charles. 1967. *The Vendee*. New York: Wiley.

Tourraine, Alain, Francois Dubet, Michel Wieviorka, and Jan Strzelecki. 1983. *Solidarity. The Analysis of a Social Movement: Poland 1980–1981*. Cambridge, England: Cambridge University Press, Paris: Editions de la Maison des Sciences de l'Homme.

Turner, Ralph H. 1964. "Collective Behavior and Conflict." *Sociological Quarterly* 5:122–32.

Wagner, David and Joseph Berger. 1984. "Do Sociological Theories Grow?" *American Journal of Sociology* 90:697–728.

Wallerstein, Immanual. 1974. *The Modern World System*. New York: Academic Press.

Walzer, Michael. 1983. *Spheres of Justice*. New York: Basic.

Weber, Max. 1958. [1920]. "Author's Introduction." In *The Protestant Ethic and the Spirit of Capitalism*. New York: Scribners.

—— 1978. [1918]. "Socialism." In W. G. Runciman, ed., *Weber: Selections in Translation*. London: Cambridge University Press.

THREE

Core Solidarity, Ethnic Outgroup, and Social Differentiation

Theorists of Western development have been hard put to account for the ethnic and racial conflicts that have created the recent wave of nationalist and separatist movements in industrial societies. For developing nations, such conflicts are to be expected; they are part of the "transition" period. But after industrial society is firmly established, it is believed such divisions will become residual, not systematic or indeed intensifying contradictions. (Marx 1848 [1955]; Tonnies 1887 [1957]; Weber 1904 [1958]; Durkheim 1893 [1947]).

This theoretical difficulty is fundamental; its roots lie in the complex history of Western development itself. Theories of nation building are products of Enlightenment thinking, generated by the twin revolutions of political nationalism and industrialism. As the analytic translation of these social developments, they have been rationalistic in the extreme, sharing a utilitarian distaste for the nonrational and normative and the illusion that a truly modern society will soon dispense with such concerns.

One antidote to this theoretical failing is increased sensitivity to secular myth and cultural patterns, phenomena with which theorists have been increasingly concerned (Geertz 1973a; Bellah 1970). But solidarity is the more crucial theoretical dimension for problems of emergent ethnicity and nationalist conflicts. The concept of solidarity refers to the subjective feelings of integration that individuals experience for members of their social groups. Given its phenomenological character, solidarity problems

I acknowledge the advice and helpful critical readings of a number of friends and colleagues: Jeffrey Prager, Seamus Thompson, Leo Kuper, Ivan Light, Dean R. Gerstein, and Ruth Bloch. I have also received invaluable aid from Maria Iosue, who was my research assistant for this project.

clearly diverge from those of economics and politics, which concern themselves, respectively, with scarcity and the self-conscious organization of goals. Yet solidarity also differs from problems of culture, which are oriented toward meaningful patterns relatively abstracted from specific time and space. Thus, although integrative exigencies are not generated by purely instrumental considerations, they are more concrete than "values." In contrast to values, social solidarity refers to the structure of actual social groups. Like religion, politics, and economics, solidarity constitutes an independent determinant of human societies and a fundamental point for sociological analysis (Shils 1975a; Parsons 1967a, 1971; Alexander 1978, 1983; cf. Nakane 1970, Light 1972).

"Inclusion" and the Paradigm of Linear Evolution

Solidarity becomes a fundamental factor because every nation must, after all, begin historically. Nations do not simply emerge out of thin air, for example, as universalistic, constitutional entities. They are founded by groups whose members share certain qualitatively distinct characteristics, traits around which they structure their solidarity. No matter what kind of future institutions this "core goup" establishes, no matter what the eventual liberalism of its social and political order, residues of this core solidarity remain.

From the perspective of the integrative problem, national development can be viewed as a process of encountering and producing new solidary outgroups (cf. Lipset and Rokkan 1967; Rokkan 1975). With religious and economic rationalization, new sects and social classes are created. With territorial expansion and immigration, new ethnic groups are encountered (cf. E. Weber 1976). In response to these developments, pressures develop to expand the solidarity that binds the core group. In this way, nation building presents the problem of "inclusion" (Parsons 1967b, 1971).

I define inclusion as the process by which previously excluded groups gain solidarity in the "terminal" community of a society. Two points are crucial in this definition. First, inclusion refers to *felt* solidarity, not simply to behavioral participation. Pariah groups that fill crucial social roles— like Western Jews in the Middle Ages or Indians in post-Colonial

Uganda—are not "included."* Second, I am concerned here specifically with a society's terminal community (Geerts 1973b). A dominant focus of the American tradition of race relations and ethnicity studies has focused almost exclusively on the primary group level, on whether individuals join the same clubs, make the same friends, and intermarry (Gordon 1964). While such questions are certainly significant, morally as well as intellectually, they cannot provide the only important focus for historical and comparative analysis. In defining the terminal community as the widest solidary group with which individuals feel significant integration, I am referring to those feelings that, extending beyond family and friends, create the boundaries of acknowledged "society." Whether this terminal community is narrow and limiting or is expansive enough to encompass a range of particular groupings—this question is as ramifying an issue as the level of economic or political development or the nature of religious belief. Inclusion, then, refers to a change in solidary status. To the degree that individuals are felt to be full members of the terminal community they have to that degree been "included."

Inclusion can be measured by the degree to which the terminal community has become more "civil" and less "primordial." The latter refer to the given, seemingly natural ties that structure solidarity—race, territory, kinship, language, even religion (Geerts 1973b, Shils 1975b). To the degree that people share any one of these traits, they will feel direct, emotional bonds. Primordial ties are necessarily few. In aboriginal society, where the "world" ended at the farthest waterhole, sex, kinship, age, and territory presented the principal axes for solidary identification.

Civil ties, on the other hand, are more mediated and less emotional, more abstract and self-consciously constructed. Instead of referring to biological or geographic givens, they refer to ethical or moral qualities associated with "social" functions and institutions. The emergence of civil ties can be seen as a process of differentiation, one that parallels the movements toward economic, political, and religious differentiation that have been the traditional foci of modernization theory. Membership in the terminal community must, in the first place, be separated from mem-

*At its extreme, such purely behavioral participation by outgroups forms the basis of "plural societies," in the terminology developed by Kuper and Smith (1969; Kuper, 1978). In their terms, I am dealing in this essay with the causes and consequences of different degrees of pluralization in the industrial West, a subject to which plural societies theory has not yet devoted significant attention.

bership in particular kinship groups and, more generally, from biological criteria. This community solidarity must also be differentiated from status in the economic, political, and religious community.

The primordial-civil continuum, then, provides an independent criterion for evaluating the inclusion process. This standard has usually, however, been applied in an artificial, linear way even by those theorists who have taken the integrative problem seriously. From Hegel and Tocqueville to Parsons, the transition from primordial to civil solidarity has been envisioned as rigidly interlocked with political and economic transformation. The ideal-typical point of origin is the narrow moral basis of Banfield's "backward society," a self-contained village where identification scarcely extends beyond the family to the town, let alone to occupation, class, or even religious affiliation (Banfield 1959). This primordial community is then transformed in the course of modernization into Durkheim's organic solidarity, Parsons' societal community, or Tocqueville's mass democracy; given the expansive civil ties in the latter societies, individuals "rightly understand" their self-interest (Durkheim 1893 [1933]; Tocqueville 1835 [1945]; Parsons 1971).

To a significant degree, such a universalizing transformation in solidarity has, indeed, characterized the modernization process. In the Western Middle Ages, the Christian Church provided the only overarching integration that bound distinct villages and estates. It was, after all, the Papal bureaucracy that created the territorial jurisdictions of Gallia, Germania, Italia, and Anglia long before these abstract communities ever became concrete groupings (Coulton 1935:28–29). It did so, fundamentally, because Christian symbolism envisioned a civil solidarity that could transcend the primordial ties of blood (Weber 1904 [1958]). Similarly, alongside the officers of the Church, the King's henchmen were the only medieval figures whose consciousness extended beyond village and clan. To the degree the King and his staff succeeded in establishing national bureaucracies, they contributed enormously to the creation of a civil terminal community, despite the primordial qualities that remained powerfully associated with this national core group (Royal Institute of International Affairs 1939:8–21; cf. Eisenstadt 1963). Economic development also has been closely intertwined with the extension of civil ties, as Marx himself implicitly acknowledged when he praised capitalism for making "national one-sidedness and narrow-mindedness . . . more and more impossible" (Marx 1848 [1955]: 13; cf. Landes 1969:1–40).

Civil solidarity is, in fact, fundamentally linked to differentiation in these other structural dimensions. Only if religion is abstracted from the earthly realm and oriented toward a transcendent, impersonal divine source can "individualism" emerge, i.e., an accordance of status to the individual person regardless of social position (Little 1969, Walzer 1965). Only with political constitutionalism, which is closely related to such religious developments (Friedrichs 1964), can groups respond to injustice, not in terms of reasserting primordial unity, but in terms of defending their rights as members of the wider community (Bendix 1964 [1977]). Only with the functional, impersonal form of industrial organization can positions be awarded on the basis of efficiency rather than in terms of kinship, race, or geographical origins. Civil solidarity cannot, however, simply be considered the reflection of these other differentiations. Not only does it constitute an independent, nonresidual dimension with which these institutional developments interact. It occurs, in addition, through particular, concrete mechanisms that, in responding to these developments, create wider solidarity: through more efficient transportation and communication, increased geographical and cultural mobility, urbanization, secular education, mass and elite occupational mobility and intermarriage, and increasingly consensual civic ritualization (cf. E. Weber 1976; Goode 1963:28–80; Lipset and Bendix 1960; Shils and Young 1975 [1956]:135–52).*

---

*Although few of the treatments of these mechanisms sufficiently relate them to the distinctive problem of solidarity, the last mechanism I have cited, civic ritualization, is rarely given any attention at all. By civic ritual I refer to the affectively charged, rhetorically simplified occasions through which a society affirms the solidary bonds of its terminal community. Such consensual rituals, microcosms of which are repeated in local milieu, include everything from the funeral ceremonies of powerful leaders to the televised dramas of national political crises (see my discussion of Watergate in chapter 5) and the spectacles of national sport championships. One crucial symbolic element often invoked by these rituals is directly relevant to the crucial historical position of any society's core group, namely, the element of "national ancestors." Every system of national symbolism involves a myth of creation, and these narrative stories must be personified in terms of actual historical persons. These ancestors become an ascriptive "family" for the members of the terminal community, as, in America, George Washington is viewed as the "father" of the American nation. As the personification of the founding core group, ethnic composition of these symbolic national ancestors is crucial, and the solidary history of a nation can be traced in terms of shifts in their purported ethnicity. In the United States, for example, there has been a struggle over whether the black leader, Martin Luther King, will be accorded such symbolic founding status. The creation of a national holiday honoring his birthday may have resolved this in the affirmative, but it is still too early for a definitive answer.

But although these systemic linkages are certainly correct, there has been a strong tendency to conflate such abstract complementarity with empirical history. Theorists of solidarity have themselves been infected by Enlightenment rationalism. From the beginning of Western society, in fact, "progressive" thinking has confidently proclaimed purely civic solidarity to be the "future" of the human race, whether this future lay in the Athenian polis, Roman law, the universal brotherhood of Christianity, the social contract, the General Will, or in classless communism.* But in historical reality differentiation is not a homogeneous process. It occurs in different spheres at different times, and these leads and lags have enormously complex repercussions on societal development (Smelser 1971, Vallier 1971, Eisenstadt 1973, E. Weber 1976). As an autonomous dimension, solidarity varies independently of developments in other spheres. As a result, civic integration is always unevenly attained. Indeed, the newly created, more expansive associations that result from differentiation will often themselves become, at some later point in time, narrowly focused solidarities that oppose any further development. This is as true for the transcendent religions and nationalist ideologies that have promoted symbolic and political differentiation as for the economic classes, like the bourgeoisie and proletariat, which after a triumphant expansion of cosmopolitanism have often become a source of conservative antagonism to the wider whole.

Most fundamentally, however, civil integration is uneven because every national society exhibits a historical core. While this founding group may create a highly differentiated, national political framework, it will also necessarily establish, at the same time, the preeminence of certain primordial qualities.† While members of noncore groups may be extended full legal rights and may even achieve high levels of actual institutional participation, their full membership in the solidarity of the national community may never be complete (Lipset and Rokkan 1967; Rokkan 1975). This tension between core and civil solidarity must inform any theory of inclusion in industrial societies.

*Even when anticivil developments are acknowledged, they tend to be treated as deviant eruptions from the purely civil mode, as in Nolte's penetrating analysis of Fascism as an "anti-transcendent" ideology or in Mosse's analysis of blood as the common denominator of German "Volk" culture (Nolte 1965, Mosse 1964).

†This general statement must be modified in applying this model to developing rather than to developed nations. Although every society does have a historical, solidary core, the artificiality of the creation of many postcolonial societies leaves several founding ethnic blocs in primordial competition rather than a single founding group.

A Multidimensional Model: The Internal and
External Axes of Inclusion

My focus here is on the problem of ethnic, not class, inclusion. I define ethnicity as the real or perceived primordial qualities that accrue to a group by virtue of shared race, religion, or national origin, including in the latter category linguistic and other cultural attributes associated with a common territorial ancestry (cf. Schermerhorn 1970:12).

Inclusion of an ethnic outgroup depends on two factors: (1) the external, or environmental, factor, which refers to the structure of society that surrounds the core group; (2) the internal, or volitional, factor, which refers to the relationship between the primordial qualities of core group and outgroup. The external factor includes the economic, political, integrative, and religious systems of society; the more differentiated these systems are, the more inclusion becomes a legitimate possibility. In contrast to this external reference, the internal factor is more volitional: to the degree that primordial complementarity exists between core goup and outgroup, members of the core group will tend to regard inclusion as a desirable possibility. Finally, although both internal and external factors can be measured behaviorally, their most significant impact is subjective and phenomenological. To the degree that the environment is differentiated and primordiality is complementary, the felt boundaries of the terminal community will become more expansive and civil.

While remaining systematic, this general model takes into account a wide range of factors. Each factor can be treated as independently variable, and by holding other factors constant, we can establish experimental control. Of course, such a general model cannot simply be tested; it must also be specified and elaborated. This can be accomplished by at least two different strategies.

Taking a purely analytic approach, we may trace the effects of varying each factor in turn. We can demonstrate, for example, that in terms of the external environment, differentiation in every social sphere—not simply changes in solidarity itself—has consequences for the structure of terminal integration. In South Africa, for example, while the divergence among primordial qualities remained fairly constant, more differentiated *economic development* ramified in ways that enlarged core and outgroup interaction and increased the pressures on the rigidly ascribed political order (cf. Kuper 1969). Similarly, while primordial anti-Semitism remained unchanged and legal restrictions were unaltered, European mercantilism created important opportunities for the exercise of Jewish financial expertise, whose recognition eventually had wide-ranging repercussions. In nineteenth-century America, on the other hand, the black outgroup was not drawn first into qualitatively more differentiated economic production. While the primordial separation between black and Caucasian Americans remained constant, the Civil War initiated changes in the *legal system* that differentiated some (if not all) individual rights from racial qualities. As an example of variation in the *political environment*, we can refer to the processes often initiated by the construction of certain great empires. By differentiating overarching bureaucracies and impersonal rules, conquerors like Alexander and Napoleon opened up opportunities for excluded groups, like the Jews, in nations where the primordial distinctions between core group and outgroup, and other structural characteristics as well, had remained relatively unchanged.

Although the relative differentiation of religion constitutes another variable in the inclusion process, as I have indicated in the first section of this chapter and will illustrate further below, the contrast between Protestantism and Catholicism, both relatively transcendent religions, is instructive for the kinds of specifications that must be introduced in applying this model to the complexity of a concrete historical case. Whereas the greater symbolic abstraction and institutional differentiation of Protestantism, especially the Puritan variety, is generally more conducive to inclusion than Catholicism, in the exclusion produced by slavery the reverse has often been true, as the contrast between Anglo-Saxon and Iberian slave conditions has demonstrated (Elkins 1969). Indeed, in the particular conditions of slavery, two of the most traditionalistic aspects of Iberian Catholicism were particularly conducive to black inclusion: (1) Its relative paternalism generated a greater concern for the well-being of outgroups than the more individualistic voluntary principle of Protestant societies did; (2) The Catholic fusion of church and state encouraged religious interference in the political and legal order to an extent unheard of in Anglo-Saxon societies.

These broad structural changes in "external environment" have affected solidarity through the kinds of specific integrating mechanisms I outlined above: through increased interaction as effected through geographic and economic mobility, increased economic and political participation, expanded education and communication, and intermarriage. Significant numbers of American blacks, for example, later used their upgraded legal status to emigrate to urban areas, where the racially based qualifications for economic and political participation could not be so easily enforced. Small but influential segments of European Jewry (the *Schutzjuden,* or "Protected Jews") used the limited political immunity generated by their economic prowess to gain access to the secular, homogenizing culture of nineteenth-century Europe. By the same token, it was participation in South Africa's differentiated economic life that produced for the non-whites increased access to universalistic culture through education, and economic and geographical mobility through, in part, expanding urbanization (Doxey 1961:85–109; Van der Horst 1965; Van den Berghe 1965:86, 279–80). In fact, it was precisely to inhibit and control these mechanisms—to protect core group domination from the effects of societal differentiation—that Apartheid was first introduced by the Akfrikaner Nationalist elite (Kuper 1960; Van den Berghe 1965; cf. Blumer 1965).

We may, on the other hand, hold environmental factors constant and trace the effects of variation in the internal factors. Probably the most significant illustration of variation in primordial complementarity and its relation to inclusion is the widespread phenomenon of finely graded color stratification (cf. Gergen 1968). In Mexico, where light Spanish or *criollo* complexion has traditionally defined the racial core, *mestizos,* or mixed bloods, are granted significantly more inclusion than the darker skinned Indians. This continuum from the light to dark color has created a finely graded series of "internal" opportunities for inclusion. The same kind of color gradation, from black to "colored" to white affects access to the internal environment in South Africa. The rule in both cases is based on the complementarity criterion: members of a solidary outgroup have access to the degree their racial traits are conceived as closer to those of the core group. Similar kinds of gradations could be established along the dimensions of religion and national origins, as I illustrate in part 3. Variation in these internal factors facilitates inclusion by affecting the kinds of structural mechanisms I have cited above. And the latter, of course, affect the way the complementarity criterion manifests itself in turn. Thus, while Peru exhibits the same grading of color, darker "mixed blood" has gained significantly less inclusion there than in Mexico. This variation can be explained by the interaction of color with the greater differentiation of Mexican social structure, produced by the contrast between Mexican and Peruvian colonial development and by the impact of the Mexican Revolution (Harris 1964:36–40).

Having outlined the major analytic features of this inclusion model, in the following I seek to demonstrate its applicability via a specific case study.[1]

The Model Applied: The Uneven Inclusion of Europeans, Asians, and Africans in the United States

In discussing the U.S. case, I compare inclusion for European and non-European immigrants and consider, within each category, the variation in both internal and external factors.

The social system that confronted mass European immigration after 1820 presented, by the standards of its time, an unusually "civil" structure. In large part, this depended on America's historial past, or perhaps the lack of one (Hartz 1955; Lipset 1965:1–233). Without an American feudalism, there existed no aristocracy that could monopolize economic, political, and intellectual prerogatives on a primordial basis. Similarly, without the legacy of Catholicism and an established Church, spiritual domination and monopolization were less viable possibilities (Bellah 1970:168–89).

As a result of this legacy, and other historically specific factors as well, institutional life in America was either unusually differentiated or, at least, open to becoming more so. Schumpeter's notion of an open class system applies more to the early American nation than to Europe, for while geographical and economic mobility did not eliminate the American class structure, they guaranteed that actual class membership fluctuated to a significant degree (Thernstrom 1974). Although America had an unusually weak national bureaucracy, the political system was differentiated in other important ways. The combination of strong constitutional principles and dearth of traditional elites generated early party conflict and encouraged the allocation of administrative offices by political "spoils" rather than according to the kind of implicit kinship criteria inherent in a more traditional status-based civil service. Wide distribution of property, plus populist opposition to stringent electoral qualifications, meant significant disperson of the franchise. Finally, the diversity and decentralized character of Protestant churches in America encouraged the proliferation of pietistic religious sects and voluntary denominationalism rather than religious establishment (Miller 1956:16–98, 141–52; 1967:90–120, 150–62; Mead 1963:12–37 and chapter 2, above). The transcendent, abstract quality of Anglo-American Protestantism also made it conducive to the secularization of intellectual and scientific discussion and to the emergence of public, nonreligious education.

This external situation must be balanced, however, against the internal one. Despite its relatively civil structure, this American nation had been founded by a strong, self-conscious primordial core. White in race, Anglo-Saxon and English-speaking in ethnicity, intensely Protestant in religious identity, this "WASP" core group sought to maintain a paradox that, though hypocritical, was rooted in the historical experience of the American nation. They asserted that American institutions, while differentiated and civil, were, at the same time, permeated by certain primordial qualities (Jordan 1968). And, indeed, although this was a basic factor in American race relations from the outset, until the 1820s and 1830s this anomaly was not severely tested within the white society. During the seventeenth century, European immigrants were almost entirely English, and though the sources of immigration varied more in the eighteenth century, the nation's English and Protestant primordial core could still conceivably be identified with the institutional structure of the nation (Hansen 1940; Handlin 1957:23–39).

Between 1820 and 1920, America experienced massive immigration from a wide variety of European nations. As the core group tried to defend its privileged position, this process produced waves of xenophobic sentiment and exclusionary movements (Higham 1969). Yet by the middle of the present century, these outgroups had achieved relatively successful inclusion (Glazer 1975:3–32), at least within the limits established by the necessarily historical roots of national identity (Gordon 1964; Glazer and Moynihan 1963).

In terms of the internal, volitional factor in inclusion, the points of conflict and accommodation in the immigration process must be assessed in terms of the congruence between primordial solidarities (Hansen 1940; cf. Schooler 1976). While the Caucasian homogeneity of outgroup and core group prevented racial conflict, significant polarization still occurred between the WASP core and non-English immigrants. The division was most intense, however, between core and Northern European immigrants, on one side, and Southern European groups on the other (Handlin 1957:75, 85; Higham 1969). Southern Europeans, after all, differed more strikingly from the core in national culture and language. Although this national conflict was partly offset by the Christianity that most immigrants shared, antipathy between Catholic and Protestant made the religious variable another significant point of ethnic cleavage.

In the actual empirical process of inclusion, these points of internal cleavage and convergence were combined in a variety of ways (Parsons 1967b; Blauner 1972:56, 68). The Irish, for example, played an important bridging role, for while sharing certain vital cultural and linguistic traits with the English core, their Catholicism allowed them to interpenetrate on the religious dimension with the later, more intensely excluded Catholic group, the Italians (cf. Handlin 1951 [1973]:116–24). Similarly, although the Jews were disliked for specifically religious reasons, this tension was partially offset by racial and national convergence, particularly in the cases of Northern European Jews like the Germans. Between the Christian core group and Eastern European Jewish immigrants, in fact, German Jews often played a mediating role like that of the Irish Catholics to the Southern Europeans (Howe 1976).

After they had become naturalized citizens, and within the limitations established by their primordial divergence, these European immigrants took advantage of the openings presented by differentiation in the external environment to contest the privileged position of America's WASP core (Handlin 1951 [1973]). According to their respective origins and special skills, groups took different institutional paths toward inclusion. Catholics used American disestablishment to gain religious inclusion and legitimacy, and Catholicism gradually became transformed into one Christian denomination among many (Ahlstrom 1972:546–54, 825–41). In the big cities, Catholics used America's party structure and spoils system to build political power. Jews, on the other hand, parlayed their urban-economic background into skills that were needed in the industrializing economic system (Blauner 1972:62–63). Later, the Jewish emphasis on literacy—which in its similar Old Testament emphasis on the "word" partly neutralized the Protestant religious cleavage—helped Jews gain access to the intellectual and scientific products of America's secular culture.

The internal and external situation that confronted America's non-European immigrants—those from Africa and Asia—was strikingly different.* In terms of primordial qualities, the divergence was much more intense. Racial differences created an initial, highly flammable cleavage, one to which Protestant societies are particularly sensitized (Elkins 1969; Tannenbaum 1969; Bellah 1975:86–112). Asians and Africans were also distinguished more sharply in the religious dimension, for few shared the majority's commitment to Christianity. In fact, as "non-Christians," blacks were in the seventeenth and eighteenth centuries as often the butt of religions slurs as they were of racial epithets. Superimposed on these religious and racial dimensions was the sharp divergence between non-Europeans and the American core in terms of national origins, viz., long-standing American fantasies about "darkest Africa" and the "exotic Orient" (Light 1972; Blauner 1972:65).

Not only were national traditions and territory more disjunctive, but also there existed no common linguistic reference or (for Africans at least) urban tradition to bridge the gap (Blauner 1972:61; Handlin 1957:80–81). The WASP core group, and indeed, the new European immigrants themselves, reacted strongly against such primordial disparity: the history of mob violence against Chinese and blacks has no precedent in reactions against European immigrants.

Equally important in the fate of these immigrants, however, was the nature of the external evironment they entered (cf. Blauner 1972). Entering as slaves in the seventeenth and eighteenth centuries, blacks were without legal rights. Because their participation in American institutional life was at every point legally fused with the biological criteria of race, they faced a closed, not an open and differentiated, social system. Although the circumstances were much less severe for the Chinese immigrants who entered in mass in the 1850s, their common status as indentured labor sharply limited their mobility and competitiveness in the labor market (Bean 1968:163–65; Lyman 1970:64–77). This external inhibition exacerbated primordial antagonism, and the California state legislature passed a series of restrictive pieces of legislation that further closed various aspects of institutional life (Lyman 1970:95–97). Similarly, whereas the Japanese did not face any initial external barriers, the primordial reaction against the agricultural success of immigrant Japanese

---

*A complete picture of the U.S. situation would have to include also the core group conquest of the native North American Indian civilization and the incorporation of the Mexican population of the Southwestern United States. Although I believe that these more explicitly colonial situations can be analyzed within the framework presented here, specific variations must be introduced. See the section that follows in the text.

farmers produced California's Alien Land Law, which fused farm ownership with naturalized citizenship, a status denied to all non-Caucasian, first-generation immigrants (Bean 1968:332–35; Modell 1970:106–10). This law partly undermined their agriculture production, forcing masses of Japanese into the cities (Light 1972:73–74). At one time or another, then, each non-European group faced a social environment that was "fused" to one degree or another. Simply in terms of external factors alone, therefore, non-European immigrants could not as easily transform their numbers into political power, their economic talents into skills and rewards, and their intellectual abilities into cultural accomplishments.

Uneven institutional differentiation and internal primordial divergence together generated massive barriers to African and Asian inclusion that protected not only the WASP core group but also the partially included European immigrants. To the degree that American blacks and Asians have moved toward inclusion, it is the result of accommodation on both these fronts. In terms of internal factors, widespread conversion not only to Christianity but also to "Americanism," the adoption of the English language, and the assumption of an urban life style have had significant impact, as have the changing religious sensitivities of the Christian majority and the continued secularization of American culture.

On the external side, institutional differentiation has opened up in different dimensions at different times. With the legal shift after the Civil War, economic and cultural facilities (Lieberson 1980:159–69) began to be available for some blacks, particularly for those who immigrated to Northern cities after the First World War. Only after further legal transformation in the 1950s and 1960s, however, has political power become fully accessible, a political leverage that in turn has provided greater cultural and economic participation. In the Asian case, discriminatory legislative enactments were gradually overturned in the courts and formally free access to societal resources was restored by the end of World War II. Two facts explain the remarkably greater rate of Asian inclusion as compared to black. First, their great "external" advantages allowed Chinese and Japanese immigrants to preserve, at least for several generations, the resilient extended-kinship network of traditional societies (Light 1972; cf. Eisenstadt 1954). Second, the core group's primordial antipathy was, in the end, less intense toward Asians (Lieberson 1980:366–67), whose racial contrast was less dramatic, traditional religion more literate, and national origins more urbanized and generally accessible.

A Note on the Model's Application
to the Colonial Situation

Although I have developed this model specifically with reference to relatively modernized Western societies, I would like to comment briefly on its relevance to the colonial situation, both because the notion of "internal colonialism" has been recently applied to these Western societies (Blauner 1972; Hechter 1975; see note 1, below) and because colonial and post-colonial societies have themselves been so vitally affected by the modernization process.

As a form of ethnic domination that usually combines a highly fused external environment with vast primordial disparity, the prototypical colonial situation must be viewed as the polar opposite of solidary inclusion. For this reason, and because colonization has involved the initial and often continual application of force, there has been a strong tendency to perceive colonialization in a theoretically undifferentiated way, as initiating a system of total domination that can end only in secession and revolution. From the perspective developed here, this perception is in error: the colonial situation is subject to the same kind of analytic differentiation and internal variation as any other relationship between core group and subordinate outgroup. Indeed, every core group, whether in the West or in the third world, rests initially upon some form of colonialization. Early Parisians colonized the territorial communities that later composed France, much as later Frenchmen tried to incorporate, much less successfully, the North African Algerian community. Similarly, the difference is only one of degree between the aggressive nation building initially undertaken with the island, now called England, by the English core group; the subsequent domination by the English nation over its neighboring communities in the British Isles; and the later English colonization of the non-British empire.

Resolution of the colonial situation, then, varies according to the same analytic factors as the inclusion or exclusion of outgroups in Western societies does. Although the rigidity of later colonial situations has often produced radicalized nationalist movements for ethnic secession (see the section following), there have been alternative developments. The case of Great Britain is instructive in this regard (for background, see Beckett 1966, Bulpitt 1976, Hanham 1969, Hechter 1975, Mitchison 1970, Norman 1968, Philip 1975, Rose 1970, 1971).

Although Wales, Scotland, and Ireland were all incorporated involuntarily, the nature of the external political factor by which this colonization was accomplished was crucial for later events. The early military domination of Ireland by the still highly traditional English state was far harsher than the later incorporation of Wales and Scotland by an English state much more committed to bureaucratic and, in the case of Scotland, constitutional organization. This initial political variation created a crucial context for the critical primordial relation of religion, helping to determine the relative success of England's attempts to incorporate these colonies into Reformation Protestantism. Scotland and Wales were successfully "reformed"; Ireland was not. In combination with the territorial discontinuity of Ireland, this internal factor created the basis for the much more passionate primordial antipathy that developed between Ireland and England. It also prevented the kind of elite intermingling that helped to further mitigate primordial antagonism between England and the other colonies. On the basis of this primordial religious antagonism, the relatively undifferentiated condition of English church-state relations became crucial to Irish development, producing the fusion of economic, political, and religious position that was unknown to Wales and Scotland. This, in turn, set the stage for the harsh settlement communities that finally transformed the Irish-English relation into the kind of rigid and exploitative situation that is so close to the traditional "colonial" one. Finally, only in this multidimensional historical context can the divergent responses to English industrialization be properly understood. Whereas the vast differentiation of the English economy that occurred in the nineteenth century produced significant leverage for the Welsh and Scots, the Irish were unable to take advantage of this opportunity for inclusion to any comparable degree. Indeed, in Ireland, this industrialization actually helped to create the internal resources for national emancipation.

In such rigid colonial situations, if economic and cultural mobilization do not lead to successful secessionist movements (see below), they may trigger, instead, extraordinary efforts at core group protection. In South Africa, Apartheid was instituted only in 1948, after intensifying economic, political, and cultural modernization threatened to open up various spheres to African participation (Doxey 1961; Van der Horst 1965). In terms of the model proposed here, Apartheid represents an attempt to isolate the "mechanisms" of inclusion—urbanization, geographical and economic mobility, education, communication, intermarriage—from the underlying processes of differentiation that produced them. Using formally legitimate coercion, Apartheid tries to link each of these mechanisms to the primordial dimension of race. It establishes racial "tracks" for job training, urbanization, education, intermarriage, sexual intercourse, spiritual action, public association, and communication (Kuper 1960). In this strategy of coping with increased differentiation through government-induced and government-legitimated racialism, the Apartheid strategy resembles the Nazi one. Just as Nazism went beyond the merely conservative antidemocratic regimes of an earlier Germany because the latter could no longer manage the strains of a rapidly and unevenly differentiating society, so Apartheid is the kind of radical, violent response to a challenge to core solidarity that occurs only in an industrial society undergoing rapid modernization. In both German Nazism and South African Apartheid, this more radical opposition to change was carried out by the more insecure older social groups, in Germany by segments of the lower middle class, in South Africa by the Afrikaner (not the British) Nationalist party.

If traditional colonization could create such different outcomes depending on the particular content of external and internal relationships, the fate of so-called "internal colonies" in contemporary industrial societies must surely be considered in an equally differentiated way. Only such a sensitivity to analytical variations, for example, can explain the kind of divergent experiences of the descendants of Mexicans, Africans, Indians, Japanese, and Chinese—all of whom have been considered colonized groups—in the United States today.

The Process of Inclusion and Ideological Strategies

Structural dislocations, of course, do not directly imply social mobilization. However, with the single exception of diaspora communities, solidary exclusion will, eventually, provoke mobilization designed to equalize outgroup position vis-à-vis the core. The nature of these struggles and the kind of ideological strategies the outgroups assume will be related closely to the structural bases of their exclusion. Three ideal-typical strategies may be distinguished.

Assimilative Movements and "Equal Opportunity." Assimilation may be defined as the effort to achieve full institutional participation through identification with the primordial qualities of the core group. Significant movement in this antiethnic direction will be a viable strategy only under certain conditions. If inclusion is reasonably to be viewed simply as a matter of closing the "primordial gap," fairly substantial external opportunities must exist. Assimilation is not, of course, a rationally calculated strategy. It emerges rather from the experience of relative commonality and from certain levels of actual sociation in institutional life. In the American case, both Christian and Jewish European immigrants have followed this path, as, more recently, have Asian Americans. In Britain, though there have been strong assimilative tendencies within the Scots and Welsh, these have been intertwined, as we will see, with more primordially sensitive strategies.

The conflicts within assimilative groups are between "traditionalists," who wish to maintain strong ethnic identity and are usually regarded as politically conservative, and "modernists" who seek to adopt the dominant ethnic style and most often are viewed as politically progressive. As for conflicts between assimilationists and the host society, assimilating solidary outgroups produce significant independent social and political movements only in the first generation. After this initial wave, however, they often constitute important cultural forces and widely influential ethnic spokesmen. The self-conscious stratificational principle that such assimilative spokesmen adopt is "equal opportunity" rather than "equality of results." The assimilationists' drive for equality is expressed in the desire for "social rights" like public education. Yet they simultaneously embrace the ideal of individual liberty for every member of the society, justifying their demand for limited egalitarianism on the grounds that it is necessary to sustain the principle of individual, meritocratic competition. This commitment to liberty only reflects their structural experience: for assimilative groups, constitutional, individualizing freedoms have been an effective lever in the inclusion process (Raab 1972, Glazer 1975).

Even in the limiting case of maximal external opportunity and internal complementarity, however, it is unlikely that the primordial gap will ever be completely closed. The failure to do so cannot, moreover, be traced only to the core group's historical advantage. Highly assimilated outgroups themselves often seek to maintain vestiges of primordial definition—what Weber cynically labeled ersatz ethnicity and what contemporary Americans admiringly call "roots." Ethnic solidarity, after all, need not have a pejorative connotation; it can contribute to the construction of social identification as such. For this reason, the concept of civil society is a limiting case. Although an assimilating outgroup disproportionately identifies with a core group, the definition of core primordiality may itself be subtly changed by the very process of assimilation (cf. Glazer 1975).

Nationalist Movements and Ethnically Conscious Inclusion. In groups that experience stronger primordial divergence and face more difficult structural barriers, assimilative strategies will not predominate. To be sure, assimilation will be one reaction to solidary exclusion, and as long as efforts at inclusion continue it will remain, if only unconsciously, a significant and important strategy in breaking down the barrier of primordial divergence. Yet where solidary groups face significantly fused external structures or possess certain primordial qualities—like race or an autonomous territorial area—that cannot easily be mitigated, they will remain primordially sensitive to a significant degree. When these groups become mobilized, the stratificational principle they advocate shifts from the "balanced" endorsement of equal opportunity to more group-oriented demands for preferential treatment. As equality of results becomes more significant, the individual rights of the dominant core receive increasingly less attention (Hentoff 1964, Prager 1978; Glazer 1975, ignores these basic distinctions in his conflation of the European and non-European aspects of U.S. inclusion). This shift reflects, of course, the *relative* failure of differentiated constitutional principles and civil rights in effecting outgroup inclusion. Such an ideological transition is reflected in the "affirmative action" demands of America's racial minorities and in the demands by groups like the Welsh and Catalanians for linguistic equality in their public education.

Contrary to the assimilationist tendency, these nationalist groups do form independent social movements. In terms of struggles for actual political power, however, they usually express themselves through institutionalized party structures and economic organizations and only sporadically create vehicles that compete for power with these dominant institutions. While primordially sensitive, these movements still seek equal institutional access. Moreover, though self-consciously committed to maintaining ethnic distinctiveness, they continue to undergo a gradual process of primordial homogenization. For example, while there is significant support in Wales for linguistic autonomy—social-psychological studies indicate much higher rates of approval for Welsh over English accents (Bourhis et al. 1973)—the actual number of Welsh speakers has greatly declined in recent years. This would seem to have been the inevitable result of meeting the other major Welsh nationalist demands, which have urged inclusion in the English core institutions of culture and economic life (Thompson 1978). Such an unintended consequence will continue to be a source of tension in nationalist movements as long as the primordially sensitive group remains committed to inclusion rather than to secession. Whether these movements continue, indeed, to seek inclusion depends on the relative flexibility of the institutional environment. In the cases of American blacks, the British Scots and Welsh, and the Spanish Catalans, these environments either have continued to be sufficiently flexible or have recently become so. Insofar as they are not, secessionist movements develop (Shils 1975a). In the case of French-Canadian Quebecois, the issue remains unresolved; their situation indicates the independent impact that social mobilization has upon basic structural dislocation.

Nationalist Movements and Ethnic Secession. Whereas efforts at ethnically conscious inclusion are only rarely committed to independent party organization, secessionist movements create political organizations that subordinate not only traditional political disagreements within the outgroup but also economic divisions.

Although the line should not be drawn too sharply, two general factors are crucial in facilitating this movement toward secession. The most basic is unusual rigidity, in terms either of internal primordiality or external environment. Among primordial qualities, independent territory seems to be the most significant factor, hence, the radical nationalism so often associated with the ideal-typical colonial case. Shared territory is an "intrinsic," quasi-permanent factor around which shifts in ethnic consciousness can ebb and flow. In points of high primordial consciousness, furthermore, it allows ethnicity to be connected to the political and economic interests of every sector of the excluded group. Territory has clearly been central, for example, in the most recent movement for Scottish secession from England, where the shifting economic opportunities of center and periphery have quickly become the focus of a new, more ethnically conscious political strategy (Thompson 1978). Such factors must interact, in turn, with external circumstances. In Ireland, for example, the secessionist drive developed much earlier and more intensively because autonomous territory was combined with the kinds of highly rigid external factors described above.

The second crucial factor in moving ethnically conscious groups from inclusive to secessionist strategies is a more idiosyncratic one: the international climate. If secessionist nationalism appears to be "the order of the day" in the mid-twentieth century, and, more recently, in industrial countries, it establishes a normative reference that will inevitably affect perceptions of the actual situation. This "demonstration effect" (Bendix 1976) or cultural diffusion (Smith 1978) is as significant for twentieth-century nationalism as for nineteenth (Kohn 1962:61–126); the anti-colonial nationalism of the postwar world is as important for explaining the timing of the European secessionist movements of the 1960s and 1970s as the upsurge in Italian nationalism was for explaining the Irish "Home Rule" movement in the 1860s. The international context can also have highly important material effects, not just moral ones, when an outside power supplies arms or financial support to national insurgents.

As the analysis in this section begins to indicate, the relation between "structural" position—in an internal and external sense—and ideological outcome is mediated in any historical situation by a series of more specific intervening variables (see Smelser 1962). Thus, although the general relation obtains, any single outgroup in the course of its development will actually experience all three of these movements. American Judaism, for example, continues to have factions that advocate Zionist secession and ethnically conscious inclusion, as well as assimilation. Furthermore, the movement toward a "structurally appropriate" strategy is never chronologically linear. American black consciousness about primordiality, for example, actually began to increase during the civil rights drives of the 1960s, when the assimilative standard of "equal opportunity" was dominant and when the legal and political orders were finally becoming differentiated from biological, particularistic standards. The particular time order of ideological strategies depends upon a series of such historically specific factors, and on this more specific level conflict itself becomes an independent variable. One also wants to consider the effects of the distinction between leadership and mass. Since strong and independent political leadership so often emerges only from middle, highly educated strata, certain initial advances toward inclusion—no matter how ultimately ephemeral—will usually occur before secessionist movements can forcefully emerge.

A similar issue concerns the actual motivation of solidary outgroups themselves. Certainly, there are periods when excluded groups do not actively desire inclusion, and a few groups never want it. The degree to which an outgroup experiences the desire for inclusion relates, in part, to the same internal volitional factors that affect core group receptivity to the excluded party; it also depends upon the length of time of mutual exposure and on the degree to which the external environment of the interaction is differentiated. Where the primordial gap is extreme, the external environment rigid, and the period of mutual exposure relatively short, exclusion is less likely to produce demands for solidarity inclusion. Even in this case, however, instrumental self-interest will usually produce demands for equal treatment, if not solidarity, as a strategy to alleviate unsatisfactory external conditions.

Conclusion

Given their rationalist bias, theories of nation building generally ignore the role of solidarity in societal development. Among those theorists who have discussed the integration problem, moreover, an evolutionary bias leads most to underestimate significantly the permanent importance of primordial definitions of the national community. In contrast to these prevailing perspectives, I have argued that because most nations are founded by solidary core groups, and because societal development after this founding is highly uneven, strains toward narrow and exclusive national solidarity remain at the center of even the most "civil" nation-state. Differences in national processes of ethnic inclusion—even in the industrial world—are enormous. To encompass the variation while retaining systematicity, I have proposed a multidimensional model. On the internal axis, inclusion varies according to the degree of primordial complementarity between core group and solidary outgroup. On the external axis, inclusion varies according to the degree of institutional differentiation in the host society. It is in response to variations in these structural conditions that ethnic outgroups develop different incorporative strategies— assimilation, ethnically conscious inclusion, and nationalist secession—as well as different stratificational principles to justify their demands.

Applying this general model primarily to special aspects of the inclusion process in the United States, I have elaborated it in important ways. Yet this effort still represents only a first approximation; much further work remains before the model could truly become a theory of the middle range. For example, it would eventually have to be specified for different classes of empirical events. Thus, within the general external and internal constraints I have established, inclusion seems to vary systematically according to the different modes of outgroup contact: indentured servitude versus slavery, economic colonization versus military, colonization over groups within contiguous territories versus more territorially distinct occupation, and so forth.* This variation in turn affects the kind of external variable that is most significant in any given situation, whether the state, the economy, religion, or law.† This factor weighting is undoubtedly also affected by the kinds of historically specific "differentiation combinations" encountered in particular national societies, i.e., which institutional sectors lead and which lag. Finally, different kinds of internal combinations might also be specified; for example, a white-Anglo Saxon Catholic core group will differ in predictable ways from the WASP and a white Catholic Southern European core from a Northern European one.

I hope it is clear, however, how such further conceptualization can fruitfully draw upon the hypotheses already set forth. At a minimum, the model proposed here demonstrates not only that fundamental cleavages in developed societies can be nonutilitarian in scope and proceed along nonlinear paths, but also that within a multidimensional framework such complex strains can be conceptualized in a systematic comparative and historical manner.

NOTES

1. In terms of contemporary sociological theory, then, the animus of this chapter is directed in several directions.

While in one sense further developing the functionalist approach to differentiation theory, I am arguing for a much more serious recognition of group interest, differential power, uneven development, and social conflict than has usually characterized this tradition. My "neofunctionalist" argument begins, for example, from the intersection between neo-Marxist and Shilsian center-periphery theory and one aspect of Parsons' system theory, modifying

---

*For a discussion of independent political effects in the South African case, see Kuper 1965:42–56.

†These are the kinds of variables that Schermerhorn makes the central focus of his analysis, virtually to the exclusion of the factors I have discussed above.

the former and energizing the latter. I also distance myself from the conflation of ideology, model, and empirical explanation that often characterizes Parsons' work.

On the other hand, by stressing the necessity for analytic differentiation and multidimensional causality, I am arguing against Marxist and structuralist analyses, which even when they formally recognize the independence of ethnic phenomena—whose inequality they rightly insist upon—continually try to root it in "last instance" arguments. Thus, even in his sophisticated version of Marxist analysis, John Rex (1970) never accepts religion or ethnicity as truly independent variables, nor, more fundamentally, does he view the problem of solidarity as an independent dimension of social life. Concentrating mainly on the activities of labor and work, ethnic domination per se becomes for Rex an extrinsic variable.

Very much the same instrumental theoretical bias reduces the value of Lieberson's (1980) impressive empirical study. In his effort to explain the relative lack of success of postslavery blacks as compared with white immigrants in the United States after 1880, Lieberson tries to conceive of the "heritage of slavery" simply as a structural barrier, i.e., one that affects only the external conditions of the competition between the two groups. In this way, despite his occasional recognition of their importance (e.g., p. 366), the subjective perception of differences experienced by the groups themselves—and by the other ethnic communities involved—becomes a residual category.

I am suggesting a general process that occurs when racial and ethnic groups have an inherent conflict—and certainly competition for jobs, power, position, maintenance of different subcultural systems, and the like are such conflicts. Under the circumstances, there is a tendency for the competitors to focus on differences between themselves. The observers (in this case the sociologists) may then assume that those differences are the sources of conflict. In point of fact, the rhetoric involving such differences may indeed inflame them, but we can be reasonably certain that the conflict would have occurred in their absence. . . . Differences between blacks and whites [for example] enter into the rhetoric of race and ethnic relations, but they are ultimately secondary to the conflict for society's goodies. . . . Much of the antagonism toward blacks was based on racial features, but one should not interpret this as the ultimate cause. Rather the racial emphasis resulted from the use of the most obvious feature(s) of the group to support the intergroup conflict generated by a fear of blacks based on their threat as economic competitors. (pp. 382–83).

Without a multidimensional framework that takes cultural patterns as constraining structures in their own right—see my discussion of "structural analysis" in chapter 1, above—Lieberson is necessarily forced to conceive of subjective "discrimination" as an individualistic variable. Indeed, he links the use of discrimination not only to supposedly "psychological" studies of attitude formation but also to analyses that find inherent racial qualities of the victims themselves to be the cause for their oppression.

Finally, by stressing the strong possibility for social and cultural differentiation in Western societies and the distinction and relative autonomy of the external and internal axes of ethnic conflict, I argue against contemporary "internal colonialist" theory. This approach too often refers to domination in an undifferentiated and diffuse way and, conversely, underemphasizes the variations that characterize the histories of oppressed groups by virtue of their distinctive primordial relations to the core group and their different external environments.

For the relation between the present argument and plural society theory—which still remains relatively unsystematized—see p. 80*n.*, above.

REFERENCES

Ahlstrom, Sydney E. 1972. *A Religious History of the American People*. New Haven, Conn.: Yale University Press.

Alexander, Jeffrey C. 1978. "Formal and Substantive Voluntarism in the Work of Talcott Parsons: A Theoretical and Ideological Reinterpretation." *American Sociological Review* (April), 43:177–98.

—— 1983. *The Modern Reconstruction of Classical Thought: Talcott Parsons.* Vol. 4 of *Theoretical Logic in Sociology.* Berkeley: University of California Press.

Banfield, Edward C. 1959. *The Moral Basis of a Backward Society.* New York: Free Press.

Bean, Walton. 1968. *California.* New York: McGraw-Hill.

Beckett, J. C. 1966. *The Making of Modern Ireland 1603–1923.* New York: Alfred A. Knopf.

Bellah, Robert N. 1970. *Beyond Belief.* Harper and Row.

—— 1975. *The Broken Covenant.* New York: Seabury.

Bendix, Reinhard. 1964 (1977). *Nation Building and Citizenship.* Berkeley: University of California Press.

—— 1976. "The Mandate To Rule: An Introduction." *Social Forces* (December), 55(2):252–56.

Blauner, Robert. 1972. *Racial Oppression in America.* New York: Harper and Row.

Blumer, Herbert. 1965. "Industrialization and Race Relations." In Guy Hunter, ed., *Industrialization and Race Relations,* pp. 220–53. New York: Oxford University Press.

Bourhis, Richard Y., Howard Giles, and Henri Tajfel. 1973. "Language as a Determinant of Welsh Identity." *European Journal of Social Psychology,* 3(4):447–60.

Bulpitt, Him. 1976. "The Making of the United Kingdom: Aspects of English Imperialism." P.S.A. Workgroup on United Kingdom Politics, University of Strathclyde (September).

Coulton, C. G. 1935. "Nationalism in the Middle Ages." *The Cambridge Historical Journal* 5(1):15–40.

Doxey, G. V. 1961. *The Industrial Colour Bar in South Africa.* New York: Oxford University Press.

Durkheim, Emile. 1893 (1933). *The Division of Labor in Society.* New York: Free Press.

Eisenstadt, S. N. 1954. *The Absorption of Immigrants.* London: Routledge & Kegan Paul.

—— 1963. *The Political System of Empires.* New York: Free Press.

—— 1973. *Tradition, Change, and Modernity.* New York: Wiley.

Elkins, Stanley. 1969. "Slavery in Capitalist and Non-Capitalist Countries." In Laura Foner and Eugene D. Genovese, eds., *Slavery in the New World,* pp. 8–26. Englewood, N.J.: Prentice-Hall.

Friedrichs, Carl J. 1964. *Transcendent Justice: The Religious Dimension of Constitutionalism.* Durham, N.C.: Duke University Press.

Geertz, Clifford. 1973a. *The Interpretation of Cultures.* New York: Basic Books.

—— 1973b. "The Integration Revolution: Primordial Sentiments and Civil Politics in the New States." In Geertz, *The Interpretation of Cultures,* pp. 255–310.

Gergen, Kenneth. 1968. "The Significance of Skin Color in Human Relations." In John Hope Franklin, ed., *Color and Race,* pp. 112–28. Boston: Beacon Press.

Glazer, Nathan. 1975. *Affirmative Discrimination.* New York: Basic Books.

Glazer, Nathan and Daniel Patrick Moynihan. 1963. *Beyond the Melting Pot.* Cambridge: Massachusetts Institute of Technology Press.

Goode, William J. 1963. *World Revolution and Family Patterns.* New York: Free Press.

Gordon, Milton M. 1964. *Assimilation in American Life.* London: Oxford University Press.

Handlin, Oscar. 1951 (1973). *The Uprooted.* Boston: Little, Brown.

—— 1957. *Race and Nationality in American Life.* New York: Doubleday.

Hanham, Harold J. 1969. *Scottish Nationalism.* London: Faber and Faber.

Hansen, Marvin Lee. 1940. *The Immigrant in American History.* Cambridge, Mass.: Harvard University Press.

Harris, Marvin. 1964. *Patterns of Race in the Americas.* New York: Walker and Company.

Hartz, Louis. 1955. *The Liberal Tradition in America.* New York: Harcourt, Brace and Jovanovich.

Hechter, Michael. 1975. *Internal Colonialism: The Celtic Fringe in British Development, 1536–1966.* Berkeley: University of California Press.

Hentoff, Nat. 1964. "Reaching Equality by Special Treatment." *The New Equality.* New York: Viking.

Higham, John. 1969. *Strangers in the Land.* New York: Atheneum.

Howe, Irving. 1976. *World of Our Fathers.* New York: Harcourt, Brace and Jovanovich.

Jordan, Winthrop D. 1968. *White Over Black.* Durham: University of North Carolina Press.

Kohn, Hans. 1962. *The Age of Nationalism.* New York: Harper and Row.

Kuper, Leo. 1960. "The Heightening of Racial Tension." *Race* (November), 2:24–32.

—— 1965. *An African Bourgeoisie.* New Haven, Conn.: Yale University Press.

—— 1969. "Political Change in White Settler Societies: The Possibility of Peaceful Democratization." In Leo Kuper and M. G. Smith, eds., *Pluralism in Africa,* pp. 169–93. Berkeley, University of California Press.

—— 1978. "The Theory of Plural Society: Race and Conquest." Unpublished manuscript.

Kuper, Leo and M. G. Smith. 1969. *Pluralism in Africa.* Berkeley: University of California Press.

Landes, David. 1969. *The Unbound Prometheus.* London: Cambridge University Press.

Lieberson, Stanley. 1980. *A Piece of the Pie.* Berkeley and Los Angeles: University of California Press.

Light, Ivan. 1972. *Ethnic Enterprise in America.* Berkeley: University of California Press.

Lipset, Seymour Martin. 1965. *The First New Nation.* New York: Vintage.

Lipset, Seymour Martin and Stein Rokkan. 1967. "Cleavage Structures, Party Systems, and Voter Alignments: An Introduction." In Lipset and Rokkan, eds., *Party Systems and Voter Alignments,* pp. 1–64. New York: Free Press.

Lipset, Seymour Martin and Reinhard Bendix. 1960. *Social Mobility in Industrial Society.* Berkeley: University of California Press.

Little, David. 1969. *Religion, Order, and Law.* New York: Harper Torchbook.

Lyman, Stanford M. 1970. "Strangers in the Cities: The Chinese on the Urban Frontier." In Charles Wollenberg, ed., *Ethnic Conflict in California History,* pp. 61–100. Los Angeles: Tinnon-Brown.

Marx, Karl. 1848 (1955). *The Communist Manifesto.* Samuel Beer, ed. Northbrook, Ill.: AHM Publishing Corporation.

Mead, Sidney E. 1963. *The Lively Experiment.* New York: Harper and Row.

Miller, Perry. 1956. *Errand Into the Wilderness.* Cambridge, Mass.: Harvard University Press.

—— 1967. *Nature's Nation.* Cambridge, Mass.: Harvard University Press.

Mitchison, Rosalind. 1970. *A History of Scotland.* London: Methuen.

Modell, John. 1970. "Japanese-Americans: Some Costs of Group Achievement." In Charles Wollenberg, ed., *Ethnic Conflict in California History,* pp. 101–20. Los Angeles: Tinnon-Brown.

Mosse, George L. 1964. *The Crisis of German Ideology.* New York: Grosset and Dunlap.

Nakane, Chie. 1970. *Japanese Society.* Berkeley: University of California Press.

Nolte, Ernst. 1965. *The Three Faces of Fascism.* New York: Mentor.

Norman, E. R. 1968. *Anti-Catholicism in Victorian England.* London: George Allen & Unwin.

Parsons, Talcott. 1967a. "On the Concept of Influence." In T. Parsons, ed., *Sociological Theory and Modern Society,* pp. 355–82. New York: Free Press.

—— 1967b. "Full Citizenship for the Negro American?" In T. Parsons, ed., *Sociological Theory and Modern Society,* pp. 422–65. New York: Free Press.

—— 1971. *The System of Modern Society.* Englewood Cliffs, N.J.: Prentice-Hall.

Philip, Alan Butt. 1975. *The Welsh Question.* Cardiff: University of Wales Press.

Prager, Jeffrey. 1978. "Equal Opportunity and Equal Protection: Ideas and Interpretation in Flux." Presentation to Annual Meetings of the American Sociological Association. San Francisco, California.

Raab, Earl. 1972. "Quotas by Any Other Name." *Commentary* (January), pp. 41–45.

Rex, John. 1970. *Race Relations in Sociological Theory.* New York: Schocken.

Rokkan, Stein. 1975. "Dimensions of State Formation and National Building: A Possible Paradigm for Research on Variations within Europe." In Charles Tilly, ed., *The Formation of Nation States in Western Europe,* pp. 562–600. Princeton, N.J.: Princeton University Press.

Rose, Richard. 1970. "The United Kingdom as a Nation-State." Survey Research Center Occasional Paper No. 6, University of Strathclyde, Glasgow.

—— 1971. *Governing without Consensus.* London: Faber & Faber.

Royal Institute of International Affairs. 1939. *Nationalism.* Oxford: Oxford University Press.

Schermerhorn, R. A. 1970. *Comparative Ethnic Relations.* New York: Random House.

Schooler, Carmi. 1976. "Serfdom's Legacy: An Ethnic Continuum." *American Journal of Sociology* 81(6):1265–86.

Shils, Edward A. 1975a. "The Integration of Societies." In Shils, *Center and Periphery: Essays in Macro-Sociology,* pp. 48–90. Chicago: University of Chicago Press.

—— 1975b. "Primordial, Personal, Sacred, and Civil Ties." In Shils, *Center and Periphery,* pp. 111–26.

Shils, Edward A. and Michael Young. 1975 (1956). "The Meaning of the Coronation." In Shils, *Center and Periphery,* pp. 135–52.

Smelser, Neil J. 1962. *Theory of Collective Behavior.* New York: Free Press.

—— 1971. "Stability, Instability, and the Analysis of Political Corruption." In Bernard Barber and Alex Inkeles, eds., *Stability and Social Change,* pp. 7–29. Boston: Little, Brown.

Smith, Anthony. 1978. "The Diffusion of Nationalism: Some Historical and Sociological Perspectives." *British Journal of Sociology* 29(2): 234–48.

Tannenbaum, Frank. 1969. "Slavery, the Negro, and Racial Prejudice." In Laura Foner and E. D. Genovese, eds., *Slavery in the New World,* pp. 3–7. Englewood Cliffs, N.J.: Prentice Hall.

Thernstrom, Stephen. 1974. "Socialism and Social Mobility." In John H. M. Laslett and Seymour Martin Lipset, eds., *Failure of a Dream?* pp. 509–27. New York: Doubleday.

Thompson, Seamus. 1978. *Dual Incorporation in British Politics: A Theory of Class and Ethnic Mobilization.* Unpublished Ph.D. dissertation. University of California at Los Angeles.

Tocqueville, Alexis de. 1835 (1945). *Democracy in America,* vol. 1. New York: Random House.

Toennies, Ferdinand. 1887 (1957). *Community and Society.* East Lansing, Mich.: Michigan State University.

Vallier, Ivan. 1971. "Empirical Comparison of Social Structure: Leads and Lags." In Vallier, ed., *Comparative Method in Sociology,* pp. 203–63. Berkeley: University of California Press.

Van den Berghe, Pierre L. 1965. *South Africa, A Study in Conflict.* Middletown, Conn.: Wesleyan University Press.

Van der Horst, Sheila T. 1965. "The Effects of Industrialization on Race Relations in South Africa." In Guy Hunter, ed., *Industrialization and Race Relations,* pp. 97–140. New York: Oxford University Press.

Walzer, Michael. 1965. *The Revolution of the Saints.* Cambridge, Mass.: Harvard University Press.

Weber, Eugen. 1976. *Peasants into Frenchmen: The Modernization of Rural France: 1870–1914*. Stanford, Calif.: Stanford University Press.

Weber, Max. 1904 (1958). "Class, Status, and Party." In Hans Gerth and C. Wright Mills, *From Max Eber,* pp. 180–95. London: Oxford University Press.

—— 1958. *The City*. New York: Free Press.

FOUR

The Mass News Media
in Systemic, Historical and
Comparative Perspective

In its search for greater precision and causal specificity, contemporary sociology has tended to neglect "society" as such, a point of reference whose empirical significance is often matched only by its theoretical obscurity. To speak of the whole invites generality and historical scope, qualities that undermine the assurance of exact verification, yet it is precisely generality and historical perspective that are necessary if the components and boundaries of society are to be understood. If to ignore the whole creates difficulty in every area of "special" sociological focus, it is particularly dangerous in the attempt to understand those institutions whose "function" is actually to address society as a general unit.* The mass media is such an institution.

I am interested in making a theoretical statement about the mass news media that is both thoroughly general and abstract and at the same time directly specifiable in empirical terms. I locate the media in terms of, first, a theory of the social system, and, second, a theory of social differentiation that provides both historical and comparative perspective. By linking analysis of news media to these broader theoretical traditions, I hope to enrich sociological thinking about the relation of the media to the

---

*My use of the concept "function" here and elsewhere in this chapter is a shorthand form that makes it easier to situate the cultural and "structural" aspects of the mass news media— their causes, effects, and institutional character—in the social system. I believe the following discussion demonstrates that there is nothing teleological, conservative, or static about functionalist analysis when conducted in a certain way. This is not to say, however, that functionalism is simply "good sociology" by another name (cf. Alexander 1985).

For their earlier comments on this paper, I thank Robert N. Bellah, Ruth H. Bloch, Donald N. Levine, Jeffrey Prager, and Neil J. Smelser.

operation of other social institutions and to issues of social change, subjects usually underplayed by more micro studies of mass communication. I hope also to throw a different light on broader implications of media practices that are either interpreted narrowly or simply taken for granted. Finally, in the course of carrying out this analysis, I hope to illuminate certain problematic moral and political issues that have been the focus of ideological debate about the role of news media in social life.

The Mass News Media in the Social System

The mass media produce symbolic patterns that create the invisible tissues of society on the cultural level just as the legal system creates the boundaries of the community on a more concrete and "real" one. In a modernizing and differentiating society, the media are a functional substitute for concrete group contact, for the now impossible meeting-of-the-whole. Indeed, as I argue below, media emerge only with social differentiation itself, and the more "modern" a society the more important its media. This dialectic between media integration and differentiation forcibly struck visitors to the early American nation. Tocqueville (1835:pt. 1, ch. 11) described newspapers as "the power which impels the circulation of political life through all the districts of that vast [American] territory," and Thomas Hamilton (1833:[2]:72–73), another visitor to the United States in the early nineteenth century, testified that "the influence and circulation of newspapers is great beyond anything ever known in Europe. . . . In truth, nine-tenths of the population read nothing else. . . . Every village, nay, almost every hamlet, has its press. . . . Newspapers penetrate to every crevice of the nation." It is certainly true, as I emphasize below, that mass media have a certain atomizing effect on the perception of social life. Yet, such fragmentation hardly exhausts its function. To the contrary, this effect is what allows the integrating power of the media to exercise its distinctive scope.

If cultural patterns can be differentiated into cognitive, expressive, and evaluative strands (Parsons, 1951:24–112; 1961), the mass media can be divided into cognitive and expressive components. In the category of expressive media, I include the narrative stories found most frequently on television. By the cognitive dimension of media, I refer to news stories that occur in newspapers, as well as television news programs. Because of these different foci, entertainment and news media have sharply different social functions; they depend on very different kinds of social resources and must be judged according to what are often contradictory criteria of success (Fass 1976). I limit myself in this effort to the news media and the cognitive dimension.

But a question immediately presents itself that touches on a critical problem in the sociological literature: is cognitive in fact a sufficient designation for the orientation of news reporting? Cognitive patterns are typically understood to concern objective definitions of social reality, definitions that are directed toward the object itself rather than toward the subject's feeling about that object (the latter, by contrast, defining the expressive patterns) or toward the relation between subject and object (an orientation that defines moral or evaluative patterns). The perception of news as providing "information" indicates this cognitive status in both lay and sociological parlance. However, as recent, postpositivist discussion in the philosophy and history of science has emphasized, even the most radically cognitive statements are bound to have evaluative or moral dimensions that, although secondary, are significant nonetheless. The empirical perceptions of scientists are influenced by their group commitments, as well as by their more general moral, cultural, and metaphysical concerns (Polanyi 1958, Kuhn 1969, Holton 1973). Professional disciplinary self-scrutiny cannot eliminate the nonempirical aspect of scientific observation; it can only change the nature of noncognitive constraint (Toulmin 1972). It follows logically that news judgments, as less controlled exercises in empirical observation, are also bound to be partly evaluative (cf. Gans 1979:39–42, 201–2).

To focus primarily on the impact of overt political bias on news reporting or on the problem of journalistic ethics, as a vast literature on the media has done (e.g., Noelle-Neumann 1978), obscures the fact that a major function of the news media is actually to produce "bias," to create through the framework of cognitive statements certain nonempirical evaluations. The problems of reportorial bias and professional ethics concern the cognitive dimensions of news, but if we accept the notion that the production of moral bias is also a "good" and necessary social function (cf. Missika 1986, 1987), the empirical and theoretical focus of analysis shifts. The problem becomes to discover what particular kinds of evaluative judgments the news media produce, under what conditions they do so, and, perhaps, to formulate the ideal and pathological conditions for the performance of this task.

There are two possible orientations of evaluative symbolic judgments, the level of values and the level of norms. Norms occupy a middle, intermediate position between general value patterns and the "raw data" or "plain facts" that are continually being produced in the course of human activity. If we do not accept the view of human life as thoroughly atomistic and discrete, we must assume that "just doing it" cannot be a major mode of self-explanation in any society (cf. Bellah 1970:261). More general and significant justifications and legitimations are necessary. Yet at the same time it is true that social life is too variegated, too fluid, too profane to be organized in a manner strictly consistent with the broad sacred tenets that provide the generalized integration that forms value patterns. A more flexibile form of integration is provided by "normative" patterns, which although sharing in the generality of the value dimension, are nonetheless more specific and contingent, more open to continuous reformulation in relation to shifting social exigencies.

What is most conspicuous about the news media is their focus on this normative level. Just as individuals continually try to organize their experience in terms of formulating different normative explanations, newspapers do this for the—or at least "a"—society at large. News stories and news commentaries can be understood as a continuous processing of raw information that makes the experience of a society comprehensible in terms of more general categories. In the early nineteenth century, a writer for the *Boston Daily Advertiser* made this link between the need for individual integration and interpretation and the functional necessity for institutional interpretation very clear. "The insatiable appetite for *news,*" he wrote in 1814 (quoted in Mott 1941:202, original italics), "has given rise to a general form of salutation on the meeting of friends and strangers: *What's the news?*" A news story, in other words, is a situationally specific, extraordinarily flexible kind of nonempirical evaluation.

It has, of course, been phenomenology that has conceptualized the ordering of contingency from the standpoint of the individual. As Husserl ([1931] 1977) and, later, Garfinkel (1967) suggested, individuals view external events as documenting, or elaborating, prior perceptions. The news media, I am suggesting, can be understood as linking such individual documentation to social events that an individual never directly encounters. They do so by reporting events in terms of more general categories.* Reporters employ this "documentary" method in their own perceptions of events, and the products of their investigations—the stories they file— allow the categories they have chosen to "document events" for their readers. The cognitive implication of "categories" is intended. News provides the social component of rational judgments about the nature of everyday life, and it does so in a uniquely standardizing way.† Law, by contrast, provides the social, standardizing framework for judgments about the morality of everyday life. Because it is expressed in what are apparently transparently cognitive terms, the normative element of news judgments is not nearly as visible as the normative component of legal ones. News, in other words, camouflages its nonempirical, interpretive aspect in the same way as science.

The categories that news stories evoke emerge from previously articulated norms and from more general values about what to expect from social life. Both the interpretative character and the nesting in broader patterns are manifest in any reporting that is subject to conflicting interpretations and that therefore becomes an object of at least covertly political contention. In March 1978, for example, twenty-one of the thirty-seven members of the House International Relations Committee of the U.S. Congress wrote a letter urging the President of the United States to reconsider his controversial arms package deal with Israel, Egypt, and Saudi Arabia. In an article reporting this event, *The Washington Post* linked it to the actions of a number of pro-Israeli groups, describing it as part of

---

*In his later writings, Goffman (1974:17) understood news media in precisely this kind of phenomenological way. Although he limits his remarks specifically to the press's reporting of human interest stories, they hold good, it seems to me, for news as such:

> Our understanding of the world precedes these stories, determining which ones reporters will select and how the ones that are selected will be told. . . . The design of these reported events is fully responsive to our demands—which are not for facts but for typifications. Their telling demonstrates the power of our conventional understandings to cope with the bizarre potentials of social life, the furthest reaches of experience. What appears, then, to be a threat to our way of making sense of the world turns out to be an ingeniously selected defense of it.

This position ignores, of course, the possibility that the media might also contribute to social change or to the achievement of rationality. That is the price of adopting a purely phenomenological understanding, and I try to avoid it below.

†Parsons (1961) provides a precise conceptual discussion of the ways in which the normative sphere of culture—which he also identifies with the integrative sphere in the social system—provides regulation over cognitive, as well as expressive and explicitly ethical, judgments.

a "determined campaign to block the package deal" (*Near East Report,* 1978, p. 46). The *Post* had characterized these congressional representatives as acting in terms of their ascriptive political bias rather than as responding to their constitutional duties or to their individual consciences. It is likely that five years earlier—when American sympathies for Israel were more firmly rooted—this "fact" would have emerged in an entirely different light, if indeed it would have been viewed as sufficiently interesting to have been reported as news at all.

A similarly revealing incident was disclosed by former Israeli Defense Minister Ariel Sharon's libel suit against *Time* magazine for its report on his involvement in the massacre of Lebanese civilians in September 1982 (*Los Angeles Times* 1/14/85:part 1). In this case two distinct levels of interpretation were involved. *Time* had reported that Sharon had "discussed . . . the need for revenge" with Lebanese leaders the day before the massacre and that the discussion was cited in a secret Appendix B of the special Israeli government commission's report on the incident. In the libel trial, Sharon's attorneys were able to force the *Time* Jerusalem correspondent, David Halevy, to admit under oath that, while he had been told about conversations between Sharon and Lebanese leaders, he had never actually been told that the crucial meeting between them was detailed in Appendix B. Rather, Halevy said, he had "inferred" this after hearing a description of what sort of material Appendix B contained. Halevy could have made such an inference only because he was looking at these Israeli events within a preexisting framework that supplied him with expectations unfavorable to Sharon. The trial did, in fact, reveal that Halevy sympathized with anti-Sharon groups in Israeli politics, though these connections were, per se, no different from those that any active reporter usually maintains. In Halevy's case, such expectations quite naturally led him to see the references made to Appendix B as documenting his suspicions and as allowing him to make connections between "facts" that are the basis of a story. The broad story he perceived, moreover, meshed perfectly not only with his own expectations but also with the outrage of his audience. Americans had reacted forcefully against the Israeli invasion, and *Time*—its earlier leanings notwithstanding—was swept along in the outrush of public feeling. It was, after all, a member of another, quite different solidary community—Ariel Sharon—who brought the suit against *Time*; his quite different normative expectations allowed him to perceive a different way in which the "facts" could have been put together.

That suspicions of Sharon and outrage at the massacre led to one particular interpretation among possible others is made even more clear in a second level of documentation revealed by the suit. All newspapers and news magazines submit news stories to editing by the home desk. In this case, it was revealed, the *Time* writer in New York had changed the Jerusalem dispatches in distinctive ways. Where the dispatch had read "we understand [that the meeting is cited in Appendix B]," the New York editor had changed that to "*Time* has learned." Where Halevy had reported that Sharon "gave them [the Lebanese leaders] the feeling . . . that he understood their need to take revenge," the home editor rewrote it to read that Sharon "reportedly discussed with . . . [Lebanese leaders] their need to take revenge." In a purely factual sense, understanding that a conversation has taken place is not different from having learned that it did so. Both phrasings assume such a conversation occurred. The second way of putting this information, however, implies a more authoritative objectivity than Halevy may have wished, given his own preceding interpretative leap. Since *Time*'s New York editor knew nothing about the internal interpretation that had produced this earlier documentation of objective phenomena, he had no more reason to hesitate before a more active formulation than his readers would themselves. Much the same can be said for the second rewriting I have noted. How could Sharon have given the Lebanese such an impression without having discussed it with them? The brute "facts" do not differ, but the frame that is used to explain them, and that they implicitly document, contrasts in a subtle but significant way.

Another typical example of how "objective" news reporting actually places raw data into a preexisting normative framework—and of how this function rests upon the documentary method of journalists' commonsense activities—is revealed by a controversy generated in Canada by Canadian reporting of a visit by the French Prime Minister. In mid-February 1979 the Premier of Quebec and ardent French nationalist, René Levesque, hosted a visit by French Prime Minister Raymond Barré. Canada's English-language papers described Levesque's behavior throughout the trip as an embarrassment, reporting that he had frequently drunk too much and had engaged in "erratic behavior." The French-language press viewed the visit far differently. The behavior, when mentioned at all, was usually treated as good fun, evidence of Levesque's informality and high spirits. The *Toronto Globe and Mail,* a leading English-language paper, accused the French-language press of a cover-up. Michel Roy, editor of Montreal's *Le Devoir,* argued, instead, that the reporting of the specific incident revealed contrasting general orientations:

The secrets and travels of Margaret Trudeau have never had the place of honor in the French-language press that they have had in the newspapers of our colleagues. . . . What comes out of the anecdote, out of private behavior, out of the digressions of conduct of a public figure—without being submitted to censorship for an instant—interests the French press much less [than the English] (*Los Angeles Times* 1979).

To the French journalist and editors, Roy is arguing, the "incidents" had simply not been news: they had not violated their general expectations of personal behavior for public figures, especially when those figures were their own.

Although the newspaper and magazine reports from which I have drawn my information treated these controversies as deviant cases, as departures from standard professional conduct, I have presented them in a way that reveals their typical features. Critics of a specific piece of reporting—be they interested observers or academic analysts—usually charge its author with bias. The primordial fact that in producing a news story all atomized pieces of data must be normatively organized is conveniently ignored. What is really happening in such instances is that these critics are arguing against a bias of which they do not approve, not against bias per se. This is not to say that one cannot differentiate good reporting from bad—there is, after all, "thick" versus "thin" interpretation (Geertz 1973)—nor is it to say that the notion of journalistic bias must be dispensed with. Later in this essay I develop a theory of "biased" and "unbiased" reporting that accepts interpretation as a primordial fact. It is to say, however, that the ordering of disparate information is an inherent feature of news reporting and that, despite the examples I have used, it is not limited to international reporting or to specifically political issues. Events must be reconstructed in an orderly and relatively coherent way, day in and day out, even when such logicality is not actually there.

Although the study conducted by Paletz, Reichert, and McIntire (1971) of city council news coverage in Durham, North Carolina, emphasizes the specifically political bias of news reporting, it can just as accurately be viewed as documenting this more neutral function of news as normative organizer and interpreter in a "typical" domestic situation. The study concludes that news reports on the council's activities invested the events with a "rationality, causality, and temporal coherence" not inherent in the events themselves. Their conclusions are worth quoting directly:

[C]onventional journalism includ[es] condensing and summarizing; investing events with rationality and coherence (even though the events may be confusing to the participants, and the reporter himself may not fully comprehend both what has occurred and its meaning); emphasizing the council's decisions at the expense of other activities . . . and treating the council and its members with respect (1971:81).

The idiosyncratic aspects of news writing and its professional mores can be viewed as geared to this intermediate level of normative production.* For example, an examination of news leads indicates that they are not only cognitively oriented to the "five w's," that is, to the traditional injunction to identify "who, what, when, where, and why." They invariably make a strong normative and moral point, and this latter function is, indeed, the implicit criterion by which good lead writing is distinguished from bad. The lead seems to be a device for summing up the significance of the data-event by relating it, implicitly, to what people would have expected to happen in similar situations or to more general value judgments what would normally be applicable.

The clarifying, and by implication the interpretative, function of news writing is revealed by journalists' self-imposed strictures about style. The

*As the term *normative production* indicates, I am looking at the normative function of the media in terms of the theory of interchange that Parsons developed in his later work (Alexander 1983b:73–118). According to this model of the social system, fundamentally different kinds of activities—economic life, political life, integrative and norm-setting activities, value maintenance and socialization—can be conceived as subsystems that produce important resources (outputs) upon which the others depend. Each subsystem relies on receiving suitable inputs in turn. This model makes it possible to conduct a fully multidimensional analysis of social system life, because it differentiates analytically the interdependence of various social system activities that in "real life" are interpenetrating and interacting simultaneously. The emphasis on reciprocity and exchange, moreover, makes this systemic analysis dynamic rather than static. My use of interchange theory differs from Parsons' own, however, in my insistence that it is an abstract model rather than an actual description of social system processes. In opposition to Parsons' "conflated" usage (Alexander 1983b:186–276; cf. chapter 2, above), I focus here on concrete institutional processes, social groups and their interested activity, structural fusion (as resulting from functional interchange), the uneven development of different sectors, and the possibility that social strain and even pathology are attendant on the differentiation process.

style books used by major news organizations universally stress simplicity of language in the service of communicability. To achieve such simplicity, of course, important details must be selected from a wide range of facts. As Harold Evans (1972:25, italics added), former editor of the (London) Sunday *Times,* writes in *Newsman's English*: "Sentences should assert. The newspaper reader above all does not want to be told what is not. *He should be told what is.*" As Evans (ibid.:17, italics added) makes clear in the rules he lays down for copy editors, to be simple and precise is at the same time to identify facts that are significant to an individual's social life. The copy editor, he writes,

must insist on language which is specific, emphatic, and concise. Every work must be understood by the ordinary man, every sentence must be clear at one glance, and every story must say something about people. *there must never be a doubt about its relevance to our daily life.*

The close relation between the interpretative function of news and its peculiar linguistic style is also revealed in the following admonition by Curtis McDougall (1968:104, italics added), professor emeritus of journalism at Northwestern University.

Vagueness and indefiniteness are avoided, and clarity obtained, by placing important ideas at the beginnings of sentences. Also by *playing up the action, significance, result or feature of the paragraph or story,* by avoiding vague and indefinite words and eliminating superfluous details, words, phrases, and clauses.

Of course, these latent functions of news style are contrary to the self-conscious, manifest professional rationale, which views stylistic simplicity simply as a means to more powerfully communicate neutral and objective truth. Sometimes this contradiction is revealed quite plainly, as when Hohenberg (1978:100), author of *The Professional Journalist,* argues, on the one hand, that instead of using platitudes and jargon the writer should just provide "a clear, simple story of what happened" and, on the other (ibid.:440), that the journalist must be an interpreter who "applies the rule of reason to the news" (cf. Harris 1978).

In fact, the entire professional concentration on what is "newsworthy," "fresh" as opposed to "stale," as well as the stratification of rewards around the ability to make news "discoveries," can be viewed as flowing from this normative function. For only by continually finding new, unfiltered, and unforeseen societal experience can the media perform their normative function effectively. This normative function also explains the occupational character and psychology of the news reporter role. The "tough," "cynical" quality of the role is usually taken as an indication that reporters have become jaded by the inundation of social experience and are concerned, as a result, only with recording the "facts" on the most pragmatic and empirical level of analysis. I would suggest, to the contrary, that reporters remain committed to evaluative judgment and that their "tough-minded" cynicism is a professional role demand requiring the particular kinds of judgments they must produce—particularized and flexible normative evaluations rather than the more generalized, self-important, and "religious" judgments that characterize spokesmen in institutions concerned with broader cultural patterns. Gans (1979:184) observes that American reporters seek to exclude "conscious values" from their work.

> The news media I have studied seem to attract people who keep their values to themselves. . . . They have no prior values about the topics which become news, nor do they always develop them about topics on which they are working. . . . They did not become journalists to advocate values or to reform society.

Still, Gans insists that "unconscious values" continue to underlay these reporters' judgments, no matter how pragmatic or situationally specific they try "consciously" to be. Indeed, this continued occupational commitment to normative evaluation is reflected in what is actually an inherent gullibility of the reportorial role, which is shown, for example, in the way that newspapers are always open to accepting "the hoax" (Shaw 1975). It is also reflected in the continual strain toward journalistic "advocacy" and activism, even under the conditions of media differentiation.

Social institutions in every social sector can be associated with different kinds of social control, can be understood as providing the society with certain kinds of resources with which to respond to social strain and social conflict. The legal system is the institution commonly associated with social control in the normative sector. Laws present contingent formulations that are both consistent with more general values and at the same time allow society to change and evolve in response to developing strain and conflict. In distinguishing the news media from the law, the significant point is the media's flexibility. By daily exposing and reformulating themseves vis-à-vis changing values, group formations, and objective economic and political conditions, the media allow "public opinion" to be organized responsively on a mass basis. By performing this function of information conduit and normative organizer, the news media provide the normative dimension of society with the greatest flexibility in dealing with social strains. In exchange for this flexibility, the news media must, in effect, eschew certain attributes that allow social control to be exercised in other ways; they cannot, for example, attain the self-consciousness, legitimacy, and enforceability of the norms associated with the legal system. Between the news media on one side, and the legal system on the other, there is a continuum of other institutions which make other kinds of normative contributions. The political party, for example, is more explicitly normative than the news media and at the same time significantly less flexible in response to social events; in relation to the legal system, the party produces norms that are more flexible and responsive while being less legitimate and enforceable.

American news coverage of the Vietnam war strikingly illustrates these distinctive characteristics: the noncognitive dimension of news judgments, the particular character of normative versus value statements, and the flexibility this function provides in terms of the operation of social control. It can be argued that throughout the long American involvement in Asia, the "facts" of the war remained relatively constant. With the passage of time, however, the war was reported very differently and came to seem like a different war. If the empirical event had not changed, what had altered were the nonempirical inputs to the American news media, particularly the normative definitions of those solidary groups that came to oppose the war and the more general value orientations supplied by the intellectual community. In a secondary but nonetheless significant manner, the news media were also responding to the domestic economic and political strains created by the war, which were filtered through the intellectual and solidary groups. Because of these changing inputs the "news facts" about the Vietnam war—the headlines, leads, interviews, and reports on direct observations—became more hostile. In a symbiotic fashion, such "new" facts contributed to the restructuring of public opinion concerning the "old" facts of the war.

Perhaps the most spectacular illustration of this shifting process of interpretation can be seen in the American news media's coverage of the 1968 Tet offensive in Vietnam. Baestrup (1978) has shown that American war reporters' perceptions of the massive strength of the North Vietnamese Army after Tet had much to do with the changing framework through which they filtered their experience of the war: their growing distrust for official U.S. military sources in Saigon; their increasing alienation from

U.S. governmental authority in general; and their ever more firmly rooted pessimism about any successful outcome of the U.S. war effort. For these reasons, U.S. reporters' descriptions of the Tet offensive emphasized the "psychological defeat" suffered by the United States and South Vietnam instead of focusing on the more purely military side of the U.S. response. In terms of the latter, Tet could, in fact, have been interpreted as a standoff or even as a limited U.S. victory given the military objectives of the North Vietnamese. The domestic impact of Tet "news" was, of course, tremendous. It was undoubtedly in part responsible for the decision of Lyndon Johnson not to seek a second term in office and indirectly contributed, therefore, to the election of Richard Nixon.

This incident demonstrates the potential autonomy that news interpretation possesses vis-à-vis other institutions and other normative pressures. Still, these war correspondents' judgments were themselves highly responsive to the changing positions of other institutions and other authoritative interpreters of publc events. There is a symbiotic relationship between the reporting of news, the discovery of new facts, the opinions of intellectuals (both elite and dissident) as expressed in intellectual journals, the contents of "little magazines," and the stories in mass news magazines. In one sense, the intellectual journals and little magazines may be seen as the creators of new orientations and the mass weeklys and daily news mediums as distributors (cf. Hirsch 1978). On the other hand, these sources of opinion are interdependent, closely linked through personal networks, as well as through channels of information to institutions in other sectors of the social system (cf. Kadushin 1975).

Another striking overt illustration of the theoretical position taken here is the American reporting of the Watergate scandal. Throughout the Watergate period, battle raged between different social groups over the proper normative framework for interpreting the break-in and electoral violations, ranging from the Republican administration's characterization—a third-rate burglary—to the Left's portrayal—a reactionary neofascist plot. Because of the balance of social groups and normative definitions before the 1972 presidential election, a situation I discuss later in this essay in a different context (see also essay 5, below) the "facts" that appeared as Watergate news before the election supported the former, moderate "observations." Only afterward, when events had changed and more universalistic national definitions had begun to reassert themselves, could the version of Watergate now accepted as real be reported as news.

In retrospect, it is clear that the facts about Watergate are not facts at all without the framework provided by notions of "constitutionalism," "impersonal higher authority," and other similar kinds of generalized value commitments. Only the combination of these emergent definitions with the raw data of changing events allowed the more critical normative conclusions to be drawn in the form of "fast-breaking" new reports.

In concluding this section, I relate the theory presented here to an approach that appears to be its diametrical opposite, the understanding of news media presented by mass society theory and, more recently, by "critical" theory (Mills 1956:298–324; Benjamin 1973:112–13; Hall and Whannel 1964:364–86; Mueller 1973:86–126; Dahlgren 1978; Golding 1978). According to this perspective, rather than perform an integrative function, the news media actually produce atomism and inhibit rather than facilitate the exercise of independent, rational, and principled social action. While the sense of atomization often produced by mass news coverage is an undeniable fact, two responses to this mass society critique seem in order. First, the diverse pieces of news informations are not, in fact, as disorganized as they appear, for as normative evaluations they are always informed by more general patterns of value orientation. Second, the lack of overall coherence among these pieces faithfully represents the actual conditions of a differentiated society. From the perspective I have outlined, atomization should be seen as the result of the commitment of the news media to organize information at a normative level in as flexible a manner as possible. To maintain flexibility, these norms cannot be tied directly to any particular sacred value or to any particular organizational form, even though either of these connections would contribute to a greater sense of overall coherence. I am arguing, in other words, that the sense of disorder created by the front page of a newspaper or by the half-hour of network news is actually composed of a series of normative statements, each of which provides integration at a situationally specific level. The sense of overall disorder is necessary if the mass news media are to perform effectively their function of "covering" with a normative net the wide range of national societal experience. Moreover, we shall see that far from creating passivity and resignation, as the mass society critics and critical theorists assume, this mode of integration creates the possibility for effective, voluntary action and for the assertion of individual rights.

This recent emphasis by mass society and critical theory on the enormous power of the media to suppress reflexivity and to enforce passivity rests upon a theoretical logic that must be strongly rejected. These theories imply that individuals can create their own interpretations of the external world without reference to social norms. Thus, the very fact that consumers of modern mass media make political interpretations linked to supraindividual "social facts" (in Durkheim's sense) is considered by critical theory to be prima facie evidence of the repressive character of mass media effects. I assume, to the contrary, that all individual decisions occur in a normatively defined environment. For this reason, the decisive issue becomes, not whether, but how and what; that is, what is the nature of this normative institution and how does it affect action? This introduces a historical and comparative perspective on the question of reflexivity and autonomy that is absent from most of the recent media literature informed by critical theory.

Whereas this recent "strong media" approach overemphasizes the power of media vis-à-vis individuals—and, correspondingly, virtually eliminates the reality of secondary institutional life—earlier classical media studies like the two-step flow model of communication (Katz and Lazarsfeld 1955) created a "weak media" model that was unrealistic in the other extreme. These studies focused on whether or not the media could influence short-run political events—and on whether media effects can be isolated from social context—rather than on their specific cultural impact on normative perception. Certainly, the media are impotent if they depart too radically from the socialized values of their audience and their primary groups (cf. Shils and Janowitz [1948] 1975). Their critical sociological contribution is precisely to relate these background values to the vast array of particular incidents that unfold in the daily life of a modern society. The relevant theoretical question at this stage of media research is not that of primary groups *versus* mass media but rather the specific function performed by mass media vis-à-vis primary groups, secondary institutions, and ongoing social events.

The third theoretical tradition of mass media research I polemically address in this chapter is the more orthodox Marxist, or ruling class, model whereby the media are viewed as instruments for the dominant economic elite to control information for their own instrumental interest (for an attempt to make this argument for the Canadian case, see Clement 1973:270ff.). The fundamental theoretical weakness of this perspective is that it overlooks the pivotal role of voluntary action in the media process— that the judgments expressed in news stories are much more the result of the socialized value orientations of reporters than the instrumental control of media owners. In historical terms, as I demonstrate below, the general movement of Western media has been to separate themselves from direct client relationships with social groups (for the Canadian case, see Baldwin's [1977] argument against Clement). The ruling-class model argues, to the contrary, not only that the media have retained their tight linkage to social interests but also that any historical analysis of media position should focus principally on social classes (cf. Golding 1974:23–29). I insist, by contrast, on a multidimensional analysis: the media have a variable, and potentially independent, relation to every major institutional subsystem. This leads to the historical and comparative discussion that follows.

The Mass News Media in Historical and Comparative Perspective

Although I have thus far described the mass news media in purely systemic terms, the exercise of this function is dependent on certain unique historical conditions, and the comparative variation in the performance of the news function can be explained in reference to the variation in these historical conditions. The very possibility of flexible normative production, for example, as distinguished from normative production per se, is dependent on the autonomy of news media from control by groups and institutions in other social subsystems. If the news is controlled by political authorities it will be much more rigid in its interpretation of political events because it will be unable to incorporate other political and normative perspectives. In addition to political differentiation, of course, the news media may also be independent, in a relative sense, of more general value-producing institutions like the church, university and party. Finally, there may be differentiation from structures in the economic dimension, particularly from social classes.

Fusion and Autonomy: A Developmental Model. This differentiation of the mass news media is a developmental process parallel to the classic cases of differentiation that have traditionally been the focus of attention, the emergence of the autonomous economic market, independent state, and independent religious and cultural activities (cf. Parsons and White 1969 and Alexander 1978). It should be viewed not as an event but as a process. Differentiation of the news media begins with the creation of the first news institution, or collectivity, where there had previously been only the circulation of rumors or improvised publication by broadside. The emergence and circulation of "La Chanson de Roland," the epic poem of medieval France, illustrates how public opinion is organized about a political event—Charlemagne's campaigns in A.D. 778–779—where public discussion has not yet taken a differentiated institutional form as "news." The relationship of such epics, and rumor and broadsides as well, to the later media is the same as the relation of court cliques to political parties in political life, trading fairs to markets in the economic sphere, and early monotheistic religions to transcendental religion in the cultural world. The earliest institutions of mass news may be traced to the "canards" in fifteenth- and sixteenth-century France (see Seguin 1961, 1964). These proto-news sheets combined a religious-magical world view with standards about "objective" reporting that typify a more modern, differentiated media. On the one hand, canards regularly reported fantastic events like miracles, visions, and various manifestations of the divine will on earth; at the same time, they tried to "verify" them, in good reportorial style, by providing impressive lists of eyewitnesses—for whom age and profession would be presented—and by providing legitimating texts from religious and secular authorities.

Even after the actual institution of a newspaper first emerged, however, differentiation in anything other than the most minimal, concrete sense did not yet exist. Despite this concrete structural differentiation, these first newspapers were tied rather directly to—in fact, they usually emerged in response to—efforts to realize specific group aims such as class demands, party commitments, or religious values. Only gradually was there movement toward more substantive autonomy, as not only institutional structures but also the goals themselves became differentiated (for this distinction, see Eisenstadt 1969:13–32). One step in this process is the creation of a free press in the legal sense, but differentiation involves freedom from more informal but equally powerful forces in the religious, solidary, economic, and political subsystems.

Because of differences in specific historical development, the mass media of different Western nations were attached to, and promoted by, different kinds of groups and institutions. Media differentiation has proceeded, therefore, at enormously different rates and with widely varying results. In France, the first real newspapers were organs of the absolutist state, to which the Church soon responded with papers of its own (Albert and Terrou 1970). In the United States, on the contrary, the differentiated state as such never had its own media, and the most important early papers were promoted by independent bourgeois like the Franklin brothers and later by political parties (Mott 1941). The relationship between institutional independence and legal freedom is similarly uneven. Whereas in the United States legal freedom of the press preceded any real institutional independence, the institutional autonomy of certain newspapers in nineteenth-century France—at least the ability of newspapers to disagree with one another and the government, to present, that is, divergent interpretations of unfolding events—preceded the legal freedom that arrived only with the Third Republic.

The emergence of more independent news media can be interpreted as the creation of an "autonomous regulatory mechanism" for the integrative dimension of society in the same manner that the emergence of representation, party formation, and constitutionalism indicates the development of regulatory mechanisms in the political sphere. And just as the resulting "generalization" of political power is basic for the achievement of substantive freedom and reformist types of social control (Eisenstadt 1969; Alexander 1978), so can the differentiation of mass news media be regarded as the generalization of normative resources. Such generalization provides society with an enormously increased flexibility in responding to changing events and contributes in a fundamental way to the attainment of increased freedom in the society at large. With political and cultural differentiation, the legitimation of political power moves from the unconditional forms of traditional support to the conditional forms of what Weber called, somewhat misleadingly, "rational-legal" legitimation. As the result of this development, the response of other social sectors to the activities of national government becomes increasingly significant for the maintenance of that power. It should be clear that the differentiation of mass news media is basic to such nontraditional legitimation, for it allows the continuous "regulation" of government action according to the more general value commitments produced by intellectual and cultural groups, as well as by the activities of political, economic, and solidary groups outside of the government itself. It is no wonder that in democratic societies the media are in constant struggle with the state: they confront the state as the populist counterpart to constitutional legal controls.

In rational-legal societies, this struggle between state and media will be a fight for position and relative strength with each side retaining its relative freedom of movement. In societies where regimes are neither fully traditional nor fully rational-legal, on the other hand, the state will become interventionist and impinge on the internal functioning of the press itself. The governments in such societies will confront the media in different ways, depending on the nature of the particular resources they possess. In various forms of political dictatorship, the governments of nineteenth-century France relied on direct political force of one kind or another. Napoleon established the first left-wing control of media with his "Décret du 27 Nivôse" on January 17, 1808, which tried to institutionalize general ideological values from which newspapers could not deviate. It forbade journals to publish articles "contrary to the social compact, to the sovereignty of the people and the glory of the armies" (Albert and Terrou 1970:30). The purpose of this tactic was to control the effects of social differentiation by preventing any independent interpretative intercession between the government and newly emerging social groups. This rationale was articulated very precisely by Napoleon in his memoirs written at Saint Helena. As he wrote about his government-controlled newspaper, *Le Moniteur* (see Albert and Terrou 1970:31): "J'ai fait du *Moniteur* l'âme et la force de mon gouvernement ansi que mon intermédiaire avec l'opinion public du dedans comme du dehors. . . . C'était le mot d'ordre pour les partisans du gouvernement" (I made the *Moniteur* the soul and the power of my government as well as my intermediary with public opinion inside and outside the country. . . . It laid down the "word of order" for the supporters of the government).

Later, when the French government of the Second Empire could not control the increase in newspapers in the face of rapid and widespread social differentiation and its own weakened control, the regulation it did achieve was still established through political means: first, by establishing "authorization" for opposition media, demanding the rights to prepublication readings (*préalables*), and by sponsoring its own official media in Havin's *Le Siècle,* the "monitor of the opposition." Despite these precautions, the existence of the "authorized" opposition papers contributed massively to the fall of the regime in the late 1860s and early 1870s.

By contrast, in a liberal if not fully democratic regime, like that in late eighteenth- and early nineteenth-century England, the government seeks to control opposition media in more voluntary ways. Thus, between 1815 and 1855 Britain's government imposed high taxes that made British papers the most expensive in Europe, three times as expensive as the French. The effect of this indirect economic control was, nonetheless, much the same as with direct political control: it cut off the ability of competing leadership from reaching the masses and, thereby, enforced a more strongly stratified political community (Albert and Terrou 1970:50).

The social forces that produce and inhibit differentiation of the news media are the same that create differentiation in other spheres. On the structural level, media differentiation is produced by the demands for more universalistic information that oppressed groups make in the course of their demands for societal inclusion and support—for example, in the demands for the end of "anti-workingman" reporting in late nineteenth-century America or the demand by black groups for "community" coverage in American society in the 1960s and 1970s. As long as state control does not become absolute—as in the ideal-typical Fascist or Communist state—social differentiation will produce (and be created by) new social groups whose position vis-à-vis other groups and unfolding events must be articulated and whose demands must be internally integrated and standardized. These tasks can be achieved only if the group has its own news medium. For this reason, in nineteenth-century France, despite the unfree status of the press, the number and varieties of newspapers increased dramatically, as did the total circulation, which grew from 150,000 to 1,000,000 between 1852 and 1870, a period entirely within authoritarian government control. Every new rupture in French society during the 1860s, even between the government and its natural supporters like the Catholics, created new papers. By 1870, even the "Normaliens" had their own organ, *Le Courier du Dimanche* (Bellet 1967).

Another structural factor producing media differentiation is the growth of professional norms and self-regulation within the journalistic profession itself, developments that lead to demands for increased prestige and autonomy in journalistic work. The growth of a journalistic profession illustrates how role differentiation must accompany institutional differentiation. In eighteenth-century America, the first newspapers were established and written by printers, who performed a number of different tasks in their local communities. The typical editor

had other affairs besides his newspaper on his hands. He was a job-printer and usually a publisher of books and pamphlets . . . often the local postmaster, sometimes a magistrate, in many cases public printer . . . frequently kept a bookstore . . . occasionally branched out into general merchandise lines. (Mott 1941:47)

There seem to have been three phases of role differentiation in the history of American media. In the first, printers themselves performed all the principal tasks involved. In the second phase, which extended from the first days of the nation into the late nineteenth century, the printers were, on the one hand, differentiated from general editors, who directed all editorial policy and were usually also the owners of the paper, and from writers on the other. Writers in this period were usually highly educated intellectuals. In the third phase, owners and editors were differentiated from each other, and correspondingly, the journalist's role became more specialized and professional, relatively more insulated from the personal intervention of the owner (Schudson 1978:61–87). These differentiating processes manifest themselves in a number of different ways, for example, in the changes in policies for hiring reporters, or in the editorial changes that often accompany generational shifts in newspaper ownership within the same family. One can also observe that there has been a significant differentiation of content along with role and institution. The contents of newspapers themselves became increasingly differentiated as they sought to integrate and interpret the events and institutions of an increasingly differentiated society. From the late nineteenth century, the sections of the newspapers throughout Western nations have become increasingly specialized into sports sections; home sections; religion and book review supplements; and business, lesiure, and travel sections. Editorial coverage has been differentiated into national, local, and foreign news.

On the cultural level, the crucial variable in producing media differentiation is the degree of universalism in national civic cultures, which depends on a range of factors from national religion to the structure of the educational system. In England, for example, the universalistic religious categories of Puritanism gave a tremendous push to the development of early English news pamphlets (Walzer 1965:255). The transcendent and impersonal orientation of the Puritans made them distrust traditional, personal sources of information, particularly as they related to outside events like foreign wars and the progress of the international Protestant movement. To remedy this situation, the Puritans issued their own, more objective news pamphlets. This early development in the mass news media also served to define the self-consciousness of a newly emerging social group, the English gentry.

This kind of multidimensional analysis of sources of differentiation makes it possible to understand a fact that is commonly misinterpreted in the literature on media, namely, the impact of decreasing economic competition among newspapers and television stations. The fact that this historical development has been accompanied by a perception of increased news objectivity indicates that although economic competition is certainly a facilitating factor, it is only one economic factor among several others in contributing to media independence. Indeed, economic competition is not nearly as important as the differentiation of media institutions from other strategic elites and from institutions in other societal sectors. Directed by a strategic elite oriented toward a unique function, the news media need enormous financial resources to support their independence from other sectors in the society, even from the industrial-corporate one. Thus, the paradox: In the period of late capitalism the media became corporatized and their markets oligopolistic; these developments, however, allowed media institutions to save themselves from being dominated by certain forms of economic power and from a dominant economic class.[1]

The French case is interesting in this regard, for it can be argued that one of the primary reasons for the historical lack of independence of the French press from various social groups and classes was its inability to produce advertising. British and U.S. (see Schudson 1978:14–31) papers relied heavily on advertising to expand circulation and news coverage and to generate capital internally; in this way, they became more independent of personal wealth and direct control. In France, however, the strong cultural bias against "bourgeois commercialization" for a long time made it impossible for newspapers to both publish advertisements and be accepted as objective media (Albert and Terrou, 1970). The differences between this French situation and the American one could not be more striking. In America, the early papers were often started precisely for the purpose of advertising, the "news" representing a later editorial addition. The felt antinomy between advertising and objectivity was virtually nonexistent in America. A vast number of newspapers in the early nineteenth century were in fact called "advertisers" even when they were principally devoted to news reporting and to political affairs (e.g., the *Boston Daily Advertiser*). The "penny press," which appeared in the 1830s, was even more openly dependent on mass advertising; yet this penny press virtually invented the modern concept of "news" as a detached and relatively independent medium (Schudson 1978:22). This perceived complementarity between news and advertising is evidenced by the announcement of intention in the Baltimore *Sun* of 1837 "to lay out before the public, at a price within the means of everyone, all the news of the day, and at the same time afford an advantageous medium for advertising" (quoted in Schudson 1978:21).

By contrast to the aristocratic distrust of commercialization ingrained in French culture, individualism informs the positive American attitude toward media advertising. As the *Boston Daily Times* replied to its critics in 1837:

Some of our readers complain of the great number of patent medicines advertised in this paper. . . . [W]hether the articles advertised are what they purport to be . . . is an inquiry for the reader who feels interested in the matter, and not for us, to make. It is sufficient for our purpose that the advertisements are paid for. . . . One man has as good a right as another to have his wares, his goods, his panaceas, his profession published to the world in a newspaper, provided he pays for it. (quoted in Mott 1941:301)

At the risk of a certain simplification, this abstract general argument can be stated succinctly in the following way. The problem of the differentiation of the news media is the problem of the realization of a democratic social order or, to use a term I have developed in other contexts (Alexander 1978, 1983a), substantive freedom. To the degree that the news media are tied to religious, ideological, political, or class grouping, they are not free to form and reform public events in a flexible way. Without this flexibility, public opinion becomes "artificial" and "biased": it will be keyed to a part over the whole.

Fusion and Autonomy: Comparative Perspectives. We are now in a position to return to the general perspective stated at the outset of this chapter and to place it in a more comparative perspective. Charges of "news bias" must not be viewed as the failure of a reporter to report what is true, to indulge in the provision of moral judgment as opposed to cognitive information. It should, rather, be understood as the failure of an activity that has a normative and evaluative character to achieve sufficiently differentiated social status. Strains produced by such fusion, dedifferentiation, and the consequent perception of "bias" are endemic, in various degrees, in all modern societies. If the mass media are "superimposed" upon (Dahrendorf 1959:206–40), rather than differentiated from, specific religious, class, political, economic, or regional groupings, they will continuously recreate these particularistic formations instead of "society" itself. The informational inputs to the media will be partial and shielded, and the normative outputs will be rooted in particularistic perspectives. Because flexibility in creating evaluative judgment is diminished, the social control function of the media is rigidified. Because opinion will be formed on the basis of partial information, efforts at reform will be less successful, strain will be increasingly unresolved, and social polarization will be exacerbated.

In such less differentiated situations, the normative definitions produced by the mass media—the news that they report as fact—are no longer perceived as objective fact, as "news," by the society as a whole. Only the members of those communities directly associated with the particular medium consider the reporting to be accurate; it is regarded as biased by all other groups, which in turn have their own version of the facts supplied by their own "client" media.

We can view this problem in static terms, comparing different Western media and relating degrees of differentiation to degrees of national acceptance of news as fact or fiction. In the United States, one newspaper, the *New York Times,* is accepted as factual arbiter by a wide spectrum of social opinion, with certain exceptions to be discussed below. In England, there is less unanimity, and the *London Times* reports facts that are often in direct contention with those reported by the more Labor- or Social Democratic-oriented *Guardian* and *Observer.* In continental countries, dedifferentiation is often more pronounced. Both national news channels in Italian television, according to Hallin and Mancini (1984:830), "have partisan and ideological attachments" that are religious and political. One is pro-Catholic, "employing managers and journalists close to the Christian Democratic party; the other is secular, and close to the parties of the non-communist left." The more general comparison these observers draw between Italian and American media is particularly to the point.

Many of the print media in Italy are oriented toward providing political commentary, a function that they share with the other institutions of political debate. And if print journalism in Italy shares the functions of the political parties, television journalism serves them. The Italian television journalist is, both in training and in terms of actual power relations, a party functionary. The journalist is trained in the party apparatus, and can be transferred by the party if his or her work displeases its leadership. American journalism, by contrast, has developed into a separate political institution, with a set of functions and an ideology that are more or less its own. American journalists are not only free of direct political control, their political loyalty is primarily to journalism itself rather than to any distinct political tendencies. (ibid.:842)

Only after the First World War did the papers of France move from direct "party" affiliations to the representation of "tendencies" (Albert and Terrou 1970:94), and the particularistic association between medium and political orientation still remains strikingly apparent. In the typical coverage of a single event in the Parisian press, one often sees very little overlap in "facts" among the several papers, which span the political spectrum from right to left. For example, on Sunday, July 30, 1978, most papers reported that the French government planned to support Spain's entry into the European Common Market. The conservative *Le Figaro* ran the news as a major front-page story, but it focused entirely on what it described as the dishonest, unscrupulous manner in which Socialist leaders had opposed the government's decision under the banner of support for southern French agricultural workers. The Communist paper, *L'Humanité*, played the story in an equally big way, but its "news" focused on the "intolerable" and irresponsible aspect of the government's decision, purportedly taken without "rational" consultation with the agricultural groups affected. Equally important to its front-page story was the announcement by Communist groups of the elaborate demonstrations against Spanish entry to be held by the agricultural workers in southern France. *Le Matin,* then the moderate Socialist daily, referred to the government's decision hardly at all, focusing almost completely in its front-page news coverage on the new political conflict between the Socialists and Communists the decision had triggered. *Le Monde* placed the story on page 20, re-presenting without elaboration the press releases of the government, Socialists, and Communists. As this brief recounting begins to indicate, the fact that interpretation occurs in France in a still relatively fused context makes it difficult to get a sense of the nature of the actual event without reading the report in every paper. In the weekend edition of *Le Figaro,* July 29–30, 1978, five out of six front-page stories were basically editorial commentaries. With the exception of the Common Market story referred to above, the first news reports appeared on page 3.

Left-wing totalitarian governments present, of course, a systematically different and much more primitive kind of media fusion. There, the lack of differentiation between state and society has pushed the media less into the role of party newspaper than party-state ideological organ. There is, however, a direct link between such a media position and the dominance of party papers in the prerevolutionary periods. Bolshevik papers began, for example, as the instruments of a struggling party, organs which, correctly, viewed bourgeois papers as similarly particularistic and ideological in orientation. The Russian Revolution, then, simply substituted one dominant class bias for another. As Lenin wrote in 1921:

Capitalism has transformed journals into capitalist enterprises, into instruments of gain for informing and amusing the rich, and as a means of duping and undermining the mass of workers. . . . *We* have begun to make the journals an instrument for instructing the masses, to teach them to live and to build their economy without the financial interests and the capitalists. (Quoted in Conte 1973, italics added)

This perspective is firmly in place today. As a leading journalist, V. Kudraiavtsev, wrote in *Izvestiia* on August 25, 1968: "Even the very term 'truth' has a class content" (quoted in Conte 1973). In 1969, 77 percent of the more than 11,000 students entering Soviet journalism schools were party members. As I have indicated by calling them ideological organs rather than party newspapers, the Soviet press actually performs more of a generalized value function than a specific normative one. They are more interested in the underlying "meaning" of events—in putting the events directly into the general ideological context of Soviet Marxism-Leninism and Russian national culture—than in the nature of the unfolding events themselves and in their immediate relation to other events in the society. It seems possible that the more detailed and concrete function of day-to-day integration and interpretation is performed by other Soviet institutions, for example, by the elaborate and profuse "letters-to-the-editor" sections contained in many newspapers.

Fusion and Autonomy: Specific Historical Paths. We can also view this problem of "biased," client-like relationships between media and particular social groups and institutions in historical terms. The different paths toward development and the uneven, discontinuous advances toward differentiation taken by different Western mass media must be seen against the background of divergent national social structures and cultures.

From the early 1600s to the Revolution, the French *ancien régime* established strong censorship and a directly political tradition of news reporting. (In this discussion of the French case, I am drawing upon Manévy 1955; Deniel 1965; Boussel 1960; Bellanger et al. 1969–1976;

Bellet 1967; Albert and Terrou 1970.) Thus, in the first period of the formally free press, 1789–1792, the perspective of the revolutionaries was that newspapers were not to be unattached but were, rather, to instruct. As Brissot wrote of the press: "It is the unique means of instruction for a large nation little accustomed to read and wanting to leave ignorance and bondage behind" (quoted in Albert and Terrou 1970:26–27). New journals formed around individual radical political leaders, expressing their personal points of view and closely connected to revolutionary clubs and societies. Equally personal counterrevolutionary news organs soon established themselves. After the end of Napoleon's rigid governmental control, the regulation became less intense, but Restoration papers continued to view themselves mainly as adjuncts to parties, classes, regions, and religious groups, and they reported news from a similarly personal editorial outlook. The Catholic Right, for example, had its own weekly journals and daily papers that regulated and interpreted its relation to the government, to the republicans, and to the Church itself vis-à-vis unfolding daily events. These interpretations occurred against the background of certain general value commitments, supplied particularly by Paulian texts as they were articulated by Bonald, Maîstre, and Lamenais. Thus, the reporting by the Catholic press of such mundane and specific events as parliamentary debates reflected the general themes of hierarchical authority, the organic unity of the state, and the need for religion in public life.

The revolutionary period of 1848 simply repeated this pattern of personal political journalism, this time shifting toward the Left: George Sand, Raspail, Lamartine, Hugo, and Proudhon all had their own news organs. And despite the broadening mass audience in the later nineteenth century, political and social conditions ensured the continuation of this sectarian style. In the Third Republic, serious senatorial candidates would often start their own newspaper as a means of bolstering their chances for election, and even in this democratic period government authority continued to interfere directly with the media's autonomy. The Republic's press law of 1881 continued to outlaw "offenses against the President of the Republic, defamations against the army and its leaders, attacks against the regime, and calls to dissolve the laws" (Manévy 1955:69). In the 1890s, this law was used freely against Socialist and Anarchist papers. In the Dreyfus case, newspapers were highly politicized. Zola, after all, had initiated the affair with his famous "J'accuse" in *L'Amore* in 1898, for which he spent one month in prison. During each day of the trial, newspapers of different political persuasions devoted their pages to the task of exposing the errors and contradictions of the opposing side. At the time of the outbreak of the First World War, fully forty of the fifty major French newspapers were frankly and openly propagandistic for different political factions. Although partisanship subsided to some degree between the wars, it was revived during the early postwar years primarily because of the effects of the Resistance, during which highly personalized and political journals flourished around individual leaders.

The American media experience differed drastically from the French for a number of reasons. (1) Although both colonial America and pre-revolutionary France were enmeshed in patrimonial systems with non-democratic states, the American experience in this regard was significantly more conducive to media autonomy. America's colonial separation made it much more difficult for England to enforce its royal restrictions than for the French king to enforce the writs of the *ancien régime*. Equally important, the English form of patrimonial rule was significantly more differentiated and controlled than the French; it left more room for de-centralized, independent estates and for dissent. (2) The subsequent revolutionary experiences of the two nations were also far different. In France, the highly personalized attacks of the dissenting newspapers on traditional authority were strongly linked to particular ideological positions; this particularism set the stage for a vicious circle of personalized journalism to continue unabated into the postrevolutionary phases. In the United States, the equally personalized attacks on authority were carried out in the name of "freedom of the press," since the colonial rebellion was one that united the whole nation and was conducted in part under the ideology of neutral "due process." The revolutionary victory, therefore, set the stage for a future American journalism that, while still highly personalistic, could be carried out under the legal auspices of a free press. (3) Postrevolutionary France remained significantly traditional and highly polarized through the early twentieth century, with more or less primor-dially defined religious, economic, and political groups vying for control of the state. The United States, by contrast, despite continuing polari-zation and the early history of confrontation between North and South, maintained a rational-legal state throughout its subsequent history and had a certain level of diffuse civil consensus.

Just as the ideal-typical model I have articulated for media development was specified in a particular way in France, therefore, so it must be modified for the American case (I draw here on Mott 1941, Commager 1950, and Schudson 1978).

The first newspaper in the U.S. colonies was published in 1689 in Massachusetts as the spokesman for the religious-political leadership of the colony; the first opposition paper, published in the early eighteenth century by the older Franklin brother, can be seen as representing the protests of the newly independent artisan group against elite control. The famous Zenger case in 1735 set the crucial course for public attitudes toward newspapers throughout the colonial struggle for independence: prosecuted by the colonial governor for printing anti-English material, Zenger published pro-American news from his jail cell throughout the nine months of his pretrial incarceration, all in the name of "freedom of the press." At the end of this time he was freed because the local grand jury would not convict him for his patriotic action. This case combined two of the factors that made American media development distinct: the relatively legal-rational English system (trial by jury, due process) and the independence provided by America's colonial status (the local grand jury). During the Revolutionary period, this same pattern was reinforced. In the name of "freedom of the press," American colonialists engaged, relatively freely, in the very kind of extremely partisan and personalized journalism that in the French situation—and, as we shall see, in the German—would have been suppressed immediately and that would have reinforced ideological, more personalized notions of journalism. Thus, the lead of the March 12, 1770, *Boston Gazette*'s story on the Boston "massacre" was the following: "The Town of Boston affords a recent and melancholy Demonstration of the destructive Consequences of quartering Troops among Citizens in a Time of Peace." Only after two-thirds of a column of such editorializing did it actually begin its news: the "circumstantial Account of the tragical Affair on Monday Night last" (quoted in Mott 1941:102).

The first daily newspapers appeared in the postrevolutionary period in response to two kind of pressures: (1) the need of the mercantile class for up-to-the-minute and wide-ranging information on sailing vessels and import offerings; (2) the need of newly emerging political parties to interpret events to their respective audiences. Freneau's *National Gazette,* for example, was initiated by Thomas Jefferson and significantly widened the breach between Federalists and their Republican opposition in the 1790s.

In 1798, the "Alien and Sedition Act," passed under the Federalist administration, sought among other things to directly link the media with state control, under the umbrella of conservative political ideology. Although the law failed for a number of reasons, its inability specifically to control news reporting had a revealing sidelight. In order to suppress a news report, the law stipulated that malicious intent had to be proven, thereby acknowledging the existence—even in the early period—of a relatively institutionalized normative standard of universalistic truth against which any partisan statement could be judged. This acknowledgment simply was never made in relationship to the French media, not even by the Third Republic.

The "penny press," an inexpensive paper well within the reach of most Americans, first appeared in the pre-Civil War years. Responding to the emergence of mass middle and working classes on the American scene, this press was sharply opposed by economic and party papers, which wanted to maintain their monopoly on information. Significantly, the penny press first pursued the "plain old news" of everyday life, and it could do so only because it was the first news medium to conceive of itself as in a relatively differentiated position. This ambition was trumpeted by the *Baltimore Sun* in a particularly lofty manner.

We shall give no place to religious controversy nor to political discussions of merely partisan character. On political principles, and questions involving the interests of honor of the whole country, it will be free, firm, and temperate. Our object will be the common good, without regard to that of sects, factions, or parties; and for this object we shall labor without fear or partiality. (Quoted in Schudson 1978:22)

Despite the emergence of this relative independence, however, the vast majority of papers in this period continued to link their "news" to economic-merchant and political-personal interests. As a spokesman for the Democratic Party press wrote in 1852, "every shade of political persuasion has its organ. . . . Each of these organs is a propagandist after its own fashion" (quoted in Mott 1941:253). In the 1850 census, only 5 percent of the country's papers were listed as neutral or independent. Although the Civil War experience continued to support the legal freedom and differentiation of the press, the particularistic style of party papers remained in full force after the war. It was an informal association of newspaper editors that placed Andrew Greely, the famous editor of the *Herald Tribune*, into the Democratic nomination for President in 1872, and when

Ochs bought the *New York Times* in 1896 he tied it publicly to the antisilver campaign.

By the last decades of the century news media were becoming more differentiated, not just in terms of how they viewed their product but institutionally as well. What contemporaries of the period called the "new journalism" was intricately tied up with sensationalism and the attempt to create for the growing industrial classes an apolitical paper that would sell. More general factors were involved than the "capitalist" factor of the potentially wider market, as any comparative reference reveals. Although native-language ethnic papers often served as protosocialist organs for first-generation immigrant groups and partisanly worker-oriented papers were a constant feature of nineteenth-century social history, it is extremely significant that there were no "labor" papers attached to working-class parties that emerged on a mass scale in the United States. By 1880, one-quarter of American papers were independent or neutral, and by 1890 one-third. Papers developed *"human* interest" stories, and for the first time defined the reporter's role as actively seeking out "news." They launched "crusades" in the name of the "public interest" against corrupt groups like New York's Tweed ring. This transition in content coincided with the birth of journalistic professionalization and the emergence of newspapers as big business. By the turn of the twentieth century, the notion of the news media as a public institution was, then, beginning to be institutionalized. The major exception to this tendency was the relation of the news media to racial groups. American media remained tightly linked to the white core group of American society until at least the mid-twentieth century.

Although I have developed this contrast in the historical specification of media development in terms of French versus American media history, nineteenth-century Germany presents a case where newspapers were even more sharply polarized around class and party than the French were. As a result of its more rigid patrimonial structure and the lateness of its industrialization, Germany produced a confrontation between proletarian and middle-class papers unmatched anywhere in Europe, one that contributed to the increasing social rigidity that led to that nation's fateful social conflict (Roth 1963:243–48). In 1873, for example, the German Social Democratic newspaper reported that the typhoid epidemic then sweeping Germany was actually a bourgeois conspiratorial tool against the working class! In their turn, middle-class papers so distorted the activities of working-class groups that their readers could learn virtually nothing of the positive sides and real political justifications for the Socialist movement. The Social Democrats responded to this situation in a revealing way. They decided to start party papers only in areas where middle-class papers already existed; only in this way, they reasoned, could middle-class readers compare news reports of the same event. But while the sectarian nature of Socialist papers certainly served the vital intraparty function of bolstering members' self-images in the face of often degrading and offensive characterizations in the middle-class press, such papers obviously presented a significant barrier to expanding the Social Democratic following. Even though more space was given to "news" and less to party affairs after the expansion of membership in the 1890s, these papers never moved beyond a highly sectarian orientation that alienated many workers, and particularly a large number of workers' wives, who remained relatively integrated with the dominant culture (particularly the religion) of the Reich. Fully 80 percent of the editors of Social Democratic papers were from the working classes, and the party prohibited its members from working for the bourgeois press.

Fusion and Autonomy: A Dynamic Process.   Finally, the problem of media "bias" can be seen not only in comparative or historical terms but also as a dynamic process that ebbs and flows with the episodic polarization produced by the strains that inevitably occur within the modernizing process of every nation, no matter how differentiated its media are in comparative or historical terms. For example, in the United States in the late 1960s and early 1970s, spokespersons for the national government acceptably portrayed the "Eastern establishment" press as presenting a biased and distorted picture of American social life. The success of this characterization was tied to the polarization of the national normative community into sharply opposed particularistic groupings (see the chapter that follows). From this perspective it is clear why, as Woodward and Bernstein reported (1974), the Nixon administration was not worried about the Watergate problem before the 1972 presidential election. They believed, quite correctly, that a sufficiently large number of Americans would not accept the news reported by the *Washington Post* as "factual." A large group of Americans perceived the *Post* as biased because, in the preceding years of social turmoil, that newspaper had become the normative spokesman of a liberal community no longer in the national majority. During this period of social conflict most of the national news media were not perceived as strongly differentiated from the positions and perspectives of particular social groups. Only after the 1972 presidential election with the defeat of McGovern and the ensuing depolarization of American society did the national media once again begin to receive the more broadly based inputs of support that allowed it to produce news about Watergate that could be judged as fact rather than opinion.

Although the parallel is not exact, a similar relationship can be seen between a later period of intense polarization in France and the emergence there of more particularistic media. In September 1977, when it appeared that the French Left coalition would come to power in the March 1979 national elections, a potentially powerful new paper, *J'informe,* appeared on the national scene. Published by a former cabinet minister close to President Giscard-D'Estaing and financed by a number of large industrial interests, the paper immediately assumed the role of spokesperson and interpreter for the government's center-Right coalition (with an initial circulation of 150,000). Although *J'informe*'s short-run purpose was to contribute to the government's reelection, its long-range goal was to provide a forum for Giscard's party and, presumably, for the social interests attached to it, after the Left took control. Once the Left coalition split apart in late 1977, and the prospect of a left-wing government receded, the need for the new and self-consciously propagandistic paper was gone. On December 18, 1977, *J'informe* ceased publication; its financial backers had withdrawn the necessary support (*New York Times,* December 18, 1977).

I would conclude by noting that whereas social scientists have studied "cleavage" problems extensively in regard to the economic, political, and cultural subsystems of society, they have rarely investigated the impact of cleavage on the integrative dimension and the production of norms. This lack of attention is largely the result of the fact that, in contrast to these other sectors, processes in the normative dimension have rarely been theoretically articulated (cf. Alexander 1978). In this section, I have indicated that sharp cleavage situations are explosive not only because they produce broadly defined economic, political, and cultural conflicts, but also because, through their impact on the news media, they produce less cognitive agreement about the "factual" nature of the social world itself. The more that this kind of disagreement occurs, the more will social strains become exacerbated and prove immutable to social reform.

Structured Strain
in Differentiated Societies

I have argued that the news media's success in performing their normative "function" is dependent on certain distinctive kinds of historical conditions. In the modern period, three ideal-typical situations may be identified: (1) a single newspaper or news network that is the voice of official state ideology; (2) news institutions representing specific social perspectives of relatively autonomous groups; and (3) news media that are structurally free of directly inhibiting economic, political, solidary, and cultural entanglements.* Only in the third situation does the national public perceive the news media as providing "facts," and only in this situation can the media's normative function be performed in a manner that maximizes the public's flexibility.

Yet even though such a differentiated situation is in a certain sense ideal, it produces certain distinctive social conflicts and is open to certain ideological criticisms. I describe these as "structured strains" or "contradictions," which are inherent in the relation between a differentiated mass news medium and its social system environment. Although my treatment of such strains cannot be exhaustive, I elaborate the problematic relationships I have in mind.

On the microlevel of role conflict, the existence of differentiation must

---

*I stress that these are ideal types. The concrete arrangements in each national case are idiosyncratic and blur these analytic distinctions in various ways. One important source of this blurring is state ownership of national news organizations. In a vulgar sense, all such institutions would have to represent the "state." In democratic societies, however, there is a distinction between the solidary community of citizens, which is constitutionally endowed with a range of power-enhancing public skills, and the actual state apparatus. The democratic situation creates the possibility for an autonomous news organization within a state-owned system—usually called "public ownership"—but it does not necessitate it. Thus, the English BBC has been relatively independent of particular governments, whereas the French national news has not. In Italy, there is a different situation still, with state ownership being combined with at least two competing party-affiliated organizations. Because the present chapter has been so historical in scope, televised news has not been a primary focus. Insofar as it becomes so—despite the recent trends toward deregulation and privatization—the factor of state ownership becomes important, for it mediates the phenomena of fusion and autonomy in situationally specific ways, for example, contrasting cultural milieux make legal control by government different in every case. For an analysis of privately owned television news that correlates fairly closely with the model suggested here, see Gans' (1979) extended research on the relationship between values and objectivity in American television news and on the often tense relationship between American news organizations and their surrounding environments.

by its very nature continually raise the problem of collusion between a news reporter and the reporter's sources. In order to function as a normative organizer, news reporters must stretch their reach into the "socially unknown," which means establishing intimate and trustworthy contacts through which to gain information that otherwise would remain private and "unregulated." Yet if to discover is to engage, to evaluate is to withdraw, and only if the latter occurs can the information garnered by the reporter be processed and judged according to independent norms. This problem must be regarded as a dilemma inherent in the very structure of the differentiated system. "Selling out" is a possibility only because differentiation has first established the partners for the transaction. On the other side of this conflict, the differentiated and legally protected status of the journalist's role raises the possibility that the narrow interest in finding "what's news" enters into conflict with important public interests, as when journalists protect the identity of illegal sources. This kind of strain has manifested itself in the increasingly acrimonious conflict between courts and media that is occurring in most Western nations.

Another, more general, structural problem for even the most ideally differentiated media is the antagonism between government and news agencies that generates efforts at news distortion and manipulation by the government and occasional episodes of irresponsible criticism of the government by the media in turn. If, as Neustadt, for example, has maintained (1960:42–63), the American president is himself a "normative" figure engaged in persuasion, as well as in command, the government's political goals become directly competitive with the goals of the mass media, for each seeks to place public events within a more general evaluative framework. The president and the media are in continual battle over the normative definitions of events. The norms the president seeks to impose, however, are those of a particular segment of the national community. In other words, precisely because the power of the state is thoroughly differentiated from the news media, the latter become vulnerable to an enormously potent political force whose aim, paradoxically, is to dedifferentiate, or fuse, the relationship. Although the prize in this battle is influence rather than power, the struggle is in deadly earnest, and to minimize the stakes in the conflict between democratically elected governments and free press—as critical theorists of the "bourgeois" press inevitably do—is a serious mistake.

In periods of political polarization, of course, this conflict is particularly acute. In his first four years in office, Richard Nixon devoted strenuous legal and illegal efforts to restrict the autonomous judgments of news reporters (Porter 1976). But even in relatively tranquil times, the war continues. When Ronald Reagan began his second term in office, in January 1985, he announced that the White House would launch its own news service to distribute presidential speeches and announcements. While liberal opponents of the conservative president's first term had viewed Reagan as having successfully tamed a now docile White House press corps, this was not Reagan's own view at all. According to the Associated Press report on the rationale for the news service (*Los Angeles Times,* January 7, 1985), "Reagan has complained to reporters that they misinterpret his words and distort his views." As one White House official explained, the president would be more effective if his views were "unfiltered" by the independent media. The effort, quite clearly, was to avoid the primordial fact of news interpretation, which in the American situation is carried out by a body with a structured antagonism to central power. In the American case, it should be mentioned, this strain goes back to the founding of the nation itself. In 1789, the U.S. Congress sharply restricted journalists' access to the Senate because of what they regarded as the latter's "misrepresentations" of recent senatorial debates (quoted in Mott 1941:143).

The controversy that developed in the early 1970s in France between *Le Monde* and its veteran economic reporter, Philippe Simmonet, offers an example of such structured conflict in a different national media environment. Claiming that Simmonet had discovered and intended to print information embarrassing to the government's relation to the international oil companies, the French government brought suit to prevent publication. Its strength in this situation is revealed by the fact that *Le Monde's* editors easily surrendered to government pressure. In fact, they joined the government's campaign to pressure Simmonet to reveal his sources, and when he would not do so, they fired him without a hearing. The firing, of course, immediately became politicized. Socialist and Communist trade union representatives joined Simmonet's suit to regain his position, and the story was interpreted in particularistic ways. It is revealing that the message Simmonet took away from his experience (Simmonet 1977) is that the idea of a "liberal," independent journal in a capitalist society is hypocritical and that newspapers should seek to develop consistent, all-encompassing political perspectives on everyday events. To the degree this does occur, however, governments simply seek to control news media in a more direct manner. Simmonet's reaction clearly illustrates how the structured strain in a differentiated situation can lead, under certain conditions, to powerful arguments for undermining media differentiation itself.

The third and most general kind of contradiction I mention concerns the manner in which the differentiated position of the media makes them vulnerable to pressures for the "inflation" (Parsons 1967) of its social system role. I describe this strain in relation to several of its specific manifestations.

Theorists from Aristotle to Marx and Weber have emphasized that the achievement of intellectual insight proceeds most effectively along a dialectical path, through the head-on dialogue of opposing perspectives. Yet, by a logic that would be contradictory to the entire implication of the preceding argument, it appears that the conditions for such dialogue occur only in those societies in which the news media are less rather than more differentiated, for only in relatively undifferentiated situations do the media produce sharply divergent perspectives of public events. This logic is apparently fortified by the charges made by intellectuals critical of the American press, who describe it as bland and simplistic, who assert that by not "facing the issues" the press contributes to the political and moral stagnation of American society. Of course, to continue the science analogy used earlier, the knowledge created by such polarized media would be subject to a high degree of paradigm conflict. Still, media differentiation appears, paradoxically, inversely related to the sharpness of public thought and the quality of intellectual insight available to the society at large.

But this connection between the relative impoverishment of public dialogue and media differentiation is, indeed, only apparent. Social scientists drawing such a connection misunderstand the media's social function, and when the same error is committed by the public at large the media become vulnerable to serious damage. The news medium's peculiar social position means that it "reflects" the conditions of the society around it, and in this respect it is, as conventional wisdom would have it, "a slave to the facts," if that phrase is taken in a noncognitive sense. Because of its very flexibility and integrative power a differentiated news medium cannot be an explicit "organizer" of norms in the way that institutions in other dimensions often are: it cannot formulate basic goals, which is a political responsibility, or basic values, which is a cultural one. In my view, the lack of sharp political focus and perspective in American political news is not a dire commentary on the impact of differentiation on the news media but rather a reflection of the inadequate autonomy achieved by the American political system, as manifest by such structural weaknesses as the atomization of executive and legislative functions and particularly the inability of political parties to articulate and maintain distinctive political positions (cf. Huntington 1968:93–139; Hardin 1974).

This specific problem provides an opportunity for formulating the contradiction we are concerned with in more general terms. To the degree the mass media sustain a differentiated position, they will absorb the weaknesses and reflect the distortions created by inadequate structural development in other social sectors. Social differentiation is always an "uneven and combined" process of development, and in one society certain sectors "lead" where in other societies these same sectors "lag" (Smelser 1970:7). The peculiarly American combination of a highly differentiated news media and less thoroughly differentiated political and intellectual institutions produces certain distinctive problems. In this situation, precisely because the media have been such effective normative organizers, they will be "blamed" for the weaknesses of these other sectors.

Such a double-bind situation creates strong centrifugal pressure for the inflation of the media's social function, which can lead, ultimately, to an equally radical deflation. The media will be asked to perform, and may well accept, a political or cultural role, and because they do not actually possess the functional resources for performing such tasks, they are bound to fail.

Illustrations of this inflationary-deflationary spiral abound in the recent history of the news media in America. In social crises, for example the 1960s, when the weaknesses of the American political system are exacerbated, pressure mounts for the media to expand their functions, to engage in critical or radical political judgment, to investigate and "clean up" the government and the society as a whole. But because the government has itself been unable to accomplishh this task, in responding to these demands, the media open themselves to devastating political criticism about their lack of objectivity.

"Media politics" presents another example of the manner in which effective media performance can be undercut by weaknesses in the political sector. By media politics, I refer to a range of politically degenerate phenomena: the generation of political support on the basis of presentation of self rather than the articulation of public issues; presidential use of television to create the charismatic, Caesarist domination of political opposition; the volatility of public opinion, which encourages the mercurial ascension of untried, inexperienced, and often incompetent political leadership. Yet, once again, these problems relate to the deficiencies of the American political system interacting with the peculiar functional position of the media, not to the problems of differentiation in the media themselves. Although the differentiation of news media does introduce a high degree of fluidity into political communication, it need not necessarily dominate other forms of political influence, as it tends to do in the United States. The real problem in the U.S. case is not the differentiation of the integrative dimension but the lack of differentiation of the political system. Because the institutions that should produce self-conscious political norms cannot do so—cannot, in terms of systemic logic, provide certain kinds of competing inputs to the media—political candidates gain popularity without articulating explicit positions. In the same manner, although "presidential politics" is facilitated by a differentiated media, the failure of organizational opposition prevents the creation of alternative, competing political symbolization. And, once again, the pervasive public criticism of what are mistakenly regarded as instances of an inflation of the media's political role can result in the deflation of what is, in itself, a relatively "healthy" social institution.

This inflationary-deflationary dilemma can occur in regard to the cultural, as well as the political, dimension. In certain situations of extreme social strain, the news media's normative orientation becomes legitimately transformed into a "value" function, although even this more generalized role is performed in a flexible and differentiated way. Such a generalization of function characterized television news at crucial points in the Watergate period, particularly during the congressional hearings when television served a key function in the ritualistic invocation of the civic culture that was one of the fundamental responses to the strain of that time. After such episodes (cf. Lang and Lang 1968; and chapter 5, below), however, the danger is that the news media will be expected to assume the permanent role of, and will accept the responsibility for, value arbiter rather than norm organizer. But this inflation can occur only to the degree that deficiencies exist in the cultural dimension itself, if moral leadership cannot generate sufficient clarity and relevance to provide the news media with the value inputs they would normally "register" in a normative manner. The performance of this inflated function makes the news media particularly vulnerable and opens the door for the destructive deflation of their normative scope, for example, in the public support for presidential legislation restricting the media's flexibility.

Finally, if our system reference shifts from the national to the international level, we can see quite clearly that even the most differentiated national medium will usually be closely linked to particularistic, national loyalties in terms of its relationship to extranational events. One way of comparing the international and national communities is in the degree to which their normative structures are, first, widely shared, and second, universalistic. On the international level there is radically less commonality and radically more particularism. Consequently, whereas the direct link between newspapers and a particular social group remains a distinct possibility on the national level, the dedifferentiated identification of newspapers with the interests of a particular national community is standard practice on the level of international social relations. Although many a national newspaper may succeed in differentiating itself from a particular government's "line" on the interpretation of an international event, it will rarely succeed in differentiating itself from the norms and values of the nation as a normative community. Events in the international arena are, as a result, almost always interpreted from the particularistic perspective of the nation within which the news medium operates. Thus, when the Western powers moved to establish wire services in the mid-nineteenth century—the Wolffe Agency in Germany, Reuters in England, L'Agence Havas in France, and the Associated Press in the United States—it was precisely in order to gain control over the information conveyed to their respective citizenries about the rapidly developing international economic and political relations of the day (for the French case, see Frédérix 1959). International particularism is revealed in a particularly acute way by the lies that are so often told, wittingly and unwittingly, by reporters in time of war (Knightley 1978). But it extends to the mundane as well. When the first American landed on the moon, the event was covered in strikingly different ways by French, Italian, and Russian newspapers (Tudesq 1973).

The fusion of national community and national media in terms of international news means that little "regulation" over government policy in this area is exercised by democratic media. The bias is not simply the result of such factors as reportorial ethics or an overreliance on government sources. It constitutes a major independent factor in the creation and exacerbation of international conflict. Although the problem of national media particularism is not created by media differentiation—the other strains I have mentioned are—it is certainly a structured strain that such differentiation does nothing to resolve.

In this chapter I have presented the outlines of a general theory of the mass news media in society. The media produce certain normative definitions, and the "success" of this production depends on the degree to which they have achieved autonomy from other social institutions and groups. Dependent media—the products of an unevenly differentiated, relatively fused society—can themselves become a significant source of social polarization and rigidification of social control. Moreover, the flexibility of the news media is such that even in a highly differentiated condition they can become a focal point of great social strain, for their very transparency makes them a highly visible conduit for the weaknesses of their external social environment. Although my argument has been abstract and condensed, it provides, I hope, a relatively specific model for future empirical elaboration and debate.

NOTES

1. This is not to say, of course, that the pressure to sell papers (or media time) is always supportive of the media's interpretative function. It is to say, however, that the results of capitalist pressures on the media have usually been greatly exaggerated, both in terms of their distorting and their dominative tendencies.

Raymond Williams is perhaps the most influential analyst of the media who has taken up the neo-Marxist position I am criticizing here. Describing corporatization of the mass media as one of the "two major factors in the modern history of communication" (Williams 1962), he condemns it as fundamentally antidemocratic. Whereas I have described the separation of editorial control from financial ownership as a phase of role differentiation that allowed news reporting to be increasingly autonomous vis-à-vis particularistic opinion, Williams describes it as having allowed "the methods and attitudes of capitalist business to have established themselves at the centre of public communications" (ibid.). Corporatization, according to Williams, means the reliance on advertising sales to finance papers, i.e., a newly economic bottom line. Relying on Marx's commodification theory, Williams (1962:25) suggests that in these conditions communications are produced, not for "use," but for exchange, a development tantamount in his view to eroding the capacity for truth.

Williams overlooks here the multidimensional context of media development, which necessitates looking at not only the media's economic links but also at political, cultural, and solidary links. This change in ownership, for example, occurred more or less simultaneously with another central phenomenon, namely, professionalization. The result was that, during the purported period of commodification, the work of the actual producer of communication—the reporting of news—was pushed toward greater concern with use. Increasingly, the reporter's work became subject to a wide range of normative controls that centered on creating more "rational" and "truthful" news.

More generally, Williams has not developed a viable sociological understanding of the conditions for "media truth." In the first place, autonomy from capital is only one of several major forms of differentiation that must be accomplished, as my discussions of the relations between media and religious groups, intellectuals, ethnic communities, and political parties indicate. Second, it is not the autonomy from capital per se that has been crucial historically but autonomy of one institutional source of capital from the capital of others. I have laid out the reasons for this above. In the text that follows, I suggest, indeed, that wide reliance on advertising actually helped American newspapers to become more democratic—e.g., more responsive to wide segments of the reading public, more flexible in its evaluations of ongoing events—than the privately controlled newspapers in France, where the possibilities for advertising were quite limited.

REFERENCES

Albert, P., and F. Terrou. 1970. *Histoire de la presse.* Paris: Universitaires de France.

Alexander, Jeffrey C. 1978. "Formal and Substantive Voluntarism in the Work of Talcott Parsons: A Theoretical and Ideological Reinterpretation," *American Sociological Review* (April), 43:177–98.

—— 1980. "Core Solidarity, Ethnic Outgroup, and Social Differentiation: A Multi-Dimensional Model of Inclusion in Modern Societies." In Jacques Dofny and Akinsola Akiwowo, eds., *National and Ethnic Movements.* Beverly Hills and London: Sage.

—— 1983a. "Max Weber, la théorie de la rationalisation et le marxisme." *Sociologie et Sociétés* 14(2):33–43.

—— 1983b. *The Modern Reconstruction of Classical Thought: Talcott Parsons.* Vol. 4 of Alexander, *Theoretical Logic in Sociology.* Berkeley and Los Angeles: University of California Press.

—— 1985. "Introduction." In Alexander, ed., *Neofunctionalism,* pp. 7–20. Beverly Hills and London: Sage.

Baestrup, Peter. 1978. *Big Story: How the American Press and Television Reported and Interpreted the Crisis of Tet 1968 in Vietnam and Washington.* New York: Doubleday.

Baldwin, Elizabeth. 1977. "The Mass Media and the Corporate Elite: A Re-

Analysis of the Overlap between the Media and Economic Elites." *Canadian Journal of Sociology* 2(1):1–27.

Bellah, Robert N. 1970. "The Systematic Study of Religion." In Bellah, *Beyond Belief,* pp. 260–80. New York: Harper and Row.

Bellanger, Claude, Jacques Godechot, Pierre Guiral, and Fernand Terrou. 1969–1976. *Histoire générale de les presses françaises.* 5 vols. Paris Presse, Universitaires de France.

Bellet, Roger. 1967. *Presse et journalisme sous le 2nd Empire.* Paris: Armand Colin.

Benjamin, Walter. 1973. *Charles Baudelaire: A Cynic Poet in the Era of High Capitalism.* London: New Left Review Books.

Bernstein, Carl and Bob Woodward. 1974. *All the President's Men.* New York: Warner Communications.

Boussel, Patrice. 1960. *L'Affaire Dreyfus et la presse.* Paris: Armand Colin.

Clement, Wallace. 1973. *The Canadian Corporate Elite.* Toronto: McClelland and Stewart.

Commager, Henry Steele. 1950. *The American Mind.* New Haven, Conn.: Yale University Press.

Conte, A. 1973. "La Presse soviètique et le premier débarquement américain sur la lune." In A.-J. Tudesq, ed., *La Presse et l'événement,* pp. 117–45. Paris: Mouton.

Dahlgren, Peter. 1978. "TV News and the Suppression of Reflexivity." Paper delivered at the Ninth World Congress of Sociology, Uppsala, Sweden (August).

Dahrendorf, Ralph. 1959. *Class and Class Conflict in Industrial Society.* Stanford, Calif.: Stanford University Press.

Deniel, Raymond. 1965. *Une Image de la famille et de la société sous la Reconstruction.* Paris: Les Editions Ouvrières.

Eisenstadt, S. N. 1969. *The Political System of Empires,* 2nd ed. New York: Free Press.

Evans, Harold. 1972. *Newsman's English.* New York: Holt, Rinehart and Winston.

Fass, Paula S. 1976. "Television as a Cultural Document: Promises and Problems." In *Television as a Cultural Force,* pp. 37–58. New York: Prager.

Frédérix, Pierre. 1959. *Un Siècle de chausse aux nouvelles—de l'Agence d'Information Havas à l'Agence France Presse, 1835–1957.* Paris: Flammarion.

Gans, Herbert. 1979. *Deciding What's News: A Study of CBS Evening News, NBC Nightly News, Newsweek, and Time.* New York: Pantheon.

Garfinkel, Harold. 1967. *Studies in Ethnomethodology.* Englewood Cliffs, N.J.: Prentice-Hall.

Geertz, Clifford. 1973. "Thick Description." In Geertz, *The Interpretation of Cultures,* pp. 3–32. New York: Basic Books.

Goffman, Erving. 1974. *Frame Analysis.* New York: Harper and Row.

Golding, Peter. 1974. *Mass Media.* London: Longman.

—— 1978. "The Missing Dimensions—News Media and the Management of Social Change." Paper delivered at the Ninth World Congress of Sociology, Uppsala, Sweden (August).

Hall, Stuart and Paddy Whannel. 1964. *The Popular Arts: A Critical Guide to the Mass Media.* Boston: Beacon.

Hallin, Daniel and Paolo Mancini. 1984. "Speaking of the President: Political Structure and Representational Form in U.S. and Italian Television News." *Theory and Society* (1984) 13:829–51.

Hamilton, Thomas. 1833. *Men and Manners in America.*

Hardin, Charles M. 1974. *Presidential Power and Accountability: Toward a New Constitution.* Chicago: University of Chicago Press.

Harris, William F. 1978. "Government Without Newspapers?" Paper delivered at the Ninth World Congress of Sociology, Uppsala, Sweden (August).

Hirsch, Paul M. 1978. "Institutional Functions of Elite and Mass Media." Paper delivered at the Ninth World Congress of Sociology, Uppsala, Sweden (August).

Hohenberg, John. 1978. *The Professional Journalist,* 4th ed. New York: Holt, Rinehart and Winston.

Holton, Gerald. 1973. *The Thematic Origins of Science: From Kepler to Einstein.* Cambridge, Mass.: Harvard University Press.

Huntington, Samuel P. 1968. *Political Order in Changing Societies.* New Haven, Conn.: Yale University Press.

Husserl, Edmund. 1977 (1931). *Cartesian Meditations.* The Hague: Martinus Nijhoff.

Kadushin, Charles. 1975. *The American Intellectual Elite.* Boston: Little Brown.

Katz, Elihu and Paul F. Lazarsfeld. 1955. *Personal Influence.* New York: Free Press.

Knightley, Phillip. 1978. *The First Casualty.* New York: Harcourt, Brace, Jovanovich.

Kuhn, Thomas. 1969. *The Structure of Scientific Revolutions.* Chicago: University of Chicago Press.

Lang, Kurt and Gladys Engel Lang. 1968. *Politics and Television.* Chicago: Quadrangle.

Manévy, Raymond. 1955. *La Presse de la IIIe Republique.* Paris: J. Foret.

McDougall, Curtis D. 1968. *Interpretive Reporting,* 5th ed. New York: Macmillan.

Mills, C. Wright. 1956. *The Power Elite.* London: Oxford University Press.

Missika, Jean-Louis. 1986. "Abstracts for Decision: The Parsimonious Elements of Public Choice in Public Controversy." *European Journal of Communication* 1:27–42.

—— 1987. "Selecting Political Controversies: Mass Media, Parties, and Public Opinion during the March 1986 Legislative Campaign in France," *European Journal of Communication,* vol. 2.

Mott, Frank Luther. 1941. *American Journalism.* New York: Macmillan.

Mueller, Claus. 1973. *The Politics of Communication*. New York: Oxford University Press.

Near East Report. 1978. Washington Letter on American Policy in the Near East (March 15), vol. 22, no. 11.

Neustadt, Richard E. 1960. *Presidential Power*. New York: Wiley.

Noelle-Neumann, Elisabeth. 1978. "Mass Media and Social Change in Developed Societies." Paper delivered at the Ninth World Congress of Sociology, Uppsala, Sweden (August).

Paletz, David, Peggy Reichert, and Barbara McIntire. 1971. "How the Media Support Local Governmental Authority." *Public Opinion Quarterly* (Spring).

Parsons, Talcott. 1951. *The Social System*. New York: Free Press.

—— 1961. "Introduction to Culture and the Social System." In Talcott Parsons, Kasper D. Naegele, Edward A. Shils, and Jess R. Pitts, eds., *Theories of Society*, pp. 967–93. New York: Free Press.

—— 1967. "On the Concept of Influence." In Parsons, *Sociological Theory and Modern Society*, pp. 355–82. New York: Free Press.

Parsons, Talcott and Winston White. 1969. "The Mass Media and the Structure of American Society." In Parsons, *Politics and Social Structure*, pp. 241–51. New York: Free Press.

Polanyi, Michael. 1958. *Personal Knowledge*. New York: Harper and Row.

Porter, William E. 1976. *Assault on the Media: The Nixon Years*. Ann Arbor: University of Michigan Press.

Roth, Guenther. 1963. *The Social Democrats in Imperial Germany*. New York: Bedminster Press.

Schudson, Michael. 1978. *Discovering the News*. New York: Basic Books.

Seguin, Jean-Paul. 1961. *L'Information en France, de Louis XII à Henri II*. Geneva: E. Droz.

—— 1964. *L'Information en France avant le périodique: 517 Canards imprimés entre 1529 et 1631*. Paris: G.-P. Maisonneuve et Larose.

Shaw, David. 1975. "Hoax: A Risk That Haunts Newspapers." *Los Angeles Times* (July 7).

Shils, Edward and Morris Janowitz. 1975 (1948). "Cohesion and Disintegration in the Wehrmacht in World War II." Reprinted in Shils, *Center and Periphery: Essays in Macrosociology*, pp. 345–83. Chicago: University of Chicago Press.

Simmonet, Philippe. 1977. *'Le Monde' et le pouvoir*. Paris: Less Presse d'Aujourd'hui.

Smelser, Neil J. 1970. "Stability, Instability, and the Analysis of Political Corruption." In Bernard Barber and Alex Inkeles, eds., *Stability and Change*, pp. 7–29. Boston: Little Brown.

Tocqueville, Alexis de. 1835. *Democracy in America*.

Tudesq, André-Jean, ed. 1973. *La Presse et L'événement*, pp. 117–36. Paris: Mouton.

Toulmin, Stephen. 1972. *Human Understanding*. Princeton: Princeton University Press.

Walzer, Michael. 1965. *Revolution of the Saints.* Cambridge, Mass.: Harvard University Press.

Woodward, Bob and Carl Bernstein. 1974. *All the President's Men.* New York: Simon and Schuster.

Woodward, Bob and Carl Bernstein. 1976. *The Final Days.* New York: Simon and Schuster.

FIVE

Three Models of Culture
and Society Relations:
Toward an Analysis of Watergate

The problem of the relationship between systems theory and social conflict remains unresolved. Within conflict theory, the problem has unfortunately been linked to the emphasis of systems theory on the relative autonomy of ideas, that is, to its emphasis on the value segment in social systems. In part, the systems theorists themselves are to blame for this false link between an emphasis on equilibrium and social values. Theorists like Parsons (1971) and Shils (1975) tended to illustrate the analytical differentiation of their systems theory by referring to societies like the United States, where there is both an empirical differentiation of institutions concerned with social values and relative consensus about the values themselves. Parsons (1969), moreover, often conflated the analytical issue of the relative autonomy of the cultural vis-à-vis the social system with the empirical question of whether there is value consensus in a particular social system.

On the one hand, Parsons employed the term *specification* in a very clear analytical way to argue that any social system configuration involved the application or the utilization of cultural patterns that were necessarily more general than any particular institutional form of concrete behavior. The way in which concrete behavior used general forms inevitably involved a process of "specification." Social system behavior, in other words, always involves some cultural reference. Yet Parsons also applied the notion of specification to the actual empirical instance of a historical

I thank Jeffrey Broadbent, Randall Collins, and the anonymous referees of *Sociological Theory* for their instructive readings of earlier drafts of this paper.

nation. He would portray the values of the political actors and social actors in the system as specifications of a common value system.

Although this may indeed have been the historical fact, the use of the same term, *specification,* to cover both analytical and empirical instances is an illegitimate conflation of a particular situation with the general analytical point.* For even if a society contained competing general value systems and no common overarching value system at all, it would nonetheless be correct in an analytical sense to say that each of the political or social subgroups in conflict with one another derived its own specific form of values by specifying the more general values of a cultural system. These more general values would, nonetheless, be antagonistic to other systems of values on the cultural level. Thus, in this kind of empirical case, analytical specification and empirical polarization and conflict are perfectly reconcilable. In this respect, conflict theory is wrong: systems theory can both allow the autonomy of values and illuminate the instability of social systems.

Once we have understood the fundamental dangers and fallacies of this conflationary strand in Parsonian work we can develop a more satisfactory approach to the analysis of values in empirical social systems.† I try to demonstrate in the remainder of this essay that the seminal theoretical advances of functionalist theory in analyzing the relationship between cultural and social systems can, in fact, help us to develop a theory of conflict in empirical historical systems.

Three Models of
Culture/Society Interrelation

I first introduce an ideal-typical schema for analyzing the relationship between values and social structure. Three models can describe the relationship between conflict and consensus in advanced societies—models

---

*"Conflation" is a concept I developed (Alexander 1982) to explain the common tendency to eliminate the relative autonomy of different levels of sociological theory. The discussion here takes off from a general criticism I made of Parsons (Alexander 1983: esp. chs. 6, 7) to the effect that he often cross-cut his differentiated understanding of order with a more reductionist and conflated one. In the conflationary dimension of his work, three relatively autonomous aspects of order are viewed as synonymous: presuppositional order (in the sense of nonrandomness), model order (in the sense of systematicity in functionalist terms), and empirical order (in the sense of cooperation and harmony). In *Culture and Agency,* Archer (forthcoming) makes extensive use of the conflation concept—which she developed independently of my own work—to defend the viability of a cultural sociology against its critics.

†Archer (1985) has made a remarkably similar argument in her recent reconsideration of the concept of cultural integration.

that refer to different relationships between the social and cultural systems. The first model assumes harmony and consistency on both the cultural and the social levels. Particular functions and groups in the social system do specify cultural patterns in concretely different ways, but these diverse value groupings are not in conflict with one another in any sense beyond the immediate one of a division of labor. I call this model "cultural specification."

The second model assumes that there are more fundamental conflicts on the social system level but still sees the cultural system as fairly integrated. In this model, conflicting social groupings and functions can and do develop antagonistic subcultures, not just complementary cultural "specifications," but because these subcultures still draw upon an integrated value system at the cultural level, there remains between these subcultures substantial if unacknowledged commonality. We might call this the model of "cultural refraction," following Evans-Pritchard's analyses of harmony and conflict among the Nuer (Evans-Pritchard 1953). Why refraction? Because we can say that in this situation different interests have been refracted through the same cultural lens.

Finally, the third model I introduce describes fundamental antagonism in both social and cultural systems. Thus, rather than simply subcultural conflicts, genuinely antagonistic cultures emerge in a society, interest groupings that have no significant common beliefs. One might call this "cultural columnization" because interest groupings occur in hermetically sealed cultural columns, vertical spaces between which there is no horizontal integration.*

*It can be argued, if only on logical grounds, that there is a fourth ideal type, one in which social system integration is maintained despite cultural conflict. This combination, indeed, seems to be implicit in much of the sociological literature on modern societies. Although formally acknowledging the cultural level, such an approach actually makes this level impotent, for it assumes that social life can proceed its merry way no matter what the condition of the cultural system. Among the classical theorists, Simmel's theorizing about conflict and the network of plural associations appears to support this view. Yet even Simmel makes residual reference to culturally integrative "forms" and "concepts"—for example, the "rules of the game," whose presence distinguishes competition from more brutal conflict. In contemporary discussions, the "politics of accommodation" evinced by Dutch society (Lijphart 1974) would seem to be another such case. I believe, however, that this fourth possibility is a logical illusion, sociologically unfounded. If social system processes bring people together in cooperative ways, they either draw on earlier cultural commonality or will soon produce some. The literature on the Dutch, for example, contains frequent references to Dutch nationalism, shared material values and a democratic ethos (Coleman 1978). Whether this process issues in refraction or columnization remains an empirical question. Even columnized societies can be stable if there is a temporary balance of forces, as Rex (1961) demonstrates in his theory of the "truce" situation.

In sociological literature the prototypical account of cultural specification is Parsons' and Platt's (1973) analysis in *The American University* of the relation of the cultural value of rationality to social systems. Parsons and Platt argue that rationality is a dominant theme in American society and that this value operates at a very general, cultural level. They suggest, further, that there are more specific, institutionalized versions of the rationality orientation in each of the four subsystems of society: economic rationality in the adaptive sector, political rationality in the polity, citizenship or solidary rationality in the integrative system, and value rationality in the pattern maintenance system.

Pluralist theorists, and theorists who emphasize the disintegrative aspects of modern life, such as those in the Frankfurt school, would portray these concrete institutionalizations of rationality as in fundamental conflict with one another, arguing, for example, that the economic rationality that emphasizes efficiency in the business world is antithetical to the cognitive rationality that inspires scientific truth in the world of the university. Parsons and Platt, by contrast, argue that although the systemic exigencies of such concrete institutions are certainly different, the cultural rationality that guides them is derived from a common "rationality" theme in the culture at large. They assume, moreover, that these social system level functions are not particularly antithetical—indeed, that they usually support one another through a process of complementary exchange. With neither functional nor cultural antipathies, then, the patterns of behavior motivated by economic rationality and political rationality are basically cooperative: there is no long-term basis for division or conflict. Such a model need not examine the detailed structure of subcultural traditions, for each more specific tradition is principally derived from the roots and structures of a single more generalized cultural theme. Not surprisingly, therefore, for Parsons and Platt, rationality itself is the object of analysis. When problems of disequilibrium are analyzed, as they are in some detail, the issue of intersystemic conflicts is given rather short shrift, for such an analysis would lead to an emphasis on cultural refraction. Disequilibrium is analyzed, rather, in terms of inadequacies in the generalized value pattern itself, in this case the overly instrumental aspects of contemporary Western rationality.

This analysis of *The American University* in terms of the specification model should not be taken as purely pejorative. To the contrary, it seems to me that in the case of American culture, instrumental rationality is, in fact, a widely shared value, one that different institutions often merely specify in different ways without substantially challenging or refracting. In part this occurs because American society is, in relative terms, functionally well integrated. This specification pattern also occurs because this particular value, rationality, is in fact widely shared in American life. Despite this empirical plausibility, however, one wonders whether Parsons and Platt may not have underemphasized the possibility that economic and political rationality may represent competing subcultures, or, similarly, have underplayed the conflict between ethical rationality and instrumental political expediency that Weber so profoundly articulated as the tension between the ethic of responsibility and the ethics of expediency and faith.*

The difficulties of such a pure specification perspective are apparent when it is more directly applied to political mobilization and group conflict. The functionalist tradition has emphasized the significance of the cultural generalization that occurs in periods of intense political and social conflict, when the anxiety produced by disequilibrium pushes significant elements of the population to focus on the most fundamental and simplified value concerns—on the general cultural themes from which the society's specific institutionalized patterns have been derived. This analytical theory of generalization is a fundamentally important contribution, but insofar as it has been applied empirically only in the context of an insistence on cultural specification, it has been treated in a flawed and partial way. The flaw is apparent in the ease with which such generalization is assumed to proceed, and, hence, the ease with which particular social crises are seen to be resolved. In Parsons' and Smelser's (1956) account of the Progressive period in the United States at the end of the nineteenth century, for example, movements to reform the business structure are presented without sufficient attention to the fundamental social and cultural polarizations of the day. In Smelser's own first book

*Schluchter (1979), for example, writes about these as the "paradoxes" of the social rationalization produced by differentiation, rather than as specifications. His Weberianization of Parsons' theory adds another dimension to it. Still, the notion of paradox should not, in my view, entirely replace the notion of empirical specification; this would make it impossible to understand one of the most powerful forms of social integration in a differentiated society—viz. my earlier comments on functionalist versus neo-Marxian views of "rationality." Specification must be retained as an analytical concept, moreover, even while its empirical application is delimited. In an analytical sense, even value paradoxes are specifications.

(1959), the problem is much the same. The issue is not whether, as Smelser rightly insists, an activist Protestant culture is widely shared, but whether the competing economic groups in the early industrial period developed sharply divergent subcultures to express this common value. If such subcultural development took place, and I believe it did, then the process of cultural generalization that Smelser describes could have occurred only under conditions that would have allowed the end of subcultural conflict: either some kind of genuine reintegration—produced, for example, by the decline of group conflict or by ritual renewal—or the dominance of one subcultural position over another. In the particular English case, I suspect, there were elements of both.

At the opposite end of the continuum from such cultural specification is what I have called cultural columnization. The situation portrayed here could not be more different, for not only is a much more fundamental conflict on the social system level portrayed, but also this conflict is seen as building upon fundamentally divergent themes in the general national culture. Such columnization brings to mind, of course, societies that have been subject to revolutionary upheaval from either the left or the right; indeed, my theory of columnization is, in part, an attempt to help illuminate such process. In his *Ancien Regime* Tocqueville portrayed France as radically divided on the cultural level between a new tradition of critical rationality, carried by the bourgeoisie and intellectuals, and a culture of tradition, deference, and hierarchy carried by the Church and the aristocracy. These cultural groupings were presented as radically heterodox, as emerging from antagonistic cultural developments like feudalism and the Enlightenment. They were, moreover, viewed as cultures that were specified by fundamentally conflicting institutional interests—estates whose economic and political positions were in fundamental functional antagonism. In this situation of columnization, it is clear, no common ground could be found. Raymond Aron's (1960) theory that modern functional elites are segmental and fragmented can be seen as the contemporary French analogue to that earlier columnization theory. That Aron completely ignores the cultures of his elites merely demonstrates that his theory is drawn from a sample of groups that are so columnized that their beliefs play no integrative role.*

*For a good contrast between columnization and specification theory, one might compare Aron's analysis with the cultural emphasis of Suzanne Keller's (1963) theory of functional elites, which argues that they carry out complementary functions of the same general culture.

The extreme polarization of columnization tends to occur in societies where traditional and modernizing cultures are carried by vigorous and contentious social groups. In Italy, for example, Bellah (1980) has found five "civil religions," suggesting that the Italian cultural system contains sharply divergent traditions that extend all the way from a form of primitive naturalism to an ultrarationalistic Marxism. The case of pre-World War II Germany has been more extensively documented. Roth (1963) has written about the "negative integration" of the German working class. It seems indisputable that in Germany sharply antagonistic class groupings became organized around traditions that were experienced as radically antagonistic. The small radical intelligentsia and the large socialist working class adhered to rationalistic and modernizing Marxism, while the middle classes, state-supported academics, and aristocracy followed a strong antimodern traditionalism fundamentally influenced by Lutheranism. Nolte (1966) has described the conservative side of this polarization as culturally "anti-transcendent," a description that effectively portrays its radical antipathy to the Enlightenment tradition.

It is no wonder that in such columnized situations the unifying "generalization" that is so necessary for the cultural and social reintegration of a crisis situation can rarely occur. It is not simply that functional interests diverge but also that the anxiety that leads to value ritualization and to the urge for renewal occurs within the "column" of divergent cultural groupings rather than within some more general and widely shared cultural belief. Cultural celebrations in 1848 revolutionary France did occur, but they engaged a cultural heritage fundamentally at odds with the commitments of a significant, if not at that time dominant, segment of the French nation. Four years later, the ascension of Louis Bonaparte allowed generalization to occur in another cultural "column," that of tradition or at least of modernity very traditionally defined. The "two cultures" in a columnized society, then, provide ritual experiences that serve merely to reinforce the different faiths and interest of already polarized groups.*

*By the time of his second book, Smelser (1963) had already realized this important fact, for he acknowledges that a significant element of revolutionary movements is their production of widely divergent value patterns. Although Smelser ascribes this value divergence primarily to structural rigidity, it should, I believe, be linked to cultural, as well as "structural," arrangements. Traugott (1985), for example, has shown that symbolism, ritual, and generalized responses to political crisis were, in a brief five-month period, crucial to the formation of the opposing armies in the June 1848 civil war in France. These cultural processes, in other words, played an independent role in columnizing France.

For the middle case of cultural refraction, divergent social tasks and interests are portrayed as drawing upon fundamentally similar cultural themes. It should not be surprising that the United States has been considered a prime example within which such refraction occurs. The famous dichotomy in American culture between "equality of opportunity," a theme that emphasizes equality in an individualistic way, and "equality of results," a theme that combines equality with more collectivist concerns, exemplifies the phenomenon of refraction. In this case the common cultural commitment to equality is accepted, while conservative and liberal groupings are described—for example, in the work of Lipset (1965)— as refracting this commitment through the more individualistic or collectivist interests of different economic and political groups. The implication is that sharp conflicts do in fact occur in American society but that even such polarized groupings as conservative businesspersons and liberal trade unionists share a commitment to the value of equality, a shared commitment that allows for some ultimate consensus and cooperation. Hartz (1955) applied something like this refraction analysis to the value of individualism rather than equality. Arguing that the bedrock of all American ideology is the commitment to a Lockean version of liberty and rights, he suggests that conflict groups in the United States offer what really are simply interest-bound refractions of individualism rather than radically antagonistic ideologies.* Similar arguments have, of course, been made for the conflict groupings of countries other than the United States. Pitts (1964), for example, has suggested that the much more radical conflicts in French society can be traced back to internally contradictory themes within Catholicism.

It should be clear that when cultural refraction is the model employed for an empirical case, the opportunity for reintegration of cultural and social conflicts is presented in a more complex and open-ended way than in the case of the two other ideal types. Because sharp subcultural conflicts exist, generalization to a shared common culture is by no means automatic; powerful general themes underpin the subcultures, and these subcultural themes may become the object of polarizing ritual and generalization. Reintegration certainly is a possibility, however, for with refraction, in contrast to columnization, strong common themes do exist.

---

*For an acute discussion of American conservative ideology as a variation on individualism, see Nakano (1981).

Whether generalization will actually lead to convergence upon these shared general cultural themes is a matter for particular analysis of specific empirical circumstances. While close attention must be paid to divergent interests and to subcultural values, common commitments cannot be ignored.

Figure 5.1 is a schematic presentation of how the three models conceptualize successive periods of normal political conflict, early political crisis, and either social breakdown or reintegration.

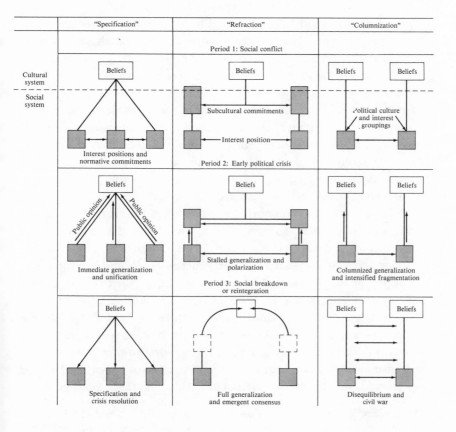

Figure 5.1. The Three Models in Social Process

Watergate: A Case Study
in Refraction and Reintegration

Although every advanced industrial society experiences elements of specification, refraction, and columnization, the structural and cultural characteristics of each national society incline it in one direction or another. For the United States, with the possible exception of racial conflicts today and the definite exception of sectional conflicts before 1865, the refraction model seems most appropriate. American conflicts have been serious, but they have rarely produced ideologies that have seriously violated the consensual framework composed by America's principal cultural themes.

The Watergate crisis must be placed into the context of social conflict in America in the 1960s.* If we want to understand the situation in America in that time, we must recognize both the intensity of social system conflict and the areas of common perception. That is, what we have to recognize is the refracted nature of conflict in that era.

In its broad outlines, the decade of the 1960s was a period of intense, modernizing social change. It was a period of rationalization and differentiation in every institutional sphere, in politics and education, family, law, religion, civic solidarity, and economic life. The reforms introduced in these spheres revolved around issues that might be called late modernization. They demanded and involved more equality, more participation, the expansion of the notion of the individual, and the rationalization and secularization of values. In sum, they revolved around a radical universalism that created and unleashed pervasive criticism of all traditions and authority and that demanded continual change of self and institutions.

The groups that initiated these changes might be called vanguard modernists—middle-class, highly educated reformers, both whites and racial minorities, government planners, intellectuals and students, liberal church men and women, and selected professionals, for example, activist lawyers and teachers. These groups sometimes draped themselves in antimodernist garb, harking back to the "lost" communal world, to the need for renewed and broadened affectivity. Although these traditionalistic

---

*The following very schematic discussion draws from a research project I have been conducting on Watergate for the last several years. A more thorough but still very partial analysis of the crisis can be found—in a slightly different theoretical cast—in Alexander forthcoming. Rather than present a full empirical study, my purpose in the following is merely to illustrate, through references to this empirical case, some of the possibilities of the theoretical model I have presented.

strands were not irrelevant, I think that, considered as a whole, the sub-cultural orientation of these groups presented a radicalized left-wing version of mainstream American political culture, critical universalism with an unusually activist twist.

Against this culture of critical rationality there emerged a reaction that was more of a departure from the dominant American civic tradition, although in no sense was it a complete repudiation. This "backlash" promoted the drastic reduction of universalism and transformative values. It promoted particularistic evaluations like loyalty to family, race, ethnicity, and nation and loyalty to the authorities that represented and ruled each of these diffuse collectivities. It was anti-intellectual and often explicitly and fundamentally, or rather fundamentalistically, religious. This reactive backlash movement promoted deference and obedience; it was called the "silent majority" to contrast its manners with those of the group that emphasized critique and dissent. It emphasized stability and order, not change.

Yet this broad outline of social division conceals common cross-cutting ties that remained salient sociologically even if they were not experientially salient to citizens of the day. The social changes that seemed so spectacular in the 1960s actually can be traced back to changes inititated in the late 1950s, in the later years of the Eisenhower administration. The establishment of the U.S. Civil Rights Commission, vigorous educational expansion and upgrading, religious ecumenicism, economic expansion and rationalization—all these initiatives commanded an extremely wide consensus. This social cohesion continued in the early 1960s, during which time the radical left and right continued to be marginal groups. In the course of the 1960s, this consensus broke down only gradually and in complicated ways.

The intensification of change in the 1960s created increasing polarization into right and left. The first phases of this division proceeded in a fairly straightforward, Hegelian way, with reformers grouped under critical universalism and reactors devoted to more conservative, backlash particularism. Liberals moved leftward, renewing their emphasis on equality and remaining united in their support of political, integrative, educational, and religious change. Conservatives united around the backlash libertarianism of the Goldwater campaign. Modernizing groups championed equality and tied their critical position to universalism; conservative groups championed liberty and tied their defensive position to particularism. Both groups, all the same, embraced at a more general level certain common notions. Opinion polls of the 1960s show that support for inclusion and economic democracy increased in every segment of society. For the emerging left, indeed, equality did not seem to deny liberty; in fact, the left often championed equality in the name of greater individual freedom. For the right, liberty was often seen merely as emphasizing a particular kind of equality, the equal rights of individuals to buy and sell and to be protected from government intrusion. The tension these commitments produced within both backlash and frontlash moralities are clear in retrospect, but at that time they had not yet surfaced.

This invisible yet real common ground became explicit and played a less passive role in the later phases of 1960s polarization. During the period from 1966 to 1969, various forms of left-wing particularism emerged within the modernizing movement, producing uncomfortable combinations of modernity and primordialism within the critical movement itself. Racial separatism and color-consciousness were promoted in the name of universal inclusion; the revolutionary culture of violence and confrontation encouraged Leninist versions of authoritarianism in the service of critical rationality; the diffuse affectivity of the counterculture tended to counteract the demand for impersonal, universalistic standards upon which other strands of the modernizing movement were based.

None of these developments, however, completely undermined the critical activism, inclusiveness, and universalism upon which so much of the earlier liberal-left movement had depended. The black power movement still demanded equal rights; the militant student left mobilized movements in the cause of critique; the hippies envisioned universal brotherhood and championed the pure autonomy of the individual.

Still, the lines of polarization had become significantly blurred. In the same period of 1966–69, partly in response to this further leftward movement in the party of reform and partly in further reponse to the structural changes that had actually initiated it, a distinctly more moderate segment of the liberal movement emerged. This more conservative group of *Commentary* liberals and centrist politicians like Daniel Moynihan vacillated between upholding the liberalism of the earlier phase and moving toward an accommodation with backlash values.

This splitting of the left was mirrored—indeed was directly connected to—equally significant changes in the right. In the wake of Goldwater's defeat and increased activism on the left, the conservative movement fissured into more and less radical forms of backlash antimodernism. In the later 1960s, an explicitly reactionary strand emerged under the banner of nationalism and a passifying civility (Walzer 1980) calling for social order even at the cost of abandoning constitutional rights. Other rightists feared not only modernism but also the loss of liberty . This latter group sought to maintain its connection to the "center," forcing its backlash views into the mainstream. This moderation allowed it to make growing alliances with the rightward-moving segment of liberal reformers, and the neoconservative movement was born.

This refracted character of the 1960s polarization is crucial for understanding the orientations out of which Watergate arose and the resources that eventually allowed it to be resolved. On the one hand, there was the fact of intensely polarized social groupings, the antagonism between particularistic backlash and vanguard modernist frontlash. Little conscious sense of commonality existed in the America of that day, and this climate of confrontation produced exclusionary and conspiratorial politics. Demands for total political control were encouraged, with each side making efforts to silence the opposition. As sectarian politics became the order of the day, the common normative rules of the game often seemed threatened and about to give way. On the other hand, this polarization camouflaged a widespread American commitment to "modernist" culture, to forms of universalistic activism that were accepted regardless of the particular political stands of any conflict group.

To see the relationship between this political-cultural refraction and Watergate, we have to turn to Richard Nixon and the presidency. Nixon brought both strands of the backlash movement to power. He had always conceived of himself as a victim of social change and a champion of grass roots movements against it. At the same time, he felt himself to be a forward-looking leader—cosmopolitan, educated, enlightened—who could be trusted to control the lunatic fringe of the right wing, as well as the left. Only this ambiguity in Nixon's position can explain the appeal of his promise, in 1968, to build a "new American majority." His administration coopted and even sponsored certain issues of the left, such as environmentalism, women's rights, and even (as in its minimum income proposal) economic equality; it brought home American troops from Vietnam; while calling for quiet in the streets, it claimed a renewed dedication to traditional forms of American activism like educational and civic reform. This was the Nixon who gained support from the growing neoconservative movement and who put Moynihan into his cabinet.

It is true, nonetheless, that Nixon was also elected in 1968 as the factional leader of the backlash culture. He appealed to patriotism over dissent, tradition over modernity; he invoked paternalistic authority and attempted to weld it against the forces of change, in the name of the nation, in the name of the family, and in the name of "the people." Drawing on the authoritarian resources of the American presidency, Nixon sought to push his "new American majority" in a backlash direction. He emphasized the pomp and circumstance of the office. He remained remote, inaccessible and mysterious. He used the extraordinary instrumental powers of executive secrecy and the powers of coercive control at his command.

Nixon wanted to set in motion a sweeping movement of "counter-change" against the agencies, leaders, and ideas of vanguard liberalism. Spiro Agnew, his Vice President, took the role of spear carrier, rallying "the folks" against "the elites." Together, Nixon and Agnew initiated a politics more sectarian than the presidency had ever seen. Indeed, they connected the powerful and factious behavior of the backlash movement to the personalistic, quasi-patrimonial form of presidential authority itself. The result was a presidency that often showed little regard for the abstract and generalized rules of the game, which, according to a consensual model, govern conflict in modern political systems. It is not surprising that this combination of power and will led to a series of illegal and potentially dangerous abuses of power.

The moderate and extreme dimensions of the Nixon presidency were by no means sharply demarcated. This was precisely its great danger. While the combination sometimes allowed right-wing, anticivil elements to be pushed toward cooperation and reform, the support of more traditional and centrist conservatism often legitimated the most anticivil trends.

With their assumption of office in 1969, Nixon and his staff began to exert control over cosmopolitan and dissident enemies. They justified their actions—some of which were public and visible, others private and concealed—on the grounds that they were dealing with enemies outside the boundaries of civil society. These actions ranged from illegal arrests and extensive bugging of subversives, to spying and provocation, to the infiltration even of their own eastern-educated staffs, and, finally, to extensive institutional maneuvers to restrain liberal institutions and their elites—for example, the news media. It is important to understand that such illegal tactics received at least passive consent from the silent majority they helped to shape. There existed a general moral code to justify these actions; they could be justified in terms of the reactionary subculture. The refraction of political morality made liberals and radicals into an "other" with whom, Nixon's supporters believed, they had little in common.

The break-in at the Democratic headquarters in the Watergate Hotel in the summer of 1972 was simply one part of this overall activity. George McGovern was the symbol of aggressive modernization and radical change, not only for Nixon but also for the silent majority itself, and it was McGovern and his potential supporters who were the object of the Watergate break-in. In this way, the refracted atmosphere of the time legitimated the break-in. Because of this legitimation, Watergate received relatively little attention and generated no widespread sense of outrage at the time. There were no cries of outraged justice. There was the acceptance of Nixon's rationalizations, respect for his authority, and the belief that his version of the facts was correct despite strong evidence to the contrary. With important exceptions, the media did not even pick up the story, not because they were coercively prevented from doing so, but because they subjectively felt it to be unimportant. Even after a long, hot election, 80 percent of the American people found Watergate hard to believe; 75 percent felt it was just plain politics; 84 percent said that what they had heard had not influenced them.

Two years later, it was generally agreed, this same incident, still called "Watergate," had initiated the most serious institutional crisis in American history. It had become a riveting moral symbol that was responsible for the resignation of a president for the first time in American history.

To understand how this crucial shift in public perception occurred, we must return to the phenomenon of "generalization" I introduced earlier in this essay. There are different levels of generality at which every social fact can be told. These levels are linked to different social resources. If public attention remains specific, it focuses on the goals of public actors. Insofar as generalization occurs, norms and ultimate values come into play. Only with such generalization, of course, can a societal sense of crisis emerge. Routine politics means that interests do not seem to violate more general values and norms. Nonroutine, or crisis, politics occurs when tension is experienced between these levels, either because of a shift in the nature of political activity or a shift in the general commitments held to regulate them.

In the period surrounding the Nixon-McGovern contest, Watergate was perceived in terms of goals, as "just politics" by 75 percent of Americans. Generalization did not occur, because no conflict seemed to exist between these specific activities and norms or values. Why not? Because each side in the initial Watergate dispute could legitimately frame its responses within the confines of their respective subcultures. The silent majority felt that the break-in was justified by the times. Since by their "anti-American" activities McGovern and the other left Democrats had abrogated the protection of civil rights, secret actions to curtail their activities could hardly be illegal, let alone immoral. Indeed, to limit their activity was one of the political mandates for which Nixon was in the process of being reelected. For the left, in turn, the break-in merely confirmed their own views about the purely political character of Nixon and the right. It was another in a long series of political activities that demonstrated, to their mind, that legal—let alone moral—regulation of American political conduct failed to exist. For both of the most active political groupings of the time, therefore, the early events surrounding the Watergate crisis remained "simply political" because they were compared only with the more polarized, refracted expectations of subcultures, not with the broader universalism and constitutionalism of the common culture itself. The latter, temporarily eclipsed by refraction, would have forced Watergate to be viewed in a much more alarmed, and alarming, way.

Two years after the break-in, public opinion had sharply changed. From purely political goals Watergate was, indeed, now regarded as an issue that violated fundamental American customs and morals. By the end, almost half of those who had voted for Nixon had changed their minds. Two thirds of all voters thought the issues had now gone far beyond politics. What had occurred was a radical generalization of opinion. It was not so much the facts that were different but the context in which they had come to be viewed. That American political culture was refracted rather than columnized had allowed the two years of national crisis to produce reintegration and renewal rather than fragmentation and further polarization.

There were, of course, critical factors other than the cultural one that were involved in the creation and resolution of this nationwide crisis. There had to be the mobilization and struggle by elites and other organized social groups, struggles often perceived, by the enemies of these groups and often by the groups themselves, as self-interested in the instrumental sense. There also had to be the continual intervention of social control forces, which often threatened coercion and sometimes carried it out.

But if such "structural" factors were going to be successful in triggering and helping to resolve a full-scale national crisis—rather than simply in creating a political vendetta—much more general cultural forces had to be involved. In the first place, some significant degree of evaluative consensus had to emerge in the American public. If not all-encompassing, this consensus still had to be powerful enough to label a broad swath of "Watergate" as deviant. Only if this labeling stuck could the event disturb more than a mere fragment of the population and "society" itself be aroused. Once the crisis was underway, moreover, broader cultural agreement was necessary if ritual processes were to emerge that could resolve it. Only on common cultural ground could polluting rituals frighten citizens into dramatic action and purifying rituals provide symbolic resources for them to carry out such action.

Of course, while refraction has more integrative capabilities than columnization, it is much more fragmenting and conflictual than specification. In the early months of the Watergate period, between the break-in and the election, the consensus necessary for common perception could not occur. This continued to be a time of intense polarization politically, though the social conflicts of the 1960s had actually begun to cool. McGovern's presence allowed Nixon to promote backlash politics, which was the key to keeping his moderate reactionary coalition together. The refracted political culture meant, therefore, that societal generalization could not take place. There could be no movement upward toward shared general values, and because there was no generalization, there could be no societal sense of crisis.

Yet in the six months following the election, the situation began to be reversed. The end of an intensely divided election period allowed the subtle left/right realignment, which I described as beginning in the late 1960s, to continue. Once McGovern left the scene, the more centrist elements in Nixon's coalition were not nearly so eager to align themselves with the tactics of the extreme right. This development fed into another, equally important phenomenon that had, in fact, barely begun to impinge on the consciousness of the political actors of the time. For some time before the break-in, the social struggles of the 1960s had been petering out. By 1972, left-wing groups had virtually disappeared from public view. Because more fundamental processes of social change had decelerated as well, purely reactive movements now had less of an immediate base. For all these reasons, in the post-1972 period, critical universalism could be readopted by more centrist forces without its being linked to the specific ideological themes or goals of the left. With this emerging consensus, the refraction of common politics into abrasive, distinctive subcultures began to dissipate. The possibility for common feelings of normative violation emerged, and with it began the movement toward generalization vis-à-vis Watergate events. This development provided a more congenial atmosphere for the struggle of interested elites and the operation of social controls, which in turn legitimated the growing public feeling that Watergate was, in fact, a serious crime.

The most important ritual event of the Watergate crisis—the Senate Select Committee's televised hearings in May 1973—forcefully demonstrated how important it is for a social system in crisis to have access to a common general culture. This event had tremendous repercussions on the symbolic patterning of the entire affair. It responded to the anxiety that had been building within large segments of the population and functioned to canalize this anxiety in a consensual and democratic way. The hearings constituted a civic ritual that revivified very general but nonetheless very crucial currents of critical universalism in the American political culture.

The senators who were the "stars" of the Watergate hearings managed to isolate and condemn the subculture of backlash values that had motivated and initially legitimated it. On the one hand, they bracketed the refracted subcultures of both left and right. On the other hand, they engaged in a ringing, unabashed affirmation of the common ideals through which both political movements had been initially refracted, invoking the universalistic myth that is the backbone of the American civic religion. Through their questions, statements, references, gestures, and metaphors, the senators maintained that every American—high or low, young or old, conservative or radical—acts virtuously in terms of the pure equality and individualism of the civic Republican tradition. Individualism never degenerates into selfishness, equality never leads to inhumanity. No

American is concerned with money or power at the expense of fair play. Team loyalty is never so strong that it vitiates the common good or neutralizes the commitment to liberty that sustains the critical attitude toward authority so essential to a democratic society.

The senators' questioning of administration witnesses focused on three principal themes, each fundamental to the moral anchoring of a civic democratic society. First, they emphasized the absolute priority of office obligations over personal ones. The frequently invoked claim, "This is a nation of laws, not men," emerged as a virtual slogan for the hearings. Second, the senators emphasized the embeddedness of such office obligations in a higher transcendent authority; as committee chairman Sam Ervin insisted, "the laws of men" must give way to the "laws of God." To quote from Ervin's famous colloquy with the treasurer of Nixon's reelection committee, Maurice Stans, "which is more important, Mr. Stans, not violating laws or not violating ethics?" Finally the senators insisted that the common culture underlying political conflict was an uncontested social fact. They claimed, indeed, that in America there was a transcendental anchoring of interest conflict that allowed the modern society to be a true *Gemeinschaft,* what Hegel called a concrete universal. As Senator Lowell Weicker, the liberal Republican from Connecticut, proclaimed: "Republicans do not cover up, Republicans do not go ahead and threaten . . . and God knows Republicans don't view their fellow Americans as enemies to be harassed [but as] human being[s] to be loved and won."

The hearings ended without laws or specific judgments of evidence, but they had, nevertheless, profound effects. They established the moral framework that would henceforth give Watergate its meaning. They accomplished this by organizing the actual political events and figures of the Watergate episode in terms of the higher antitheses between the sacred and profane elements of the more general American civic religion. The hearings re-sacralized the liberties of the Constitution, unwritten mores of fair and egalitarian treatment, and sentiments of social solidarity. They profaned authoritarianism, self-interest, particularism, and with these polluted elements they aligned Richard Nixon, his staff, and backlash values in general. The presidential party and the elements of civic sacredness became antithetical to one another. Over time, the American public found it impossible to bring them back together.

That "Watergate" did not prevent conservatism from continuing—after

Carter's four years of ambiguous respite—its relentless assault on liberal reform misses the most important implication of that fateful crisis. No society can avoid oscillations between reforms and reaction, change and stasis, left and right. The decisive sociological question is not whether this occurs but how. Will the polarization produced by social change be so severely divisive that intense social conflict is transformed into anti-democratic civil war? This has, indeed, been the fate of most modern and modernizing nations. Why it has not yet been so for the United States is a cause for study. One place to begin, I have suggested, is Watergate.

That the first elected conservative president to succeed Nixon, Ronald Reagan, sometimes felt drawn to anticivil extremism should not be denied. Yet neither can it be denied that very strong barriers were set against such inclinations. Such limits reside not only in social "structures" but also in the minds of men and women. They represent common values that in the midst of social crises are reproduced, extended, and internalized in turn. That Reaganism was democratically controlled as compared with unbridled conservatism is, at least in part, thanks to how the Watergate crisis turned out.*

This essay began with a rather esoteric theoretical problem and concluded with a detailed case study of a gaudy and famous political scandal. My point has been, first, that social system conflict cannot be analyzed without reference to deeply felt social values, and, second, that the relation between such values and social integration can by no means be easily understood. I have offered three ideal-typical models of this relation, each of which presents different possibilities for reintegration in social crisis. I have indicated, with this concluding analysis of Watergate, not only some of the empirical details that such models imply but also the more specific social processes upon which the institutionalization of what I have called specification, refraction, and columnization depend.

REFERENCES

Alexander, Jeffrey C. 1982. *Positivism, Presuppositions, and Current Controversies,* vol. 1 of *Theoretical Logic in Sociology.* Berkeley and Los Angeles: University of California Press, 1983.

*The Iran-Contra affair, which has emerged since the completion of this essay, demonstrates both of these points—the Reagan administration's continuing attraction to anti-civil extremism and the strong barriers that American society continues to erect against it. Without the "memory of justice" provided by Watergate, it is doubtful that the administration's actions would have so easily and quickly been transformed into an "affair."

—— 1983. *The Modern Reconstruction of Classical Thought: Talcott Parsons*, vol. 4 of *Theoretical Logic in Sociology*.

—— forthcoming. "Culture and Political Crisis: 'Watergate' and Durkheimian Sociology." In *Durkheimian Sociology*. New York: Cambridge University Press.

Archer, Margaret. 1985. "The Myth of Cultural Integration." *British Journal of Sociology* 36:333–53.

—— forthcoming *Culture and Agency*. London: Cambridge University Press.

Aron, Raymond. 1960. "Social Class, Political Class, Ruling Class." *European Journal of Sociology* 1:260–81.

Bellah, Robert N. 1980. "The Five Religions of Italy." In Bellah and Phillip E. Hammond, *Varieties of Civil Religion*, pp. 86–118. New York: Harper and Row.

Coleman, John A. 1978. *The Evolution of Dutch Catholicism 1958–1974*. Berkeley and Los Angeles: University of California Press.

Evans-Pritchard, E. E. 1953. "The Nuer Concept of the Spirit in Its Relation to the Social Order." *American Anthropologist* 55:201–41.

Hartz, Louis. 1955. *The Liberal Tradition in America*. New York: Harcourt Brace.

Keller, Suzanne. 1963. *Beyond the Ruling Class*. New York: Random House.

Lijphart, Arend. 1974. *The Politics of Accommodation*. Berkeley and Los Angeles: University of California Press.

Lipset, Seymour Martin. 1956. *The First New Nation*. New York: Doubleday.

Nakano, Hideichiro. 1981. "Conservatism as a Political Ideology in Contemporary America." *Kwansei Gakuin University Annual Bulletin* 30:95–108.

Nolte, Ernst. 1966. *The Three Faces of Fascism*. New York: Holt, Rinehart.

Parsons, Talcott. 1969. "On the Concept of Value-Commitments." In Parsons, *Politics and Social Structure*. New York: Free Press.

—— 1971. *The System of Modern Societies*. Englewood Cliffs, N.J.: Prentice-Hall.

Parsons, Talcott and Neil J. Smelser. 1956. *Economy and Society*. New York: Free Press.

Parsons, Talcott and G. M. Platt. 1973. *The American University*. Cambridge, Mass.: Harvard University Press.

Pitts, Jesse. 1964. "Continuity and Change in Bourgeois France." In Stanley Hoffman, ed., *In Search of France*. Cambridge, Mass.: Harvard University Press.

Rex, John. 1961. *Key Problems in Sociological Theory*. London: Routledge and Kegan Paul.

Roth, Guenther. 1963. *The Social Democrats in Imperial Germany*. New York: Bedminster Press.

Schluchter, Wolfgang. 1979. "The Paradoxes of Rationalization." In Schuchter and Guenther Roth. *Max Weber's Vision of History*. Berkeley and Los Angeles: University of California Press.

Shils, Edward. 1975. "Charisma, Order, and Status." In Shils, *Center and Pe-*

riphery: Essays in Macrosociology, pp. 256–75. Chicago: University of Chicago Press.

Smelser, Neil J. 1959. *Social Change in the Industrial Revolution.* Chicago: University of Chicago Press.

Smelser, Neil J. 1963. *Collective Behavior.* New York: Free Press.

Traugott, Mark. 1985. *Armies of the Poor.* Princeton, N.J.: Princeton University Press.

Walzer, Michael. 1980. "Civility and Civic Virtue in Contemporary America." In Walzer, *Radical Principles,* pp. 54–72. New York: Basic Books.

SIX

The University and Morality

The problem of the "university and morality" has been a recurrent one in the Western world ever since the university stopped being an institution of clerical dispensation. It will continue to be one as long as universities do not become ideological handmaidens of the state. The problem is created by the process of social differentiation itself. Once the university becomes specialized in its cultural aims, once it loses the legitimation of church and state, the question inevitably arises: what should the morality of the university be?

The search for an answer to this question is unending. It is only asked, indeed, insofar as the university has given up claims to justification by a clear-cut particular moral creed, that is, when a reassuring, once-and-for-all answer to the question cannot, in fact, be made. There are certain historical periods, however, when at least a provisional answer must be given. In these times, the question, "what is the morality of the university?" becomes more urgently asked, and the responses are stridently forthcoming. The 1960s was the last such period when the question was raised, mainly by the New Left. We have now entered another period in which the question is being raised, this time particularly by opponents of South African apartheid. In this essay I develop an initial answer to the question of university and morality. It provides a revised framework for thinking about contemporary issues and also indicates a way of thinking about the long-term processes involved.

This essay was initially prepared as a contribution to mark the fiftieth anniversary of the California State University at Northridge (CSUN). I thank Reba Soffer and the other members of the CSUN faculty and administration for their comments. I also acknowledge the helpful criticisms of an anonymous reviewer for the *Journal of Higher Education*.

In the argument about the university and morality two main positions have been advanced. Proponents of the first position argue that because the university is scientifically specialized, it is not a moral institution, for the only way to be moral is to be committed to a clear-cut, particular moral creed. To be morally committed in this way leads to direct involvement in political conflicts. The logical conclusion of this argument is that, if the university is to become moral, it must align itself directly with a particular creed and a political cause. Historically, this argument has been made by conservatives and radicals. I will call it the "critical position."

Those who have advanced the second position agree that the university is not "moral" in the sense of being committed to any particular moral creed. They argue, however, that because technical specialization is socially productive in many different ways, it is morally justifiable. The logical conclusion of this argument is that the university must be disengaged from moral creeds and political commitments. Historically, this argument has been made by liberals. I will call it the "established position." Max Weber (1973) advanced a strong case for it in the turn-of-the-century period, and Talcott Parsons (Parsons and Platt 1973) elaborated this position in the postwar climate. Derek Bok (1982) has formulated the established position in the context of the renewal of controversy in the present day.

This conflict between critical and established positions raises the following questions. Does the university have an obligation to take explicit ethical or political positions vis-à-vis the society at large? If the university chooses to remain disengaged, is its position in society a moral one? How might a morality of disengagement be justified? Are there limits or conditions to a disengagement position? Although these questions raise issues of justice and political obligation, they cannot be answered in a purely abstract way. To achieve what Rawls (1971) has called "reflective equilibrium," every theory of justice must be tempered by an empirical assessment of actual possibilities and by a sensibility that respects the commitments particular to each social sphere (see Walzer 1983).

To answer these questions in a responsible manner we must begin with the internal structure and values of the university. Everything that is said about the university and society comes back to questions about the university itself, about the desirability of maintaining the integrity of its internal processes, and about whether in doing so special obligations to society are entailed.

I begin by affirming the contention of the established position that the technical specialization of the university is morally justified. Although the moral justification derives from the utilitarian consequences of scientific specialization—the greatest good for the greatest number—this utility itself rests upon a normative base: the technical specialization in science can be achieved only if its practitioners allow themselves to be regulated by the impersonal morality of cognitive rationality (Parsons and Platt 1973). I will suggest later, indeed, that this cognitive specialization is itself deceptive and that in practice it is combined with rationality of a more evaluative, value-specific kind. At this point, however, I explore the nature and utility of cognitive rationality itself.

The notion that academic life is governed by cognitive rationality is upheld by sophisticated proponents of the established position and by ideologists of the university alike. To uphold cognitive rationality is to create impersonal standards of judgment and evaluation, standards that give decisive power to what is agreed at any particular point to be empirical truth. Insofar as society becomes secular, bureaucratic, and egalitarian, such impersonal standards become increasingly central. To be cognitively rational is to possess expert knowledge. The bureaucratic form of organization is based upon expert knowledge. The expertise of officials who direct bureaucracies is legitimated by the value of cognitive rationality. This is the argument from efficiency, but there is a fairness argument as well. Cognitive rationality is a norm to which all have access; its abstraction promotes inclusion and allows the truth to be contested by all.

Although cognitive rationality takes different forms in different disciplines, in each one it maintains its universalistic form. In the humanities and natural sciences there are rules of evidence that everywhere apply, rules about verification and falsification and standards of what constitutes legitimate explanations and interpretations. In the ideal-type case, these rationality rules apply to every member of the university community, to students and faculty alike. They govern the allocation of prestige, money, and power within the university and, in principle, the allocation of everything that is relevant to the academic occupational sphere.

It is a tremendous historical achievement to have institutionalized such an elusive and impersonal norm, one that so often violates tradition, challenges authority, and constrains personal impulse while abnegating any particular moral creed or political belief. Of course, this norm has never been fully accepted or continuously applied. The university exists in real life, and the organizational and personal exigencies of real life make particularism impossible to stamp out.

Still, cognitive rationality is not only the formal but the practical norm of the university. Whether its scope can be expanded depends, in the first place, on whether it can be maintained. Cognitive rationality can be maintained only by the collegial, self-governing structure of faculty control. The special integrative and allocative processes of academic life must be protected from other standards more representative of community, student body, or state. If these other group interests intervene—no matter in how well-meaning a way—the delicate mechanisms for sustaining cognitive rationality can easily break down.

It seems obvious that the best way to protect these standards of rationality is for the university to remain completely agnostic regarding power and value conflicts in the "outside" world. What follows from this is the strong argument for university autonomy. Autonomy, it is argued, must be absolute because the rationality that governs the university is purely cognitive. What academics do—the kind of rationality they pursue—is completely different from what people do in the outside world. Therefore, let us not bother them and they will not bother us. This liberal position, formulated by Weber and Parsons and forcefully argued by Harvard's Bok, has provided the justification for university inaction in the present period.

This is a serious position, for which much can be said, and I accept it in important respects. I suspect, however, that in this strong form the autonomy defense fails because, ironically, it is too easy to make. It underestimates the forces with which university autonomy must contend. When the autonomy position is stated, the question immediately arises why, after all, anybody would want to intervene in such a purely cognitive community, a community concerned only with the pursuit of empirical truth. There are, of course, religious and political fundamentalists of the left and right who do oppose scientific rationality. But the influence of these groups has shrunk significantly in the twentieth century, and even now, despite the right-wing revival, fundamentalists are not the principal actors in ideological debate. The same kind of question, moreover, can be asked of those inside the university as of those without. Why should the members of such a purely cognitively rational university want to make any social commitments anyway? If they are concerned only with empirical truth, what is all the fuss about? After all, they are still citizens, and they have ample opportunity to pursue political commitments outside the university context.

I argue that this strong version of autonomy cannot be maintained, and I support university autonomy on very different grounds and in a much more qualified way. The different grounds lead to the consideration of areas and occasions where autonomy cannot hold. I outline my "revised autonomy" position by introducing three problems I have with the established position described above.

The first problem concerns the notion of purely cognitive rationality. Although this notion certainly characterizes one special and distinctive dimension of the university, it does not describe academic life in an ample enough way. What the members of the university really pursue is not empirical but value rationality. Here I take over Weber's term but use it in a slightly different sense. Scientific rationality is not neutral but also committed. It is not only concerned with truth in a cognitive sense but with truth in the moral sense. The faculty accept the discipline of cognitive rationality, of being true to the nature of the empirical world. Within the confines of this discipline, however, academics pursue substantive, a priori, political and cultural values. Because of their simultaneously evaluative and cognitive thrust, the term *value* rationality holds.

Despite their commitment to cognitive rationality, then, the university faculty produce enormously value-laden, particularistic arguments. Their aim—and the ambiguity is intended—is to rationalize their values. Academics support constitutionalism; they do not only explain constitutions. They oppose or seek to contribute to revolutions; they do not simply analyze their course. They support or condemn urban renewal; they do not merely analyze the costs it entails. They champion secularism; they do not simply explain evolution.

The nonempirical commitments that inevitably form and inform rational scholarly debate, then, go beyond the explanatory presuppositions to which recent postpositivist philosophers and historians of science have pointed; they extend to ideological evaluations of the world. The university is not only a place for cognitive science; it is also a central place for ideological debate. Academic books and articles form the intellectual basis for political conflict in the modern world. Those who are outside the walls of the university—the William F. Buckleys, the George Wills—are popular but not intellectual ideologues. Although the university is certainly the primary source of objective expertise in modern life, this knowledge is not as abstracted and cognitive as both the critical and established positions assume. Particularly in the humanities and the social sciences, but in subtle ways often in the natural sciences as well, scientific knowledge is connected to the expression of particular political and cultural values.

Only now can we see the extent of the moral problem that the modern university faces, for what is taken to be the epistemology of academic work, becomes, inevitably, the basis for judgments of what its political stance should be. It is not nearly so easy to maintain the strong autonomy argument when we realize that activities of the university are to an important extent ideological and, indirectly, political. In this sense Parsons (Parsons and Platt 1973) was wrong. The university does not simply lend its rationality to an institutionally separated value realm, informing the work of intellectuals (a few of whom are academics) who define themselves in an explicitly ideological way. Weber (1949) errs in much the same way. He defends the independent vocation of the university by limiting scientific rationality to technical knowledge that defines means but not ends, to purposive rationality, or *Zweckrationalität*. Because Weber limits value rationality, or *Wertrationalität*, to actions that are morally absolutist and do not accept the discipline of cognitive rationality, he cannot conceive the actual intermixing that defines the modern university. Bok's case for strong autonomy is too easily made for the same reason. He (1982:20) describes university activity simply as "the search for knowledge and new discovery," i.e., as concerned only with objective, cognitively rational knowledge. I would suggest, to the contrary, that the real university is a dangerously political place.

But if we accept the value basis of academic activity, does the argument follow that the university is not and should not be autonomous? I believe it does not. Here I introduce my second departure from the established position. My first departure concerned what the university does; the second one concerns what the university is. It is simplistic to speak of "the university," for there are really two universities; or at least it should be said that the university—like the medieval kings of old—has two bodies. There is the corporate institution—the legal body, which answers to the state or to a private group—and the collegium of the faculty. Because of its value rationality, the faculty body is never insulated from society, nor should it try to be. The corporate body of the university must, however, behave in a quite different manner from the collegium. The corporate university should seek to insulate itself as thoroughly as possible from any social commitment. In order to do so, its spokespersons usually employ an ideological ruse, presenting the university as concerned only with cognitive reality. Although these spokespersons may be perfectly sincere in this presentation, it remains a form of false consciousness, even if an extremely useful one. When critical outsiders counter that academic work does take value positions, spokespersons for the corporate body argue for objective rationality in a slightly altered way. In the process of producing objective knowledge, they suggest, reasonable scientists can often disagree. It is the free pursuit of knowledge, not the connection between knowledge and value, that leads to disagreement. The argument for autonomy rests in this way on the need for cognitive rather than ideological pluralism.

Yet even if this cognitive fig leaf is discarded, the argument for autonomy can still be made. It must simply be made in a different and ultimately more restricted fashion. The pressures on the corporate university for political commitment—moral pressures from faculty, students, and the public—are enormous. For those inside and outside the university the citizenship of the faculty cannot easily be separated from their intellectual vocations. These pressures only make all the more urgent the necessity for the corporate university to desist from commitment to particular values or interests. In a complex and contentious society, to adopt a particular position is to open the university to powerful political and cultural attack. Such attacks will eventually seek to restrict the faculty's freedom of thought. This sounds like the established position, but it differs in its rationale. It is to protect ideological particularism that the university must remain ideologically neutral. It is to encourage ideological communication that the corporate body must refrain from itself participating in ideological communication.

The political neutrality I am describing is clearly a "compromised position," not simply a "compromise position." Weber pointed out that the purity of moral absolutism is very short lived. A responsible vocation is always a rational compromise between ideals and reality. The regrettable fact is that the university must be willing to tolerate unpleasant and sometimes downright evil social facts without taking a corporate position against them. There can be no such thing as a pristine university untouched by the world's evil. Like Shaw's clergyman, the university must either share the world's guilt or go to another planet. It is not only absurd to ask the university to embody only good and holy things, it is sociologically naive and politically counterproductive.

At this point I introduce my third reservation about the established position, just when it would seem that I am endorsing so much of it. The university should not make autonomy into a universal, abstract principle that holds good for all occasions, for autonomy is not an end in itself but a pragmatic protection. Corporate commitments are renounced so that powerful extrauniversity forces will not be legitimated in taking a position against the ideological discourse of the faculty collegium. But what if it is impossible for the university not to take a position, what if certain conditions in the external society, no matter what the university does, thrust a position upon it? The established position views this question as an exotic possibility, a topic for speculation; President Bok (1982:265) refers, for example, to the "extraordinary circumstances" of German universities in the 1930s. I suggest, to the contrary, that the question of social commitments is, even in its limited version, an issue that is vital for the life and health of every university today and for the society in which it seeks not only to live but also to thrive.

Two kinds of occasion thrust a commitment upon the university, the subjective and the objective. The subjective occasion is less clear-cut and, therefore, more easily obscured in contemporary debate. It goes back to the evaluative character of internal academic discussion. In every society, powerful moral feelings sometimes develop within the public, which make a particular issue take on overriding importance. In such times of political and cultural polarization, a moral decision is eventually made, whether or not any institutional step actually occurs. As citizens of their societies, faculty share the widespread moral feelings, and because of the inherently ideological dimension of their activity, these feelings are significant factors in motivating their work. However these controversial issues are resolved, the moral motivation of the faculty is powerfully affected. When significant enough, therefore, moral controversy can deeply affect the internal operation of the university itself. To defend itself on these occasions, the corporate university must make particular moral commitments.

The objective occasion is more obvious but not less important for that. Cultural and political polarization often result in politically coercive powers threatening to impinge on the university in both its forms. As compared with the subjective situation, on these occasions university autonomy is jeopardized without motivated action on the university's part. Either the government seeks to force the university to adopt a certain organizational position or the university is faced with a situation in which other major social institutions upon whom it depends will be forced to do so. In the latter case, continued university neutrality is simply commitment by another name, for a neutral university passively throws its weight behind whichever side has the most political power. In either case, autonomy will be effectively set aside and commitment will occur without the university's having chosen for itself.

Before becoming more specific about how the university might initiate responsive value commitments in such situations, I make two brief points. Both underscore what Weber would call the university's ethic of responsibility rather than conviction. First, the corporate university must never take the lead in seeking to advance substantive commitments. The need to make a commitment must be thrust upon it. The university acts negatively, to preserve itself. Second, the justification for university commitment is an extremely relativistic, situational one. There are no issues that inherently violate the university's ethical vocation to society. Even anti-Semitism and racism in the larger society cannot be viewed as automatic commitment-producing facts. For the university, every commitment is a dangerous one; it should be undertaken only when threats to university functioning are unavoidable. Thus, in a consensually racist society—the American South in the antebellum period for example—for the university to make an issue out of affirmative action would succeed only in rupturing the university/society relation. The result would undermine the ability of its less racist faculty to advocate the very ideology that corporate action had been taken to uphold. By contrast, in a society deeply divided over racism—American society in the 1960s, for example—a similar neutrality about racial recruiting would place the corporate university at odds not only with powerful faculty sentiment but also with significant institutional forces in the society and state.

When social commitments cannot be avoided, what are the criteria the university should employ to choose sides? What are the mechanisms, moreover, by which the general will of the university can come to be expressed? The university must align itself with whichever position more clearly supports the principle of value rationality. There are certain social conditions upon which the pursuit of such evaluative rationality clearly depends. First, there must be a substantial intellectual freedom, that is, freedom of thought. Second, there must be intellectual self-regulation, that is, as much academic control as possible over the conditions of academic work. Third, there must be full communication, that is, the widest possible opportunities for the exchange of ideas.

In times that demand corporate value commitment, then, the university must act to increase freedom and control and to extend the scope of communication, for these conditions are the basis of the value rationality it seeks to defend. The university lives off commitments to value rationality in the general population. It does, of course, contribute to the attractiveness of this value by the vigor of the way its faculty exemplify it. There are also occasions, however, when the university must defend the conditions of value rationality directly.

There can be no formal rules that determine when the conditions of value rationality must be defended. What is involved is a sociological process, a process of opinion formation that gradually crystallizes the collegium's public will. The dynamics of this process proceed from the fact that the collegium is composed of intellectuals who are also value-committed citizens. Yet while formal rules are impossible, formal procedures might be desirable. At present, the only group legally empowered to formalize university commitments to the outside world is the corporate governing board, composed almost exclusively of nonacademic and nonstudent personnel. It is clear, of course, that this board does not control intrauniversity commitments. Ownership and control are separated in the academic world as they are in the corporate one. Moreover, there is a clear rationale for the nonacademic nature of such governing boards. They represent the society's fiduciary interest in overseeing academic work. They may not, however, be nearly so effective at presenting the university's own interests vis-à-vis society.

The nonacademic and nonstudent nature of university governing boards often makes them too timid or too aggressive in deciding the relationship between university and society. Why? Because they themselves are not deeply in touch with the value rationality that the university must protect. Because of this, dangerous situations can arise, situations in which university interests are threatened in ways that nonacademic governing boards could not have foreseen. Formalized faculty and student input, by contrast, could alert the corporate community to impending threats to the conditions for value rationality and to the need to establish social commitments to defend against them. Formal and explicit advisory powers should be assigned to student bodies and faculty senates, according to which a vote by a certain percentage would require that an issue be discussed and eventually voted upon by university governing boards. Once again, my position may be contrasted with the established one. President Bok (1982:248–53) notes the extensive Harvard faculty debate about the Vietnam War, but he dismisses the discussion as burdensome and time-consuming. This observation fails to appreciate, however, the close affinity between such discussions and "real" academic work. It also fails to see the need for a sociological rather than a formal approach to university/society commitment. Whether such discussions are burdensome must be left to the sensibilities of the faculty to decide. As a rule, they will devote extraordinary time only in extraordinary circumstances. It is just such circumstances, of course, that may call for corporate university commitment. Obviously, such expressions of intrauniversity will may not finally decide the regents' or overseers' vote. A strongly felt issue could, however, come up again, and the reiteration of such a theme would send a powerful message to the extrauniversity community from which the governing boards arise.

The foregoing outlines a theoretical perspective within which the general issue of university-society relations may be reconsidered. In my conclusion, I briefly consider how this perspective might be useful in thinking about issues in the present day.

According to my earlier argument, threats to value rationality can activate university commitment in one of two ways. On the one hand, there can be objective, coercive action that arouses the faculty collegium and the students. On the other hand, there can be a subjective threat that although not producing an institutional challenge, activates commitment because the moral feelings of the faculty collegium are perceived by them to be threatened in a fundamental way. Equally real limitations of value-rational discourse may occur, of either an objective or a moral type. They will not create or justify university commitment, however, if they do not arouse the indignation of the faculty collegium itself.

Consider, for example, the history of the university's commitment to affirmative action. Here the university faced a direct government policy, which, if it had not acted, would have committed it passively. Faced with this objective reality, the university decided to implement affirmative action on its own rather than to stall compliance. It did so, I believe, in accordance with the stricture to expand intellectual communication. The range of value-rational discourse in the university is inhibited by racially tinged hiring and admissions, just as it once was by anti-Semitic barriers. Now, it has been argued by conservative opponents of this commitment that this step beyond autonomy undermined one of the other bases of value-rational discourse, namely, intellectual self-regulation. The committed university has responded that it has merely broadened its own criteria for employment, not abandoned self-control, and it has everywhere sought to keep direct government intervention outside of even affirmative academic hiring. The commitment to maintaining all the conditions for value-rational discourse has, indeed, been the principal source of contention between university and government in arguments over university compliance with racial guidelines.

Although university commitments to affirmative action were made in the face of an objective constraint, they occurred against the background of a giant movement of public opinion. This movement raised the racial consciousness of American citizens, and it was as citizens that faculty, students, and administrators made this particular objective constraint a major issue. By contrast, the university's reaction to government-imposed penalties for those who failed to register for the draft—recently lifted— indicates a very different situation.

This latter threat by the government certainly constituted an equally objective situation, an attempt by coercive powers to force the university into a political commitment of great importance, into support for the draft and, indirectly, for American foreign policy. This coercively produced support ran directly contrary to the condition of self-regulation upon which value-rational discussion is based. To enforce draft registration, the government took federal financial aid away from graduate and undergraduate students who failed to comply. By supplying records to the federal government, universities forced students to indicate whether or not they had registered. In so doing, universities acquiesced to policies that undermined their ability to allocate rewards according to purely scientific criteria. In the sociology department at UCLA, for example, an excellent graduate student was substantially delayed in his dissertation research because his work-study grant was withdrawn when he failed to register.

In this recent case of draft registration, the university has maintained its neutrality but has been forced to assume a position passively. Why the contrast with its actions on affirmative action? Because the sociological process of opinion formation decides which threat to value rationality will be crystallized. In the midst of the great popular upheaval of the 1960s, major universities refused to comply with government pressures to enforce draft laws. The change in public consciousness in the 1980s makes this commitment "unnecessary." Because students are not fighting in an unpopular war, the draft has not aroused the collective consciousness of faculty or students. The issue does not "feel" like a critical one to the members of the university community. Hence it is not, in fact, an issue in which commitment becomes a sociological necessity.

Since World War II, powerful interconnections have developed between universities and defense work, both private and public, and more recently, growing connections have emerged between universities and biotechnology industries. In both cases, it seems clear, the self-regulation of the collegium is restricted. When the corporate university allows such economic and technological relations to be established, scientists cannot be hired according to strictly value-rational criteria. Classified research, proprietary information, and patent rights considerations, moreover, restrict the freedom of communication upon which the extended scientific community depends. It might even be argued that "mission-oriented" research, by skewing scientific resources toward short-term applications at the expense of basic research, restricts freedom of thought. None of these threats represents directly coercive action against the university by the state, because in every case the corporate university has entered into such relationships voluntarily. Once entered into, however, they represent real and coercive restrictions on academic life.

Few of these instances, however, have triggered university commitments to a moral or political stance. The reason is that in the postwar climate they have not aroused sufficiently widespread faculty and student concern. In the University of California system there has been continual protest against the university's connection to the Livermore weapons laboratory. Yet the protest has not been widespread. Indeed, even when a popular governor—Jerry Brown—sought to make Livermore an issue, he failed to crystallize sufficient public attention. By contrast, in 1984 the faculty at the California Institute of Technology held a series of mass meetings to protest the Caltech president's plans to sponsor an Air Force think tank. Faced with threats by the faculty to seek his dismissal and, no doubt, sincerely surprised by the depth of faculty feeling, the president found a diplomatic way to withdraw his initial offer. The difficulties of the recent effort to petition scientists against "Star Wars" research provides another example of the contingency and importance of experienced indignation. So far, this massive influx of restricted research money for "Star Wars" has aroused relatively little opposition, and there have certainly been no signs of university commitment to an anti-"Star Wars" stance.

The South African divestment movement is responding to a much more subjective threat than any that I have discussed so far. It is not, in the first instance, the real or actual danger to the society or the university that is the stimulus for action; rather, it is the danger to the university's moral reputation, which, of course, can ultimately have real consequences for both. For many years, the existence of South African apartheid did not seem related to the exercise of value rationality in American universities in a substantial way. For many years, moreover, students and faculty were complacent about the issue. In the last two years, however, the small number of activists who have long campaigned for divestment have begun to exert a far-reaching moral effect. They have succeeded in creating a deep symbolic identification between American students and faculty and the disenfranchised racial groups in South Africa. Indeed, not to take university action against apartheid is now experienced by many faculty as a threat to the collegium's own intellectual life. The result, it is feared, would be the restriction of the moral authority of collegium faculty and of university students alike. In this situation, to maintain university autonomy would, in fact, reduce the integrity of value rationality inside the American university itself. Apparently, some university commitment against apartheid must be made if the motive for value-rational behavior is to be maintained. The conflicts that have once again arisen between faculty and students, on the one hand, and governing boards, on the other, make evident the need for more rational and consistent procedures to formally express noncorporate university opinion.

In this essay I have steered a middle course between long- and short-term considerations, between conviction and practicality, and between advocacy and explanation. For Weber, this middle ground was called "responsibility." Only by revising the liberal position on university autonomy can a truly responsible position be maintained.

REFERENCES

Bok, Derek. 1982. *Beyond the Ivory Tower: Social Responsibilities of the Modern University*. Cambridge, Mass.: Harvard University Press.

Parsons, Talcott and Gerald Platt. 1973. *The American University*. Cambridge, Mass.: Harvard University Press.

Rawls, John. 1971. *A Theory of Justice*. Cambridge, Mass.: Harvard University Press.

Walzer, Michael. 1983. *Spheres of Justice*. New York: Basic Books.

Weber, Max. 1949. "The Meaning of 'Ethical Neutrality' in Sociology and Economics." In Weber, *The Methodology of the Social Sciences*, pp. 1–49. New York: Free Press.

Weber, Max. 1973. "The Power of the State and the Dignity of the Academic Calling in Imperial Germany." *Minerva* (April 1973), 11:571–632.

PART III

The Micro-Macro Link

SEVEN

Social Differentiation and Collective Behavior

Eisenstadt and Curelaru (1976:180) begin their masterful analysis of the structural-functional school of sociological theory with the following admonition: "Despite many claims to the contrary, especially by opponents, the structural-functional school was neither uniform nor unchanging." Indeed, they warn that there emerged "within this school, many internal controversies, disputes, and 'openings.'"

These words should introduce every discussion of structural-functional theory. They are an acknowledgment, by one of the most distinguished "functionalists" of our time, of the need for revision experienced by even the most representative and able members of every great theoretical tradition (see Alexander 1979). As such, they provide a key for evaluating both Eisenstadt's contributions to functionalism and the functionalist tradition more generally. They are also vital to a proper understanding of the relationship between this tradition and others.

In this chapter we propose, first, to identify the "openings" that Eisenstadt himself created within the functionalist school. After doing so, we trace how his revision of social differentiation theory, in particular, creates an opening toward developments within a tradition often considered to be antagonistic to functionalism—symbolic interactionism. This opening, we believe, allows critical elements of Eisenstadt's revisionist theorizing to be expanded significantly. Such expansion is vital to the creation of a neofunctionalism, that is, the emergence of a self-critical strand of functional theory that seeks to broaden functionalism's intellectual scope while retaining its theoretical core.

Written with Paul Colomy.

I

Every great social theory is ambiguous on certain critical points, and Talcott Parsons' was not less so than others. On the most general and presuppositional level, Parsons' theory at its best was motivated by a genuinely ecumenical ambition, articulating a frame of reference that synthesized idealist and materialist modes of analysis, allowing each independent but only partial determination of action and order. Using a sophisticated functional model and a complex yet precise conceptual scheme, Parsons defined culture, society, and personality as analytically differentiated systems, a notion that mandated interpenetration but that also legitimated conflicting aims. He also applied these general theoretical orientations to the social system itself, arguing that it, too, is composed of internally differentiated systems that, while analytically interchanging with one another, can be powerfully at odds. After specifying equilibrium and integration as significant analytical points of reference, Parsons dedicated much of his empirical analysis to tracing the process of differentiation and separation among actual historical groups and institutions, a process often produced by conflict and often producing conflict in turn.

Yet this ecumenical ambition was cross-cut in Parsons' work by a more sectarian and reductionist strand of analysis (see Alexander 1983, chs. 6–9). While the ecumenical strain of Parsons' analysis embraced the materialist segments of Weber's work, and through them certain crucial aspects of Marxism, the more one-dimensional strand of his writing was largely confined to exploring the implications of Durkheim and Freud. In this Durkheim-Freud reduction, the normative-evaluative dimension of personal orientation—which exerts moral control, among other things, over cognitive-instrumental orientations and acts—is said to control such orientations and actions not just in the analytic sense of morality as normatively regulated order but substantively, i.e., in the moral interest of collectivities and societies as a whole. Inevitably coupled with this reduction is Parsons' redefinition of "institutionalization." In the ecumenical strain, institutionalization is defined simply as the intersection of often conflicting demands from the systems of personality, culture, and society. But in the Durkheim-Freud reduction the disjunction created by the autonomy of the social system drops away: institutionalization becomes the internalization by personalities of common value patterns (e.g., Parsons 1951:36–45). This idealist reduction of presuppositions and models, in turn, corresponds to an empirical reduction. If normative regulation is to be taken as collectively moral, and if the problem of scarce social resources drops away, then the differentiated subsystems in society will surely exchange resources in a reciprocal and mutually supporting manner. Moreover, equilibrium becomes not just an analytical reference point for the analysis of social process but also a description of the empirical status of that process itself (cf. essay 5, above).

II

It is at the reductionist strand of Parsons' legacy that Eisenstadt has always taken him. A loyal student, he has for the most part carefully camouflaged his departures, averring as recently as 1976 that Parsons' "heavy systemic emphasis" indicated neither an idealist reduction nor an anticonflictual tone (Eisenstadt and Curelaru 1976:182). Yet, the evidence of a vast if subrosa revisionist effort is not hard to find.

In his little-known but extremely interesting introduction to *Max Weber on Charisma and Institution Building,* a piece that ostensibly placed Weber squarely into the Parsonian camp, Eisenstadt insists that in functionalist theory values are viewed as the disruptive foundation of personal and collective struggles for fulfillment (1968:42). In *The Political System of Empires,* a work that for the first time translated Weber's theory of patrimonialism into functionalist language—even while, as we later emphasize, "Weberianizing" functionalism in turn—the implicit challenges to Parsons' reductionist strand are omnipresent. (1) Parsons' interchange model is here cross-cut by the "ecological" dimension of stratification (1963:69–93). (2) The empirical differentiation modelled by interchange is viewed as creating problems and not simply or even primarily as adapting to them (ibid.:224). (3) The differentiated parts of an interchanging society, e.g., the political system, are conceived as producing not just complementary but dominating institutional forces of their own, as, for example, in Eisenstadt's discussion of the disruptive qualities of the early bureaucracies (1963:273–99). (4) The "generalization" of such differentiated systems and their media of exchange is defined simply in terms of institutional autonomy and independent power rather than in terms of symbolically produced, moral, and fundamentally integrative legitimation (1963:18–20). (5) The processes that result from such differentiation and generalization are analyzed in terms of their contentiousness and the struggles they involve, rather than primarily as forms of reequilibration (ibid.:304).

Clearly, it was the ecumenical and incorporative dimension of Parsons' work that Eisenstadt took most strongly to heart. Rather than attempt to defend the fortress-like distinctiveness of the Parsonian corpus against all critics hither and yon, Eisenstadt expanded the theory to encompass the critics' best points. For classical theorists, this pertained primarily to Marx's emphasis on struggle and class, which Eisenstadt (1971) sublated into his broader theory of differentiation and ecological segmentation (1971); it pertained also to the instrumental aspects of Weber's political analysis, which he (1963, 1968) incorporated into a more muscular, multi-dimensional theory of interest group exchange.

In terms of contemporary theorizing, this ecumenical ambition reached out to the reified, incomplete theories of conflict, exchange, and symbolic interaction. Far from merely dismissing Homans, Eisenstadt (1971b) dwelled not on the inadequacies but on the insights that exchange theories generate about the concrete and processual aspects of what Homans called subinstitutional behavior. Rather than emphasize the analytic inadequacies of instrumental conflict theories, Eisenstadt (1965:1–68; 1976:245–95) used them to expand and make more systematic his investigation into the inequalities generated by allocation and by the merely formal aspects of legitimation. And while criticizing the individualistic dimension of symbolic interaction, he tried, at the same time, to utilize its insights to expand his understanding of the communicative and contingent aspects of interaction processes and role behavior (1976:273–77). What a more strictly analytical and purely critical approach (see Alexander 1987) might have legitimately called the residual categories in these traditions—e.g., Homans' theory of distributive justice—Eisenstadt called openings, and rather than decrying the fragmentation of contemporary sociology, he tried to document what he described as the "broadening" of the sociological tradition.

Though Eisenstadt's early work, for example, *From Generation to Generation* (1956), represented functionalism in almost a pure form, his revisionist impulses began to manifest themselves soon after. Rarely were they explicit. They usually took cover behind a subtle combination of the functionalist framework and formulations and models from competing traditions. This should not be surprising. The same pattern is evident in revisionist efforts by other distinguished students of great masters—in those Marxists who combined Marxism with Hegel and Freud, in those Durkheimians who melded their maître's theories with Simmel and Marx (Alxander 1982:chs. 9, 10).

In considering Eisenstadt's work as a whole, his revision of Parsons may be said to have four distinct emphases: (1) process and innovation; (2) the role and the significance of interests; (3) the omnipresence of conflict; (4) the disruptive aspects of culture. In his early revisions, these challenges were articulated by the extraordinary "Weberianization" of functionalist theory I mentioned above. On the one hand, *The Political System of Empires* (1963) demonstrated how Parsons' theory could unravel the often confused relationships between class, state, and religion in Weber's monumental theory of political modernization. Yet, at the same time, this work demonstrated another ambition: to use the antithetical emphases of Weber's theory to push the functionalist framework in new directions. Eisenstadt firmly linked, for the first time, the different functional exigencies of social systems to the interests of concrete social groups and their desires for control (1963:8, 315). In this way, he could demonstrate that social change is a process involving the differentiation of power and efforts at mobilization of resources and control (ibid.:14) while insisting, nonetheless, that the political goals and interests of the mobilizing and controlling rulers were always mediated by overarching cultural patterns (ibid.:222–50).

The introduction of economic classes into functionalist theory comes naturally from this emphasis on different concrete groups. The boundary relations between functionally differentiated subsystems can now be seen as social relations between different groups, and the groups that articulate the "adaptive function" are, at least in early periods, economic classes (ibid.:120 and ch. 8, passim). From this innovation, Eisenstadt could powerfully extend class theory in turn, for he demonstrated that the development of different economic classes is related not just to economic development but to the level of social differentiation. Indeed, Eisenstadt developed in this work a systematic, historically specific theory of group development for each functionally differentiated subsystem. On this basis he articulated a detailed theory of social, not just economic, contradictions for the imperial period. This theory suggests, for example, that the great communist revolutions of the modern period have been triggered, not by forms of property, but by dominant political relationships that could not escape the contradictions of an imperial bureaucracy (on this point, see also Eisenstadt 1966:67–74 and passim).

Whereas these earlier revisions were couched in the language of Weber, Eisenstadt's later revisions were most conspicuously articulated in the theoretical language of Shils. Shils' center/periphery theory, on the one hand, allowed Eisenstadt to make even more concrete and subtle his earlier concentration on the interest relations that govern exchanges between political and extrapolitical groups. At the same time, Eisenstadt powerfully sublated Shils' theory by defining the center in a more pluralistic and Parsonian way, systematically linking it to differentiated spheres in the social system. Yet Shils' broadening of the charisma concept proved still more important, for it enabled Eisenstadt to give a more innovative and disruptive twist to Parsons' theory of culture. Eisenstadt could use charisma to open Parsons' value conceptualization to the more mercurial qualities of sacredness. This allowed him to establish a fateful dialectic. Eisenstadt argued that while according to Shils' broadening of the concept charisma is omnipresent, it can be produced only by specialized actors and specific and discrete aspects of the social structure (1968:xli–xlii). The narrow access to sacred power, however, must somehow be responsive to the "quest" for participation in the symbolic order by the population as a whole. Eisenstadt concludes that "the quest for participation . . . does not necessarily constitute a focus of consensus—it may easily become a focus of dissension, conflict, and change" (ibid.:xlii). On this foundation, he can formulate a new theory of the relationship between functionally differentiated groups, in which the terms of exchange are set not only by a group's dominating interest or relation to an overarching symbolic order but also by its capacity to create and crystallize broader symbolic orientations and norms (ibid.:xxxix; see also Eisenstadt's Shilsian recasting of Weberian revisions of functional theory in his introduction to the paperback edition of *The Political System of Empires* [1963 (1971)]:vii–xxii).

Eisenstadt's efforts to revise functionalism may be said to have reached theoretical maturity in two different forms. The first is his theory of institutionalization, which he developed in the 1960s in various papers and made more detailed in book-length treatments over the subsequent decade. The second is a more metatheoretical conceptualization of the relation between social order, social systems and culture, and social change, a formulation that came to fruition in his work with Curelaru, *The Form of Sociology*, in 1976. We consider the latter theory first, not only because it supplies a framework for Eisenstadt's more specific considerations of institutionalization but also because this institutionalization theory provides an effective link to our empirical discussions in the latter part of this chapter.

From the perspective of his intellectual development, Eisenstadt's *The Forms of Sociology* is a richly revealing work, for he and Curelaru developed an analytic history tracing sociological theory from the classical figures to the present. Because they made claims for the stready advancement and accumulation of social-scientific knowledge, their analysis is fearfully Whiggish in its approach to science (Alexander 1977). Yet like many other presentist treatments, it proved extremely useful for Eisenstadt's developing sociology. It allowed him to look "forward" from classical theory to functionalism and in this way to argue for the advances Parsons made and to look "backward" from more contemporary debates to Parsons' functionalism in order to argue that these later developments responded effectively to real shortcomings in Parsons' work. The final chapter in *Forms*, "The Broadening of the Sociological Tradition: Some Preliminary Indications" (1976:347–75), marked the first time that Eisenstadt theorized explicitly from a perspective outside of functionalism. It presents, in addition, the most abstract and purely theoretical statement he has ever made. This chapter, like so much of Eisenstadt's work, makes difficult reading. It is clear, however, that this discussion systematically reformulates Eisenstadt's ad hoc and implicit functionalist revisions, as well as the equally camouflaged openings he earlier made to the prefunctionalist and postfunctionalist traditions. This systematic theory, therefore, marks one of the principal starting points in Eisenstadt's revisionist career. With Smelser's (e.g., 1974) own work in the early 1970s, it marks the beginning of neofunctionalism. It must be understood both in relation to the ambiguities of Parsons' original work and to Eisenstadt's own agenda for ecumenical revision.

While the fundamental elements of Parsons' synthesis remain, Eisenstadt forcefully integrates them, in this concluding chapter, with a focus on process, group action, interest, conflict, and cultural disruption. The potential for disorder and conflict, he maintains at the outset, is rooted in the very givens of human nature. The genetic code of human beings is an open one; it must be arbitrarily structured by symbolic forms and technical organization. Yet this very act of structuring produces an openness to change and disruption, for the details of symbolic forms and instrumental techniques cannot be determined in advance. They unfold only in concrete interaction. This openness, in turn, creates powerful anxieties about the randomness and changeability of people's goals and activities, about the control of personal impulses, about the scarcity of valuable resources, and about the duration of human life itself (ibid.:352). Given the human tendency toward symbolization, such anxieties become transcendentalized, giving rise to various forms of cultural expression like religion, philosophy, science, and art. Yet these uncertainties also give rise to organizational effort and conflict. Because the distribution of human labor is not genetically coded, this conflict becomes, in its most general expression, a struggle over the division of labor. More specifically, it is a conflict over three different kinds of organizational indeterminacies: (1) the indeterminacy of solidary relationships, i.e., "the lack of specification of the range of actors who are admitted to a situation—that is, of the boundaries of interaction and of criteria of participation [i.e., membership] in it"; (2) the indeterminacy of power, i.e., "the lack of genetic specification of universal or general human goals and of goals that can or should be sought by participants in any particular situation"; (3) the indeterminacy of wealth, i.e., "the lack of fixed specification of the range of access of different actors to the major resources which are being produced, exchanged, and distributed" (ibid.:354).

These overwhelming contingencies, Eisenstadt believes, make the development of mutual trust the central issue for all human societies. To pursue this end, societies develop organizational frameworks and mechanisms to regulate the division of labor and detailed symbolic codes that can structure the situation in accord with more general given cultural concerns. Yet there is by no means a perfect fit between the meaningful obligations and codes that societies develop and the organizational frameworks and mechanisms that regulate the division of labor. This tension between structures that develop to promote trust has the effect of assuring that trust cannot be maintained. This tension produces new symbolic codes that transpose the felt inadequacies of the division of labor into critical ideologies emphasizing the disorder and arbitrariness of organizational life. Moreover, because these critical codes must be defined concretely in each instance, differences soon develop among carrier groups that exacerbate the tensions.

In this unsatisfactory situation, Eisenstadt argues, groups of actors seize access to critical resources and positions and promulgate rules that support their own perspectives and interests. Such rules themselves often seem arbitrary, coercive, and unjust to members of society outside these groups. The group conflict that ensues is fought on the following grounds: hierarchy vs. equality, effectiveness vs. legitimacy, authority vs. solidarity, exploitation vs. justice, and spontaneity vs. control.

In response to such conflicts, there emerge in all societies detailed ground rules that control not only symbolic interaction but also access to valued resources. These ground rules form what Eisenstadt calls the "deep structure" of society, and they are set up and maintained by conscious and unconscious coalitions of different types of "entrepreneurs," or institutional innovators. These coalitions seek to control the flow of resources, symbolic and material, that are crucial for determining the structure of society. Eisenstadt's conclusion to his metatheory is as dialectical as the arguments that compose it. While the establishment of ground rules "copes with the problems of social order," he warns, "it does not solve them; it only transposes them to a new level" (ibid.:369).

Since this metatheory formalized notions that had evolved over the entire course of his work, it should not be surprising that Eisenstadt's more specific theory of institutionalization fits securely within it. By institutionalization, Eisenstadt means, in the first place, the process by which organized, "societally described" behavior is established (1964a:235). But he also uses the concept to refer to the movement of specification from general, background conditions to specific and concrete social arrangements, i.e., to "the processes by which the various predispositions engendered in given structural, cultural, and organizational settings, are taken up and crystallized into specific organizational and symbolic patterns" (1956 [1971]:xlvii). While this second meaning emerges more directly from Eisenstadt's attention to contingency and social process, both definitions refer to the problem of social change. From within his empirical and theoretical studies of social change, Eisenstadt issues this fundamental challenge to the reductionist strands of Parsons' work. It was, after all, the idealism of Parsons' own theory of institutionalization—its failure to recognize sufficiently the "social" disjunction between personality and culture—that undermined the original functionalist theory of order and made it appear to be antagonistic to the processes of social change.

Parsons identified social change and, more particularly social differentiation, with general processes like value generalization, adaptive upgrading, and inclusion. Although references to the specific causes of differentiation can be found throughout his work, most of the time Parsons was content with the general causal designation, "strain." What he was more interested in was differentiation's effects. He described these effects very precisely, but these descriptions—like his descriptions of the processes of differentiation themselves—tended to be highly generalized (for an important exception, see Parsons 1971:ch. 4, passim). Equally significant, these descriptions of effects assumed that the processes of differentiation that responded to the initial strain would, in the last instance, reestablish equilibrium (see essay 2, above).

Eisenstadt's position on the effects of differentiation could not be more different. "Recognition of the integrative *problems* that are attendant on new levels of differentiation," he insists, "constitutes the main theoretical implication of the concept of differentiation" (1964b:377, italics added). He also differs emphatically with Parsons on the relevance of causes. While in the following statement Eisenstadt (1964b:375) purportedly is discussing only "older evolutionary models," it seems clear that he also has Parsons' own evolutionary model in mind: "Very often [such models] confuse . . . general tendencies with the causes of change." Eisenstadt quite clearly believes, in other words, that the integrative problems which differentiation produces can be understood only if the causes of differentiation are specified in a concrete and systematic way.

The process of differentiation refers to tendencies that societies have, when certain background conditions are present, to respond to social conflicts or abrupt disruptions by developing more specialized structures. Yet, even if such responses occur, Eisenstadt believes, social conflict and disruption may not be resolved: "The emergence of a solution, i.e., the institutionalization of a social order congruent with the new range of problems, is not necessarily given in the process of differentiation" (1964b:378). How can it be possible that the process of differentiation may not "solve" the problems—resolve the strain—which in some sense caused such differentiation in the first place? Because the actual process of differentiation is activated by factors much more specific than the general strain that caused the prior social disruption. Tendencies to differentiation are activated, Eisenstadt insists, "by the occupants of strategic roles within the major institutional spheres" who "attempt to broaden the scope and develop the potentialities of their respective spheres" (ibid.). He puts the matter more succinctly at a different point: "These things are done by people who are placed in or attempt to achieve strategic positions and who aspire to certain goals" (1964a:245). The fact that newly differentiated structures are established only by groups acting in their "self-interest" explains why the institutionalization produced by social change can in turn produce new problems of its own. To maintain the structures they have established, Eisenstadt believes, these entrepreneurial groups will make "continuous attempts to mobilize resources from different groups and individuals, and to maintain the legitimacy of the values, symbols and norms of the system" (ibid., 246). Such efforts, however, will obviously "affect the positions of different groups in the society, giving rise to continuous shifts in the balance of power among them and in their orientations to the existing institutional system and its values" (ibid.). Because differentiation is carried out by particular groups, and because the maintenance of newly differentiated institutions depends upon resources that can be acquired only from other groups, the differentiation process inherently produces group conflict. "Most groups within any society or collectivity," Eisenstadt insists, "tend to exhibit some autonomy in terms of their attitudes toward any such institutionalization and they vary greatly in the extent of their willingness or ability to provide the resources demanded by the [new] system" (ibid.:246). The groups most unwilling or unable to supply the needed resources, moreover, will develop organizations and ideologies even more antagonistic to the newly dominant group's demands.

Differentiation, then, actually may "facilitate the development and 'maturation' of certain inherent tendencies in the structure and orientation of key groups . . . which may then develop beyond the basic premises of the system" (ibid.). Differentiation, in sum, is a process beset by contradictions. Though it responds to an initial conflict, the subsequent development of a new institution often leads "to the depletion of the resources necessary to maintain" it and may, indeed, create forces that "seek to create a new institutional system" altogether (ibid.:247).

In the course of the last decade, Eisenstadt's analysis of this institutionalization process became in crucial respects more culturally sensitive and precise. In part, this further reveals the influence of Shils, but more significantly it indicates the response that Eisenstadt made to the structuralism of Lévi-Strauss. This response takes seriously the autonomy and internal systematicity of "codes," but it relates them much more forcefully than structuralism to the level of the social system itself. In this later work of Eisenstadt's, the carriers and promoters of differentiation become also the creators and articulators of distinctive cultural languages (1976:250ff.). These codes are linked (1973:119–50) to the complex conceptual scheme articulated in *The Forms of Sociology*: to the levels of organization and symbolic specificity, to the antinomies around which conflicts are formed, and to the concrete and detailed ground rules that Eisenstadt lays out. Eisenstadt has also tried to identify "rules of transformation" that govern the relationships between the different levels and kinds of institutionally specific codes.

Though Eisenstadt's study of codes is still far from completion, the general impact of his increased sensitivity to cultural life can be assessed in a preliminary way. While "socializing" the purely cultural emphasis of structuralism, Eisenstadt's work now stresses, at the same time, that in certain historical periods possibilities exist for a direct, suprainstitutional relationship between socialized personalities and symbolic patterns. In the process of institutionalization and change, he suggests, this relationship creates possibilities for social disruption as significant as the more purely socially generated tensions described in his preceding work (1973:132–33, 325–27). The existence of such a direct relationship also means that periods of disruption and transformation will be permeated by episodes of ritual behavior, and such ritualization makes societies even more dramatically open to change (1976:248–52). Indeed, Eisenstadt has argued (1978) that the impact and independence of cultural codes actually makes them the single most powerful creator of revolutionary transformations. Although this presents a dramatic change from his earlier, more purely political theory of revolution, it represents an expansion of explanatory emphasis rather than a change of type. The multidimensional character of his general theory, which he inherited from Parsons along with his ecumenical ambition, allows Eisenstadt's cultural turn to enrich his earlier writing on institutionalization rather than contradict it.

III

We now indicate how some of these openings in differentiation theory can be extended by linking them with developments in one branch of the symbolic interactionist tradition.

While contemporary interactionism suffers from an astructural and individualist bias, it contains, nonetheless, a strand that can be seen as "open" to the analysis of institutional and structural change. This strand is collective behavior.* The interactionist approach to collective behavior overemphasizes its emergent character, yet the end point of such unstructured behavior is held to be structure itself. Antistructure is said to lead to structure, while structure itself is never considered in a systemic way as a thing-in-itself. This paradox appears in Blumer's (1951 [1939]:214) early statement on the area, which recommends that social movements

can be viewed as societies in miniature, and as such, represent the building up of organized and formalized collective behavior out of what was originally amorphous and undefined. In their growth a social organization is developed, new values are formed, and new personalities are organized. These, indeed, constitute their residue. They leave behind an institutional structure and a body of functionaries, new objects and views, and a new set of self-conceptions.

But can structure simply "appear" out of collective behavior in an automatic way, unaffected by any surrounding, i.e., structural environment? Wouldn't the products of earlier collective behavior affect later episodes in turn? The attempt to develop this line of reasoning leads back to Eisenstadt's work. Antistructure and structure can be combined if neofunctionalism is systematically related to one strand of the theory of collective behavior.†

Early students of collective behavior described the crystallization of these new institutional and cultural orders as the invariable outcome of developments purely internal to a social movement. This is clearly evident in efforts to construct a "natural history" of all social movements, which assumed that movements traversed a series of stages culminating in the realization of new institutional frameworks. Blumer identifies, for example, the stages of social unrest, popular excitement, formal organization, and institutionalization. In the latter stage the movement "has crystallized

---

*In this analysis we focus on publics and social movements and do not examine how more "elementary forms" of collective behavior, such as crowds or panics, affect institutional change.

†John Wilson (1973:332–63) argues that as social movements persist they become more routinized and structurally differentiated. He does not, however, explicitly link the origins and development of such movements to the subjective, voluntaristic, and conflictual elements of neofunctionalism or, indeed, to the symbolic interactionist treatment of collective behavior. Our discussion attempts to articulate these links in a detailed and systematic fashion.

into a fixed organization with a definite personnel and stucture to carry into execution the purposes of the movement" (ibid.:203; also see Edwards 1927; Hopper 1950).

More recent analyses of collective behavior have moved away from the simplistic natural history approach and, in contrast, have emphasized the contingent nature of movement development (Turner 1964:123–25; Turner and Killian 1972:252–55; Jackson et al. 1960). Arguing that movements do not invariably move through a set of fixed stages, these interactionists have sought to identify the conditions necessary for movements to develop and endure. Ironically, this very increased emphasis on contingency has opened the possibility for connecting the collective behavior approach to more structural concerns, for once the institutionalization of a social movement is seen as problematic, it is seen also to depend on a variety of social and cultural conditions.

The major theorists of this later collective behavior tradition, Turner and Killian* (1972:245–425), write, for example, about the tension between competing value, power, and participation orientations within movements; a movement's success in generating material and ideological support from the community; the public response and the reaction of social control agents to the movement; and the strategies and tactics of the movement's leadership. The relation between these conditions of collective behavior and Eisenstadt's innovations in the functional tradition are clear and unmistakable. As we have summarized these above, they include an emphasis on process and innovation, on the significance of group and individual interests, of conflict, and the disruptive aspects of culture. If the continuing emphasis on contingency in this later collective behavior perspective is taken as illuminating a level of empirical analysis rather than as articulating a systematic theory, then it clearly complements some of these neofunctionalist concerns; the later theory's openness to

---

*In our view, Turner and Killian's *Collective Behavior* (1972) is among the most comprehensive treatments of the field. Surely, it is the most thoroughly interactionist treatment. With regard to the latter point, it seems clear that Turner and Killian's "emergent norm" approach is more consistent with the basic interactionist tenets about the character of social action than is, for example, Blumer's depiction of "circular reaction" (Turner 1964:128–32). For this reason, we employ Turner and Killian's text as the most authoritative interactionist treatment of collective behavior.

impinging structures promises, in turn, to elaborate and complete neo-functionalism's more structural emphasis.*

Yet there are substantive, not just analytic, reasons for seeking to combine neofunctionalist theory with this strand of interactionism, for the phenomenon of collective behavior seems to embody much of what differentiation theory conceives of as modern life. With the differentiation of a public sphere in the late eighteenth and early nineteenth centuries, and the increasing impingement of the periphery on the centers, collective behavior became an increasingly important vehicle for aggregating and articulating societal demands; it also became an ever more important mechanism for introducing change in a continuous, self-regulating way.

In the following discussion, we suggest how key concepts developed by these later students of collective behavior—communication and a sense of injustice, the public, countermovements and general movements—can extend the subjective, voluntaristic, and conflictual elements of Eisenstadt's theory of social differentiation and change. Our theoretical argument is illustrated with examples drawn primarily from political development in the early United States.

Strain and the Sense of Injustice. We have shown how Eisenstadt's approach to strain makes several important advances. First, he replaces a broad and often vague notion of strain with a reference to specific tensions generated by particular groups and their interests. In doing so, he allows that general strain and disequilibrium is not enough: institutional entrepreneurs must emerge to identify this dislocation with some positive personal gain. Strains, in other words, do not "reveal themselves"; they must be defined before they can be acted upon. This definition will depend not just on material position but on contingent cultural sensitivities, and will develop in an atmosphere of contingent conflict between individuals and groups.

In interactionist terms, Eisenstadt is suggesting that strain is a product of communication and collective definition. If a strain is perceived, and

---

*There is a significant parallel between our analysis and the one presented in Neil Smelser's *Theory of Collective Behavior* (1962). Like Smelser, we seek to demonstrate how functionalism can be extended through the examination of noninstitutionalized conduct. Despite this shared intention, however, our theoretical strategy is somewhat different. Whereas Smelser sought to incorporate the analysis of collective behavior within the functionalist paradigm, we hope to show that functionalism can be enriched by opening itself to some of the insights generated by another sociological tradition.

an individual or group wants to act on it, proposed remedies require the cooperation of others. Institutional entrepreneurs must "persuade" others, then, that an important social problem exists that deserves immediate attention. It is upon these processes of definition and persuasion that interactionist accounts focus (Blumer 1971; Spector and Kitsuse 1977:73–96).

If strain is to precipitate collective action it must be transmuted into a "sense of injustice" (Turner 1969; 1981:18–19). The simple recognition of systemic problems or perceived threats to a group interest is rarely sufficient to generate sustained collective mobilization oriented to institutional change. Eisenstadt believes there must also exist a sense of cultural disruption or possible disruption. Interactionists like Turner and Killian (1972:259) allow us to put the matter more precisely: if differentiation is to occur, these conditions must be defined as unjust. For example, the development of the first mass political party in the United States is an important instance in American history of institutional differentiation. Yet it did not occur simply because the traditional mode of selecting presidential candidates—the Congressional Caucus—broke down. It depended, in large part, on mass mobilization supporting a new party structure, a movement that depended in turn on a deeply felt sense of injustice. This sense of injustice emerged from the widespread belief that the Adams/Clay/Jackson presidential election was decided by a "corrupt bargain" in which Clay exchanged his electoral votes for assurances that he would be appointed Adams' secretary of state. This "deal," it was widely believed, enabled Adams to secure the presidency even though he had considerably fewer popular votes than Jackson (Dangerfield 1952:331–45, 415–35).

Eisenstadt is aware that, even beyond these considerations, students of social change must consider additional historically specific and contingent conditions. Once again, interactionists provide more systematic explication. While enduring strain or perceived injury to group interests is a necessary condition for the emergence of a sense of injustice, it is not sufficient (Turner and Killian 1972:259–68). Other conditions must exist: the presence among those directly or indirectly affected by the strain of an established communication network, a viable group identity, and an embryonic subculture; an established (often, high-status) group that legitimates and supports the growing sense of injustice; an "independent" intellectual stratum that effectively articulates a sense of injustice; and the identification of an "oppressor" or "culprit" who appears to benefit from and is deemed responsible for existing conditions. To the degree that these conditions are combined with a recognized and enduring systemic strain, the more likely it is that a sense of injustice will be articulated and diffused, and the more likely that movements oriented to differentiation or dedifferentiation will arise.

For Eisenstadt, "institutional entrepreneurs" are both the cause and effect of such a successful response to strain. He portrays such movers and shakers, furthermore, as both interest-seeking and culture-creating elites. The interactionist usage of the concept of "ideological primary groups"* seems to sustain and elaborate this understanding, though, typically, it relates primarily to the normative rather than structural dimension. As Marx and Holzner (1977:426) put it, ideological primary groups "focus the energies of their members on the construction and legitimation (through consensual validation) of a shared symbolic apparatus that publicly interprets a problematic or incomprehensible reality and invents (or defines) it into existence." Given the affective support it generates and the high degree of control at its disposal, the ideological primary group is particularly effective when movements not only fuel a sense of injustice but also when they aspire to restructure members' identities vis-à-vis other collectivities. Such groups, for example, have been a conspicuous feature of the movement toward more universalist structures that has been generated by the contemporary women's movement (Cherniss 1972).

Finally, Eisenstadt insists that whatever the success of group formation, differentiation will meet opposition from the outside. Reactive groups may be insulated from the social positions in which strain is most intense; they may be beneficiaries of the existing social arrangements and fearful of alterations; or they may simply be convinced that certain deprivations or inconveniences are an inevitable part of life and that little good is done by unnecessarily stirring up discontent. Eisenstadt is aware of such reactive possibilities. What remains is to link this focus, as interactionism does, to the problem of collective definition. If reactive groups are successful in convincing others that serious deprivations do not exist, then the process of differentiation will be inhibited. The problem is conceptualized by interactionism as follows: the development of a widespread sense of injustice is typically opposed by other groups and collectivities

---

*Nahirny (1962) introduced the notion of ideological primary group into sociological discourse. Marx and Holzner broaden the scope of the concept considerably by examining it from an interactionist perspective.

that, for a variety of reasons, deny that the existing institutional order is a source of legitimate grievance (Hall and Hewitt 1970). These groups often attempt to defuse the growing sense of injustice by attributing the expansion of discontent to a small group of self-interest agitators or outsiders (Blumer 1971, Spector and Kitsuse 1977).

In sum, Eisenstadt's recognition of the subjective and contingent dimensions of strain suggests that our understanding of this concept and its relation to differentiation can be advanced by considering strain in conjunction with a sense of injustice and by viewing both as, in part, the products of communication, collective definition, and definitional conflict. Eisenstadt's revision of functionalist strain theory suggests a basis for linking "objective" strains and contradictions to processes of collective redefinition. Such redefinition processes, interactionists believe, are essential if "objective" conditions are to be recast as so inequitable and unjust that they legitimate the collective mobilization necessary for social differentiation and institutional change (Zurcher and Snow 1981:469–72).

Respecification and the Public. Eisenstadt's description of the symbolic activities of institutional entrepreneurs presents another area where the interactionist emphasis on collective redefinition can extend neofunctionalist thought. Eisenstadt argues, we recall, that the establishment of social institutions is the product of creative individuals or groups who not only procure and exchange resources, establish organizational frameworks to implement collective goals, and mobilize support but also exhibit a heightened sensitivity to order-giving, charismatic principles. Innovating groups are pressed by their own special needs for contact with the sacred and by the necessity, as well, of demonstrating to their potential supporters the vital connection between the new institution they are bringing to life and fundamental dimensions of the cultural order.

Yet, while Eisenstadt notes some of the situations in which a generalized sensitivity to the charismatic is heightened, he does not fully explore the contexts or mechanisms through which connections between the burgeoning institution and broader symbolic orientations are established. His suggestion that a coalition between institutional entrepreneurs and representatives of various collectivities "selects" the ground rules of social interaction and establishes the institutional specifications of those rules should be followed up, particularly his remark that this coalition acts "in special institutional-ritual, legal, and communicative frameworks" (Eisenstadt 1978:33; also, Eisenstadt and Curelaru 1976:364–67). A more detailed examination of such contexts and mechanisms is especially crucial because institutional entrepreneurs are often not charismatic individuals—Eisenstadt invokes here Shils' attenuated sense of the term. They are not, therefore, able to compel compliance by virtue of extraordinary personal qualities. Instead, they must either borrow the aura of charisma or generate new and more compelling specifications of accepted cultural codes. The interactionist treatment of publics indicates one context through which such "borrowing" and "respecification" occurs.

Differentiation theory explains how an independent public comes into being (Parsons 1971), but theories of collective behavior explain how the public actually works. Presupposing constitutional guarantees for freedom of association, expression, and publication of opinion, the public is conceptualized by interactionists as an emergent collectivity engaged in extended public discussions and debate (Turner and Killian 1972:179–98). Precisely through such discussion, one may reason, groups establish the connection between an emerging institution and basic cultural beliefs.*

The structure and process of publics then, is of vital concern for the neofunctionalist theory of change. Public discussion, interactionists observe, is conducted by two opposing factions, with each faction being assumed by others to represent the position of an established, usually larger group. Despite this perception, however, the debates and arguments within the public provide a basis for new strategic groups and coalitions (Blumer 1948; Shibutani 1966:37–40). Each public faction develops a rudimentary division of labor between an opinion leader and those who support the leader. These leaders may be drawn from persons of established prestige and reliability, but they may also be chosen because they personify certain values or are known to be closely associated with a charismatic person (Turner and Killian 1972:202). As a public debate endures, disparate issues become solidified into a single matrix, and the legitimate alternatives on an issue are successively narrowed (ibid.:192–93). In the course of this consolidation and simplification, public debate becomes "generalized" in the sense that Eisenstadt and other functionalists use this term to imply the heightened symbolic and charismatic importance of the debate. In this compacted and generalized phase, the mean-

---

*Jeffrey Prager's (1986) study of public dialogues in a macro sociological context articulates clear links between functionalist and interactionist treatments.

ings of abstract cultural codes and their relation to concrete practices are addressed. Established practices and institutional forms not previously considered in relation to fundamental structuring principles can now be scrutinized for possible inconsistency (Blumer 1978:27–30; Gusfield 1979); if they are delegitimated, institutional entrepreneurs can publicly argue that new structures are better able to preserve basic principles in turn. This, indeed, is functionalism's "value respecification" by another name, though it is a more detailed and systematic conceptualization.

One elaboration of the interactionist treatment of publics has identified three types of publics in which this connection between emerging structure and charismatic principle can be made (Colomy 1982:103–10). The connection is most explicit when the institution itself becomes the topic of public discussion. Opponents of the new institution deny that it faithfully represents the community's code, arguing, for example, that if it is allowed to persist, the community's sacred traditions will be subverted. Proponents, in contrast, attempt to describe how the burgeoning structure is designed to uphold these traditions, suggesting that without this innovation the very integrity of the society is at stake.

The second type of public context makes the object of discussion the entrepreneurial groups and individuals themselves, not the institution they seek to create. While the intent of those who initiate such discussions is to discredit and publicly embarrass the innovators, the attacks usually afford the entrepreneurs an opportunity to respond at a similarly generalized, "all or nothing" level. In these responses, entrepreneurial groups may associate themselves with contemporary or historical exemplars of a society's transcendent order. By so identifying themselves with a charismatic figure, they may contend that the institutions they propose are designed to preserve at all costs the traditions such charismatic figures struggled to attain.

Finally, the developing institutional framework can become linked to a still broader discussion about the fate and future of the entire community. In such a debate the new structure is treated as prototypical of a general movement away from established principles, a reactive position that engenders counterarguments that seek to demonstrate that the same structure actually is vital if cherished traditions are to be sustained.

All three types of publics, we might note, were deeply involved in the differentiation of the American mass party structures we mentioned earlier. On the reactive side, the new parties were condemned as cancers on the social order; the men instrumental in constructing the new organizational frameworks—particularly Van Buren and the leading members of the Albany Regency—were castigated as self-interested, untrustworthy, licentious, and greedy, and the emergence of party was treated as symptomatic of America's declension from the sacred legacy of the founding fathers. On the innovative side, party structures were championed because they performed essential functions for the political and social order; leading institutional entrepreneurs defended their actions by declaring their personal identification with such charismatic figures as Jefferson and Madison; and it was widely contended that new parties were essential to revitalize the sacred principles of the "revolutions" of 1776 and 1800 (Wallace 1969, 1973; Hofstader 1969).

This integration of neofunctionalist and interactionist understandings may be clarified further by returning, once again, to Eisenstadt: such communication processes can never be separated from the ideal and material interests of the factions involved. Because the innovative groups, as well as their reactive opponents, aspire to gain the support of other groups in the community, the manner in which they connect their arguments to cultural concerns is bound to have a "strategic" dimension. Arguments are often made with particular subcommunities in mind, and every attempt at cultural respecification is sensitive to the subcommunity's various interpretations of a society's cultural codes. The task of making a convincing connection between the proposed structure and a subcommunity's interpretations of a basic organizing principle stimulates entrepreneurial groups to modify their original conception of the structure. In order to make this proposed structure palatable to important constituencies, compromises are often introduced that, in effect, combine new elements with established institutional arrangements. More generally, if new ideas are to be combined with divergent but enduring interpretations, the "creativity" of institution builders is constrained. Ideas that cannot be linked to the community's fundamental codes are unlikely to generate sufficient support. The ability to make this connection is also, of course, partly dependent on the talents of the entrepreneurs themselves.

In summary, then, Eisenstadt argues that differentiation is partially the product of the "symbolic" activities of institutional entrepreneurs. If they are to successfully institutionalize new structures, entrepreneurial groups must link emerging organizational frameworks to new or established cultural codes. The interactionist treatment of the public provides a useful analytic tool for examining a key area where such entrepreneurs seek legitimation and where their efforts are contested. This discussion brings us to our final substantive discussion. Eisenstadt insists that conflict can be both cause and byproduct of differentiation. This proposition can be further developed by drawing upon the analysis of what interactionists call countermovements and general movements.

Conflict, Countermovements, and General Movements. In contrast to more benign versions of differentiation theory, Eisenstadt's analysis of differentiation emphasizes conflict and opposition. Most of his discussion is historical and focuses on the more autonomous polity. Our purpose here is to generalize this discussion and, simultaneously, to make it more analytically differentiated.

In modernizing societies, where public spheres are institutionalized and where peripheries impinge substantially on the center, social differentiation, as we noted above, usually involves social movements. Interactionists have consistently observed that social movements mobilized for change stimulate the opposition of vested interests, which organize into countermovements. Countermovements can impede the effectiveness of initial movements, prompt substantial modification of the initial movement's program, and/or generate intense polarization within a society (Mottl 1980; Turner and Killian 1972:317–21; Lo 1982). These varying outcomes, all of which inhibit differentiation, depend not only on the relative balance of movement and countermovement resources but also on such considerations as the intensity of the original strain that gave rise to the initial movement, the strategic skill of leaders, the level of relative general public support, and the response, if any, of social control agents.

Two aspects of this movement/countermovement dynamic have special theoretical interest. The first obtains when the relationship between the initial movement and countermovement assumes a competitive form. If the initial movement appears to have considerable support and resources, countermovements that initially arise to defend the existing institutional and normative order may often adopt elements from the program and goals of the original movement. In this way, as Turner and Killian (1972:318) point out, a countermovement attempts to use for its own ends some of the generalized discontent and also to force the opposed movement to focus on the most extreme portions of its original program (also see Lo 1982:119). Yet by coopting elements of the initial movement's program and advocating changes in the normative order that were originally opposed, the countermovement actually promotes the institutionalization of new, more differentiated structures. Competitive countermovements, then, are often transformed into agents of social change.

Once again, early American political development provides a dramatic example of this phenomenon. The first attempts to construct differentiated mass party organizations, which made the civil service less ascriptive and created a more inclusive polity, were undertaken by Democratic leaders, especially by Jackson and Van Buren. The incipient Whig leadership vigorously opposed these organizational and normative changes, particularly the extension of egalitarian standards to political leadership, and it sought to mobilize a large constituency in defense of traditional, deferential patterns. This adherence to conventional patterns of authority involved the repudiation of populist egalitarianism and for this reason was largely responsible for the Whigs' inability to compete effectively against the Democrats for political office. By 1840, important elements of the Whig leadership decided not merely to adopt but to improve the innovations introduced by the Democrats; the presidential campaign of that year marked the first genuine institutionalization of mass political parties and the ascendence of the egalitarian style as the unquestioned mode of political leadership (Marshall 1967, Hofstader 1969, Wallace 1969).

At the same time, however, the acquiescence of countermovements often has a "strategic" character; in this case, the institutionalization of new levels of organizational and normative differentiation masks continued opposition to new forms. This is especially true if acquiescence follows upon a "split" in the ranks of the countermovement, with one faction arguing for accommodation and a pragmatic acceptance of "new realities," another for shunning the desertion of principle and tradition. In any case, opposition to new forms of differentiation may persist even after new institutions appear to have become firmly entrenched. That opposition may resurface and assume significance in later episodes of differentiation or dedifferentiation, as Eisenstadt notes, for example, in his discussion of counterrevolutionary groups in *Revolution and the Transformation of Societies* (1978:41–42). In the American case, the civil service reform movement emerged in part as an attack on the mass party and the "corruption" it promoted. This movement resulted in the further differentiation of administrative structures, yet it was initiated and led by descendents of the "Conscience Whigs," men who had always eschewed notions of party loyalty and discipline because of their general antagonism to the differentiation of the mass party system itself (Hofstader 1962:172–96; Blodgett 1966; Josephson 1938:158–70, 345–65, 374–84).

Another aspect of the movement-countermovement dynamic that deserves serious consideration stems from Blumer's (1951 [1939]:199–202) distinction between general and specific movements. General movements refer to broad cultural drift, to gradual but significant changes in value orientations that supply a common formula for many varied, goal-oriented movements. A specific movement, by contrast, posseses organizational structure, is oriented toward a program, and provides a sense of identity for its members. Often goals and programs of distinct specific movements are derived from the broader cultural orientations of the same general movement. Indeed, insofar as similar cultural themes pervade specific movements, their adherents and the public at large often recognize them as constituent elements of a "cultural gestalt," as sharing a similar orientation and as promoting compatible goals.

This interactionist conceptualization promises to extend and elaborate certain key elements of differentiation theory. In a period of intense historical change, opposing general movements often emerge. These general movements give rise to an array of specific movements and countermovements, each "set" battling for, and against, differentiation in an array of institutional spheres. Students of Jacksonian America, for example, have discovered that behind the discrete conflicts over differentiation in the political, educational, religious, economic, and stratification spheres lay two opposing sets of internally coherent cultural themes. One set stressed modernization (especially in the economic and cultural spheres), self-control, qualitative improvement, societal hierarchy, cultural uniformity, achievement, and social reform; the other emphasized personal liberty and expressiveness, quantitative expansion, equality, cultural heterogeneity, and individual reform (Walters 1978, Howe 1979).

The compatible cultural orientations of adherents to the same general movement, and the sense that each confronts a similar opponent, often constitute grounds for the exchange of material resources and support between different specific movements (Lo 1982:126–29). Further, the international, societal, and local responses to a particular movement are at least partially dependent on the perceived relationship between this movement and more general social shifts. In terms of both resources and social control, therefore, the relationship between general and specific movements affects the forces mobilized for and against differentiation.

The distinction between specific and general movements underscores the need for a conception of culture capable of comprehending contradiction and opposition in turn. Eisenstadt's work on cultural codes is promising in this respect, for he contends that the very construction and institutionalization of the ground rules of social interaction create the possibility for tensions and contradictions leading to change (1978:40), and he also relates these conflicts closely to group and institutional life. Eisenstadt's discussion of the uneasy fit between established ground rules and the conflict-generating features of the social division of labor, for example, identifies some of the central themes and the cultural-institutional axes around which general movements arise. His analysis provides a broad framework within which more fruitful examinations of general movements and the specific struggles they inspire can proceed.

V

We began our discussion by noting Eisenstadt's "invisible" but powerful revision of Parsons' theory. We followed that detailed analysis by demonstrating how certain strands of symbolic interactionism can contribute to a crucial elaboration of some of Eisenstadt's central themes. It seems fitting to close our analysis with a brief comment on the opening Eisenstadt's neofunctionalism presents for the development of symbolic interactionism in turn. Interactionists working at many different analytic levels are now striving for a rapprochement with macrosociology (e.g., Lewis and Smith 1980, Stryker 1980, Handel 1979, Maines 1977, Strauss 1978). These efforts suffer from two limitations. First, by elaborating notions of process, bargaining, and negotiation, some interactionists aspire to build a macrosociology entirely from within the interactionist tradition. Yet by transforming conventional notions of structure and constraint beyond recognition, these efforts fail to reconcile interactionism with the vital corpus of macrosociology (see the critique by Meltzer et al. 1975:109–10). Other writers in this tradition have, quite rightly in our view, acknowledged interactionism's failure to generate a viable corpus of macrosociological concepts. Yet their efforts to adopt ideas about structure from other sociological traditions have often employed concepts primarily suited to the analysis of stability and stasis. The efforts to link such concepts with interactionism, which traditionally has stressed process, adaptation, and change, has a forced and unconvincing quality. (Similar objections, e.g., are made in the recent reviews of Stryker [1980] by Warshay [1982], Weinstein [1982], and Overington and Maugham [1982]; see also Turner's [1982] critical assessment of Handel's attempt to unite interactionism with structural sociology.)

We share the conviction that interactionism has not generated a viable macrosociology. It appears to us, however, that the most congenial macrosociological traditions for interactionists are those that focus on change and that are open to notions of process, temporal development, and the capacity of individuals and groups to define and redefine their situation. We believe that Eisenstadt's corpus provides just such a macrosociological model, and we have tried to demonstrate the possibilities for linkage. Eisenstadt's implicit revisions of Parsons, we have suggested, amount to a call for a major redirection of functionalist theory. Eisenstadt's critiques of Parsons must be read as, simultaneously, openings to other traditions. By aggressively searching out complementary aspects of what are usually considered antifunctionalist traditions, important steps toward a new and fully multidimensional theory can be made.

REFERENCES

Alexander, Jeffrey C. 1977. "Review Essay of Eisenstadt and M. Curelaru. The Forms of Sociology." Contemporary Sociology. 6(6):658–61.
—— 1979. "Paradigm Revision and 'Parsonianism.'" Canadian Journal of Sociology 4:343–57.
—— 1982. The Antinomies of Classical Thought: Marx and Durkheim. Vol. 2 of Alexander, Theoretical Logic in Sociology. Berkeley and Los Angeles: University of California Press.
—— 1983. The Modern Reconstruction of Classical Thought: Talcott Parsons. Vol. 4 of Alexander, Theoretical Logic in Sociology.
—— 1987. Twenty Lectures: Sociological Theory Since World War Two. New York: Columbia University Press.
Blodgett, Geoffrey. 1966. The Gentle Reformers. Cambridge, Mass.: Harvard University Press.
Blumer, Herbert. 1948. "Public Opinion and Public Opinion Polling." American Sociological Review 13:542–54.
—— 1951. "Collective Behavior." In A. M. Lee, ed., Principles of Sociology,

pp. 165–222. New York: Barnes and Noble. Blumer's essay was originally published in 1939.

—— 1971. "Social Problems as Collective Behavior." *Social Problems* 18:298–306.

—— 1978. "Social Unrest and Collective Protest." *Studies in Symbolic Interaction* 1:1–54.

Cherniss, Cary. 1972. "Personality and Ideology: A Personological Study of Women's Liberation." *Psychiatry* 35:109–25.

Colomy, Paul. 1982. *Stunted Differentiation: A Sociological Examination of Virginia's Political Elite, 1720 to 1850.* Unpublished Ph.D. dissertation, UCLA.

Dangerfield, George. 1952. *The Era of Good Feelings.* New York: Harcourt, Brace, Jovanovich.

Edwards, Lyford P. 1927. *The Natural History of Revolution.* Chicago: University of Chicago Press.

Eisenstadt, S. N. 1956 (1971). *From Generation to Generation.* New York: Free Press.

—— 1963 (1969). *The Political System of Empires.* New York: Free Press.

—— 1964a. "Institutionalization and Social Change." *American Sociological Review* 29:235–47.

—— 1964b. "Social Change, Differentiation, and Evolution." *American Sociological Review* 29:375–86.

—— 1965. *Essays on Comparative Institutions.* New York: Wiley.

—— 1966. *Modernization: Protest and Change.* Englewood Cliffs, N.J.: Prentice-Hall.

—— 1968. "Charisma and Institution Building: Max Weber and Modern Sociology." In Eisenstadt, ed., *Max Weber on Charisma and Institution Building,* pp. ix–lvi. Chicago: University of Chicago Press.

—— 1971a. *Social Differentiation and Stratification.* Glenview, Ill.: Scott, Foresman.

—— 1971b. "Societal Goals, Systemic Needs, Social Interaction, and Individual Behavior: Some Tentative Explorations." In Herman Turk and Richard L. Simpson, eds., *Institutions and Social Exchange,* pp. 36–55. Indianapolis: Bobbs-Merrill.

—— 1973. *Tradition, Change and Modernity.* New York: Wiley.

—— 1978. *Revolution and the Transformation of Societies.* New York: Free Press.

Eisenstadt, S. N. and M. Curelaru. 1976. *The Forms of Sociology: Paradigms and Crises.* New York: Wiley.

Gusfield, Joseph. 1979. "The Modernity of Social Movements: Public Roles and Private Parts." In Amos H. Hawley, ed., *Societal Growth,* pp. 290–307. New York: Free Press.

Hall, Peter M. and John P. Hewitt. 1970. "The Quasi-Theory of Communication and the Management of Dissent." *Social Problems* 18:17–27.

Handel, Warren. 1979. "Normative Expectations and the Emergence of Meaning as Solutions to Problems: Convergence of Structural and Interactionist Views." *American Journal of Sociology* 84:855–81.

Hofstader, Richard. 1962. *Anti-Intellectualism in American Life.* New York: Vintage.

—— 1969. *The Idea of a Party System.* Berkeley: University of California Press.

Hopper, Rex D. 1950. "The Revolutionary Process: A Frame of Reference for the Study of Social Movements." *Social Forces* 28:270–79.

Howe, Daniel W. 1979. *The Political Culture of the American Whigs.* Chicago: University of Chicago Press.

Jackson, Maurice, Eleanora Peterson, James Bull, Sverre Monsen, and Patricia Richmond. 1960. "The Failure of an Incipient Social Movement." *Pacific Sociological Review* 3:35–40.

Josephson, Matthew. 1938. *The Politicos.* New York: Harcourt, Brace, and World.

Lewis, J. David and Richard L. Smith. 1980. *American Sociology and Pragmatism.* Chicago: University of Chicago Press.

Lo, Clarence Y. H. 1982. "Countermovements and Conservative Movements in the Contemporary United States." *Annual Review of Sociology* 8:107–34.

Maines, Davis. 1977. "Social Organization and Social Structure in Symbolic Interactionist Thought." *Annual Review of Sociology* 3:235–60.

Marshall, Lynn. 1967. "The Strange Stillbirth of the Whig Party." *American Historical Review* 72:445–68.

Marx, John and Burkart Holzner. 1977. "The Social Construction of Strain and Ideological Models of Grievance in Contemporary Movements." *Pacific Sociological Review* 20:411–38.

Meltzer, Bernard, John Petras, and Larry Reynolds. 1975. *Symbolic Interaction: Genesis, Varieties, and Criticism.* London: Routledge and Kegan Paul.

Mottl, Tahi. 1980. "The Analysis of Countermovements." *Social Problems* 27:620–35.

Nahirny, Vladimir C. 1962. "Some Observations on Ideological Primary Groups." *American Journal of Sociology* 67:397–405.

Overington, Michael and Iain Maugham. 1982. "Dr. Stryker's Fabulous Booke Where a Beaste With One Wynge Taketh a Predictable Course." *Symbolic Interaction* 5:157–65.

Parsons, Talcott. 1951. *The Social System.* New York: Free Press.

—— 1971. *The System of Modern Societies.* Englewood Cliffs, N.J.: Prentice-Hall.

Prager, Jeffrey. 1986. *Building Democracy in Ireland: Political Order and Cultural Integration in a Newly Independent Nation.* New York: Cambridge University Press.

Shibutani, T. 1966. *Improvised News: A Sociological Study of Rumor.* Indianapolis: Bobbs-Merrill.

Smelser, Neil J. 1962. *Theory of Collective Behavior.* New York: Free Press.

—— 1974. "Growth, Structural Change, and Conflict in California Public Higher Education, 1950–1970." In Smelser and Gabriel Almond, eds. *Public Higher Education in California,* pp. 9–142. Berkeley and Los Angeles: University of California Press.

—— 1962. *Theory of Collective Behavior.* New York: Free Press.

Spector, Malcolm and John I. Kitsuse. 1977. *Constructing Social Problems.* Menlo Park, Calif.: Cummings.

Strauss, Anselm. 1978. *Negotiations: Varieties, Contexts, Processes and Social Order.* San Francisco: Jossey-Bass.

Stryker, Sheldon. 1980. *Symbolic Interactionism: A Social Structural Version.* Menlo Park, Calif.: Cummings.

Turner, Ralph. 1964. "Collective Behavior and Conflict." *Sociological Quarterly* 5:122–32.

—— 1969. "The Theme of Contemporary Social Movements." *British Journal of Sociology* 20:390–405.

—— 1981. "Collective Behavior and Resource Mobilization as Approaches to Social Movements: Issues and Continuities." *Research in Social Movements* 4:1–24.

—— 1982. "Unanswered Questions in the Convergence Between Structuralist and Interactionist Role Theories." Paper presented at the International Sociological Association Convention, Mexico City.

Turner, Ralph and Lewis Killian. 1972. *Collective Behavior.* Englewood Cliffs, N.J.: Prentice-Hall.

Wallace, Michael. 1969. "Changing Concepts of Party in the United States: New York 1815–1828." *American Historical Review* 74:453–91.

—— 1973. *Ideologies of Party in the Antebellum Republic.* Unpublished Ph.D. dissertation, Columbia University.

Walters, Ronald. 1978. *American Reformers. 1815–1860.* New York: Hill and Wang.

Warshay, Leon. 1982. "A Tough-Minded Interactionism." *Symbolic Interaction* 5:141–47.

Weinstein, Deena. 1982. "Versions of Symbolic Interaction." *Symbolic Interaction* 5:149–56.

Wilson, John. 1973. *Introduction to Social Movements.* New York: Basic Books.

Zurcher, Louis A. and David A. Snow. 1981. "Collective Behavior: Social Movements." In Morris Rosenberg and Ralph Turner, eds., *Social Psychology,* pp. 447–82. New York: Basic Books.

EIGHT

The "Individualist Dilemma" in Phenomenology and Interactionism

In this essay I delineate the positive accomplishments of the schools of phenomenology and symbolic interactionism while, at the same time, exposing the limitations that have prevented either from becoming a fully satisfactory theoretical tradition of contemporary social thought. I demonstrate that while each can enrich the collectivist understanding of social order developed by the classical tradition of sociology, neither can replace it. Yet the classical approach to collective, "social" order can be powerfully enhanced by incorporating the "individual moment" of phenomenology and interactionism, even if the collectivist tradition cannot completely defer to it.

The distinctiveness of what follows rests with the general framework of analysis that I bring to bear on the topics at hand. Although the nature of this framework should become increasingly clear in the course of my analysis, I present its essentials at the outset.*

Introduction: Some Analytical Considerations

It is possible to make theoretical explorations of social thought at very different levels of analysis. I could, for example, explain the problems of phenomenological analysis by examining specific empirical studies con-

---

*This general framework is much more elaborately discussed in *Positivism, Presuppositions, and Current Controversies* (Berkeley and Los Angeles, 1982a), the first volume of my *Theoretical Logic in Sociology,* though in the present context I am specifying it in relation to a problem not directly considered in that work.

I thank Lewis Coser, David Lewis, Victor Lidz, Melvin Pollner, and Emanuel Schegloff for their instructive readings of this essay, and Harold Garfinkel for his instructive conversation.

ducted from the phenomenological point of view, examining the particular *propositions* advanced about the detailed structure of empirical "reality." Or, to consider another level, I could focus on the distinctively *methodological* issues involved in producing such propositions. I could also look at the *models* employed, or I could look at the *normative-ideological assumptions* phenomenologists make, if, in fact, they make them in a consistent way. Although each of these different levels of analysis will reveal significant aspects of theory and of the relative power of different theories, I focus here on a level of analysis more general and, I believe, more generally ramifying than any of these, namely, the level of analysis I call the "presuppositional."

The presuppositions of any social theory are the positions a theory takes about the nature of human action and the manner in which plural actions are interrelated. The problem of action refers basically to epistemological questions: to problems of idealism and materialism, which are usually formulated sociologically in terms of the relative "rationality" of the prototypical actor in any theoretical system. The problem of order, on the other hand, refers to the problem of how consistent patterns of such rational or nonrational actions are created: are patterns of action the result of continuous negotiation between relatively separated individuals or is this patterning—at least in part—the result of the imposition (either consensually or coercively) on individuals of a sui generis, prior structure or pattern?

While the options for "the problem of action" are rational versus nonrational (not irrational), the theoretical options for addressing the order problem are individual versus collective. It is possible to develop a synthetic approach to action, which would attempt to integrate materialist and idealist concerns without adopting either in an exclusive way. *It is not possible, however, to adopt a synthetic approach to the order question if this implies that the alternative approaches be regarded as theoretically symmetrical.* To do so would be to adopt a theoretical agnosticism precisely the opposite of the truly synthetic position required. Social theorists must, and do, choose either collective or individualist positions, though within the context of either choice, theorists may be more or less receptive to the problematics of the counterposition. Thus, a collectivist theorist may be concerned to incorporate into a conceptualization the (relatively small) element of negotiation that goes into the creation of any specific historical construction of a particular social order, for only in this way, it might be argued, can the processes of creativity and change that characterize any empirical order be clearly analyzed.

As these comments indicate, I believe strongly that a successful social theory must be synthetic vis-à-vis the problem of action and collectivistic vis-à-vis the problem of order.* At the same time, I believe that collectivist theories can and must incorporate some of the empirical insights of more individualistic theories if they are to succeed as empirical descriptions of the actual historical world. These statements raise two final general considerations that must be explicated before more detailed analysis can proceed: the problem of the "individualist dilemma" and the problem of "levels of empirical analysis" versus "kinds of presuppositional commitments."

One advantage that accrues from focusing on the most general presuppositional level of social theory is that problems of the most ramifying and complex empirical character can be discussed in the general and abstract terms of theoretical logic. One such problem will be vital for the discussion that follows. I call it the "individualist dilemma," and its logical structure follows from the nature of the presuppositional issues I have described above. To maintain an approach to order that is individualistic in a clear, consistent, and honest way, a theorist must introduce into a construction a level of openness to contingency that, in the final analysis, makes the understanding of order approximate randomness and complete unpredictability. Most theorists of society, of course, unless they are "closet psychologists" or absolute nominalists, will simply not be satisfied with such randomness, even if they consciously feel they should live with it and, indeed, promote it. Because of this dissatisfaction, individualist theorists will move toward the more collective moment by embracing, in one way or another, some aspect of supraindividual pressure or sustenance.

The individualist dilemma is created because this "theorist with second thoughts" will not give up on formal claims to a thoroughgoing individualism; for this reason, the "collectivist moment" introduced must be camouflaged by residual categories. Because it cannot be part of the systematic and forthright argument of the theory itself, the collectivist ref-

*The collectivist position on order must be regarded as the major, and least disputed, contribution of the classical tradition initiated by Marx, Weber, Durkheim, and Simmel and carried forward by numerous "schools" and followers today, including, perhaps most conspicuously, the functionalists.

erence will be indeterminate and vague. This indeterminacy and vagueness make it theoretically and empirically frustrating and incomplete. To resolve this problem, obviously, the dilemma itself (i.e., the choice between randomness or residual indeterminacy) must be transcended; this can come about, however, only if the formal adherence to individualism is abandoned. Only with the movement toward an explicitly collectivist theory can the sui generis autonomy of social order be clearly stated rather than camouflaged in an ambiguous way. Only in this way, moreover, can the contingent and individualistic elements of order be inserted into a collectivist theory as significant insights into specific levels of empirical analysis and as nothing more.

This raises the second general issue I would like to clarify. I regard as fundamental the distinction between empirical-level-of-analysis and pre-suppositional-approach-to-order. Stated in less oblique terms, I insist that it is one thing to focus on the individual as the point of one's empirical analysis and quite another to adopt an "individualistic" position in terms of one's presuppositions about the sources of patterned action in general. A collectivist theorist may, indeed, focus empirically on the level of individual interaction or even at the level of the personality itself. Likewise, an individualistic theorist may focus, not on the isolated individual, but on a collectivity or even a nation-state. The point is the more general *analytical* assumptions made about such empirical individual interaction or collective processes, e.g., how relatively important are a priori socialized attitudes as compared with historically specific, completely contingent individual signals and responses?

One cannot argue, then, that symbolic interactionists or phenomenological theories are preferable because they focus empirically on individual interaction, for this could quite plausibly be—and indeed, has often been—the province of collectivist theories as well. What I argue in this essay is that, while the general framework for social theory can be derived only from a collectivist perspective, the empirical analysis of individual interaction should incorporate wherever possible the empirical insight of individualistic theories into the concrete operations, structures, and processes of the empirical interactions of concrete individuals. I believe these insights are substantial even if, in more general theoretical terms, they are incapable of supplying the presuppositions of theoretical analysis itself.

"Phenomenology" Strictly and
Traditionally Perceived

In terms of Hegel's debate with Kant, in terms, that is, of strictly philosophical usage, phenomenology might be applied to any theory that accepts the independent structuring power of consciousness while denying
the dualism Kant posited between phenomenal and noumenal worlds.
Insofar as a theory claims that objects (the noumenal in Kant's terms) are
constituted purely by consciousness (the phenomenal realm of subjectivity), it is phenomenological. In terms of its approach to action, then,
phenomenology is radically and thoroughly idealist. Any theory that
would hope to go beyond the confines of an idealist, or materialist, theory
would have to incorporate and transcend Kant's dualism rather than reject
it out of hand.

The question that remains is the approach that such phenomenology
strictly considered takes to the problem of order. Hegel's theory must be
considered the prototype of a collectivist phenomenology, though in its
specific form it certainly does not exhaust all possible shapes of the genre.
Hegel focused on the structure, continuity, and development of supraindividual *Geistes*—"spirits" or "cultures." His method was descriptive and
reductionist, and it is not surprising that in the supple hands of Dilthey
his phenomenology of the spirit could become the basis for a science of
the spirit, or *Geisteswissenschaft*. Dilthey called this science "hermeneutics," and both as method and as theory this commitment to the structuring power of ideational patterns has in the ensuing years become a
central current of collectivist-idealist thought. We can see the Dilthey-
Hegel tradition of phenomenological hermeneutics in significant aspects
of Weber's work; in the superb if little noticed writings of Weber's contemporary, Jellinek; in much of Parsons' sociology; and in such contemporary "post-" or "neo-Parsonians" as Clifford Geertz and Robert Bellah.
For most of these collective phenomenologists, the individual actor is
conceived as a representation of the broad cultural types. Through a
process of internalization, the individual becomes identified with the collectivity, and through externalization the collective becomes identified
with the individual. As Hegel (1977 [1807]:110) describes "the experience
of what spirit is" in the chapter on Lordship and Bondage in his *Phenomenology of Spirit*: it is "the unity of itself in its otherness . . . the unity

of different self consciousness which, in their opposition, enjoy perfect freedom and independence: 'I' that is 'We' and 'We' that is 'I'."*

It is possible, on the other hand, to adopt a more individualistic approach to the phenomenal realm, and it is to this approach that the term *phenomenology* has traditionally been applied in social theory. Such theory begins, of course, with Husserl. Husserl accepted the structured, patterned quality of reality, but he insisted that the source of such structure must be found in the constituting processes of the human mind itself. After Husserl, the legacy of phenomenology as traditionally understood moved in two quite different directions, each movement addressing itself to the individualist dilemma. Moving toward rapprochement with more collectivist theory, Merleau-Ponty, Scheler, and Schutz, among others, formulated the notion of tradition-bound "life worlds." In so doing, they tried, either directly or indirectly, to reconcile phenomenological hermeneutics with the more traditionally understood phenomenology in its individualist sense.

At the same time, however, another school of Husserl followers moved toward the dramatically less structurally sensitive, more purely individualistic phenomenology of existentialism. Alongside his notion of *"lebenswelt,"* which inspired movement in a collectivist direction, Heidegger emphasized historicity and immediate experience (existence) in opposition to Husserl's insistence on structure and essence. Sartre completed this "purification" of Husserl by insisting that it is out of the individual experience of nothingness that all consciousness arises. Existential phenomenology takes the dynamism of Hegel's dialectical emphasis on movement and change and separates it from any consideration of overarching "spirit." The result is an individualistic theory par excellence—the "I" without a "we," self-consciousness without any society. Once existence is accepted as the ultimate arbiter of society and structure, the relation between individual and structure becomes in principle irresolvable; the va-

---

*It is precisely this "strict" tradition of phenomenological analysis that, we will see later in this chapter, provides the justification for allowing so much of sociology the designation "phenomenological." This is the philosophical rationale for Tiryakian's (1965, 1970, 1978) position over the years, one that has drawn much criticism from those who would defend the individualism of a more "traditional" phenomenological position but that, nonetheless, is absolutely correct in terms of the synthesis of "phenomenology" and "sociology" that must be carried out.

garies, inconsistencies, and dead ends of the argument between existentialism and structuralism amply attest to this rupture.*

This dead end can be avoided only by combining a sensitivity to the individual operations that constitute ongoing "existence" with an appreciation for the structuring qualities of mind: both moments must be inserted moreover, into the theory of more inclusive life-worlds and traditions toward which some of Husserl's students haltingly moved and which has been articulated independently by the collectivist tradition of hermeneutics of Hegel and Dilthey. For several years this seemed, in fact, precisely the promise of the American school of phenomenological sociology called "ethnomethodology," but, though the movement has yielded brilliant empirical insights, this more general theoretical promise was never fulfilled.

I now look more closely at the movement from Husserl through Schutz and his followers. In the vicissitudes of this theoretical development, I believe, one can discover precisely what needs to be done if theoretical reintegration and synthesis is to be attained, even if such synthesis would be anathema to some of phenomenology's recent practitioners.

---

*The debate between Sartre and Levi-Strauss shows how the traditions of phenomenology traditionally and strictly perceived have been so taken to their extremes that their leading proponents believe they have nothing in common at all. In *Being and Nothingness* (1966:46) Sartre individualized the phenomenological movement traditionally understood: "My freedom is the unique foundation of values. . . . As a being *by* whom values exist, I am unjustifiable. My freedom . . . is itself without foundation." Freedom, therefore, "is characterized by a constantly renewed obligation to remake the Self which designates free being." In reacting against such thought, Levi-Strauss in *The Savage Mind* collectivized the idealist tradition so far that he suggested that cultural themes proceeded without being internalized by individuals and, in fact, had nothing to do with "meaning" per se.

Linguistics . . . presents us with a dialectical and totalizing entity but one outside (or beneath) consciousness and will. Language is human reason which has its reasons and of which man knows nothing" (1966:252).

Or as he insists (1970:64) at another point, "in my perspective meaning is never the primary phenomenon. . . . Behind all meaning there is a non-meaning." Whereas Sartre (1971:111) in his later years tried to hedge his bets, he would not give up his individualism; the result was a frustrating series of residual categories and theoretical indeterminacy, e.g., "What is essential is not that man is made, but that he makes that which made him."

Husserl's Individualistic
Phenomenology

Though I insist that Husserl illuminated individual processes from within an individualistic presuppositional framework, it is important to recognize from the outset that Husserl was, indeed, very aware of the existence of structure and patterning in the real world: he simply argued that phenomenology correctly understands that this order proceeds from consciousness, and from consciousness understood in a decisively individualistic way. This order must come from, and somehow be completely produced by, the individual: "The Objective world, the world that exists for me, that always has and always will exist for me, the only world that ever can exist for me—this world, with all its Objects . . . derives its whole sense and its existential status . . . from me myself" (1977 [1931]:26).

To understand the role that individual consciousness plays, one must make the "phenomenological reduction"—one must place into radical doubt the realness of the world as such: "The world is for us something that only *claims* being" (p. 18, italics added). The "sense of reality" or "sense of structure" comes only from the individual person: "It is given to the consciousness *perceptually* as it itself" by me (p. 19, italics added). To understand the process of perception by which a sense of reality is constructed—in another phenomenological vocabulary, the process of reification that objectifies the otherwise random stream of subjective perceptions—involves stepping outside of the "natural" or "naive" attitude.

Daily practical living is naive. It is immersion in the already-given world, whether it be experiencing, or thinking, or valuing. Meanwhile, all those productive intentional functions of experiencing, because of which physical things are simply there, go on anonymously. The experiencer knows nothing about them, and likewise nothing about his productive thinking. The numbers, the predicative complexes of affairs, the goods, the ends, the works, present themselves because of the hidden performance; they are built up, member by member; they alone are regarded. . . . The intentional performances from which everything ultimately originates remain unexplained (pp. 152–53).

Husserl focuses, in other words, on those productive intentional functions that go on anonymously as hidden performances, and as a result of which, in his view, there is an external world. He calls this the realm of "transcendental subjectivity," for it focuses on the objectivity-creating functions of the mind that exist apart from the particular nature of any historically specific or context-dependent reality. Only by bracketing such particular details, indeed, can the realness of existence that stems from the essential intentional structures of mind be discovered. This definition of the phenomenological reduction is the source of Husserl's distinctive program and of his enormous empirical contribution; it is, at the same time, the source of his—and his students' and followers'—greatest theoretical weakness.

What Husserl accomplished was to outline some of the essential "constitutive techniques" of consciousness. Through intentional analysis, he discovers "a mode of combination exclusively peculiar to consciousness" (p. 39) by which the streams of atomized experience are transformed into an apparently transcendental and authentic reality. Husserl suggests that these are, in the first instance, techniques by which consciousness arranges the experience of ongoing space and time. Rather than "incoherent sequencing," for example, the mind assumes that spatial connections exist between elements of perceived reality even when these connections cannot, in fact, actually be seen. Consciousness establishes a "horizon of reference" such that one always connects things one sees to things one has not yet perceived but anticipates that one will see or must see if shapes and forms are to be completed. Such spatial abilities rely on temporal capacities as well. Only because of memory can temporal sequences be connected to each other instead of seeming like random occurrences. The capacity for connecting past, present, and future provides that "new evidences are restituting of the first evidences" (p. 60), i.e., that the mind constitutes a whole from successive sequences that seem merely to be parts. More generally, this constitutive technique means that "the object is always met expectantly as having a sense yet to be actualized; in every moment of consciousness it is an 'index' of prior expectations" (p. 46).

To allow newly encountered objects to maintain this status as index, specific techniques are required. There is the constant use of analogizing: "Each everyday experience involves an analogizing transfer of an originally instituted objective sense to a new case, with its anticipative apprehension of the object as having a similar sense. . . . At the same time that sense-component in further experience which proves to be actually new may function in turn as institutive and found a pregiveness that has a richer sense" (p. 111). There is, further, constant association and "pairing" of things with other things, people with other people, and each with the other.

The suggestiveness of such insights into the order-creating capacities and order-creating activities of the mind should be obvious for all who would wish to understand the sociological structure of the world around us. These contributions will be examined further when Husserl's contemporary followers are discussed below. At this point, however, some of the limitations of this position must be discussed.

First, of course, there is the problem of idealism itself. Husserl does not shirk from the idealist label: "I . . . have objects solely as the intentional correlates of modes of consciousness of them," he asserts (p. 37), and he describes his method as "transcendental idealism." Even though purposefully one-sided, however, this method is one-sided nonetheless, for although objects may, in fact, always be mediated by consciousness, they are not by any means always created by it; any theory that looks only at such subjective mediation will leave unexplored structures of power and cultural constraint through which some aspects of this object became constituted before its conscious mediation.

But even within the framework of idealism, there is the problem of Husserl's choice of an individualistic versus a more collectivist mode of proceeding. Husserl looks into the structure-producing capabilities of the individual mind rather than into the typical structures and processes of culture or collective world-view. Whereas Hegel and Dilthey developed the latter kind of idealism, Husserl proceeds in an individualistic mode that has some of the intellectual weaknesses of traditional religious thought. Indeed, in one of his last major works, Husserl approvingly quotes Augustine: "Do not go out; go back into yourself. Truth dwells in the inner man" (p. 91).

Husserl was not completely unaware of such shortcomings. Toward the end of his life, in published and unpublished (e.g., Husserl 1965) work, he indicated a desire to combine his insights with an account of the sui generis social element. Borrowing from some aspects of Heidegger, he suggests that the intentional construction of meaning results in, and is made from within, *lebenswelten* or "life-worlds"—cognitive styles, symbolic patterns, communities that are given. It is important to see, however, that, while achieving this illumination about the limitations of his work as a social theory, Husserl did not succeed in reconceptualizing the presuppositions of his theory as such. He was so consistent a thinker, indeed, that, for the most part, he succeeded in introducing *"lebenswelt"* into his theory without even making it into a residual category. This external, collective world, he insists, is constituted merely by the extension of the techniques individuals use to construct their individual worlds—through analogy, pairing, and other techniques that make things similar to the experience of one's past. One creates, in this way, the understanding of a "normal" world of others who are like oneself (pp. 99, 119, 125).

But this is still a mode of consciousness, and it still starts with oneself. What Husserl has concluded is simply that "not all my own modes of consciousness are modes of my *self*-consciousness" (p. 105). The "others" who are the objects of such associational techniques are still completely unexplained. Husserl can say only, "let us assume that another man enters our perceptual picture" (p. 110). Although he acknowledged, after reading the work of the Durkheimian-manqué Levy-Bruhl, that cultural analysts—not simply phenomenologists—could also illuminate a reality beneath the "natural attitude," he still insists that understanding the structure of the *lebenswelt* (the task of cultural analysts like Levy-Bruhl and Durkheim, as well as of the hermeneuticists like Dilthey and Hegel) is only "preparatory" to showing how *lebenswelt* itself is the result of transcendental consciousness and abstract intentionality (see the unpublished statement cited in Merleau-Ponty 1978 [1960]:154). In such moments, it seems even Husserl himself succumbed to the temptation of transforming the collectivist moment from a logical part of his theoretical individualism into an unexplained residual category.

Husserl's Collectivist Revisers

Some of Husserl's most important students and followers transformed these later references of his work from residual categories into theories about the relation between intentionality and the impact of supraindividual collective order. Merleau-Ponty, for example, writes about Husserl's "dilemma," which concerns, in fact, precisely whether the *lebenswelt* will remain a residual category or a source of independent determination vis-à-vis the objects produced by individual consciousness. Intentionality, Merleau-Ponty suggests (1978 [1960]:153), operates only in reference to the culturally given: "It is not the mere sum of expressions taken in isolation." Another significant revisionist, Alfred Schutz, argued that "our everyday world is, from the outset, an intersubjective world of culture" (1978 [1940]:134-35). Schutz develops what he calls a mundane rather than transcendental phenomenology: he inserts transcendental intentional activity into the context of supraindividual culture and gives both important roles (e.g., Schutz 1967 [1932]). Schutz and Merleau-Ponty issued strong and perceptive programmatic statements about the individual-order relationship, and Schutz, much more than Merleau-Ponty, conducted detailed empirical studies that were so programmatically informed. That there remained even in Schutz's efforts an "amalgamizing" rather than a completely "theoretized" quality is clear from the summarizing statement offered in the first, and perhaps still most famous, article he published in English:

The naively living person . . . automatically has in hand, so to speak, the meaningful complexes which are valid for him. From things inherited and learned, from the manifold sedimentations of traditions, habituality, and his own previous constitutions of meaning, which can be retained and reactivated, his *store of experience* of his life-world is built up as a closed meaningful complex. The experience of the life-world has its special style of verification. This style results from the process of harmonization of all single experiences. It is co-constituted last but not least, by the perspectives of relevance and by the horizons of interest which are to be explicated (1978 [1940]:137).

The last three sentences refer to Husserl's techniques for "verifying" the familiarity and objectivity of the external world: through spatial and temporal consistency, through analogizing from oneself to other people, through pairing, through expectant meanings, and through indexing, the culture that is already shared is made more widely applicable to new actors and to ongoing events. The first two sentences refer, by contrast, to collective cultural complexes that precede such individual constitution. The relation between the two is posited, but it remains unexplained.

Early Ethnomethodology: Garfinkel's Revolutionary Pursuit of Theoretical Compromise

In the early and early-middle phases of his career, Harold Garfinkel continued this camouflaged effort to resolve the individualist dilemma by transforming its polar choices: to restore a social, supraindividual moment that is neither a residual category nor a vaguely defined indeterminacy.

Husserl's mathematical background gave him the false sense of order as "just being there"; Merleau-Ponty's political activism and socialism gave him a more accurate understanding of historically specific supraindividual order that could, in principle, include collective constraint; Schutz trained within the collectivist idealist tradition and absorbed from Weber the notion of collectively rooted idealist tradition and normative patterns. Garfinkel was trained by Parsons, as well as by Schutz. He could more easily understand, therefore, that order is given and persistent and outside of any individual actor. Yet while acknowledging this order as based upon institutionalized culture, he could see that it had to be, and was, continuously revived through individual practices.

Though Garfinkel produced a variety of articles in the 1950s and 1960s, the most powerful statement of his initial, and I believe his most successful, position was his magnificent essay, "A Conception of and Experiments with 'Trust' as a Condition of Concerted Stable Actions" (1963), where he introduced an entire conceptual schema in the context of a series of ingenious empirical tests. Was it merely an accident that this great attempt to incorporate individual intention into the study of supraindividual order was devoted to the study of "games," the very prototype of institutions that link individual desires to social needs and that civilize intense rivalry by submitting it to the mutual acceptance of common rules?

Garfinkel's work has so rarely been properly understood as central to the classical sociological tradition that it is worthwhile to study this first and most important article at some length.

Garfinkel identifies the games he is studying as supraindividual "normative orders" and "disciplines." Trust occurs to the degree that this normative order is maintained. How is it sustained? To answer this question Garfinkel tries to synthesize the traditions of Parsons and Durkheim, on the one hand—the traditions, that is, of phenomenological hermeneutics—and the phenomenological tradition more traditionally conceived, which goes back to Husserl through Schutz.

Rules are, and have to be, internalized. But they must also be "worked at," because norms, or rules, are effective only because they operate in conjunction with "consciousness" in a phenomenological sense: they produce expectations and behaviors that mesh with the order-creating functions of consciousness in Husserl's sense. A game's rules rely on certain intentions; they create certain "constitutive expectancies" among the players. Rules exhibit, therefore, the following characteristics: (1) Players in the game (i.e., the members of a group) expect the rule to be unquestionably accepted—they assume the natural and naive attitude toward them which, as Husserl suggested, is part of everyday life. (2) Players expect all other participants in the game to exhibit the same attitude.

How are these expectations confirmed: how is this natural attitude maintained? Actors must constitute reality to conform with their expectations. If rules provide "categorical possibilities," then they are also intended events. People work to bring "all actual observations . . . under the jurisdiction of intended events as particular cases of the intended event" (p. 194). Every new situation in a game is therefore referred for definition and interpretation to "rules," which are viewed as embodying past experience, and which, in fact, helped produce and direct this prior experience just as they are doing so with this new event in turn. There is, then, in every game an ongoing process of "normalization," the depiction of all new events as normal and consistent with past events and with the overarching rules. The specific techniques of normalization, Garfinkel follows Schutz and Husserl in suggesting, are comparability, typicality, analogy, association, and most interestingly of all, the "etc. clause," which holds that no given set of rules can be expected to refer beforehand to every possible kind of event. In this way, every given set of rules can be extended and reformed to cover new situations. Because these intentional techniques are continuously employed, the "natural attitude" can be maintained toward rules by members of social groups: rules exist, they work, we believe them, and so does everybody else. If what really happens is that we elaborate and extend rules to fit our new situation and thereby force the rules to fit the objective reality rather than limit each reality to the rules—this is the nature of normativizing action.

What threatens social order is the violation of constituent expectations in such a drastic way that the new event cannot be normalized. The new event, in this case, produces senselessness rather than sense, and though Garfinkel does not say so, in such periods radical or revolutionary norms would have to be produced that would allow a new and different game to be played. Senselessness in this subtle use follows an operational, sociological definition: it implies an event that defies analogizing. When this occurs, there has been, in Garfinkel's words, a "breaching [of] the congruency of relevances" and of the "interchangeability of standpoints." The "etc. clause" is not plastic enough: collective memory malfunctions; it cannot traditionalize reality. Normative order breaks down.

Because of his commitment to supraindividual social order, Garfinkel's sensitivity to phenomenology more traditionally understood has produced some remarkable results. He has shown that normative order, i.e., cultural integration, does—as Durkheim himself insisted—depend on the processes of individual representation.* In important ways such integration is sustained from event to event through the normalizing processes Husserl first described. For this reason, Garfinkel can insist that rules exist within rather than without actors, and he can argue that sociology should pay careful attention to such "accommodative work." Although from this perspective collective order does indeed have the quality of an emergent product, Garfinkel clearly realizes, at this stage of his career, that this accommodative work occurs only with reference to internalized rules: constitutive expectations exist, and intentions are carried out, only in relationship to an internalized culture that produces a sense of the nature of a legitimate order. When discussing the breakdown of order, therefore, Garfinkel does not point merely to individual failures of typification—though these certainly would, perforce, have to be involved—but rather to social processes: to the "modifications of real environments" that occur because new cultures are introduced that demand new learning and create new ceremonials or because instrumental transformations have been carried out by coercion or force.

The "Individualist Dilemma" and Later Ethnomethodology's Return to an Anticollectivist Stance

To appreciate the difficulties that Garfinkel tentatively overcame in this early work we must remind ourselves of the dilemma that individualistic thought involves. To maintain individualism in a clear and honest way,

---

*One typical case of the frustrating, and entirely inappropriate, theoretical distance that has developed between the phenomenological traditions strictly and traditionally defined has been the inability of most theorists and interpreters to understand that Durkheim himself relied heavily on a theory of individual "intention," or "signification," to develop his later theory of symbolic collective order (Alexander 1982b:247–50). Durkheim discovered that through "representation" individuals continuously "named" external objects (ideal or material); this naming specified some prior expectations and traditions, and it simultaneously internalized and externalized the object it created. I suggest that Durkheim articulated here much the same phenomenological, subjective process as Husserl and his followers.

theorists must introduce fantastic randomness into their picture of the world, basically denying that patterning exists outside specific situations. Most theorists, however, unless they are psychologists or nominalists, will not be satisfied with such a position and will move toward embracing the collectivist moment. Yet as long as formal commitments to individualism are maintained, such a collective moment can be introduced only in a residual way: it will inevitably be indeterminate and theoretically and empirically frustrating. The tension generated by being stranded on the horns of this dilemma—being pulled between randomness and indeterminacy—usually produces resorts to "last instance" arguments, which suggest that, though collective dimensions may exist, "in the last instance" individual negotiation actually creates social order.

Garfinkel, by contrast, offered some tentative steps at true theoretical resolution. His detailed attention to intentional practices seemed designed to show how omnipresent collective, supraintentional rules really were; his emphasis on the significance of rules, on the other hand, was used to testify to the absolute ingenuity with which individuals must continuously "work" if this order is to be maintained. On the one hand, a priori trust is fundamental to the very sensicality of an individual's life, on the other this trust relies completely on the normativizing actions of single individuals. What Garfinkel has been able to do, and here I return to a distinction offered in the introduction of this chapter, is to embrace the contingent, purely individualist element as a level of empirical analysis rather than as a presupposition of social order itself.

Despite this general synthetic thrust, even in this earlier work there are some troubling ambiguities in Garfinkel's approach. Though he has clearly argued that collective rules are, in fact, sui generis and not reducible to intentions and practices, he suggests in several programmatic statements an exactly opposite point. "The way a system of activities is organized *means the same thing as* the way its organizational characteristics are being produced and maintained" (1963:187, italics added). Can Garfinkel really mean here that rules (the way a system of activities is organized) are the same thing as practices (the way these organizational activities are produced and maintained)? He seems tempted here to return to the individualism of Husserl. The ambivalence about whether contingency is, in fact, an empirical-level-of-analysis or a presuppositional position is strikingly revealed in the following statement from that early work: "Structural phenomena . . . are emergent products of . . . accom-

modative work whereby persons encountering from within the environments that society confronts them with establish the social structures that
are the assembled products of action directed to these environments"
(p. 187). Now if structural phenomena are, indeed, merely emergent
products, then they are, it is true, simply the assembled products of
action; but such structures cannot, at the same time, confront individuals
from without.

In these studiedly ambiguous statements, Garfinkel has moved back
within the horns of the individualist dilemma: to retain a commitment to
individualism, evidently, he has felt compelled to make his assertions of
collective constraint extremely indeterminate. This strain in his early work
emerges full blown in *Studies in Ethnomethodology* (1967), and his more
recent work moves toward a decisively individualistic position.

But before examining this desynthesizing movement, it is important to
recognize that in *Studies* there remains a strong thrust of valuable synthetic conceptualizing and, especially, of empirical investigation informed
by it. Garfinkel here declares that his subject is "accounts." Actors believe
they must be able to account for new events, and they can do so only in
terms of their prior expectations and normatively structured common
sense. But these accounts, Garfinkel suggests, are actually constitutive of
the settings they purport to merely describe. Precisely this circularity
allows us to understand the reproduction of norms and rules in the face
of continuously changing external events and situations. The necessity
for accounts, of course, is merely another way of saying that action is
"indexical," that new objects are treated as signs of prior knowledge: this
quality of "indexicality" is basic if a smooth and continuous normative
order is to be maintained. Through "members' practices," therefore, social action is an "accomplished familiarity." All such practices must still,
however, be conceived as occurring in relation to "background assumptions." Intentional actors, Garfinkel often still maintains, "consult institutionalized aspects of the collectivity." There is, he acknowledges, a
"common culture" from which intentional action must always draw.
Thus, in discussing how a public health staff investigates suicides, Garfinkel argues that they employ the "documentary method": they use the
scraps of information they find not to "induce" in an objectivist way what
"really happened" but to "document" the prior expectations they had.
This practice of "ad hocing" is fundamental, he suggests, to the maintenance of any common culture.

There are currents in contemporary ethnomethodolgy that, despite their individualistic and iconoclastic self-presentation, continue this train of Garfinkel's work, maintaining the attempt to synthesize individual intentional techniques with the power of normative culture. In this work the attention on "members' practices" is important as an illuminating new level of empirical analysis: it is not the basis for an alternative to collectivist sociology; that is, it is not taken as the necessary presupposition for a completely individualistic understanding of social order. Perhaps the most systematically developed example of such ethnomethodology is Cicourel's. In *Cognitive Sociology* he criticizes collectivist sociologies for "not address[ing] *how* the actor perceives and interprets his environment, *how* certain rules govern exchanges, and *how* the actor recognizes what is taken to be standard, 'familiar,' 'acceptable' . . ." (1974:16, italics added). He is suggesting, in other words, the need for a new level of empirical analysis to be brought into play. Of course, Cicourel exaggerates the importance of such intentional rules, arguing that they supply the "deep structure" of norms and values and the "critical" feature of all role behavior. He ignores, further, the illuminations of intentionality that have been developed outside of the Husserlian tradition, e.g., in Freud's theory of defense mechanisms and Mead's theory of the "act." Nonetheless, Cicourel has used the middle period conceptualizing of Garfinkel to explore significantly new aspects of normative order in the social world. Molotch (1974) and Tuchman (1978) have similarly made good empirical use of these insights, suggesting that newspaper reporters do not so much discover new empirical facts as normalize them, that they use the documentary method to demonstrate and specify preexisting expectations. Leiter (1976) has shown how teachers, without knowing their students, read in expectations and interpret their actions in ways that sustain the often self-defeating normative order of the classroom. Zimmerman (1969) has shown how welfare agencies transform client records that are fragmentary and doubtful into hard and fast records that simply reproduce conventional expectations about their behavior. Kitsuse (1969) (and Cicourel, of course) have shown how the social control of deviance is often no more than finding ways of documenting prior expectations. Other analysts, like Zimmerman and Pollner (1970), have described how even objective social science relies on concepts that are indexical not only for the scientists but also for the subjects and that for this reason tend to reproduce the commonsense knowledge of a given society rather than studying it from a truly independent position.

I must now turn to the developments in Garfinkel's *Studies* that failed to transcend the individualist dilemma, for in the very midst of this richer and more elaborate conceptualization of a new level of empirical analysis— the level of contingency and individual intentionality—Garfinkel simultaneously suggests that ethnomethodology should, in fact, be viewed, not as an empirical illumination, but as a countertheory of order: as an individualistic theory that is an alternative rather than a complement to the classical sociological tradition.

To understand the difference between these two versions of what is apparently, in Garfinkel's and his followers' minds, still the "ethnomethodological" tradition, it is sufficient to examine closely Garfinkel's treatment—or rather his two treatments—of the intentional practice he calls "ad hocing." On the one hand, he uses this notion in a way that makes it parallel to what semioticians call "signification": an actor, encountering an object, uses it as a sign, or symbol, to "represent" or "signify" the relation of a more general system of meaning to this particular circumstance. To engage in ad hocing, then, is to use some new object indexically. This approach clearly exemplifies Garfinkel's synthetic ambition, for it is a way of neatly combining contingency with the importance of sustaining collective order. Thus, Garfinkel describes how a graduate student "coder" engages in ad hocing in the course of the research he is doing on a clinic's files:

He treats actual folder contents [i.e., the material he is to code] as standing in a relationship of trusted signification to the "system" in the clinic activities [i.e., the organization to which the folder contents refer]. Because the coder assumes the "position" of a competent member to the arrangements that he seeks to give an account of, he can "see the system" in the actual content of the folder (1967:22).

[The coder] must treat actual folder contents as standing proxy for the social-order-in-and-of-clinic-activities. Actual folder contents stand to the socially ordered ways of clinic activities as *representation* of them; they do not describe the order, nor are they evidences of the order. It is the coder's use of the folder documents as *sign-functions* to which I mean to be pointing in saying that the coder must know the order of the clinic's activities that he is looking at in order to recognize the actual contents as an appearance-of-the-order (1967:23, original italics).

Yet only a few pages later, Garfinkel suggests that this vital connection between the practice of ad hocing and the broader referent upon which it is based should be broken.

Suppose we drop the assumption that in order to describe a usage as a feature of a community of understandings we must at the outset know what the substantive common understandings consist of. With it, drop the assumption's accompanying theory of signs, according to which a "sign" and "referent" are respectively properties of something said and something talked about, and which in this fashion proposes sign and referent to be related as corresponding contents. *By dropping such a theory of signs we drop as well, thereby, the possibility that an invoked shared agreement on substantive matters explains a usage.* If these notions are dropped, then *what* the parties talked about could not be distinguished from *how* the parties were speaking (p. 28, italics altered).

In this statement Garfinkel makes a sharp and, I believe, fateful move toward individualism. He is suggesting that the contents of what people talk about—the meaning of what they are saying—can be understood without reference to the broader normative or cultural framework within which they speak. If the sign can be separated from the cultural referent, then to understand the meaning of the sign we are left only with the techniques of individual intentionality themselves. Garfinkel maintains, indeed, that the meaning of a sign is the product of interactional techniques, the constitutive gestures Husserl called analogy, normalization, shared perspective, to which Garfinkel adds some more of his own.

An explanation of what the parties were talking about would then consist entirely of describing *how* the parties had been speaking; of furnishing a method for saying whatever is to be said, like talking synonymously, talking ironically, talking metaphorically, talking cryptically, talking narratively, talking in a questioning or answering way, lying, glossing, double-talking, and the rest (pp. 28–29, italics added).

"The recognized sense of what a person said," Garfinkel now concludes, "consists only and entirely in recognizing the method of his speaking, of *seeing how he spoke*" (p. 29, original italics).

Yet this movement toward embracing individualism as a presuppositional position rather than simply as a level of empirical analysis transforms an important, synthetic insight into a dubious, one-sided presumption. The fact that a speaker uses synonym, irony, and metaphor actually tells us nothing about what was said; it simply allows us to understand how this "what" was produced. Yet it is precisely by this insistence on breaking apart signs and their referents—practices from rules—that Garfinkel can insist in *Studies* that social structures are completely emergent from practices; it follows from this, he reasons, that ethnomethodology need not follow "sociology" in its analysis of rules and institutionalized culture. "Organized social arrangements," Garfinkel writes, employing phraseology that became a byword of the ethnomethodological movement, "*consist of* various methods for accomplishing the accountability of a setting's organizational ways" (pp. 33–34, italics added).

This radical individualism completely contradicts the more synthetic strand of Garfinkel's work, a strand that, we have seen, was still very visible in *Studies* itself. When Garfinkel argues, for example, that "recognizeable sense . . . is not independent of the socially organized occasions for their use" (p. 3), he is denying the very phenomenon of indexicality he had earlier labored to conceive, for according to the notion of indexicality, a priori notions of recognized sense are precisely the means by which the meaning of any particular occasion is ascertained. When he argues that "rational features *consist of* what members do" (p. 3, italics added), he is similarly eliminating the very collective referents that had allowed him to avoid the randomizing, asocial qualities of earlier phenomenology: he had once assumed that cultural rationality set a standard of legitimate order to which ongoing "members' actions" had necessarily to be compared. Garfinkel has reduced his theory to a pragmatism of the purely experiential kind. As he writes in the very first line of *Studies,* introducing a chapter that was clearly written just before publication: "The following studies seek to treat *practical* activities, *practical* circumstances, and *practical* sociological reasoning" (p. 1, italics added). As we will more clearly see in the latter part of this chapter, this reduction to the "practical" makes Garfinkel's later work fundamentally similar to the tradition of symbolic interactionism that he has always despised.

Before turning to the interactionist tradition, however, let us follow out the implications of the individualist turn that occurred in Garfinkel's middle period work. What was critical about this turn was that it established the official self-understanding of the ethnomethodological movement. Garfinkel's *Studies,* after all, were conducted during the decade of the 1960s, the same period in which "ethnomethodology" first gained controversy and attracted to itself younger students. The most rebellious and apparently revolutionary thrust of this approach, as these younger students viewed it in relation to the reigning functionalist sociology of that day, was, ironically, precisely the individualistic and antinormative quality that undermined the potentially most significant parts of Garfinkel's contribution. To champion "ethnomethodology" was to reject "sociology," that is, to reject a discipline committed to a more collectivist thrust. Whether or not this individualism correctly characterized ethnomethodological studies in fact, therefore, it certainly informed their self-understanding. Indeed, each of the more synthetic studies I have referred to above—by Cicourel, Zimmerman, Kitsuse, Pollner, Leider, et al.—articulates its findings, not in terms of the relation between intentionality and belief, but in terms of practices alone. In the later period, the actual conduct of ethnomethodology conformed more closely to this self-understanding.

Probably the most conspicuous corpus of later work that has given up the theory of signification is the language analysis first initiated by Sacks and now carried on by a network of researchers who constitute a self-conscious school of "Conversation Analysis." For this group it is entirely the nature of the conversational interaction itself that determines the actions of each speaker: the necessity for exchanging speakers without excessive gaps or overlaps, the problem of changing a subject without losing continuity, the number of speakers, the visibility or lack of visibility of the partners in a conversation. Not only is the a priori meaning of language considered irrelevant—the intertwined culture of the "language game" in Wittgenstein's sense—but also meaning itself has dropped completely from concern. Not surprisingly, this branch of later ethnomethodology is more positivistic and latently materialistic than any other, though it can range from the focus on individual decisions (Pomerantz [1980]) to the elaboration of "speech exchange systems," which are held to allocate turns according to an economy of interaction (Sacks, Schegloff, and Jefferson [1974]).

More revealing perhaps of Garfinkel's later individualist turn is the work by Pollner, for it continues to preoccupy itself with meanings as such. In "Explicative Transactions: Making and Managing Meaning in Traffic Court" (1979), Pollner provides an elegant description of the enormous interpretive efforts that everyday life entails, even in the well-institutionalized location of a court of law. Because of the contingency produced by temporality, actors employ a repertoire of techniques to enable meaning to proceed: they make examples, they take exception, they make things visible, they arrange and rearrange temporal sequences, they carefully try to maintain the "horizons" of their actions. Yet Pollner wishes to do more than describe intentional techniques in an ethnographic setting: he wants to describe how the meaning of the courtroom experience is created as such. He is proposing that the meaning of what goes on in a traffic court is, quite simply, the product of the interactive techniques he has described. "What one does next," he writes, "will be seen as defining the import or significance of what another did before."

But can significance really be so shorn of referent? A succeeding action can define my own only insofar as both mine and the succeeding act refer to, and can be clearly interpreted by, an elaborate and complex cultural system of prior meaning. Is the judge in a court "constituting" meanings, as Pollner would like to suggest, or is he, with significant individual variation, "enacting" them? When a judge expresses incredulity at a guilty plea that is lodged in an awkward and illegitimate way, is he "inventing" a legitimate guilty plea, or is he merely using normalizing techniques to ensure that ongoing events conform to well-established norms about what guilty pleas "should be"? That Pollner concludes this paper by lauding Mead's insistence that the meaning of an act is determined by the response to it—a position, we will see, that is not necessarily representative of the main line of Mead's thought—shows, once again, how later ethnomethodology has moved back toward the tradition to which it was originally opposed.

It has been a long time since Garfinkel himself has provided published work in which the later individualist strand could be examined in "pure" form: he has confined his public efforts, in the main, to be a *maître* of students who have themselves articulated his later position in effective ways. What Garfinkel and his students now study is "work," the details of "practical" action in highly circumscribed natural settings. Garfinkel's own recently published essay on science, however, allows some insight into what this new vocabulary implies. In studying how the initial scientific observations of the optical pulsar came to be made, Garfinkel et al. (1981) insist that they are concerned only with the "*in situ* . . . efficacy" of the scientists' actions. Without reference to scientific norms, either formal or informal, or to the paradigmatic or thematic prior expectations of the scientists themselves, they suggest that "the properties that their [i.e., the scientists'] competent practices have in local production" are completely "interactionally produced." This study is concerned, indeed, with the tools and instruments the scientists used, the words they spoke, and the notes they took, with the "worldly objects" that allowed "embodied practice" and that, together, created "the pulsar's existing *material* shape" (italics added). Garfinkel's later ethnomethodology, it is clear, has become more like the conversational analysis that his individualizing movement first stimulated: it is a study of situated material practice without reference to meaning, let alone to the traditions of culture by which, according to Garfinkel's earlier work, such meaning would have to be informed.

Mead's Interactionism: The Individualist Dilemma Resolved or Reinstated?

George Herbert Mead's theorizing developed from American pragmatism, and this quintessentially American philosophy, as Lewis and Smith have recently affirmed, was itself sharply, if subtly, rent between more individualistic and more collectivist understandings of action. Most well known, of course, is the strand of pragmatic individualism. James developed a personalized theory of meaning that claimed that a concept *means* the experience to which it leads. The mandate of the pragmatic method is, from this perspective, to test all conceptual beliefs with practical experience, in James' words "to determine the meaning of all differences of opinion by making the discussion hinge as soon as possible upon some practical issue." Though Dewey's work is more ambiguous, it often showed a similarly exclusive focus on the "here and now" and evidenced a similar opposition to the notion of the existence of overarching tradition and idealized, a priori commitments. His "American" individualism often decisively colors his thought: subjectivity is "initiative, inventiveness, varied resourcefulness, and the assumption of responsibility in choice of belief and conduct" (1957:200). Individuals, he often holds, are not simply morally but *theoretically* responsible for their choice of beliefs. Social order must therefore be continually started over anew: "Society is one word, but infinitely many things." When he writes in this vein, Dewey's theory precludes the symbolic generalization upon which any notion of a subjective supraindividual order must rest. He writes, for example, that "the new pragmatic method, takes effect by substituting inquiry into these specific, changing and relative facts for solemn manipulation of general notions" (1957).

Against this nominalist strand in Pragmatism there stands a more collectivist and synthesizing strain that is well known. The work of Charles Peirce has not been given its due, yet it was he who actually founded Pragmatic philosophy and who was acknowledged as its most original and systematic thinker by his contemporaries. Although Peirce's theory will not be considered systematically here, its fundamental point can, nonetheless, be stated in stark and relatively simple terms. Peirce strove mightily to reconcile the need for, and the empirical existence of, a community of ethics and obligation with a pragmatic emphasis on experience in the real world as the basis of truth. To pursue this synthesis, he developed the first elaborate theory of signs, and he argued that such systems of symbols would have to provide the context for every experiential act. Peirce was not wholly successful in this synthetic effort, but there can be no doubt about the nature of his ambition or the synthesizing thrust of this work. Far from separating signs from referents—the problem we find in the later ethnomethodology—Peirce developed his theory of signification to better explain practical reason. We can understand the nature of this accomplishment by examining the thought of Mead, for while Mead was only indirectly affected by Peirce (particularly via Royce), his relationship to more individualistic pragmatism was much the same (see, e.g., Mead's discussion of Realism and Pragmatism in Mead 1936:326–59).

In the work of Blumer and most of contemporary symbolic interactionism, "symbolism" as such seems to have completely disappeared, and with it the possibilities for any integration of interactionism with the collectivist tradition. What must be understood, however, is that, contrary to the thrust of contemporary interactionism, symbolism was, in fact, absolutely central to Mead's thought. He did not accept contingency as a presupposition; he preserved it as a vital empirical moment. He realized, indeed, that supraindividual symbolic systems were the most important creators of an individual's objects. It is "symbolization," he wrote, not the individual per se, which "constitutes objects not constituted before," and he asserted that "objects . . . would not exist except for the context of social relationships wherein symbolization occurs" (1964 [1934]:165).

Language does not simply symbolize a situation or object which is already there in advance; it makes possible the existence or the appearance of that situation or object, for it is part of the mechanism whereby that situation or object was created. . . . Objects [are] dependent upon or constituted by these meanings.

At the same time, however, Mead emphasized, more than those in the tradition of phenomenological hermeneutics, the significance of concrete individual interaction, what he called the "conversation of gestures." Gestures are every kind of movement or expression in which people engage, including language. With gestures, Mead entered the pragmatists' world of experience and activism, but he entered in a distinctive, synthesizing way.

"Gestures" can, in principle, be treated as dependent for their meaning either on individual stratagem or on more generalized symbolic frameworks. It is this latter position that Mead takes, though we will see that he does not foresake the former as a significant empirical dimension. The meaning of gestures, Mead insists, is not open to individual manipulation in a major way: "Gestures . . . are significant symbols because they have the same meanings for all individual members of a given society or social group, that is, they respectively arouse the same attitudes in the individuals making them that they arouse in the individuals responding" (1964 [1934]:159). Far from providing the rationale for a return to individualism, then, Mead actually views his theory of gestures as a means of understanding how the contingency of individual action is enmeshed within symbolic structure. Gestures, he believes, make possible "the symbolization of experience" within the broader field of meaning (p. 128). Gestures allow people to link their ongoing, novel experience to social categories, in Durkheim's words to "represent" the world to themselves in the process of objectivizing themselves in the world. It was, in fact, to emphasize and elaborate the social character of gestures that Mead developed the notion of the "generalized other."

The individual experiences himself as such, not directly, but only indirectly, from the particular standpoints of other individual members of the same social group or from the generalized standpoint of the social group as a whole to which he belongs. . . . The individual [brings] himself into the same experiential field as that of the other individual selves in relation to whom he acts in any given social situation. Reason cannot become impersonal [a development upon which this inter-individual experience depends] unless it takes an objective, non-affective attitude toward itself; otherwise we have just consciousness, not self-consciousness (p. 202, original italics).

The socializing impact of this generalized other is critically elaborated in Mead's theory of the game, an analysis that makes the same kind of profound contribution to empirical integration as Garfinkel's early essay on trust in experimental games. When children are very young, Mead believes, the sense of other individuals has not become generalized; as a result, children engage in "play" rather than in games. They take the role of other children, moving from one kind of behavior to another in an individualistic way. Children at this early point in their development, then, can only put themselves in place of another. With further development, however, children incorporate into themselves an abstract understanding of the roles that other members of the game assume. This incorporation constitutes the "rules" of the game, or the "generalized other," which now invisibly regulates the behavior of all. Only with rules are real "games" possible, for only with the rules that a generalized other provides are individualized interests and goals pursued in a simultaneously social way. When an older, game-playing child gestures, Mead insists, he is gesturing for himself but for others too, for he has automatically taken into account—by virtue of his personal identity and his actual perception—the positions and obligations of his fellow players.

The baseball player who makes a brilliant play is making the play called for by the nine to which he belongs. He is playing for his side. A man may, of course, play the gallery, be more interested in making a brilliant play than in helping his team to win, just as a surgeon may carry out a brilliant operation and sacrifice the patient. But under normal conditions, *the contribution of the individual gets its expression in the social processes that are involved in the act, so that the attachment of the values to the self does not involve egoism or selfishness* (p. 239, italics added).

The taking of all of those organized sets of attitudes gives him . . . the self he is aware of. He can throw the ball to some other members because of the demand made upon him from other members of the team. That is the self that immediately exists for him in his consciousness. He has their attitudes, knows what they want and what the consequences of any act of his will be, and he has assumed responsibility for the situation (p. 230).

The game for Mead is an analogy, or microcosm, of all social systems and groups. His understanding of the nature of gestures in games, therefore, allows him to maintain that gestures *are* social institutions. Institutions are conventionally understood as structured and objective orders, but Mead has shown that such collective order corresponds to the generalized others of its members. "An institution," he can then suggest, "is, after all, nothing but an organization of attitudes which we all carry in us" (p. 239).

Yet the contingent and individualizing aspect of action still has not been expressed. Mead attends to gestures not simply because they show how the social is specified but also because they show how the social is changed. The gesture involves an element of freedom because it involves the passage of time, and temporality is, for Mead as for Heidegger, the essence of contingency. Mead talks about the "temporary inhibition of action," which signifies thinking. In carrying out his act the individual is presented in his consciousness with "different alternative ways of completing [what] he has already initiated" (p. 169). For this reason, every new gesture has an emergent property that distinguishes it from those preceding:

That which takes place in present organic behavior is always in some sense an emergent from the past and never could have been precisely predicted in advance—never could have been predicted on the basis of a knowledge, however, complete, of the past, and of the conditions in the past which are relevant to its emergence (p. 177).

The "I" and the "me," then, are "two distinguishable phases" of the same act. In describing the genesis and constitution of acts, Mead carefully outlines the alternation of contingent and determined phases. The "attitude," in Mead's terms, constitutes the first part of the response by another's gesture, and he insists that one's "attitude" is socially determined by the nature of the internalized symbolic order: the meaning an actor gives to another's gestures is immediately given in a completely unconscious way. Yet, Mead cautions, this does not constitute one's "response" to a gesture. Within the context of the act—unconsciously, preconsciously, or consciously—one performs various rehearsals, feeling and seeing imagery of various kinds, exploring the ramifications of this or that response. Only after such "rehearsal" does one make one's response. Afterward, one evaluates the relation between the meaning given to the other's gesture and the effect of the response on the immediate and generalized others involved.

To the degree that Mead so separated "attitude" from "response"—without, in other words, reducing one to the other*—he made a fundamental contribution to the integration of individualist and collectivist phenomenologies, for by doing so he significantly elaborated how contingency becomes incorporated in the moment-to-moment specification of collective order. Though empirically different, this contribution parallels in its implications those of Garfinkel in his earlier work. Yet, although Mead's position was more stable than Garfinkel's, not even Mead is able to maintain such a synthetic and integrated position in a completely con-

*I have benefited greatly in my understanding of this distinction from the excellent piece by Lewis (1979).

sistent way. There are significant places in Mead's work where the autonomy of attitude and response is collapsed. He proclaims, in these instances, that the meaning of a gesture is determined by the response itself, that is, by contingent and purely "pragmatic" individual considerations.*

The response of one organism to the gesture of another in any given social act is the meaning of that gesture and also is in a sense responsible for the appearance or coming into being of the new object. . . . The act or adjustive response of the second organism [therefore] gives to the gesture of the first organism the meaning which it has (p. 165).

This individualistic strand in Mead's work is, in part, the result of problems inherent in the philosophy of pragmatism itself, which is too anti-Kantian and anti-Hegelian to fully transcend an individualistic point of view. Whatever its source, this individualism came home to roost in a way that eventually undermined Mead's synthetic accomplishment. It did so because the interpreter of Mead's thought for contemporary interactionists has been a pragmatist so infected by individualism that when reading Mead's work he evidently could perceive the individualistic strand alone. This man was Herbert Blumer.

Blumer as Mead's Misinterpreting Interpreter: "Symbolic Interactionism" as the Reinstitution of Individualism

The history of the interactionist tradition foreshadowed in eerie ways the more recent history of ethnomethodology: this tradition, which initially promised to transcend the individualist dilemma, concluded by actually reinstating it. Mead's thought contained certain deep-seated ambiguities, much as did Garfinkel's early work. The difference is this: the internal transformation into an unambivalent and radical individualism, a change which Garfinkel carried out for ethnomethodology within the context of his own earlier thought, was accomplished for interactionism more by Mead's followers than by the founder himself.

When Blumer defined Mead as a "symbolic interactionist" in his famous article on "Social Psychology" in 1937, he tainted him with the brush of

---

*The reference to this individualistic strain in Mead in Pollner's work (cited above) clearly reveals the link between the individualistic "practical" emphasis of later ethnomethodology and the contemporary reading of Mead.

individualism from which the interactionist tradition has never recovered. Until recently, Blumer remained the principal interpreter of Mead's thought and the most forceful teacher of interactionism's most promising students. Of course, the "reason" for the reinstatement of individualism in this quintessentially American tradition certainly cannot be the fault of a single person alone; the roots lay in deeper historical developments and in fundamental, unresolved problems of theoretical logic itself. The structure of Blumer's thought is, nonetheless, worth examining. The manner in which he has reinstated the individualist dilemma provides fascinating evidence for the universal, "structural" status of theoretical problems: Blumer's forceful individualism, though conceived entirely from within the intellectual traditions of American culture, bears a striking resemblance to the individualism that emerged in Garfinkel's later version of phenomenology, a tradition originally conceived in a very different time and place.

Blumer collapses the autonomy of "attitude" and "response" upon which any successful integration of contingency and order depends. In doing so he returns to the pragmatic emphasis on practical experience and quasi-Darwinian adaptations: "Culture," Blumer writes, "is clearly derived from what people *do*" (Blumer 1969:61; emphasis added). It is the response to the gesture that determines meaning, not the pre-given cultural background within which the gesture itself is initiated: "Meaning is derived from or arises out of the social interaction that one has with one's fellows" (Blumer 1969:2); "the meaning of a thing grows out of the ways in which other persons act towards the person with regard to the thing" (Blumer 1969:4).

To argue that action and response so directly determine meaning is, of course, to insist on an absolute individual control over meaning: "The *actor* selects, checks, suspends, regroups, and transforms the meanings in the light of the situation in which *he* is placed and the direction of *his* action" (Blumer 1969:5; emphasis added). Whereas Mead usually, though not always, spoke of meaning as the product of an unconscious attitudinal specification of general cultural patterns, Blumer proposes, in direct contrast, that "self-indication" is the basis of meaning attribution. Through "self-indication," the individual organism "makes an object of what it notes, gives it a meaning [and] uses the meaning as the basis for directing its action" (Blumer 1969:15). Blumer's individual is given incredible control over the meaning of his acts—a control contested only by the presence of other, equally separated selves. The individual, in Blumer's world, consciously "takes account of," and decides the rational appropriateness of, his "wishes and wants" and even his "images of himself" (Blumer 1969:15). Individuals are given the ability to stand against not only the entire external world but their internal world as well.

> Self-indication is a moving communicative process in which the individual notes things, assesses them, gives them a meaning and decides to act on the basis of the meaning. The human being stands over against the world, or against "alters," with such a process. . . . The process of self-indication cannot be subsumed under the forces . . . which are presumed to play upon the individual to produce his behavior. . . . It stands over against them in that the individual points out to himself and interprets the appearance or expression of such things, noting a given social demand that is made on him, recognizing a command, observing that he is hungry, realizing that he wishes to buy something, aware that he has a given feeling, conscious that he dislikes eating with someone he despises, or aware that he is thinking of doing something. By virtue of indicating such things to himself, he places himself over against them and is able to act back against them, accepting them, rejecting them, or transforming them in accordance with how he defines or interprets them (Blumer 1969:81–2).

We are in the midst, here, of the "I" without the "we," of the childlike self who can put himself "in the place of the other" but who does not carry within himself the "generalized other" which allows him automatic and unconscious resource to the meaning of others' acts. As in the later Garfinkel, the symbolic language of signification completely disappears in Blumer's work; it is not surprising that when he mentions "interpretation"—the process by which in hermeneutical theory new events are related to background assumptions—he always subordinates it to practical purpose and to the need for immediate results. "Interpretation," he says, "is a formative process in which meanings are *used* and revised as instruments for the guidance and formation of *action*" (Blumer 1969:5; emphasis added). What we have left is the same world of "local production" that is the focus of later ethnomethodology: "The sets of meanings that lead participants to act as they do . . . have their own setting in a localized process of social interaction" (Blumer 1969:19–20).

Blumer is caught firmly between the horns of the dilemma that Mead had shown a way of transcending: his thought moves back and forth uneasily between the unattractive choices of randomness and residual indeterminacy. On the one hand, Blumer posits a radical uncertainty about the course of every interaction, a randomness which he not only accepts as the price for absolute freedom but usually seems to glory in. Structural factors, he writes, are "matter[s] the actor takes into account. [But this] does not explain how they are taken into account in the situation that calls for action" (Blumer 1969:16). How could one, then, explain how they are taken into account, an explanation which obviously would be basic if the patterned processes of interaction were to be understood? Blumer suggests merely that "one has to get inside of the defining process," a process he has defined as completely within the moment of contingency itself. The evanescent, indeterminate quality of this accounting for structures comes through even more clearly when Blumer writes that one must "catch the process of interpretation through which actors construct their actions" (Blumer 1969:82). Even Blumer, however, does not entirely escape "second thoughts" about such randomizing implications. One can find in the interstices of even his theorizing residual references to supra-individual structures, references which Blumer attempts to camouflage by indeterminate and often extremely vague formulations (see, e.g., Blumer 1969:17–19).

In the double shadow of Blumer's own work and his misinterpretation of Mead, the tradition of symbolic interactionism has produced compromise formations that constitute a continuum from pure individualism to its purely social critique. One strand of interactionism has simply focused on events and "one time only" processes like historical episodes or collective outbursts. In another strand, external structures are acknowledged but they are treated as parameters which become, in effect, glaring residual categories. In still another strand, the social self of Mead becomes the entire focus of analysis, an interactionism from which any focus on the "I" and on contingency has completely disappeared. Finally, there are some attempts, as in the best works of Goffman, where under the guise of explicit obeisance to astructural individualism a forceful and illuminating integration of contingency and structure is conceived. Only in this last and much too infrequent genre is the potential for theoretical synthesis pursued that Mead originally introduced.

Conclusion

The preceding analysis has sought to demonstrate that such supraindividual elements are not, in fact, necessarily absent from the "individualist" traditions. When we look at the most sophisticated and most successful strands of phenomenology and interactionism, we see that they were not intended to be epistemological and ontological confrontations with theories that posit supraindividual order; rather, they were intended to give greater urgency to an empirical aspect of order that has been neglected by most such collectivist theories, at least post-Hegel: the relationship between the prior, supraindividual order and the moment-to-moment unfolding of real historical time. The relations between order and contingency, these traditions have argued, can be illuminated only by a more detailed empirical understanding of the processes of individual consciousness. Garfinkel and the phenomenologists discussed the intentional strategies by which normative order is specified in each concrete situation; Mead analyzed the social self and the nature of gestures—which did much the same thing. Both traditions emphasized that this contingency introduces change even while it ensures specification. These changes are usually far outweighed by the impact of collective normation, but they are individual innovations nonetheless.

The initial development of ethnomethodology, the subsequent strains and schisms within it, have revolved precisely around this question of empirical versus presuppositional individualism. The conceptualization and empirical studies of Garfinkel's earlier work synthesized a focus on empirical contingency with an analysis of social order. In this work, and in subsequent strands of the ethnomethodology school, which considered these studies paradigmatic, the integration of the two phenomenologies strictly and traditionally considered was powerfully begun. Yet in the more individualistic work Garfinkel created after, and alongside, this synthetic work, a paradigm was established through which ethnomethodology sharply separated signification from the signified. With this movement, the effort at theoretical integration was just as powerfully opposed.

The same kind of fateful dialectic occurred in the history of interactionism. Mead created a powerful, individually focused theory that precisely interrelated contingent creation and collective constraint. But when Blumer interpreted Mead, he drew upon an anomalous strand of individualism to elaborate, in the founder's name, the radically anticollectivist theory he has called, incongruously, symbolic interactionism. The followers of Blumer, with rare if important exceptions, have been caught within the individualist dilemma ever since.

It is precisely this individualist dilemma that sociology must transcend if the individual is to be "brought back in" to the classical tradition of sociological thought. If this individual cannot be the isolated, pristine individual that Homans wanted to bring back long ago, we are all so much the better for it.

REFERENCES

Alexander, Jeffrey C. 1982a. *Positivism, Presuppositions, and Current Controversies*. Vol. 1 of *Theoretical Logic in Sociology*. Berkeley and Los Angeles: University of California Press.
—— 1982b. *The Antinomies of Classical Thought: Marx and Durkheim*. Vol. 2 of *Theoretical Logic in Sociology*. Berkeley and Los Angeles: University of California Press.
Blumer, Herbert. 1937. "Social Psychology." In E. D. Schmidt, ed., *Man and Society*, pp. 144–98. New York: Prentice-Hall.
—— 1969. *Symbolic Interactionism*. Englewood Cliffs, N.J.: Prentice-Hall.
Cicourel, Aaron V. 1974. *Cognitive Sociology*. New York: Free Press.
Dewey, James. 1957. *Reconstruction in Philosophy*. Boston: Beacon.
Garfinkel, Harold. 1963. "A Conception of and Experiments with 'Trust' as a Condition of Concerted Stable Actions." In O. J. Harvey, ed., *Motivation and Social Interaction*, pp. 187–238. New York: Ronald Press.
—— 1967. *Studies in Ethnomethodology*. Englewood Cliffs, N.J.: Prentice-Hall.
Garfinkel, Harold, Michael Lynch, and Eric Livingston. 1981. "The Work of a Discovering Science Construed with Materials from the Optically Discovered Pulsar." *Philosophy of Social Science* 11:131–58.
Hegel, G. W. F. 1977 (1807). *Phenomenology of Spirit*. Oxford: Clarendon Press.
Husserl, Edmund. 1977 (1931). *Cartesian Meditations*. The Hague, the Netherlands: Martinus Nijhoff.
—— 1965. "Philosophy and the Crisis of European Man." In Husserl, *Phenomenology and the Crisis of Philosophy*, pp. 149–92. New York: Harper and Row.
Kitsuse, John. 1969. "Social Reactions to Deviant Behavior." In Donald Cressey and David Ward, eds., *Crime and Social Process*, pp. 590–602. New York: Harper and Row.
Leiter, Kenneth. 1976. "Adhocing in Schools." In Aaron Cicourel et al., *Language Use and School Performance*, pp. 17–73. New York: Academic Press.
Levi-Strauss, Claude. 1966. *The Savage Mind*. Chicago: University of Chicago Press.
—— 1970. "A Confrontation." *New Left Review*, vol. 62:57–74.
Lewis, J. David. 1979. "A Social Behaviorist Interpretation of the Meadian 'I'." *American Journal of Sociology* 84:261–87.
Lewis, J. David and Richard L. Smith. 1980. *American Sociology and Pragmatism: Mead, Chicago Sociology and Symbolic Interactionism*. Chicago: University of Chicago Press.
Mead, George Herbert. 1964 (1934). "Selections from Mind, Self, and Society."

In Anselm Strauss, ed., *George Herbert Mead on Social Psychology*, pp. 165–282. Chicago: University of Chicago Press.

—— 1936. *Movements of Thought in the Nineteenth Century*. Chicago: University of Chicago Press.

Merleau-Ponty, Maurice. 1978 (1960). "The Philosopher and the Sociologist." In Thomas Luckmann, ed., *Phenomenology and Sociology*, pp. 142–60. London: Penguin.

Molotch, Harvey. 1974. "News as Purposive Behavior." *American Sociological Review* 39:101–12.

Pollner, Melvin. 1979. "Explicative Transactions: Making and Managing Meaning in Traffic Court." In G. Psathas, ed., *Studies in Everyday Language*, pp. 227–55. New York: Irvington.

Pomerantz, Anita. 1980. "The Social Organization of Enforcement Systems" (unpublished paper). Department of Sociology, UCLA.

Sacks, Harvey, Emmanuel A. Schegloff, and Gail Jefferson. 1974. "A Simplest Systematics for the Organization of Turn-Taking for Conversation." *Language* 50:696–735.

Sartre, Jean-Paul. 1966. *Being and Nothingness*. New York: Philosophical Library.

—— 1971. "J. P. Sartre répond." *Telos* 9:110–15.

Schutz, Alfred. 1978 (1940). "Phenomenology and the Social Sciences." In Thomas Luckmann, ed., *Phenomenology and the Social Sciences*, pp. 119–41. London: Penguin.

—— 1967 (1932). *The Phenomenology of the Social World*. Evanston, Ill.: Northwestern University Press.

Tiryakian, Edward M. 1965. "Existential Phenomenology and the Sociological Tradition." *American Sociological Review* 30:674–688.

—— 1970. "Structural Sociology." In Tiryakian and McKinney, eds., *Theoretical Sociology*, pp. 111–36. New York: Appleton-Century-Croft.

—— 1978. "Durkheim and Husserl: A Comparison of the Spirit of Positivism and the Spirit of Phenomenology." The Hague: Joseph Bien.

Tuchman, Gaye. 1978. *Making News*. New York: Free Press.

Zimmerman, Don H. 1969. "Tasks & Troubles: The Practical Bases of Work Activities in a Public Assistance Agency." In D. A. Hansen, ed., *Explorations in Sociology and Counselling*. New York: Houghton Mifflin.

Zimmerman, Don H. and Melvin Pollner. 1970. "The Everyday World as a Phenomenon." In Jack Douglas, ed., *Understanding Everyday Life*, pp. 80–103. Chicago: Aldine.

NINE

From Reduction to Linkage:
The Long View of
the Micro-Macro Debate

Our aim in this essay is to take the "long view" on the micro-macro debate by providing a historical and theoretical framework within which current arguments can be read. This debate has gradually emerged as a key issue in contemporary sociological theory, transcending paradigmatic boundaries and fostering communication between different theory traditions and disciplinary integration. Although the micro-macro theme has entered sociological theorizing as a distinct and firmly established issue only in recent decades, its prehistory can be traced from late medieval thinking through postwar metamethodological debates over science, epistemology, and political philosophy.

We argue below that the micro-macro dichotomy should be viewed as an analytic distinction and that all attempts to link it to concrete dichotomies—such as "individual versus society" or "action versus order"—are fundamentally misplaced. Only if it is viewed analytically, moreover, can the linkage between micro and macro be achieved. During its intellectual prehistory, however, the very distinction between micro and macro was superseded by other conceptual oppositions. Powerful philosophical dichotomies conflated this more analytically differentiated notion with deeply entrenched disputes that were often supported by political and social conflicts. This overlapping of the micro-macro theme with epistemological, ontological, and political distinctions gave rise to fierce disputes demanding that decisions be made between incompatible alternatives. Such an all-or-nothing choice precluded any attempt at reconciliation.

Written with Bernhard Giesen.

Transmitting the micro-macro theme from general, all-encompassing philosophical and political debates into the disciplinary realm of social science, we believe, gradually qualified the oppositions and conflicts implied in presociological statements of the problem. The effort to constitute sociology as a scientific discipline helped to close the border to ontological and metaphysical issues. The result was that for the first time the problem could be treated in a distinctly sociological rather than philosophical or political manner. We show that in its initial, classical phase, sociological theory recast the conflated dichotomies into arguments about the general character of empirical processes. The questions came to focus on whether action was rational or interpretive and whether social order was negotiated between individuals or imposed by collective, or emergent, forces.

Translation into sociological theory did not, however, fully "secularize" the micro-macro debate. Although the imposition of empirical discipline closed off certain philosophical extremes and pointed to certain synthetic possibilities, in the main the controversy was simply shifted to another level. Indeed, the postclassical period witnessed a resurgence of philosophical debate that polarized the issue anew. Political and explanatory issues were once again conflated, the very possibility of emergent properties was sharply challenged, and metamethodological controversy erupted concerning the boundaries of sociology as a scientific discipline.

This philosophical debate was followed by a new round of dichotomizing argument in sociology. The response to this phase, in turn, depended upon the attempt to conceptualize the micro-macro theme as a distinction between different levels of empirical reality. This, we believe, has been the distinctive accomplishment of sociological debate in its most recent phase. Rather than confront incompatible conceptions about the constitution of social reality, the most important contemporary theoretical arguments seek to discover empirical relations among different levels of social reality. This analytical differentiation of the micro-macro relation has generated a new level of interparadigmatic discourse and a new statement of the problem: the conflict over reduction is being replaced by the search for linkage.

The path toward linkage and the implied possibilities for theoretical synthesis were prepared by the earlier theorizing of Max Weber and Talcott Parsons. Their theories resist classification as either micro or macro. The current movement from reduction to linkage is inspired by the example set by these first great attempts at micro-macro synthesis, even when it does not follow the theories themselves.

Philosophical Background

Despite the current effort to overcome the rigorous opposition between micro and macro approaches through analytical differentiation and theoretical synthesis, it is impossible to overlook the fact that current debate bears the unmistakable imprint of earlier controversies. In our view this does not represent a weakness of contemporary theorizing; it suggests, rather, its strength and vigor in the face of demands for reasoning of a purely inductive kind.

Although superseded and, to some extent, transformed by classical sociological ideas, the micro-macro distinction ranks with the core oppositions in Occidental thinking, at least since the late medieval differentiation between the individual and the state. Entering academic discourse and political debate as part of the nominalism versus realism dispute, it helped form the background for such enduring controversies as whether the whole is more than the sum of its parts, whether state and society can claim ontological and moral primacy over individuals, and whether the meaning of concepts can be reduced to their empirical referent or involves some transcendental ideal.

Although connected to one another by reference to a common ontology and frequently intertwined during the history of modern thought, the epistemological dimension of this dichotomy can be distinguished from the political and constitutional dimensions. After the turn of the century, neopositivism, and the growing pressure on antipositivist philosophy to cope with epistemological presuppositions, generated new formulations of the old theme. Vitalism in biology and Gestalt theory in psychology defended the macro position against radical psychological behaviorism and rigorous scientific physicalism. The philosophical background for the micro position was provided by the neopositivist postulation of a unified science based on the atomistic ontology and experimental methodology of modern physics. The repercussions of these early epistemological and ontological disputes continued to be felt in postwar metamethodological debates and in confrontations over the mind-body problem of contemporary philosophy of social science.

The political branch of the micro-macro dichotomy dates from the controversy over constitutions versus divine rights of kings. It was also related to arguments that the newly emerging nation should be the prime basis for political loyalty as compared with the societal community composed of individuals. The contractual thinking of the Scottish moralists, as well as John Stuart Mill's liberalism, established the individualist tradition in political philosophy. This so-called Anglo-Saxon tradition has formed the background for the micro orientation in classical and contemporary sociological debate. That it took shape against the mainstream of continental political thinking must not be forgotten. The German idealism of Fichte, Hegel, and Herder and the French revolutionary naturalism of such thinkers as Rousseau provided the holistic orientations upon which classical and contemporary macroformulations arose. Although the development of sociological thinking in the past 100 years has tended to undermine this relation between geographical, cultural, and theoretical concerns, national styles continue to canalize the theoretical conflict over mico and macro today.

The Micro-Macro Split in Classical Sociological Theory

In the latter part of the nineteenth century and the early years of the twentieth, these philosophical dichotomies came to be reproduced in the founding statements of a new, more empirical mode of discourse: sociological theory. Although general and abstract, sociological theory differs from philosophy in its explicit commitment to empirical science. In sociological theory nonempirical concerns such as metaphysics and morals become implicit parts of discourse; they rarely define its explicit character. They become the "presuppositions" of sociological argument. Onto this general, presuppositional level, the philosophical debate about individual and society comes to be translated, and even this presuppositional debate is often conducted in terms of the nature of concrete, empirical facts.

Although Marx eventually produced the most influential argument for a purely macroperspective in sociology, the emphasis in his early writings was on consciousness and action. Bringing Hegel's transcendental idealism "down to earth" via Feuerbach's critical materialism, Marx brought the force of critical rationality into play by insisting on the centrality of human activity (praxis) over objective force. He argued in "Theses on Feuerbach" (Marx 1965 [1845]) against "the materialist doctrine that men are products of circumstances" and that "changed men are products of other circumstances." Such a doctrine forgets, he insists, "that it is men who change circumstances." This radical emphasis on the activist changing of circumstances clearly gives to the micro level pride of place. When Marx goes on to argue against "the materialist doctrine" on the grounds that it "necessarily arrives at dividing society into two parts," one begins to wonder just how radical this early sociological call for micro analysis might be. Does the critique of materialism mean that we must conceive of individuals and consciousness alone, without any reference to supraindividual structures?

This, of course, was not at all the case. Why it was not, moreover, can tell us something important about how the micro-macro link can be conceived sociologically. From the very beginnings of Marx's sociological writings it is clear that he never conceived of the actor individualistically, and because he did not do so he would never suggest a purely micro focus. The praxis that changes circumstances in Marx's early writings is a form of interpersonal communication that achieves its critical leverage by appealing to deeply held, universalistic systems of belief, that is, beliefs that unite isolated individuals. As Marx 1967 ([1842]:135) explains in one of his earliest essays from this period, "Ideas, which have conquered our intelligence and our minds, ideas that reason has forged in our conscience, are chains from which we cannot tear ourselves away without breaking our hearts." Focusing on individual consciousness—in a cognitive, moral, or affective sense—and the micro level, in other words, does not necessarily imply an *individualistic* position that sees this individual consciousness as unrelated to any distinctively social, or collective, process. What it does mean, however, is that such collective force must be subjectively conceptualized.

The empirical micro analysis to which such subjective formulations of collective order might lead is suggested by Marx's focus on alienation in the *Economic and Philosophical Manuscripts*. In contrast to purely philosophical writing—for example, earlier idealist and later existentialist traditions—alienation is not viewed here as an ontological condition, a conception that guarantees the irredeemable dichotomy of individual (micro) and society (macro). Marx describes alienation, rather, as a contingent empirical fact. This allows him the possibility of thinking in terms of interrelated levels. Arguing that alienation is, indeed, an individual experience of estrangement, he suggests that it can be seen simultaneously as a "translation" on the individual level of interpersonal, structural conditions. In these early writings, however, Marx does not insist on complete homology, on the replication of macro in micro conditions. He has vigorously called our attention to the micro level of alienation for a reason.

He believes that it reveals a relatively autonomous mediation of collective order that must be studied in its own right. When Marx (1963 [1844]:131) insists that alienation creates private property, and not that private property creates alienation, he is arguing that individual experience can be a significant independent variable in macro sociological analysis even when it is not considered to be the source of social order in a presuppositional way.

Marx moves in his later theorizing to a more exclusively macro focus, but he does not do so because he has moved from an individualistic to a collectivist philosophical position. His focus earlier was on emergent properties located at the empirical level of the individual; his focus later is on emergent properties located at the empirical level of the group, collectivity, and system. He continues, in other words, to recognize emergent properties, and this means that his presuppositions about order—whether order is "individualistic" or "collectivist" (see Alexander 1982a and chs. 1 and 8 above)—remain the same. What has changed is not his approach to order but his understanding of action. However, this shift can have significant consequences for the micro-macro link. Because he has shifted from an expressive conception of action to an instrumental one in the writings after 1845, Marx uses alienation neither to underline emotional estrangement nor to establish, on this basis, the necessity for a micro focus. He uses it, rather, to emphasize the objectified, antiemotional quality of action in capitalist society and to establish, on these grounds, the irrelevance of the micro, "motivational question" to sociological analysis (see Alexander 1982b:48–53).

Because commodification is "in the saddle" and exchange value rules, the concrete, particular sensibility that Marx believes underlies human interpretation in noncapitalist societies is impossible. Because actors are reduced to beings that calculate their external environment mechanically, theoretical attention shifts entirely away from the microanalysis of consciousness, motive, and intention. Capitalists and workers are ruled by the naturalistic laws of social life. The inevitable movement from absolute to relative surplus value propels them to socialist revolution. Objective circumstances now change people.

Marx's brilliant empirical elaboration of instrumental action and of the way it is restricted by macro structures made late Marxism paradigmatic for every sociological theory that sought to privilege macro over micro analysis. This structural emphasis in turn has created fundamental problems for Western neo-Marxism, which has tried to reinstate the centrality of consciousness to critical theory.

The classical alternative to such a structuralist approach to collective order was established by Durkheim, who, from the beginning of his career, searched for a way to combine awareness of society with commitment to the individual. Durkheim's connection to the philosophical traditions of holism and realism is abundantly clear, as in his famous declaration in *The Rules of Sociological Method* (Durkheim 1938 [1895]) that "social facts are things" that have a "coercive" relation to the individual. The same cautionary statement must be made about Durkheimian structuralism as was made about Marxian and for the same reason. Even in his most dramatically macro vein, Durkheim's commitment to sociological as opposed to philosophical realism led him to root society in interaction, an effort that allowed him to avoid the maximal antiindividualist extreme. In *The Division of Labor in Society* (Durkheim 1933 [1893]), for example, he locates the macro, social force in the "non-contractual elements of contract," and he sees these as emerging from the functional interventions of an order-seeking state. The historical origins of modern social structure are similarly linked, in Book Two of that early work, to concrete interaction, in this case to the increasing density of population and the resulting struggle for survival. In *Suicide* (1951 [1897]), Durkheim links reified "suicidogenic currents," which he treats as fields of force in a purely macro sense, to patterns of interaction in different kinds of solidary groups.

Although Durkheim's commitments to empirical reasoning may have prevented him from the realist excesses of philosophical theorizing, it is nonetheless true that in these earlier writings he conceptualized emergent properties as exclusively macro. Only as his thinking developed in the 1890s did Durkheim find a way to avoid the later Marx's antithesis between individual (micro) and social (macro) determination. In a sense he rediscovered the insight of the early Marx. He came to understand that if action were conceptualized as symbolic and emotional, then collective order could be seen as exercising constraint by its ability to inform the exercise of these voluntary capacities. This led Durkheim to acknowledge, in principle, that a social theory premised on emergentism could have an empirically micro focus.

Thus, as Durkheim moved toward a fundamentally "religious" theory of society, he insisted that the most powerful elements of symbol systems depended upon sacredness, that they were effective only because they drew upon the most protective feelings from individual personalities (see Alexander 1982b:259–98). When Durkheim (1965 [1912]) described how Aborigines, in their ritual ceremony, transformed themselves into figures of the totem animal, this was theoretical, not merely ethnographic, description. He had discovered how individual action reproduced social control. Action consisted of unending representations, symbolic activity that conceptualized collective representations in an appropriately individual way.

Micro analysis was certainly justified by this later mode of Durkheim's theorizing, for the illumination of perceptual processes and emotional and symbolic exchanges was believed to be at the heart of collective life. Durkheim never, however, developed even the rudiments of a social psychology that could explain such micro process satisfactorily. This failure, combined with his positivist commitment to observable, "lawful" regularities and his missionary zeal to defend the autonomy of the sociological discipline, meant that the strikingly micro qualities of his later theorizing were never brought systematically to light, by Durkheim, his followers, or his interpreters on the contemporary scene. Just as Marx's later writings became paradigmatic for macro theorists writing within a rationalistic and materialistic tradition, Durkheim's later theory became the "classical" referent for sociologists who believed in the subjectivity of action but considered it to be ordered in a strictly macro, antivoluntaristic way.

Durkheim and Marx, then, for all the complexities and possibilities of their work, produced strongly polemical arguments for a one-sidedly macro emphasis (Alexander 1984 [chapter 1, above]). Given the range of philosophical discourse that lay in the background of this classical debate, it was inevitable that their positions would be challenged by theories polemicizing just as strongly in a micro, antistructural way. Just as Durkheim and Marx conflated the presuppositional defense of the collective, or emergentist, approach with extratheoretical issues such as ideology, so would the individualism of these "anticollectivist" approaches be underlined by latent political points.

American pragmatism developed in direct antagonism to transcendental idealism in both its Kantian and Hegelian forms and, at least in its Jamesian mode (Lewis and Smith 1980), presented as strong a reaction to realism of any kind. Individual experience, in the pragmatist perspective, is the source of ideas, and meaning arises from interaction rather than vice versa. Mead's work represents the most significant translation of pragmatic philosophy into sociological theory. Inspired by American ideology, which insisted on the fluid and malleable character of its democratic society, Mead (1964 [1934]) likened society to a game. The move by any given actor is drawn forth in response to the action of another; it cannot be seen as the product of some a priori collective force. The reaction of another player, moreover, defines in significant ways the very meaning of the action to which that player responds. In the contingency of such game situations, actions and responses become the critical source for patterning social order. So conceived, Meadian theory leads to a micro sociology devoid of macro reference. Mead wrote, in fact, almost nothing about institutional processes or the internal constitution of cultural systems.

To present Mead in this way, however, is to emphasize only one side of his work, albeit the side that has been picked up and emphasized by his successors in the interactionist tradition. Although meaning can grow only out of interaction with others, Mead believed, actors' perceptions of these others gradually become so generalized that they carry a "slice" of society around in their heads. He was convinced, moreover, that the very spontaneity and randomness of interaction guarantee that this generalized other will not differ radically from one actor to another. Thus although games are contingent and proceed through responses, every intention and every understanding is filtered through the layered expectations that constitute rules. Mead's actors interpret reality by referring to social standards, and the very idea of standards implies some interpersonal regularities.

Mead's work, then, presents a micro analysis that is open to more collectivist concerns (Alexander 1985 [chapter 8, above]), much as Durkheim's theory presented a macro perspective that opened to the individual. Mead's theory, moreover, promised to get beyond the "homology" or "reproduction" position that limited the scope of micro theory of a Durkheimian kind. Just as Durkheim completely lacked a social psychology, however, Mead lacked an institutional theory. For Durkheim this meant that the possibilities for macro-micro linkage went unnoticed; for Mead it meant exactly the same thing. None of Mead's followers was able to discern in his micro analysis a collective link; experience, not individually mediated structure, became the hallmark of interactionist micro analysis.

Similar problems affected the other major development in micro analysis that viewed action in a subjectivist manner. Although Freud was certainly not a philosopher, his focus on the individual reflected broader intellectual movements, such as Darwinism and vitalism, that were significant challengers to realism in his day. The explicitly sociological theories of early psychoanalysis, as articulated, for example, in *Group Psychology and the Analysis of the Ego* (Freud 1959 [1921]), *Future of an Illusion* (Freud 1928 [1927]), and *Civilization and Its Discontents* (Freud 1961 [1930]), described extraindividual group processes as threats to individual action that should be neutralized whenever possible. Not only did the psychoanalytic theory of society deny that any necessary function was served by groups and collectivities, but also it linked the very existence of the latter to individual fantasy and pathology. It conceived of them as distortions of reality that could be eliminated if individuals became more rational. From this theoretical foundation there followed the dictum that all collective phenomena—wars, revolutions, institutions, cultural life—must be explained as manifestations of individual personalities. This reductionist epiphenomenalism has been responsible for the radically micro focus of most psychoanalytically informed social science to the present day.

In dramatic opposition to this reduction stands Freud's more fully developed and more empirically substantiated clinical theory of the personality (e.g., Freud 1961 [1930]). Starting from the primordial fact of an actor's need to cathect external objects, Freud described an unending series of object internalizations. As cathexis spreads to objects that are further away from the nurturant, primary ones, personality growth is propelled by successive internalizations. On the one hand Freud sees the subject as constituted through such introjections; on the other he sees socialized actors as independent inputs to the structure of the very objects they encounter in turn.

Freud's clinical theory, then, by giving both extraindividual and individual-contingent elements their due, laid the basis for a systematic reconstruction of the micro-macro link. But this theoretical possibility was never pursued within the orthodox psychoanalytic tradition itself. The problem was not so much the absence of an institutional theory—the problem for pragmatism—but the presence of an institutional theory whose presuppositions were in radical opposition to those informing the clinical work.

Mead and Freud outlined the "other side" of Durkheim's macro theory, portraying micro subjective processes that could be orderly without coercive constraint. There also developed a "micro mirror image" for the other classical macro tradition, the theory of constraint without subjectivity produced by Marx. Rather than emphasize interpretation or emotion, this micro theory portrays action as objective, mechanistic, and rational. The Marxian image of action as exchange is maintained, but the ideological critique that bound this theory to the capitalist period is discarded. The point is not that actors do not engage in social life but that when they do so they are not conceived as being socialized before that interaction. As a result, they calculate their relation to external reality rather than interpret the nature of their attachment to it. Because calculation is assumed to be an inherent, natural capacity, actors do not need to be supplied by society with interpretative standards. This assumed rationality, moreover, undermines the possible emotionality of action, for the latter is thought to have irrational, hence incalculable, implications. For rational action theory is committed to the notion that behavior can be predicted in standardized, objective ways.

This rational action approach, though just as instrumentalist as Marx's, differs by being aggressively individualistic. Indeed, Marx conceived of his own theory as a "critique of political economy" because while accepting its presuppositions about action he rejected its individualism. Rational action theory brings the argument full circle; its proponents often conceive it as a response not only to subjectivist thinking but also to the coercive implications of theories such as Marx's, which insist on encasing the rational actor in a collective frame.

This rationalistic version of micro theory did not present itself in nearly as cohesive a manner as interactionism or psychoanalysis, nor can it be related to intellectual developments so central to the twentieth century. At least three different traditions fed into it. The most important development for its contemporary form has been behaviorism, the "psychology without consciousness" developed by Watson and reinforced by the experiments of Pavlov. Behaviorism follows the Darwinian emphasis on adaptation and experience but excludes the pragmatic emphasis on interpretation. It portrays action as stimulus and response and views learning as the agglomeration of material experiences through physical reinforcement. That these stimuli and reinforcements were often orderly, and produced orderly behavior in turn, was viewed by behaviorism as the happy but unintended consequence of an endless chain of individual interactions.

The same emphasis on the unintended order of rational actions was, of course, at the heart of the rational choice theory articulated by classical economics. Beginning with the work of Adam Smith (1776) and extending into neoclassical thinking in the twentieth century, economic theory has developed a simple yet powerful calculus for predicting individual action. Once again, motivational rationality and significant environmental parameters are assumed as givens. Prices play the role of stimulus; purchases and investments, the role of response. Social order emerges from actions that have an entirely individual, self-interested bent. Markets structure opportunities so that transactions can be mutually profitable and reciprocity established. Because of this "invisible hand," the micro focus of rational choice is considered sufficient unto itself.

In the history of sociology, the micro emphasis fostered by behaviorism and rational choice theory was given powerful support by Simmel's sociology (e.g., Homans 1958). This is ironic given that Simmel's philosophical position was antinominalist and that he sharply rejected any antisubjective understanding of action. The peculiarities of Simmel's reception can be traced to the artificial divisions he established between different dimensions of his theorizing, particularly the distinction between formal sociology and metaphysics or cultural sociology (Simmel 1950). Whereas metaphysics deals with subjectivity and speculates about generalities, sociology properly so called must abstract away from the particular content of experience and speak only about forms. Formal relationships such as conflict or exchange must, Simmel insisted, be looked at purely in terms of their quantitative characteristics—for example, the number of people involved and the number and rate of interactions. Within the confines of such objective parameters, then, the structure of social order can be portrayed as emerging from individual action and choice.

Although Simmel acknowledged that general concepts such as "the individual" exist and may even be significant regulators of interaction (Simmel 1977), he portrayed them as standing outside and above the heads of individual actors. As a result, he often portrays interaction as if it proceeded without any reference to "concepts" at all (e.g., Simmel 1955). It is not surprising, then, that significant aspects of his formal sociology could be taken up by behaviorists and exchange theorists as justifications for pursuing a purely micro sociology.

This discussion of the classical sociological translations of philosophical debates about individual and society, brief and schematic as it has been, suggests that from the very beginning sociological thinking offered the promise of more synthetic, less resolutely antagonistic conceptualizations of the relationship between the two. On the one hand, the explicit disciplinary commitment to "society" created an inherent interest in the connection between individual and collective behavior even among such reductive sociological theorists as the behaviorists. On the other hand, the explicitly empirical emphasis of the new discipline forced even such macro theorists as Marx and Durkheim to seek to ground their references to collective forces in the activities of observable, acting individuals. If a sociologist, for disciplinary *cum* presuppositional reasons, emphasized the significance of collective or group forces, this did not mean that he or she denied the existence of acting individuals in an ontological sense. In fact, this did not even mean that he or she would deny that individual, micro process had a critical role to play in the maintenance of macro order. Because the collective forces Durkheim conceptualized were "ideal" but also empirical, they had to reside, in ontological terms, in the internal states of human individuals.

As this suggests, sociological theorists separated questions of ontology from questions of epistemology and reformulated both issues in more strictly sociological terms (Alexander 1982a:64–112). For sociological theory, epistemology becomes "the problem of action": is the knowing actor rational or interpretative? Yet, however action is postulated, the ultimate source of this knowledge remains to be decided. It may be located inside or outside the knowing individual. This is the problem of order, and it indicates the sociological recasting of the ontological question. The question of order for sociology concerns the ultimate source of social patterns; it does not concern the ontological question of whether these patterns or the individuals who may or may not support them are real. The origin of patterns may be conceived individualistically, in which case the "credit" for social patterns, the role of independent variable, is given to micro process in a contingent way. Conversely, the origin of patterns may be conceived as emanating from some source outside any particular individual, in which case the individual actor, whose existence per se is still acknowledged, may be conceived as the victim of collective circumstances or their more or less willing (because socialized) medium.

The emergence of sociological theory from philosophy, then, makes the micro-macro issue significantly more complex. For sociological theory, the micro may be conceived as a level of analysis that deserves independent consideration even though the individual may not be considered, either ontologically or metaphysically, as the source of order in his or her own right. Because sociology insists on an empirical focus, and because its disciplinary vocation is directed to society, the issues of contingency and freedom are not inherently connected to a focus on the individual per se. It is for this reason that empirical dispute ranges so widely.

Because of such presuppositional complexity, at least five major approaches to the micro-macro relation have been taken up. Sociological theory has maintained that (1) rational, purposeful individuals create society through contingent acts of freedom; (2) interpretative individuals create society through contingent acts of freedom; (3) socialized individuals re-create society as a collective force through contingent acts of freedom; (4) socialized individuals reproduce society by translating existing social environment into the micro realm; and (5) rational, purposeful individuals acquiesce to society because they are forced to by external, social control.

To explain this range of possibilities, it is vital to understand that in sociological theory the question of action is separated from the question of order. A collective position may be adopted that denies the primary responsibility of individuals and therefore negates a primarily micro focus. This position on order, however, may be associated with either of two different understandings of action: the instrumental-objective or the interpretative-subjective. The collective theory that takes an objectivist approach to action denies to subjective perceptions of order any empirical role at all, militating against any particular focus on the micro or individual level itself. This is option 5. The collective theory that takes an interpretative approach, in contrast, makes subjective perception central, although it insists that the contents of this perception lie beyond the contingency of individual acts. In this theoretical tradition micro processes may well become central points of empirical interest, if only because phenomena such as personalities and interaction are conceived as central "conveyer belts" for collective facts. If individual subjectivity is so conceived as mere reproduction, we have option 4. If, however, subjective collectivist theory gives to the micro level analytical autonomy—if, that is, it recognizes that the socialized individual re-creates in the process of reproducing—then we have option 3.

For theoretical positions that stress the complete contingency of social action, moreover, even analytical autonomy is not enough. The micro is equated with the individual, and the latter is viewed as the primary source of order itself. To understand the relevance of even this latter tradition to the micro-macro debate, however, it is not sufficient to focus on the issue of individualism alone. Individualistic conceptions of order, just like collectivist ones, are always informed by different understandings of action. Individualistic theories may stress the rational and objective character of action, in which case microanalysis focuses on empirical phenomena such as costs, investments, and opportunities (option 1). If, in contrast, the subjectivity of individualistic order is stressed, the micro focus is shifted to the processes of interpretation and to how they are conducted in a contingent manner. This marks option 2.

In our discussion in this section we have suggested that classical political economy and behaviorism pursued the first option, whereas pragmatism and psychoanalysis embraced the second. Durkheim largely embraced the fourth possibility, and in his later and most influential writings Marx pursued the fifth. Contained in the theorizing of almost all of these figures there exists the outlines of a more synthetic link. Depending on the theorist, this link points to combining several options, embracing option 3, or both.

The First Synthetic Formulation:
Max Weber

Although each of the positions we have described took up the relationship between micro and macro dimension in its own particular way, and some made genuine contributions to outlining their actual interpenetration, all remained burdened by overcommitments to one side or the other. Of all the classical sociologists, only Weber seemed to see a clear way out of this traditional dilemma. Although in the end Weber's formulations are still not entirely satisfactory—and even their precise nature is subject to dispute—his contributions have remained central for every subsequent effort at establishing a micro-macro link.

As a German progressive strongly influenced by the Enlightenment and liberal traditions, Weber was particularly forceful in his rejection of organicist formulations. Because of this heightened sensitivity, which contrasts, for example, with the relatively complacent attitude of Durkheim, one finds no trace of an ontologically collectivist position in Weber's work. He insists over and over again that all that "really" exists is social action.

This insistence has often, however, misled his interpreters to portray his theory as nominalistic. For this reason the rubric "action theory" is often applied to his work. To interpret Weber in this way, however, is to ignore not only the empirical mediation of ontology that is at the foundation of sociological theory but also the specifically antiindividualistic thrust of Weber's own work.

Collective order was still Weber's point of departure. What he managed to avoid was conceptualizing this order in a manner that would imply the insignificance of acting individuals. Rather than speak about "forces," Weber was careful to talk about "uniformities of action." A uniformity is not something that happens to an actor but a shorthand way of talking about what is actually a series of actions. "Within the realm of social action," he wrote in *Economy and Society* (Weber 1978:29), "certain empirical uniformities can be observed, that is, courses of action that are repeated by the actor or (simultaneously) occur among numerous actors." What sociology is concerned with is "typical modes of action," not individual action as such.

Although empirical and action related, uniformities are "orders" in the sense that they are not reducible to free and contingent acts. "Orders" refer to arrangements that are not contingent in the framework of any given act. Such arrangements can also be called "structures," and structures, in all their historical and comparative variation, are what Weber's sociology is all about. Weber wrote about religious systems, legal institutions, political frameworks, modes of production, and urban associations. He devoted himself to exposing the structural patterns that are internal to each of these institutional spheres—the internal logic of theodicies, for example, and the inherent contradictions of patrimonialism.

Weber never assumed that such a system emphasis excludes the individual. His theorizing moves back and forth, naturally and fluidly, between the macro analysis of ideational complexes and institutional systems and the micro analysis of how individuals within such situations make interpretations and purposefully act. Theodicies develop only because the human concern with death makes intellectual speculation about salvation a fundamental form of social activity (e.g., Weber 1946 [1916]). Religious rationalization is possible only because the cognitive, affective, and moral constitutions of individuals lead them to respond to typical situational exigencies in an abstracting and systematizing way. Patrimonial systems can be contradictory because motives for status and power are omnipresent and because individuals' sense of their ideal interest emerges only within the context of local and concrete interactions.

Still, the recognition of individuals in societies is not, as we have seen, sufficient by itself to define a sociological position on the micro-macro dispute. Durkheim and Marx, although in much less sophisticated ways than Weber, held views on this issue that were not fundamentally different from Weber's. How does Weber differ from them? Where does Weber stand in terms of the five ideal-typical positions outlined above? To find out, it is necessary to explore his understanding of action separately from his understanding of order and to see whether this understanding blocks or facilitates an appreciation of contingency.

We argued earlier that the micro level can be forcefully brought into more collective theorizing only if subjective interpretation is considered a major characteristic of action. In much of his work Weber does, in fact, make interpretation central to his understanding of action. In *Economy and Society* (1978:4) he wrote that sociology is "a science which attempts the interpretative understanding of social action in order thereby to arrive at a causal explanation of its course and effects." In an earlier essay, *Roscher and Knies,* he insisted that to "understand" an action one must "identify a concrete 'motive' or complex of motives 'reproducible in inner experience,' a motive to which we can attribute the conduct in question with a degree of precision" (Weber 1975:25).

When these statements are juxtaposed, it is clear that Weber was making two central and interrelated points. First, subjective motivation is central to conduct. Second, because of this centrality sociology must involve a micro analysis of the course of concrete, individual interaction. Such an analysis may not necessarily reveal the unique contingency of individual action. If the motives discovered through micro analysis are typical or "uniform," then the micro analysis will illuminate how individual action is crucial for the reproduction of ideational structures (option 4), not for their re-creation (option 3).

Weber devoted a major portion of his sociological energy to a historical and comparative analysis of the social requisites of individuality, to demonstrating that social reproduction increasingly comes to focus on the autonomous individual. Analyzing the transition from sib societies to entrepreneurial capitalism, he demonstrated how collective structures—from religion to law to family—affect the individual actor's capacities for individuality. He showed that individual autonomy is neither ontologically given nor the product of material sanctions and rewards but, rather, dependent upon the socially given perceptions of self and on socially structured motivation. The very fact that a reductionistic micro sociology can be proposed in modern social theory, Weberian analysis suggests, may itself be evidence of this millennia-long social reconstruction of the individual. If the modern individual is indeed capable of resistance to social pressure, it is because of an inner strength that is historically and socially derived.

Weber, then, clearly articulated the fourth theoretical position on the micro-macro link presented earlier: he showed that the social environment relies upon its reproduction via socialized individual action. Weber did not merely render a theoretically sophisticated, historically amplified demonstration of this essentially Durkheimian point, however; he went beyond it in a significant way. His insistence on the centrality of action made him extraordinarily sensitive to contingency. This pushed him toward option 3, to the recognition that socialized individuals re-create society through their contingent action.

Historiographically, this comes through in Weber's insistence on developmental as opposed to evolutionary history. He stresses the role of historical accident (e.g., Weber 1949 [1905]) and how the inherent temporality of action makes every general pattern dependent on specific, open-ended, individual decisions. Sociologically, the emphasis on contingency comes through in Weber's insistence on the role of leadership in politics and charismatic innovation in religion. What each of these emphases—accident, leadership, and charisma—entails is not simply empirical recognition of the micro level but also an acceptance of its relative autonomy. Events, not just situations, become subjects of sociological analysis.

Given the power of Weber's insight, it is strange that so little micro analysis actually appears in his work. We find little in Weber about the processes of individual socialization, the dynamics of family interaction, the phenomenon of political persuasion, and the emotional and moral underpinnings of social movements. Indeed, Weber's systematic sociology of modern twentieth-century society depicts a structural "iron cage" that produces adherence regardless of individual motive or inclination. In terms of the micro-macro link, this later sociology of modern society is not much different from that of Marx. Both are organized around theoretical option 5: autonomous individuals acquiesce to society because they are forced to do so by coercive social control. This perspective makes reference to the micro level irrelevant, although it does not, of course, imply any ontological collectivism in the philosophical sense.

How has Weber arrived at such a position, a position that denies the very linkage between micro and macro he devoted so much of his work to sustain? He does so, we suggest, because of presuppositional tendencies (Alexander 1983a) in his work that counteract his interpretative understanding of action. There are strains of *Realpolitik* and liberal utilitarianism in Weber that often lead him to presuppose action in a materialistic, objective, and instrumental manner. If action is so conceived, motive becomes irrelevant. What matters is the external environment of action and the pressures it mounts. Even in Weber's sociology of traditional life, clear manifestations of such an antisubjectivist theory occurred. In his analysis of contemporary rationalization, these tendencies came to dominate his work. This is the source of Weber's ambiguous legacy to general sociology. It is also the reason that Weberian sociology has done so little since Weber to link the levels of micro and macro debate.

The Renewal of Philosophical Dichotomies in the Postwar Period

Although we have argued that sociological theory made significant advances over earlier philosophical considerations of the micro-macro problem, it certainly did not put an end to philosophical attempts to consider it anew. For one thing, there is an inherent link between sociological theory and philosophy. For another, the efforts of classical sociology in no sense could be seen as having resolved the micro-macro polarization. To the contrary, we have shown that in crucial respects the classical efforts can be seen as reproducing this polarization on another plane.

It should not be surprising, then, that after World War II there emerged a new round of philosophical argument that reinstated the links among ontological, metaphysical, and presuppositional issues and, in so doing, sought to frame the micro-macro argument in the most rigorous either-or terms. The focus has been on the problem of emergence. Individualists such as Hayek (1952), Popper (1958, 1961), Berlin (1954), and Watkins (1952, 1959) claimed that the concept of emergence should be reserved for the relation between mind and body. It serves to demarcate the realm of autonomy, free will, and deliberation from the realm of material nature and determinism. To speak of emergence as referring to the relation between individuals and collectivities, they argued, is to deny individual autonomy and to subject human beings to the will of supraindividual powers. Social entities such as institutions and collectivities cannot exist without the individuals who create and support them. They must, therefore be regarded as ontologically dependent on actions and cannot, for this reason, exhibit emergent properties. Any conception of supraindividual entities transcending the scope of individual actions is a mistaken category. There was a metaphysical dimension to the individualists' argument as well. They regarded collectivist ontology as implying antiliberal ideology. As political liberals, they condemned emergentism as a menace to Western ideas of democratic and economic freedom.

The opposition to these arguments for micro reduction, developed by philosophers such as Mandlebaum (1955, 1957) and Goldstein (1956, 1958) insisted on differentiating metaphysical from ontological issues (see also Giesen and Schmid 1977). Even if we concede the existence of supraindividual entities, our position with respect to them is by no means fixed. Just as faith in the existence of God need not automatically entail obedience to His will, the conception of supraindividual entities does not involve submission to them. We can admit that only individuals are capable of autonomous actions yet argue simultaneously that the products of human actions exhibit emergent properties (Mandlebaum 1955).

This defense of emergentism against the suspicion of metaphysical collectivism, though in no sense ending the debate, set the stage for a more delimited, methodological version of the philosophical dispute. Methodological individualists such as Nagel (1961), Opp (1972), and Malewski (1967) argued that micro theories are superior because the attributes of individuals are more directly observable than complex, theoretical attributes such as "stratification," "legal authority," or "class." On these grounds they argued that sociological terms must be translated into observable attributes of individual actors. This neopositivist design for the social sciences wished to follow the reductionist program of modern physics, for example, the successful reduction of chemical theories to physical laws. It was hoped that on the basis of a universal observational language, sociological terms could be translated into psychological terms and that on this basis a unified science of human behavior would emerge.

Methodological holists attacked these arguments for their naive empiricism. Without questioning the attraction of observability and reduction in principle, they nevertheless doubted the possibility of reducing existing sociological theories to psychological ones. Terms referring to social structures or institutions, they argued, can never be defined by individual behavior without enclosing other macro terms inside these new definitions (Mandelbaum 1955; Giesen and Schmid 1977). Even if this translation could be achieved, moreover, it would certainly not support the case for methodological individualism unambiguously. Translations and definitions established only a relation of equivalence; such a relation could be used to reduce micro to macro theories. Even the requirement of observability does not unequivocally justify micro theorizing. Attributes such as motive, personality, and biography can by no means be regarded as plainly observable; they are themselves informed by theoretical concepts. By the same token, in societies that have developed specialized institutional records and accounting procedures, macro structural properties such as legal systems or income distribution can, in fact, be observed.

This defense of the autonomy of sociology and the integrity of its subject matter, however, provided new grounds upon which individualistic philosophy sought to make its case. It was argued that even if we accept the notion that sociologists, and actors more generally, do use holistic notions about institutions and collectivities in their everyday practice, we cannot understand the meaning of such notions unless we recognize that they are merely the aggregate of individual actions. A satisfactory sociological explanation, then, must refer to the actions of individuals, to their intentions, and to their definitions of the situation. Indeed, Popper, Hayek, and Watkins went so far as to contend that the centrality of human action in the social sciences limited theoretical options much more sharply than in the natural sciences. They maintained that the only viable framework for social science is the paradigm of rational action, in which "rational" and "action" are viewed as inherent properties of the autonomous individual.

This justification of micro reduction through action theory leads us naturally to the sociological theory of Talcott Parsons. His work emerged at virtually the same time as this revival of postwar philosophical debate and, we believe, represented its most sophisticated sociological rejoinder.

The Second Synthetic Formulation: Talcott Parsons

Although this philosophical argumentation certainly affected sociological thinking about the micro-macro relation—and clearly played a major role in bringing the problem itself to theoretical center stage—its tendency to resuscitate conflationary and dichotomous modes of thinking about the problem did not necessarily reflect the level of sociological debate. For in the midst of this renewed controversy about the possibility of emergence, Talcott Parsons was elaborating a theory that went beyond even Weber in showing exactly how such emergence proceeds.

A sophisticated commitment to emergence—to the empirical and naturalistic quality of "collective" control—marked Parsons's theory from the outset. In this respect he benefited from Weber's remarkable sensitivity to this issue and from Durkheim's manifest mistakes. In *The Structure of Social Action*, Parsons (1937) called for a voluntaristic theory of action. He defined voluntarism only conditionally in an individualistic way. On the one hand, he insisted on the centrality of action in the liberal and utilitarian sense. This marked the micro aspect of his analysis. Throughout the book, for example, Parsons conceptualizes collective order in terms of "means/ends chains." On the other hand, Parsons insisted on distinguishing between what he called the "analytical" and the "concrete" individual. When he wrote about the "actor" in his concept of the "unit act"—the theoretical model of actor-means-ends-situation to which Parsons refers throughout the book—he meant to refer only to the analytical individual, not to a real individual in his or her concrete empirical form. What defines the analytical individual is the utter contingency of his or her acts, a quality Parsons identifies as effort. What defines the concrete individual, however, is not only effort but also all manner of social constraints. Parsons believed that the concrete empirical individual must be made a significant part of social theory if the latter is to be voluntaristic. This voluntarism, like the concrete individual, combines contingency and control and implies the need for a micro-macro link.

Parsons's sophistication about collective control was evident throughout his early work, but his focus was not on the structure of collective systems as such. He focused, rather, on the boundary between action and order. He wanted to know the precise mechanism that links micro, individual action to macro, collective context. He discovered this mechanism in the phenomenon of internalization, a process he believed lay at the heart of the most important accomplishments of Durkheim and Weber. Through recognizing internalization, a collective theory becomes voluntaristic.

Although Parsons discovered internalization in this early period, there is no discussion in *The Structure of Social Action* of the actual mechanisms by which such a process might be carried out. This was, in fact, the principal objection Parsons lodged against Durkheim: that he lacked a social psychology—in our terms, a micro theory—that could operationalize his subjectivist theory of order in a plausibly voluntaristic way. The need to supply such a mechanism defined the middle period of Parsons's career.

In the period that extended from the mid-1940s to the mid-1950s, Parsons developed the most important formulation of the micro-macro link since Weber. He did so by finding a way to combine two of the most important representatives of the micro-macro split: Freud and Durkheim. Durkheim had developed a theory of collective order implying that this order would be carried in the heads of individuals; his theory faltered, however, because he was unable to describe these interpreting individuals convincingly. Freud had demonstrated that interpretative, feeling individuals are formed from object internalizations of the external world; in his explicitly sociological work, however, he tried to explain this external world as if it were only the projection of personality.

Parsons sociologized the psychoanalytic theory of the personality and used these insights to psychologize fundamental macro processes in turn. In key chapters of his *Essays in Sociological Theory* (1954:89–102, 177–96, 298–322), *Family, Socialization, and Interaction Process* (and Bales 1955:3–186), and *Social Structure and Personality* (1963:passim), Parsons demonstrated in systematic empirical detail how the affective, cognitive, and moral development of the personality depend on the existence of group structures. The ecology and culture of an actor's environment structure the responses that can be made to his or her unfolding psychological needs. These responses, which are macro from the perspective of the personality, enter the actor's perceptual world, or micro environment. After being mediated by preexisting personality structures, they become new parts of the personality. The macro has thus become the micro. This dialectic continues in subsequent interactions. Because projections of the socialized personality affect the social world in strategic ways, the micro will almost immediately become macro again.

Parsons demonstrated this micro-macro dialectic for "pathological" and "normal" development alike. He showed, for example (e.g., Parsons 1954:298–322), that the distance between work and home in modern society, a macro fact, made the young male child overly dependent on his mother. One result of this is an exaggerated Oedipal complex, a micro development that makes it more difficult for adult males to control their dependency needs. Uncontrolled dependency produces frustration, and the anxiety is often displaced through aggression. The path of this displacement, however, can never be decided by this micro development alone. It is affected by the nature of group conflict in any particular society. Depending on the particular macro environment, it can be channeled into individual competition, into racial or class conflict, or into war between national units. Although this macro side is independent of psychological conditions, through the social channeling of aggression these conditions enter and transform the macro environment in turn.

In terms of normal development, Parsons showed that social differentiation makes individual autonomy possible. The separation of father from teacher, for example (Parsons 1963:129–54), makes rebellion against authority more possible and more controllable, which encourages decathexis from the parent and a full resolution of the Oedipal stage. Because successful resolution of this stage makes control of emotions and dependency more likely, it constitutes a micro basis for the development of universalistic culture. The original differentiation of teacher from parent, however, is itself dependent upon the existence of some overarching universalistic culture and some opportunities for mobility based on achievement rather than ascription. Micro structures are built on internalizations; macro structures depend on externalizations in turn.

As a result of his insight into the micro-macro link, Parsons elaborated the concept of "role." Roles are translations of macro, environmental demands onto the level of individual behavior. Roles are not collective in the ontological sense; they consist of internalizations, expectations, and resources that enter the contingent situation from some preexisting environment. The invisibility of roles allowed Parsons to insist that the apparently "purely micro" nature of individual interaction actually occurs within collective constraints.

In the sociological work that unfolded under the Parsonian rubric, the linkage between micro and macro was a central theme. Merton made the "role set" pivotal to a whole range of macrosociological processes (1968:422–40), and Goode (1960) demonstrated how systemic contradictions often made themselves felt only insofar as they created role strain. Family structures were investigated and systematically linked to social structure (Slater 1968, Levy 1949, Bellah 1970); the dynamics of group interaction processes were mapped (Bales 1951, Slater 1966), and this map was used as the basis for the "interchange" model of social systems at large (Parsons and Bales 1955). Models developed to explain sequences of family socialization were used for studying social change (Smelser 1959) and collective behavior (Smelser 1962), and the differentiation of familial roles was connected to differentiation between systems such as economies and polities (e.g., Parsons and Smelser 1956).

Although Parsons conceptualized the micro-macro link in a more sophisticated manner than ever before, he did so in what remained a limited way. The problem was that despite his concern with the individual, he ignored contingency. Durkheim was interested in nesting individual action within social constraints. Freud was intent on reducing individual action to organized personalities. Both of the thinkers upon whom Parsons drew for his own conception of the micro-macro link, in other words, were intent on exploding the myth of the autonomous individual. For Parsons this meant pursuing, as Durkheim did, micro-macro option 4, because he denied Freud's claim that organized personalities were not themselves reflections of social structure. Following both Freud and Durkheim, however, Parsons ignored the strands of the classical tradition that were concerned with contingency, either pragmatic or utilitarian. Both pragmatists and utilitarians recognized a space between actors and their environments, the former because interpretation intervened between every new moment and what was given before it (option 2), the latter because rational motivation objectified the environment of action in a manner that made it seem outside the acting individual (option 1).

Parsons was correct that sociology could not exist if the analytical individual were taken as the topic of micro analysis. He was incorrect, however, to think the very concept of contingency could be replaced by the relatively socialized, concrete individual alone. True, he had discovered the social psychology that Durkheim lacked, but he used this micro analysis only to root the social firmly in the individual. Although the concept of contingent "effort" existed in his earliest formulations of action, his neo-Durkheimian position left him unconcerned with action-as-effort—and therefore unable to conceptualize option 3—in all but a few segments of his subsequent work. Furthermore, his tendency to make action normative made it impossible to consider the possibility that order could be objectified and exert coercive control over action (option 5).

The Renewal of
Multiparadigmatic Debate

In the phase of sociological theorizing that followed this second major effort at synthesis, the controversies that had been rekindled earlier in philosophical discussion found their way back into sociological theory itself. In part this represented dissatisfaction with the limits of Parsons' understanding of linkage, both because of its idealist bias and because of its anticontingent stance. This motive represented, as it were, the "progressive" reason for the revival of the micro versus macro debate. From the perspective of the contemporary period (see, e.g., Alexander 1987), however, it is clear that these post-Parsonian debates can be considered regressive as well. Influenced by the revival of philosophical calls for dichotomization and by theoretical confusion about the meaning of Parsons' work, this new round of theorizing often failed to come to grips with the sophistication of Parsons' argument—and Weber's before him—that the interpenetration of micro and macro can be made.

Reconstituting the Dichotomies in American Sociology. In the period that extended roughly from the early 1960s to the early 1980s, sociological theorizing in the United States gradually severed the link that Parsons had laboriously constructed between micro analysis and macro analysis. On the one hand, there developed the most vigorous and creative renewal of micro theorizing in the history of sociology. On the other hand, there emerged a form of "structural analysis" that emphasized macro constraints at the expense of action. Because of historical circumstances such as the renewal of social conflict; because of American ideology, with its emphasis on freedom; and because of autonomous theoretical considerations, it became difficult for American theorists to accept Parsons' emphasis on the socialized individual. They demanded new conceptualizations of action, new models of order, and new formulations of contingency.

When Homans (1958, 1961) introduced exchange theory, he was renewing the very utilitarian theory that had constituted the basis of Parsons' influential early critique. He rejected the collective, emergentist tradition in classical sociology entirely, as well as the interpretative strand of the micro tradition. Drawing upon Simmel and Smithian political economy, he developed a sociological form of behaviorism in Skinnerian terms. Homan insisted that the "elementary forms" of social life were not extraindividual elements such as symbol systems, as Durkheim had argued in his later work, but individual actors of a decidedly rationalist bent. Rejecting the notion of emergentism, he focused on what he called "subinstitutional" behavior, and he considered the behavior of "actual individuals" to be entirely separated from the stipulations of norms. Intention and individual decision became the focus of analysis, first because individuals were considered to be encased in contingency and second because the assumption of absolute rationality meant that the social forces impinging on them were viewed, by both actor and analyst, as objectified and external to any act. This, of course, represents option 1.

Exchange theory became enormously influential in reviving the case for an interactionally based micro sociology. Its simple and elegant model facilitated predictions; its focus on individuals made it empirically operational. It also caught hold of a fundamental insight that Parsons had ignored: contingent participation in exchange decisions is the path by which "objective conditions" become translated into the terms of everyday life. The price for such insights was high, however, even for theorists inside the paradigm itself. Theorists such as Blau (1964) and Coleman (1966) tried to introduce significant revisions, and such efforts are continued in the contemporary German scene.

The other strands of the micro revival have taken up the interpretative side of action. Blumer (1969) is the general theorist most responsible for the revival of Meadian work, although the tradition he called "symbolic interactionism" took up pragmatism only in its radical contingent form. Blumer insisted, in opposition to macro analysis of the interpretative type, that meaning must be seen to be simply the result of individual negotiation. It is determined by others' reactions as much as by the individual act. The actor, moreover, is not viewed as bringing some previous collective order into this contingent situation. Situational relevance, not previous socialization, decides what the actor brings into play. "Selfindication" is the concept Blumer developed to describe actors' promethean ability to make an object out of themselves. The actors' temporally rooted "I" determines what elements of their past will be brought into play from moment to moment.

Blumer's call for getting into actors' heads, for a methodology of direct observation, became a second significant focus for the revival of sociological theory in an entirely micro mode. The most important empirical theorist in this movement, Erving Goffman, seemed to most observers of the time merely to point interactionist theory in a more problem-specific and dramaturgical direction. Indeed, in his early work Goffman (1959) emphasized the "presentation of self" as opposed to the significance of social roles and tried to explain institutional behavior as emergent from the direct face-to-face behavior of concrete actors. Goffman's later work turned more to the micro-macro link, but his greatest impact was to revivify an anticollective micro sociology.

Ethnomethodology, the American version of phenomenology, makes a more complicated story. Garfinkel was a student not only of Schutz but also of Parsons, and his earliest work (1963) begins where Parsons left off. He accepts Parsons' equation of internalization and institutionalization, and he made the autonomy of the macro level of social order the starting point of his micro sociology. What Garfinkel explored in his early work, then, were the methods by which actors made social norms their own—their "ethno" methodology. From phenomenology he accepted, in a way that Parsons never had, the utter contingency of action, and he described cognitive techniques such as indexicality and "ad hocing" (1967) by which binding rules were specified situationally and modified in turn. He pursued, in other words, the relatively unexplored theoretical option 3.

As ethnomethodology became a major theoretical movement, however, its dichotomous rather than synthetic approach to the micro-macro link became increasingly predominant (Alexander 1985). The mandate came to be seen as a call for producing an alternative to sociology, one that would raise "members' own practices" to the level of governing focus. The omnipresence of such practices as indexicality and ad hocing were now seen as evidence for the utter contingency of order. The practice of orderly activity came to be identified with order itself (Garfinkel et al. 1981). Microanalysis now assumed center stage, the macro perceived not as a level of empirical analysis but as an antagonistic presuppositional position. "Conversational analysis," the offshoot of ethnomethodology developed by Sacks and Schegloff (1968), conceptualized speech in quite a different manner, as interpretation governed by constraining interactional rules. Even though conversational analysts usually insisted that these rules emerge simply from the practice of speech, the openings between their perspective and macro analysis were more distinct than developments in other late ethnomethodological work.

This revival of microsociology reintroduced the first and second theoretical possibilities outlined earlier: (1) the notion that free, rational individuals create order in a completely contingent way, and (2) the position that sees order as the contingent creation of free, interpretative individuals. This was the individualist direction taken by the post-Parsonian theorizing that challenged Parsons' limited version of the micro-macro link.

The other challenge attacked Parsons' synthesis from the opposite direction. Rather than claim that Parsons was overly macro because he had ignored contingency, this development challenged him because he had overemphasized voluntarism and individuality, because, that is, he had been overly micro. This formula, too, had a significant element of truth, for in his insistence on the homology of subjective motive and social control Parsons had underplayed the manner in which instrumental motives allow social control to be objectified in an apparently coercive manner. Rational actors—albeit actors socialized to the capacity for objectification—are indeed often tied to macro environments mainly because of the external power of those environments.

This is a micro reworking of the fifth theoretical option. In emphasizing this option as the principal form of the individual-society relation, however, the post-Parsonian "structuralist" challenge broke the micro-macro link completely. It made an argument for an antimicro form of macro theory.

The most important theoretical statements of this position have come from Europe, particularly from the French structuralist school of Althusser. We analyze this theoretized structuralist position in our discussion of Germany below. America has, however, provided the most influential macro structuralist theories of the middle range. The mainly empirical reference of this American theory should not obscure its ambitious theoretical bent. No doubt the most imposing single work has been Skocpol's States and Social Revolutions (1979), which polemicized against all "subjective" and "voluntaristic" theories of revolutions in the name of a structuralist theory that focused exclusively on external environments. Wright's (1978) class analysis takes up the same antimicro theme, arguing that ambiguities in a group's class consciousness come from "contradictory class locations." Treiman (1977) similarly produced a "structural theory of prestige" that converted cultural into organizational control and denied any independent role to subjective volition. In still another influential work, Lieberson (1980) argued that racial inequality in the United States could be explained only by "structures of opportunity" and that the subjective inclinations of actors must not be given the status of independent variables.

The Structuralist Revival in Continental Sociology. In Central European sociology, the reaction against the predominance of Parsonian functionalism during the 1950s took quite a different turn. The collectivist view of functionalism was maintained, but its attempt to link structural processes to patterns of consciousness was broken. The most influential formulation of this Marxist alternative was provided by Althusser and his students (Althusser and Balibar 1970; Godelier 1967). "Objective social structures" above and beyond subjective consciousness are postulated. Historical developments, social conflicts, and collective actions are analyzed as particular variations, transformations, and incarnations of fundamental structural principles. Rather than start with the empirical and phenomenal diversity of social actions and life-worlds, as contemporary micro theorists advised, structuralists gave ontologial and methodological primacy to the "totality": one starts with fundamental structures and relates phenomenal diversity to it. Although individual actions may deviate from structural imperatives, the objective consequences of these actions are determined by these structures, which exist beyond the actors' control.

The major effort to counter this disregard for the micro level also emerged from within the Marxian camp. Exegetically based on the philosophy of the young Marx (see above), "praxis philosophy" (e.g., Thompson 1978), and "critical theory" (e.g., Habermas 1970) stressed the revolutionary role of subjectivity, reflection, and dialectical fantasy in opposition to the "repressive structures of society." Because Parsons took the micro as homologous with social structures, he could reason from social consensus to system equilibrium. Structural Marxism took system conflict as its first principle, and its severing of the micro-macro link allowed it to disregard subjective consensus in turn. Critical, or praxis, theory agreed with functionalism that a system's structures might be temporarily intact (Marcuse 1963), but the break it postulated between micro and macro allowed it to maintain the omnipresence of rebellion nonetheless.

Because of the scarcity of theoretical resources within Marxism, and because of ideological constraints as well, this micro movement within Marxism was eventually charged with being scarcely more than a critical methodology. Some of the key participants in the earlier subjectivist movement returned to orthodox structuralist assumptions and political economy (Offe 1984 [1972]; Hirsch 1974). They focused on the function of the state in capitalist accumulation and derived social problems and crises from "inevitable" state intervention. These interventions, it was maintained, uncoupled the antagonistic structure of capitalist societies from class conflicts and social movements.

Marxist theorizing in the 1960s and 1970s, then, seemed to have an inherent tilt toward the macro side. This persistent disregard for structures of consciousness, for contingency, and for patterns of concrete interaction eventually produced a reaction in German sociology, which occurred for disciplinary, as well as scientific, reasons. When the interest of sociology with respect to social action is reduced to discovering the traces and imprints of all encompassing economic macro structures, then sociology is on the verge of being reduced to a subdiscipline of economics. The effort to counteract the predominance of Marxist political economy has led to a renaissance of Weberian and Parsonian theorizing in German sociology on the one hand and to a growing interest in phenomenological and interactionist theories on the other. Both tendencies set the stage for the thrust for linkage that we believe has characterized the most recent phase of sociological debate.

Toward Linkage

Although the differences forcefully articulated by this multiparadigmatic debate continue to inform sociological theory today, it is our belief that the vital and creative phase of this movement has now come to an end. We suggest that in the present decade a quite different phase of theoretical debate has emerged, one marked by the serious ongoing effort within every theoretical tradition and from both sides of the great divide (see the essays in Alexander et al. 1987) to link micro and macro perspectives. We are under no illusion that this new development will replace theoretical disagreement with some Newtonian synthesis, but we are convinced that the scope and intensity of this search for linkage is without precedent in the history of sociology.

There are social and institutional, as well as intellectual, reasons for this new phase in contemporary sociological theory. Certainly one important factor is the changing political climate in the United States and

Europe. Most radical social movements have faded away, and in the eyes of many intellectuals Marxism has been morally delegitimated. The ideological thrust that fueled anti-Parsonianism in both its micro and macro form in the United States and that stimulated Marxist structuralism on the Continent has now been spent.

This political shift, in addition to the simple passage of time, has created new generational circumstances. In the United States and England there is a new generation of theorists for whom Parsons was never a dominant figure and who therefore feel no particular attraction to the polemic against him. By standing outside the fray, these younger theorists are committed to neither the micro nor the macro anti-Parsonian alternative, and, indeed, their new theorizing has often returned to Parsons' commitment to linkage, if not to the substance of his theory. In Germany the younger, post-Marxist generation has been forced to look elsewhere for theoretical ideas. Many of these came, in fact, from the United States. When individualistic theories made the transoceanic transition, however, they were taken up in a less polemical way, and the migration of Parsonian ideas to Germany (see Alexander 1984b), rather than inspire divisive debate, has been part of an effort at renewed theoretical integration.

There has been the passage of intellectual time as well. One-sided theories are provocative, and at various points they can be enormously functional in a scientific sense. Once the dust of theoretical battle has settled, however, the cognitive content of their theorizing is not particularly easy to maintain. The multiparadigmatic debate succeeded in eclipsing early efforts at theoretical synthesis. Moreover, the postwar philosophical revival of individualism that fueled this debate has now died out. The legacies of Weber and Parsons remain, however, presenting an enduring demand for linkage that calls sociological theory to task. For internal reasons of theoretical logic, as well as for external reasons of social and institutional life, a new and unprecedented thrust of contemporary debate toward linkage has begun.

In terms of macro theories, the shift toward linkage can be seen in each of the major theoretical schools. Giddens' earliest work (1971) was continuous with the structuralist thrust of anti-Parsonian theory and neo-Marxism, but later in the 1970s his work fundamentally changed course. He became convinced of the need for a complementary theory of action. Building from, among other traditions, the ethnomethodological insistence on the reflexive, contingent nature of action, Giddens developed a theory of structuration that tries to interweave action and order (Giddens 1976, 1979). Collins' development shows a similar trajectory. Although more interested in ethnomethodology from the beginning of his career than Giddens, Collins, in his early work (1975), presented primarily a case for structuralistic conflict sociology. In recent years (Collins 1981) he has embraced radical microsociology, both phenomenological and Goffmanian, developing the notion of interaction ritual chains as a means of mediating the micro-macro link.

Habermas, too, began his career with a more typically macro structuralist model of social dynamics (Habermas 1973). Although there are clear references to moral claims and to different types of action, these remained residual to his argument. In his recent work (Habermas 1984), however, he explicitly and systematically developed theories about the micro processes that underlie and sometimes oppose the macro structures of social systems. He has used individual moral and cognitive development to anchor his description of world-historical phases of "social learning," descriptions of speech acts to develop arguments about political legitimacy, and the conception of an interpersonally generated life-world to justify his empirical explanation of social strain and resistance.

Giddens and Collins have tended to bring theoretical options 1 and 2 (instrumental and interpretive individualism) into contact with option 5 (objective structuralism). By contrast, Habermas' sensitivity to cultural gestalts has led him to connect option 5 with linkage arguments that stress homology and socialization (option 4). As his critics have argued, although he has embraced the micro, his theory is still not really open to contingency, particularly to historical processes such as individual and collective rebellion, which have been stressed by Marxism in its more historical and political forms. Eder (1983) developed a theory of "specific evolution" in order to push Habermasian theory in this direction, that is, toward the more contingent options 1–3. A sharper departure from the determinism of macro evolutionism has been made by Schmid (1982) and Giesen (Giesen and Lau 1981, Giesen 1980). They have argued that progress, directional development, and societal growth must be seen as macroprocesses that are contingent on the micro processes of variation and selective reproduction, although the latter are themselves subject to selective pressures exerted by macro structures like stratification.

In Habermas' efforts at linkage he has been influenced by new developments in Parsonian and Weberian theories. Although Luhmann (1979) has certainly raised the radically macro concept of "systems" vigorously and influentially, it must not be forgotten that he explains the very existence of systems by referring to fundamental microprocesses, which he identifies as existential needs to reduce complexity. His more recent work (in Alexander et al., 1987) on autopoietic systems, moreover, makes the dialectic of micro and macro into the very essence of modern societies. Indeed, he wishes to argue that the micro-macro split, properly understood, is not a theoretical issue but an empirical reflection of the historical differentiation of interaction and society.

This emphasis has had a major influence on Münch's effort (1981–82) to reshape Parsons' systematic theory. Unlike Luhmann, Münch has returned to Parsons' more analytical notion of systemic interpenetration, not only of norms and interests, but also of micro and macro. Indeed, Münch (1981) has extended and much more systematically elaborated Parsons' notion that socialization lays the moral basis for social integration and control. Although he generally criticizes individualistic theory and thereby maintains theoretical option 4, Münch has incorporated contingency into his four-dimensional models in a way that Parsons never contemplated.

Although Alexander's initial work (1982a,b, 1983a,b) argued that action and order, taken together, are the inescapable presuppositions of social thought, he did not identify these positions with micro and macro emphases respectively. Indeed, he argued that only by presupposing collective or emergent order could theory encompass the mutuality of contingency and constraint in social life. At the same time, however, this early work did not entirely escape Durkheim's and Parsons' identification of action theory with the differentiation of homologous personalities and societies (option 4). Since that time, he has given action *qua* contingency a more systematic role, outlining syntheses between structural theory and ethnomethodology, symbolic interaction, and theories of exchange (Alexander 1984a, 1985, Alexander and Colomy 1985 [essays 1, 7, and 8 above]; cf. chapter 10 below).

The mirror image of this development has been produced within Weberian theory by Schluchter (1979, 1981). He has insisted from the beginning of his work that the decoupling of individual action and society is at the heart of Weber's achievement and that this Weberian understanding (reflecting options 2 and 3) is necessary to perceive the significance of individuality and responsibility in modern society. At the same time, however, Schluchter has relied heavily on Parsonian and, later, Habermasian formulations about moral and cultural evolution, and his notion of individual autonomy seems to rely implicitly on theoretical option 4 as well. This has set the stage for renewing the more synthetic position (option 3), whose initial formulation was such a singular contribution of Weber himself.

The same shift toward linkage marks recent developments in each of the major micro traditions. Striking developments have occurred, for example, in symbolic interactionism. Although Goffman (1959) began his career more or less within the radically contingent tradition of Blumer (option 2), in his later writings there emerged a dramatic shift toward the more structural concerns of positions 3 and 4. The creative strategies of actors were still Goffman's target, but he was now concerned with them insofar as they illustrated the instantiation of cultural and stratificational structures in everyday life (e.g., Goffman 1974). Similarly, whereas Becker's (1963) early impact on deviance theory derived from his emphasis on contingency and action, his most recent work takes an emphatically systemic view of creativity and its effects (Becker 1984). Indeed, recently a spate of formal efforts by symbolic interactionists to systematize the links between actors and social systems has appeared. Haferkamp (1986) added to Mead's individual construction of meaning an objective-material basis for action (combining options 2 and 5), and Lewis and Smith (1980) argued that Mead was actually an antinominalist who took what we have called the reproductionist position (4). Stryker (1980:52–54, 57–76) has gone so far as to present interactionism as if it were basically a modification of social systems theory itself (see also, in this regard, Handel 1979; Maines 1977; Strauss 1978).

Similar developments can be seen in the rational action model revived in Homans' exchange theory. The pressure to demonstrate that this polemically micro approach (option 1) could cope with macrosociological explanation (see e.g., Lindenberg 1983) gradually shifted the focus of analysis from individual actions to the transformation from individual actions to collective effects, and, by extension, to unintended rather than purposive activity. Thus, Lindenberg (1977) and Coleman (1987) rejected the notion that the connection between individual actions and macro phenomena could be viewed as a causal relation between discrete empirical events. If there were only empirical simultaneity, then the linkage between micro and macro would have to be seen as an analytical one sustained by invisible processes in the larger system. Such an analytical linkage was achieved by the application of "transformation rules" (e.g., voting procedures) to individual actions.

Theorists were led by this focus on transformation to consider individual actions not as subjects for analysis in their own right but as initial conditions for the operation of structural mechanisms (combining options 1 and 5). In this way structural explanations—about the rules of constitutions, the dynamics of organizations, the system of prestige allocation— began to replace utility arguments within the rationalistic tradition (Coleman 1966; Goode 1979). There emerged extensive theorizing about the unintended effects of individual actions (Boudon 1977; Wippler 1978) and even about the genesis of collective morality.

Although Garfinkel, the founder of ethnomethodology, continues to advocate a radically micro program (option 2) for the school (Garfinkel et al. 1981) and although the movement toward linkage is less developed here than within the other micro traditions, it seems impossible to deny that a similar crisis and a similar movement permeate phenomenological sociology as well. Cicourel, for example, certainly one of the key figures in the radical early phase, has sought a more interdependent approach (Knorr-Cetina and Cicourel 1981). A phenomenologically based "social studies in science" movement has emerged that, while arguing for a micro base to science studies, systematically acknowledges the framing effects of social structure (Knorr-Cetina and Mulkay 1983; Pinch and Collins 1984). Although Smith (1984) and Molotch/Boden (1985) have both insisted on the indispensable autonomy of ethnomethodological practice, they have produced significant studies detailing how this practice is structured by organizational context and the distribution of power (combining options 2 and 5). Oevermann (1979) has demonstrated how practical action is confined by cultural codes (combining options 2 and 4), and Luckmann (1984) has linked it to social evolution.

We are not suggesting here that the widespread acceptance of a new theory of micro-macro articulation is imminent. We have no doubt that sociological debate will continue to be organized around competing versions of action and order. In this sense the debates we have just recounted are more about the secondary and peripheral circles of theoretical traditions than about their central core. Notwithstanding Blau's (1977) dramatic switch from micro to macro sociology—a switch that is actually more incremental than appearances would indicate—few of the recent advocates of linkage have ever "jumped ship."

Indeed, it is this very loyalty to initial starting points, we believe (Alexander 1985, 1987), that limits the success of most of these linkage proposals in fundamental ways. It is our view that only by establishing a radically different theoretical starting point can a genuinely inclusive micro-macro link be made. This inclusive model would not simply combine two or three of the theoretical options in an ad hoc manner. Rather, it would provide a systematic model in which all five of the options are included as analytical dimensions of empirical reality as such. This can be achieved on the basis of an emergentist, or collective, understanding of order, a multidimensional understanding of action, and an analytic understanding of the relations among different levels of empirical organization.

Our purpose in this chapter, however, has not been to argue for or against any one of these proposals for linkage. Our purpose has been to draw a circle around all of them, to demarcate them as a new phenomenon in sociological discourse, and to commend this new discourse to the community at large.

REFERENCES

Alexander, Jeffrey C. 1982a. *Positivism, Presuppositions, and Current Controversies*. Vol. 1 of *Theoretical Logic in Sociology*. Berkeley and Los Angeles: University of California Press.

—— 1982b. *The Antinomies of Classical Thought: Marx and Durkheim*. Vol. 2 of *Theoretical Logic in Sociology*. Berkeley and Los Angeles: University of California Press.

—— 1983a. *The Classical Attempt at Synthesis: Max Weber*. Vol. 3 of *Theoretical Logic in Sociology*. Berkeley and Los Angeles: University of California Press.

—— 1983b. *The Modern Reconstruction of Classical Thought: Talcott Parsons*. Vol. 4 of *Theoretical Logic in Sociology*. Berkeley and Los Angeles: University of California Press.

—— 1984a. "Structural Analysis: Some Notes on Its History and Prospects." *Sociological Quarterly* 25(1):5–26.

—— 1984b. "The Parsons Revival in Germany." *Sociological Theory* 2:394–412.

—— 1985. "The Individualist Dilemma in Phenomenology and Interactionism: Towards a Synthesis with the Classical Tradition." In S. N. Eisenstadt and

H. J. Helle, eds., *Perspectives on Sociological Theory,* vol. 1. Beverly Hills, Calif.: Sage.

—— 1987. *Twenty Lectures: Sociological Theory Since World War II.* New York: Columbia University Press.

Alexander, Jeffrey and Paul Colomy. 1985. "Towards Neo-Functionalism: Eisenstadt's Change Theory and Symbolic Interactionism." *Sociological Theory* 3(2):11–23.

Alexander, Jeffrey, Bernhard Giesen, Richard Münch, and Neil Smelser. 1987. *The Micro-Macro Link.* Berkeley and Los Angeles: University of California Press.

Althusser, Louis and Etienne Balibar. 1970. *Reading Capital.* London: New Left Books.

Bales, Robert F. 1951. *Interaction Precess Analysis.* New York: Free Press.

Becker, Howard S. 1963. *Outsiders: Studies in the Sociology of Deviance.* Glencoe, Ill.: Free Press.

—— 1984. *Art Worlds.* Berkeley: University of California Press.

Bellah, Robert N. 1970. "Father and Son in Confucianism and Christianity." In Bellah, *Beyond Belief,* pp. 76–97. New York: Harper and Row.

Berlin, Isaiah. 1954. *Historical Inevitability.* New York: Oxford University Press.

Blau, Peter. 1964. *Exchange and Power in Social Life.* New York: Free Press.

—— 1977. *Inequality and Heterogeneity.* New York: Free Press.

Blumer, Herbert. 1969. *Symbolic Interactionism.* Englewood Cliffs, N.J.: Prentice-Hall.

Boudon, Raymond. 1977. *Effets pervers et order social.* Paris: Presses Universitaires de France.

Coleman, James. 1966. "Foundations for a Theory of Collective Decisions." *American Journal of Sociology* 71:615–27.

—— 1987. "Title of Article." In Alexander et al., eds., *The Micro-Macro Link.* Berkeley and Los Angeles: University of California Press.

Collins, Randall. 1975. *Conflict Sociology.* New York: Academic Press.

—— 1981. "On the Microfoundations of Nacrosociology." *American Journal of Sociology* 86:984–1014.

Durkheim, Emile. 1933 [1893]. *The Division of Labor in Society.* New York: Free Press.

—— 1938 [1895]. *The Rules of Sociological Method.* New York: Free Press.

—— 1951 [1897]. *Suicide.* New York: Free Press.

—— 1965 [1912]. *The Elementary Forms of Religious Life.* New York: Free Press.

Eder, Klaus. 1983. "The New Social Movements in Historical Perspective, or: What Is New in the 'New' Social Movements?" Unpublished paper. Munich.

Freud, Sigmund. 1928 [1927]. *Future of an Illusion.* New York: Norton.

—— 1959 [1921]. *Group Psychology and the Analysis of the Ego.* New York: Norton.

—— 1961 [1923]. *The Ego and the Id.* New York: Norton.

—— 1961 [1930]. *Civilization and Its Discontents.* New York: Norton.

Garfinkel, Harold. 1963. "A Conception of and Experiments with 'Trust' as a Condition of Concerted Stable Actions." In O. J. Harvey, ed., *Motivation and Social Interaction*, pp. 187–238. New York: Ronald Press.

—— 1967. *Studies in Ethnomethodology*. Englewood Cliffs, N.J.: Prentice-Hall.

Garfinkel, Harold, Michael Lynch, and Eric Livingston. 1981. "The Work of a Discovering Science Construed with Materials from the Optically Discovered Pulsar." *Philosophy of Social Science* 11:131–58.

Giddens, Anthony. 1971. *Capitalism and Modern Social Theory*. London: Cambridge University Press.

—— 1976. *New Rules of Sociological Method*. London: Hutchinson.

—— 1979. *Central Problems in Social Theory*. London: Macmillan.

Giesen, Bernhard. 1980. *Makrosoziologie*. Hamburg: Hoffman and Campe.

Giesen, Bernhard and C. Lau. 1981. "Zur Anwendung darwinistischer Erklärungsstrategien in der Soziologie." *Kölner Zeitschrift für Soziologie und Soziopsychologie* 33(2):229–56.

Giesen, Bernhard and Michael Schmid. 1977. "Methodologischer Individualismus und Reduktionismus." In E. Eberlein and J. J. Kondratowitz, eds., *Psychologie statt Soziologie*, pp. 24–47. Frankfurt/New York: Campus.

Godelier, Maurice. 1967. "System, Structure, and Contradiction in 'Capital.'" In Ralph Miliband and John Saville, eds. *The Socialist Register*. New York: Monthly Review Press.

Goffman, Erving. 1959. *The Presentation of Self in Everyday Life*. New York: Doubleday.

—— 1974. *Frame Analysis*. New York: Doubleday.

Goldstein, L. 1956. "The Inadequacy of the Principle of Methodological Individualism." *Journal of Philosophy* 53:801–13.

—— 1958. "The Theses of Methodological Individualism." *British Journal for the Philosophy of Science* 9:1–11.

Goode, William J. 1960. "A Theory of Role Strain." *American Sociological Review* 25:483–96.

—— 1979. *The Celebration of Heroes: Prestige as a Social Control System*. Berkeley and Los Angeles: University of California Press.

Habermas, Jurgen. 1970. *Toward a Rational Society*. Boston: Beacon.

—— 1973. *Theory and Practice*. Boston: Beacon.

—— 1984. *Reason and the Rationalization of Society*. Vol. 1. *Theory of Communicative Action*. Boston: Beacon.

Haferkamp, Hans. 1986. *Soziales Handeln. Theorie elementarer internationalen und komplexer Handlungszusammenhange*. Bremen.

Handel, Warren. 1979. "Normative Expectations and the Emergence of Meaning as Solutions to Problems: Convergence of Structural and Interactionist Views." *American Journal of Sociology* 84:855–81.

Hayek, Frederick. 1952. *The Counter-Revolution of Science: Studies on the Abuse of Reason*. Glencoe, Ill.: Free Press.

Hirsch, J. D. 1974. *Staatsapparat und Reproduktion des Kapitals*. Frankfurt: Suhrkamp.

Homans, George. 1958. "Social Behavior as Exchange." *American Sociological Review* 63:597–606.

—— 1961. *Social Behavior: Its Elementary Forms.* New York: Harcourt, Brace, and World.

Knorr-Cetina, Karin and Aaron Cicourel, eds. 1981. *Advances in Social Theory and Methodology: Towards an Integration of Micro and Macro Sociology.* London: Routledge & Kegan Paul.

Knorr-Cetina, Karin and Michael Mulkay, eds. 1983. *Science Observed: New Perspectives on the Social Study of Science.* Beverly Hills, Calif.: Sage.

Levy, Marion. 1949. *The Family Revolution in China.* Cambridge, Mass.: Harvard University Press.

Lewis, J. David and Richard L. Smith. 1980. *American Sociology and Pragmatism: Mead, Chicago Sociology and Symbolic Interactionism.* Chicago: University of Chicago Press.

Lieberson, Stanley. 1980. *A Piece of the Pie.* Berkeley and Los Angeles: University of California Press.

Lindenberg, Siegward. 1977. "Individuelle Effekte. Kollektive Phänomene und das Problem der Transformation." In K. Eichner and W. Habermehl, eds., *Probleme der Erklärung sozialen Verhaltens,* pp. 46–84. Misenheim/Glan: Hain.

—— 1983. "The New Political Economy: Its Potential and Limitations for the Social Science in General and for Sociology in Particular." In Wolfgang Sudeur, ed., *Ökonomische Erklärung sozialen Verhaltens,* pp. 7–66. Duisburg: Sozialwissenschaftliche Kooperative.

Luckmann, Thomas. 1984. "Bemerkungen zu Gesellschaftstruktur Bewusstseins Formen und Religion in der modernen Gesellschaft." Paper presented to Soziologen Tag, Dorfenund.

Luhmann, Niklas. 1979. *Trust and Power.* New York: Wiley.

Maines, David. 1977. "Social Organization and Social Structure in Symbolic Interactionist Thought." *Annual Review of Sociology* 3:309–17.

Mandelbaum, M. 1955. "Societal Facts." *British Journal of Sociology* 6:309–17.

—— 1957. "Societal Laws." *British Journal for the Philosophy of Science* 8:211–24.

Malewski, A. 1967. *Verhalten und Interaktion.* Tübingen, West Germany: Mohr.

Marcuse, Herbert. 1963. *One Dimensional Man.* Boston: Beacon.

Marx, Karl. 1963 [1844]. "Economic and Philosophical Manuscripts." In T. B. Bottomore, ed., *Karl Marx: Early Writings.* New York: McGraw-Hill.

—— 1965 [1845]. "Theses on Feuerbach." In Nathan Rotenstreich, ed. *Basic Problems of Marx's Philosophy.* Indianapolis: Bobbs-Merrill.

—— 1967 [1842]. "Communism and the Augsburg Allgemeine Zeitung." In Lloyd D. Easton and Kurt H. Guddat, eds., *Writings of the Young Marx on Philosophy and Society.* New York: Doubleday.

Mead, George Herbert. 1964 [1934]. "Selections from *Mind, Self, and Society.*" In Anselm Strauss, ed. *George Herbert Mead on Social Psychology,* pp. 165–282. Chicago: University of Chicago Press.

Merton, Robert K. 1968. "Continuities in the Theory of Reference Groups and Social Structures." In *Social Theory and Social Structure,* pp. 334–440. New York: Free Press.

Molotch, Harvey and Deirdre Boden. 1985. "Talking Social Structure: Discourse, Domination, and the Watergate Hearings." *American Sociological Review* 50:273–288.

Münch, Richard. 1981. "Socialization and Personality Development from the Point of View of Action Theory: The Legacy of Durkheim." *Sociological Inquiry* 51:311–54.

—— 1981–1982. "Talcott Parsons and the Theory of Action. Parts I and II." *American Journal of Sociology* 86–87:709–39, 771–826.

Nagel, Ernest. 1961. *The Structure of Science.* London: Routledge & Kegan Paul.

Offe, Claus. 1984 [1972]. *Contradictions of the Welfare State.* Cambridge, Mass.: MIT Press.

Oevermann, Ulrich. 1979. "Die Methodologie einer objektiven Hermeneutik." In H. G. Soeffner, ed., *Interpretativen Verfahren in den sozial und Textwissen Schaften,* pp. 353–434. Stuttgart: Publisher?

Opp, K. D. 1972. *Verhaltenstheoretische Soziologie.* Stuttgart: Enke.

Parsons, Talcott. 1937. *The Structure of Social Action.* New York: Free Press.

—— 1954. *Essays in Sociological Theory.* New York: Free Press.

—— 1963. *Social Structure and Personality.* New York: Free Press.

Parsons, Talcott and N. J. Smelser. 1956. *Economy and Society.* New York: Free Press.

Parsons, Talcott and Robert F. Bales, eds. 1955. *Family, Socialization, and Interaction Process.* New York: Free Press.

Pinch, T. J. and H. M. Collins. 1984. "Private Science and Public Knowledge." *Social Studies in Science* 14:521–46.

Popper, Karl. 1958. *The Open Society and Its Enemies.* London: Routledge & Kegan Paul.

—— 1961. *The Poverty of Historicism.* London: Routledge and Kegan Paul.

Schegloff, Emmanuel. 1986. "The Routine as Achievement." *Human Studies* 9:111–151.

Schluchter, Wolfgang. 1979. "The Paradoxes of Rationalization." In Guenther Roth and W. Schluchter, *Max Weber's Vision of History,* pp. 11–64. Berkeley and Los Angeles: University of California Press.

—— 1981. *The Rise of Western Rationalization.* Berkeley and Los Angeles: University of California Press.

Schmid, Michael. 1982. *Theorie sozialen Wandels.* Opladen: Westdeutscher Verlag.

Simmel, Georg. 1950. "Fundamental Problems of Sociology." In Kurt H. Wolff, ed., *The Sociology of Georg Simmel,* pp. 3–25. New York: Free Press.

—— 1955. "Conflict." In *Conflict and the Web of Group Affiliation,* pp. 11–123. New York: Free Press.

—— 1977. *Problems of the Philosophy of History.* New York: Free Press.

Skocpol, Theda. 1979. *States and Social Revolutions.* New York: Cambridge University Press.

Slater, Philip. 1961. "Parental Role Differentiation." *American Journal of Sociology* 67:296–308.

—— 1966. *Microcosm.* New York: Wiley.

—— 1968. *The Glory of Hera.* Boston: Beacon.

Smelser, Neil J. 1959. *Social Change in the Industrial Revolution.* Chicago: University of Chicago Press.

—— 1962. *Theory of Collective Behavior.* New York: Free Press.

Smith, Adam. 1776. *The Wealth of Nations.*

Smith, Dorothy. 1984. "Textually Mediated Social Organization." *International Social Science Journal* 36:59–75.

Strauss, Anselm. 1978. *Negotiations: Varieties, Contexts, Processes and Social Order.* San Francisco: Josey-Bass.

Stryker, Sheldon. 1980. *Symbolic Interactionism.* Menlo Park, Calif.: Benjamin Cummings.

Thompson, E. P. 1978. *The Poverty of Theory and Other Essays.* London: Merlin.

Treiman, Donald. 1977. *Occupational Prestige in Comparative Perspective.* New York: Wiley.

Watkins, J. 1952. "The Principle of Methodological Individualism." *British Journal for the Philosophy of Science* 3:186–89.

—— 1959 [1957]. "Historical Explanations in the Social Sciences." In P. Gardiner, ed. *Theories of History*, pp. 503–14. New York: Free Press.

Weber, Max. 1946 [1916]. "Religious Rejections of the World and Their Directions." In Hans Gerth and C. Wright Mills, eds. *From Max Weber*, pp. 324–59. New York: Oxford University Press.

—— 1949 [1905]. "A Critique of Eduard Meyer's Methodological Views." In M. Weber, *Methodology of the Social Sciences*, pp. 113–63. New York: Free Press.

—— 1975 [1903–1906]. *Roscher and Knies.* London: Routledge & Kegan Paul.

—— 1978. *Economy and Society.* Berkeley and Los Angeles: University of California Press.

Wippler, Reinhard. 1978. "Nicht-intendierte sozial Folgen individuelle Handlungen." *Soziale Welt* 29:155–79.

Wright, Erik Olin. 1978. *Class, Crisis, and the State.* London: New Left Books.

PART IV

The Problem Restated

TEN

Action and
Its Environments

I begin this concluding essay with some reflections on the micro/macro distinction in sociological theory and, on the basis of this critical reflection, suggest that some of the most illuminating and important innovations in this recent discussion need to be reconstructed and brought together. After suggesting a mode of interrelating some individualistic theories, the essay moves from the hermeneutical to the theoretical. A microempirical model of individual action is suggested, according to which action is viewed as interpretation and strategization. A microempirical model of order is then developed on this basis, in which society, culture, and personality are conceived as action's immediate environments.

Terminological Concerns

In the last decade the discipline of sociology resuscitated an old dilemma in a new form—a form, unfortunately, that has done little to resolve the dilemma itself. The perennial conflict between individualistic and collectivistic theories has been reworked as a conflict between microsociology and macrosociology. The distinction, of course, refers to size, and the implication of attaching these adjectives to "sociology" is to suggest that social theory and its empirical correlates involve clear choices between units of different size: small units versus big units. If this were all that has been implied, however, there would be little problem. In truth, much more has been suggested, for micro (small size) has usually been linked to a specific empirical focus, the focus on the individual in his or her interactions with other individuals. Although throughout much of this chapter I, too, will be examining precisely this empirical issue, I begin by suggesting that this equation of micro with individual is extremely misleading, as, indeed, is the attempt to find any specific size correlation with the micro/macro difference. There can be no empirical referents for micro or macro as such. They are analytical contrasts, suggesting emergent levels within empirical units, not antagonistic empirical units themselves.

The history of the life sciences gives ample illustration of how relative any imputation of macro and micro can be. Physiology, one of the robust life science disciplines, defined its field in terms of determinate interrelations of bodily organs and blood. Biochemistry, a much later development, suggested that interorganic functioning involves significant changes in the chemical properties of the elements from which these bodily organs are composed. More recently, molecular biology has introduced an entirely new level: fundamental life processes can be understood in terms of molecular and atomic interaction, an understanding that connected biology not only to chemistry but also to physics and mathematics. This historical declension from large units to small has illuminated new bases of physical organization and further complicated science's understanding of life. It has also enlarged the disciplinary base of the life sciences. It has not, however, except perhaps in the minds of some scientific entrepreneurs, succeeded in privileging one empirical arena over another. The autonomy and integrity of physiological functioning still holds: basic biological events can be understood in terms of the relations between organs and blood. So can they be understood in terms of chemical shifts, molecular interaction, and, indeed, in terms of the physics of elementary particles.

The issue for contemporary life science is not which level is determinate or which discipline is "right" but, rather, at what level a given life phenomenon should be explained. The properties specific to a given level of life process are taken as the variables for a particular discipline; for other disciplines they are considered parameters, not denied as such. If the explanation for an empirical phenomenon at one level leads to the concentration on processes that have been taken as parameters (dummy variables), then a different level of analysis is sought. Although this particular search for scientific knowledge may not be able to proceed until these parameters are more fully explored, the significance of the original variables is not eliminated. For example, heart disease is related, in the first instance, to inoperative valves or the breakdown of muscle, but the full causation of this physiological, functional breakdown is incomprehensible without understanding the biology, chemistry, molecular biology, and, ultimately, the physics involved. Still, the latter remain dependent on our knowledge of the heart as an organ and its relationship to blood. Or, to take another example, human reproduction can be explained physiologically in terms of mechanical activities of the genital organs. More microscopically, however, it can be explained in terms of the biology of sperm and egg; in terms of the biochemistry of acids, alkalines, and background solutions; in terms of the molecular bonds of genetic material and the mathematical probabilities of recombinant materials; and in terms of the magnetic properties of elementary units and forces.

These layers of life science are, of course, very gross; between them one could introduce a much more fine-grained picture of interdependent levels. This is precisely my point. The terms *micro* and *macro* are completely relativistic. What is macro at one level will be micro at another. Different properties associated with different levels and specific problems may demand the conversion of parameters into variables by moving toward larger or smaller units of reference. Each level, however, is homologous with every other, and there is no empirical life process that could subsist on any one level alone. Paradoxically, every empirical phenomenon can be accounted for at every level of analysis; it is simply accounted for in different ways. These different accounts reveal important new properties of the life process itself.

This complex notion of autonomy and interdependence has not been sufficiently understood by the social sciences. The tendency, rather, has been to equate micro with a specific level—the level of individual interaction—and this level has been portrayed as if it were in some kind of competition with all the others. The notion of homology has been lost and, with it, the possibility of integrating the results of this new sociology of individual interaction with more traditional understandings of social life at other levels. Such an integration can proceed only by disregarding the equation of individual interaction with microscopic. There are significant socially related processes that are "smaller" than, or "below," interaction, for example, the complex (largely unconscious) working of the personality and the open program of the individual's biological substrate, which involves not only quasi-instinctual genetic material but also the socially related prestructuring of organs such as the hemispherically specialized brain. Equally significant, there are levels of analysis "larger" than that of individual interaction—for example, the level of institutional exchange—which themselves can be viewed as micro processes relative to structures and processes of still larger scope.

The issue is not whether individual action and interaction are significant but whether theory should focus on this level in a manner that resists the rule of homology and analytic interpenetration. New insights into the structuring of individual action and interaction must be accepted. They must be articulated, however, in a manner that allows them to be interlarded with systematic understandings at every other level. Only in this way can the insights they provide be preserved while a broader, truly general theory of society is maintained.

Reconstructing Micro Theories

The challenge is to convert the empirical insights of recent micro theorizing into analytical elements of more general theories. This conversion rests on two tasks. First, the claims of such theorizing to have discovered a completely new subject must be thrown into doubt; second, its claims to a completely empirical method must be skeptically examined.

Although the emphasis of "classical" sociology—of Marx, Weber, Durkheim, and Parsons—has undoubtedly been on larger units of social life, it has been the claims of postclassical, micro theorizing, not the proclamations of the classical theorists, that suggested that the objects of this traditional theorizing were antiindividual and antiinteractional as such. This negative claim is merely the other side of a positive one: the assertion, made by all those who have participated in this micro revival, that their emphasis on individual action and interaction represents a new and revolutionary *empirical* discovery. This insight into a completely new phenomenal realm, moreover, has usually been conflated with (i.e., seen as infused by) decisive new formulations at the level of ideology, method, and epistemological presuppositions.

In *Critique of Dialectical Reason,* for example, Sartre (1976) claimed to have discovered, in opposition to all previous Marxism, the realm of individual existence, individual freedom, and contingency. This differentiated empirical realm, he believed, establishes a new form of historical reason, a new theory, that is simultaneously more revolutionary and more tolerant, more sensitive to cultural forms, and more open to historical unpredictability. This new realm also produces a new method (Sartre 1963), one that allows for the past, present, and future to be seen from within every individual act. Touraine (1977) and Bourdieu (1977) have taken up these Sartrean claims, naming (respectively) social movements and social action as new empirical arenas that, by their reference to intention and experience, promise to revolutionize our understanding of the reproduction of society.

Writing in an entirely different tradition, Schutz (1967, 1978a [1940], 1978b) took up much the same claims for his own particular micro area. The "life-world," he believed, is an area never previously perceived by social science, let alone illuminated in a systematically theoretical way. Only the perception of this life-world, the subjectively experienced horizon of individual action as defined by the actor, allows for a voluntaristic theory, a theory of motive, a theory of self. It provides, Schutz believed, a perspective drastically at odds with even the most ostensibly interpretative sociology, and it implies not only a new method but also an entirely new theory of social life. Berger and Luckmann (1966) and, much more extensively, Garfinkel (1967) later elaborated these claims in a more polemical form, suggesting that phenomenology had discovered an empirical object that justified a new social science itself. Building particularly on Garfinkel's claims, Giddens (1976, 1979) suggested that the discovery of individual reflexivity warrants the formulation of completely "new rules" of sociological method. Habermas (1984), returning to Schutz and linking him with pragmatism, raised the life-world to new empirical and ideological heights (see Alexander 1985a). Not only is it a phenomenon sharply separated from such supraindividual structures as norms, institutions, and systems, but also it allows for the immediate and satisfying personal experience that can ameliorate the alienation of late capitalist life.

From more distinctly American traditions, similar claims have been established for symbolic interactionist and exchange theory. Purportedly building on Mead, Blumer (1969) claimed that the phenomena of individual interpretation and contingent understanding have been entirely overlooked by every other tradition of sociological work. Once this new empirical realm is recognized, methodological and epistemological perspectives (and perhaps even ideological ones) will end up in a very different place. Although he never implies such theoretical extremism, Goffman (1959) suggests at various times in his work that the dramaturgical element in everyday life—the phenomenon of face-to-face interaction—will revolutionize sociology and overthrow its previous forms. Homans (1961), writing from his later, antinormative perspective on exchange, clearly promises the same thing. Exchange is an empirical phenomenon that has been ignored by almost every earlier form of sociological theorizing; it represents a distinctive realm that is determinate over all others; it demands a new method, makes new presuppositions, implies a new ideology. Collins' (1981) recent arguments urging the microtranslation of macrosociology have followed in Homans' footsteps, although Collins bolstered his claims for the scientific newness of interaction with the "discovering claims" of Goffman and Garfinkel.

I suggest that the insights of these micro theorists, though much more elaborated and detailed than what has appeared before, are neither as new nor as purely empirical as they would like to contend. For all of his emphasis on the mode of production, Marx (1962a [1867]) still devoted the lengthy tenth chapter of *Capital* to the interactional dimension and strategy of class struggle, and in his political writings (e.g., Marx 1962b [1852]) he often described individual strategy and politically contingent decisions. Weber's macrosociology of religion goes even further in this direction, resting upon quite nuanced descriptions of human personality needs (e.g., Weber 1946 [1916]). His structural theory of patrimonialism, moreover (Weber 1978:1006–1110), includes detailed disquisitions on the decision-making processes of political actors and their staffs. Durkheim's (1965 [1912]) religious theory refers continually to his understanding of the life-world of the true believer, just as his study of suicidogenic currents (Durkheim 1951 [1897]:227–94) depends on the phenomenological reconstruction of individual loneliness and despair. Parsons' functional analysis of the American university (Parsons and Platt 1973:163–222) includes a detailed portrait of student-teacher interaction, and his general theory of polarization and social change depends upon a specific understanding of the psychological deprivation experienced by traditionalist groups (e.g., Parsons 1954).

True, Marx, Weber, Durkheim, and Parsons do not concentrate for long on such smaller units of analysis, but as these examples indicate, prototheories of more microscopic levels are implied throughout their works. Usually these implicitly theorized microprocesses operate as parameters, allowing larger units to be explicitly variable. At certain times, however, the analysis even of these traditionally macro theorists takes a decidedly micro shift, taking up directly the behavior of smaller units such as individual personality, individual experiences, and individual interaction. My point here is that every macro theorist of social systems or institutions makes assumptions about how individuals act and interact; these assumptions are crucial to their large-scale theories even when they are not made explicit—as, indeed, they usually are not. It is no wonder, then, that traditional sociological theorizing has occasionally made the behavior of these smaller units an explicit object of analysis and that the discussions of more recent, self-consciously "microsociology" are not entirely new.

This leads to my second point: the focus on micro-level processes is not, in fact, entirely an empirical decision to make. Any micro sociological analysis refers not merely to an overwhelming empirical fact but also to an analytically differentiated, theoretical decision. Sociologists make presuppositions about the nature of social order—about the relative importance of different levels of analysis—and it is often this nonempirical presumption that shifts the burden of empirical discussion toward contingency and interaction and away from social structure. I am suggesting here not only that the individualist emphasis of recent micro sociology is not entirely new but also that it may, despite its great empirical insight, be theoretically misplaced. To privilege the arena of micro process may involve more than an empirical discovery; it may also involve a theoretical mistake. It may rely upon assumptions that deny to the macro parameters of interaction any real determination of this interaction itself.

Before exploring this possibility more fully, I suggest that the impact of nonempirical assumptions is actually still more complex. Sociological theories presuppose more than an understanding of the source of structure, or social order. They also proceed from a priori commitments about the nature of human action, particularly assumptions about action's relative rationality. This assumption about action separates microtheories from one another, given that they usually *share* assumptions about order, and it often confounds their predictions about micro effects. No theory is simply a theory of size: collective (macro) or individual (micro) order can be conceived as operating in radically different ways. In principle individuals can be portrayed as rational and objective or irrational and subjective (and in practice they often are); actors can also be viewed in a more synthetic way (which is rarely the case).

As I have indicated in my earlier work on theoretical logic (Alexander 1982–83, 1984 [chapter 1, above], each of these decisions about action is ramifying in significant and radically different ways. Rationalist assumptions lead to the underplaying of value components and set the stage, when action is considered at a collective level, for the elimination of the voluntaristic element in social order. Nonrational assumptions rescue subjectivity and voluntarism, but they may idealize action and neutralize the impediments that stand in its way. Because neither of these implications is desirable, the first step toward achieving a truly satisfactory general theory of action is to synthesize rationalistic and nonrationalistic modes of theorizing.

The three great micro theories of the postwar period are symbolic interactionism, phenomenology/ethnomethodology, and exchange/rational choice. Each views itself as a sui generis explanation of individual behavior and interaction, as an empirical explanation that covers the entirety of what Parsons called the "unit act." If we examine their presuppositional positions, however, we will see that each theory is no more than a partial description of this primordial micro unit. Such a critical examination, moreover, sets the stage for transforming the concrete empirical emphases of each theoretical tradition into analytical dimensions of a more broadly conceived unit act. We can find the theoretical resources for this reconstruction in Parsons' (1937) early description of the unit act, despite the fact that Parsons' own collectivist bias prevented him from ever conceiving of this unit act in a truly micro sociological way. Given that the very use of Parsons' theory demands the recognition of its antiinteractionist thrust, our synthesis of micro theories within this "action" framework will lead us, finally, to a critical discussion of the presuppositions about order itself.

The action frame of reference that Parsons set out in 1937 includes the following elements: effort, means, ends, norms, and conditions. An action is made with reference to two environments: norms (ideal elements) and conditions (material elements). Means and ends, by contrast, are the products of action. What impels this action is effort. Norms and conditions are macro sociological elements, and by far the greater part of Parsons' systematic theory is related to elaborating their nature and interrelation. Ends and means are situationally specific, given that they are produced by individual action in the world. Every end is a compromise between individuals' effort, their objective possibilities, and their normative standards of evaluation; every means represents some aspect of individuals' conditional world that they have succeeded in putting to use according to their objective possibilities and internalized needs. What carves means and ends from conditions and norms is effort, but it is precisely this ineffable individual effort that for Parsons remains an unexamined black box. Effort is the contingent element of action, the consciousness that Sartre (1956), in *Being and Nothingness,* calls the undetermined "pure event." Effort is the motor, the micro process, that drives the combination of the other elements. Because Parsons rarely had much to say about action as effort, he can tell us little about this important part of the story of ends and means, the part that sees them as "microtranslations" (cf. Collins 1981) of norms and conditions. Parsons' analytic differentiation of action still holds, however. It provides the background for a theoretical synthesis of micro sociological theories even while it can tell us little about these theories as such.

Effort is the real object of exchange theory, ethnomethodology, and symbolic interactionism. Each explains one analytic dimension of effort and in so doing contributes one crucial element to our understanding of ends and means. Each contributes, in turn, to the micro explanation of norms and conditions. Exchange theory explains action as instrumentalizing efficiency and offers an account of how, given ends, norms, and conditions, effort produces usable means through the calculation of immediate costs. Phenomenology and ethnomethodology explain action as an order-seeking activity; they suggest how, given means, norms, and conditions, actors employ cognitive processes in open, contingent situations to establish ends that are consistent with, though not exclusively derived from, overarching rules. Interactionism focuses on neither means nor ends but on the utter contingency of individual interpretation itself. Viewing the latter pragmatically as a response to the intentions and activities of other actors in the situation, it further demonstrates how effort is concerted into means and ends.

Synthesizing microtheories with Parsons' unit act, then, exposes the interactional level of social life as systematically related to more macro structure. It makes this level variable in a manner that allows the contingent properties of social structure to be discussed in a systematic way. If Parsons' black box of effort is opened up and each micro theory's exclusivist understanding of action is denied, we are directed toward elements that richly complement macro analysis. Whether parameters or variables, each element can be related to dimensions of collective structure in a way that allows the latter to be seen as products of contingent action without being reducible to it. Exchange theory demonstrates that the material conditions of action are not fixed in some ontological manner outside the acting individual. True, conditions are defined for the purposes of macro analysis as material elements that cannot be changed, but this "cannot," exchange theory demonstrates (when the shift is made to micro analysis), is only the end result of what is in the first instance a contingent, not a determined, event. Actors have a finite amount of time, energy, and knowledge that they can apply to changing their external situation. What they decide cannot be changed (in light of these limitations), they allow a conditional (i.e., purely material and external) status. Environments become "conditional"—they exert a "determinate" force—precisely because they demand so much time and energy if they are to be changed. It is not that a worker *cannot* change his or her class position; the contingent nature of action means that he or she certainly has the freedom to do so. The problem is that the time and energy required to alter the work environment are so demanding that the probabilities of the worker's changing it are very small. In this way the worker's economic environment becomes an "objective" condition.

Ethnomethodology and phenomenology indicate, similarly, that the continuity and inertia of cultural patterns—which is emphasized by one stream of macro analysis—rely on the continued operation of what Husserl (1977 [1931]) called certain "transcendental" features of human consciousness. Culture may be analytically conceived as existing outside any individual mind, but its supraindividual status depends on individual mental features, particularly on the inclination that consciousness has to make each new mental impression part of the horizon of the impressions that preceded it. If this "horizonal" property of consciousness is placed in a situation where it cannot be successful, where the break between incoming impressions is simply too great, then the orderly consistency of culture (its "determinateness") breaks down, as Garfinkel (1963) demonstrated in his famous experiments on trust. Symbolic interactionism has shown, finally, that the response of others to an actor's activity can sometimes change the interpretation an actor gives even to that activity itself. The power of culture and conditions, then, depends on maintaining pragmatic continuities between actors and situations.

To conclude this hermeneutical reconstruction I must now return explicitly to the problem of order. I have shown that micro theories are not simply empirical discussions; to the contrary, they make a priori assumptions about action's relative rationality. I have suggested that only a synthesis of rational and interpretative micro theory gives action its due, and

I have outlined this synthesis by relating each micro theory to a different element of Parsons' unit act. Each theory not only opens up Parsons' black box of effort but also relates the now illuminated contingency to normative or conditional elements of a systemic kind. One clear implication of this exercise is that Parsons' macro theory may be expanded by making variable what it left as parameter—namely, the contingent element of effort. There is another implication of equally great importance. The synthesis of unit act and micro theory demonstrates that the referents of contemporary micro theories are only the fluid or open element in larger, more crystallized units. These micro theories, then, cannot be considered theories of social order in themselves. It would be as absurd to deduce norms and conditions from transcendental consciousness and exchange as the other way around.

Each micro theory we have considered has, however, made precisely this claim. In the hands of Homans, Garfinkel, and Blumer, each has been proposed as an empirical theory of society as such. I have argued, to the contrary, that the theoretical reconsideration of these claims makes it clear that the processes these theorists posit must be combined with the exposition by the great macro traditions of collective material and ideal forms. Conflict theory and Marxism describe the allocation of conditional elements that are "declared determinate" by exchange. Cultural studies— hermeneutical, structural, Durkheimian, or Weberian—describe the integrated normative traditions from which "horizonality" and interpretation are constructed and which crystallize it in turn. This, I propose, is precisely what Parsons intended when, in his middle-period work, he made allocation and integration the central macro processes of his social system theory, whereas means, ends, and effort remained the contingent elements in his conception of the unit act (see Alexander 1987).

This concludes my hermeneutical reconstruction of the micro-macro link. In the remainder of this chapter I suggest that this interpretative reconstruction implies a systematic model of action and order as empirical processes, processes in which contingency plays a different role according to specific historical and institutional conditions.

A Micro Empirical Model of Action

In searching for a general term to describe the openness of individual action, such theorists as Giddens (1976) and Gouldner (1970), drawing on Garfinkel, developed the concept "reflexivity." Although it is certainly important to talk in general terms about the quality of action in the free space of contingency, I find this concept not only too general and opaque but also redolent of polemical traditions that imply one-sided commitments. Reflexivity is too Sartrean, both in its cognitive emphasis on self-consciousness and in its positive valuation of the individual's separateness—even alienation—from the world. It may also be too idealist, in the sense that it poses a tension between reflexivity and external material conditions, whereas, in my view at least, any general characterization of action must include the sources of conditional behavior within the process of contingency itself.

What might be a more complex way of conceptualizing the basic components of contingent action—the negotiation with the reality that Sartre (1956) calls "consciousness as pure event"—while maintaining a commitment to this generalized mode? I conceive of action as moving along two basic dimensions: interpretation and strategization. Action is understanding, but it is also simultaneously practical and utilitarian. These two dimensions of action should be conceived as analytic elements within the stream of empirical consciousness. They do not represent different kinds of action, nor do they represent different emphases within a single line of action at different points in time. Every action is both interpretation and strategization; each process ensues at every moment in time.

Interpretation itself consists of two different processes: typification and invention. By the former I invoke the phenomenological insight that all actors take their understanding of the world for granted.* They do so because they fully expect that every new impression will be "typical" of the understanding of the world they have already developed. This "typicality" does not operate merely at the gross level of tradition. Even if we encounter something new and exciting we expect this newness and excitement to be understandable: it will be known by us within the terms of reference we already possess. We cannot separate ourselves—except in the fantasy of psychotic experience—from our classification system. The

---

*The notion that perception—which for all practical purposes in the phenomenological tradition is action—involves a process of typification derived most directly from Schutz's (1967:139–214) recasting of Weber's "ideal-type" method in phenomenological form. This recasting goes far beyond anything Weber envisioned, the considerable deepening being due, I believe, to the real intention of Schutz, which is to use Weber to make Husserl's theory more social. Typification, then, can be traced back to the "intentionality" and "constitutive practices" Husserl noted (1977 [1931]); it is also related to the "indexicality" discussed by Garfinkel (1963, 1967).

most modern mind therefore is no different from the savage one exalted by Lévi-Strauss (1966), for like the "native" in a premechanical civilization, we are forever—irredeemably, with or without consciousness and intention—turning all that is new into all that is old.

Socialization means learning to typify within the framework provided by one's particular world. Every member of the collectivity must learn to explain, to name, to discover the typical terms of every possible situation. The most basic rule for acquiring sociological citizenship is "no surprises," and typification is the characteristic of consciousness upon which such inclusion depends. Similarly, typification is the hinge upon which later, more particular entries into group life depend, entries that can be seen as secondary socializations. You are a surgeon when you typify the world surgically, a woman or man when you can typify in the appropriately gendered way, and so forth. To be socialized into a world is to take your understanding of it for granted, and to live in that world is to document every new object as evidence for this ontological certainty.

Typification, finally, is part of interactional process, not merely a quality within individual consciousness. When we interact with our children we are teaching them what to typify, although we make the assumption that they already know how to do it. Communication between adult persons is not simply aimed at rational consensus, nor is it simply a process of rewarding or sanctioning; it is a deeply hermeneutical process of understanding that proceeds through gestures that typify a tiny selection of ongoing experience, gestures through which we seek to exact from others the same typifications we apply to them in the course of communication.

As this last consideration implies, however, interpretation involves more than the reproduction of an internalized classification scheme. True, even a structuralist like Lévi-Strauss (1966:161–90) has acknowledged that reproduction involves not simply universalization (putting the small into the large—what I have called typification) but also particularization (putting the large into the small). Still, it is reproduction as such that needs amending. The reality our contingency confronts is not quite the same as anything we have encountered before. We are convinced that it is just one more example of the past, but it can never be that alone. Because it is always new and because each successive representation of reality must, indeed, bring past generalization into contact with new object, there is always something different, something invented, in each successive conceptualization of reality. If we could, by the very act of our consciousness, transform reality so that it would be no more than what we have known, then understanding would involve typification alone. Reality is resistant, however. To make it typical is a creative act and not merely a reproductive, typifying act, for we are usually (unconsciously) finding ways of understanding in a slightly new key. Typification actually camouflages shifts in classification. These shifts are what invention is all about. Only because invention is hidden within phenomenological conformity can culture be so plastic and individual action proceed in such an extraordinarily fluid way.

It was, I believe, to just this inventive element that Durkheim (1974 [1898]) referred when he defined representation as composed not only of an "externalization" of prior symbolic expectation but also of an "internalization" of the newly encountered objects themselves. It was also what he referred to when he (1965 [1911]:217, 243) insisted on the transforming role "religious imagination" plays within every ritual process. Dilthey (1976 [1910]) implied invention when he stressed the ultimate incomprehensibility of individuals to one another. One tries to make the other's gestures typical, but the irredeemable separateness of human beings ensures that others' gestures retain an element of mystery. This mystery is created by others' invention, and it stimulates ours in turn, for if we can only guess at what "something other" really means we must create some partially new categories of understanding (cf. Maffesoli 1979:75–91). Interpretation is certainly, therefore, a way of reducing the complexity of the world, as Luhmann (1980) suggests, but the understanding of typification and invention presented here makes them far more active existential interventions than his concept seems to imply.

There is still another major dimension of human consciousness, one that eludes the idealist framework altogether and sets contingent action on a much more "complexifying" course. This is strategization. Action is not merely understanding the world, it is also transforming and acting upon it. Actors seek to carry out their intentions through praxis (Marx 1965 [1845]), and for this reason they must act with and against other people and things. Such practical action certainly occurs only within the confines of understanding, but within the terms of clearly understood events it introduces the strategic considerations of least cost and most reward. To act against the world requires time, energy, and knowledge. One cannot expend time and energy indefinitely; every expenditure in one direction is a loss in another. We seek the shortest path to our goal, for this will be the least costly in terms of time; but if the shortest path is not really the straightest line, if the objects in our path are piled up or much larger than expected, this time saving may be too costly in terms of energy. Time and energy, then, must be allocated according to least expense.

Every strategic calculation, moreover, involves relevant knowledge. Keynes has shown that knowledge of our environment and the consequences of our action are hardly "perfect" in the classical economists' sense. In his *Treatise on Probability* (1973 [1921]), he demonstrated that every strategic and economizing action depends on calculations about probable consequences, calculations that in turn depend upon our knowledge of the future. This knowledge can only be very sketchy, however; there is simply too much contingency (nothingness in Sartre's sense) to make any safe bets. People cannot know the future, even if they pretend that they are confident about it. Probability, then, cannot be calculated in a mathematical way; it is an empirical proposition dependent on partial and fragmented knowledge. Keynes translated these insights into his book, *The General Theory of Employment, Interest and Money* (1965 [1936]):135–64, 194–209), by suggesting that if calculations about profit (time and energy in my terms) depend on limited future knowledge, then inevitably introduced into investment decisions are subjective elements relating to confidence and trust. The "state of long-term expectations" influences investment. This puts rational calculation into a relationship with "irrational" understanding.

Strategization, then, comes back to interpretation. To the degree that we assume that the future will be like the past, we may calculate a given cost-benefit ratio as profitable, but if we sense that the future may be disjunctive, then the same profit will seem too low to proceed. Understanding not only provides the environment for strategization; it profoundly affects the calculation of strategic interest itself. One must immediately add, however, that this interactive effect works both ways: to some degree interpretation is itself a strategic phenomenon. We do not try to "understand" every impression that enters our consciousness. Considerations of nearness and farness, time, energy, and the extent of possible knowledge all come forcefully into play. They push typification and invention in this direction or that. What is understood, moreover, will not be equally valued. Our ranking of conceived impressions, I believe, is partly affected by which will be easier to act upon—that is, which segment of reality is more likely to be institutionalized in the future environments of contingent acts.

I have now presented a model—schematic as it must remain at this point—of action in the empirical sense of individual activity. This meets half the obligation I incurred in my hermeneutical reconstruction of the micro/macro debate, for the model seeks to describe the nature of action *qua* action (action in its contingent mode) that was left as a black box by Parsons and filled polemically by his individualist critics. The obligation that remains concerns what micro elements order this individual action. From the model I have presented, as from my earlier discussion of the diverse orientations of current microtheorizing, it is clear that the very description of contingent action implies the noncontingent environments within which it occurs. To understand contingency is to understand that it must be oriented to constraint, and to understand the dimensions of contingency is to understand the variation within such constraining environments. The collective environments of action simultaneously inspire and confine it. If I have conceptualized action correctly, these environments will be seen as its products; if I can conceptualize the environments correctly, action will be seen as their result.

A Micro Empirical Model of Order

To produce a model of these environments I turn once again to Parsons. I will reconstitute what I regard as his most important contribution: the three-system model of personality, society, and culture through which he reconceptualized the legacies of Weber, Durkheim, and Freud in "functional" terms. It is necessary, however, not simply to appropriate this vital distinction (which most of contemporary social science still has not done). One must also, given the theoretical resources now at hand, seek to develop it in more sophisticated ways than Parsons was able to do himself. I start, moreover, from a position Parsons did not share. I do not conceive this three-system model as a substitute for conceptualizing action in itself. Concrete action cannot be analytically broken down into these three systematic elements. These systems, rather, enter action as its more or less ordered environments. This very departure, of course, allows us to conceive systemic order in a micro way. Only by conceptualizing contingent action explicitly can we learn how to present the systems of collective order as real environments.

The social system constitutes one major environment for action by providing actors with real objects. These can be physical or natural objects such as forests, fences, automobiles, and horses, which, because of their location in society, attain much more than purely nonhuman status. More often, or at least more significantly, these objects are human beings. The division of labor and institutions of political authority provide crucial settings for individual interpretation and strategization. The division of labor results from the historically specific mode of allocating and distributing personnel, whereas the authority system is derived from the intersection of this allocative system with social control and integration. My concern here, however, is not with the macroscopic question of how these systems function in their own right but with their impact on action. Surgical residents in a university teaching hospital, for example, must typify, strategize, and invent within the confining limits of the authority and power of the staff surgeon directing their rotation (see Bosk 1979). Power, authority, and control are allocated to this staff director, not to the residents. The director sets the standards that residents seek to typify in their patient conversations and surgical interventions; it is through the director and the facilities he or she controls that energy, time, and knowledge are distributed in such a way that the resident's strategizing will be more costly if it steps outside established medical and neophyte roles. Conversely, the same division of labor and authority makes the resident fairly inconsequential to the action of the staff surgeon in turn. The resident does not set significant standards for the staff surgeon's interpretative procedures, nor does he or she exercise significant control over the surgeon's costs and rewards. The residents stand, of course, as superordinates in relation to others. Surgical nurses and hospital orderlies do not significantly affect the residents' interpretative procedures, nor are they important objects for their strategic consideration.

Solidarity is another significant dimension through which the social system exercises its environing effects. Those with whom we stand in some community significantly affect our action. This community may be conceived both quantitatively, in terms of the number of its constituents, and qualitatively, in terms of the nature of the bonds that unite them. As Simmel (1955), Blau (1977), and modern-day conversation analysts (e.g., Sacks et al. 1974) have shown, we strategize and possibly even interpret differently depending on the size of the group with which we are interacting and according to whether the members in this group are defined consensually or conflictually. Similarly, whereas primordial ties lead the costs of conflicts to be calculated in one direction, civil and impersonal ties allow social objects to enter strategic thinking about the consequences of action in quite another (Alexander 1980 [Chapter 3, above]). Typification in a caste society extends the horizon of action in a persistently hierarchical way; cultural reproduction in a more egalitarian society leads, by contrast, to the extension of citizenship, to the reproduction of the salutation *citoyen*. Invention, too, is fundamentally affected by the experienced definitions of community that the social system provides (see Prager 1985).

In a relatively differentiated and fluid society, of course, actors can never be members of every solidary group at once. Even while they remain members of the national societal community, they move in and out of smaller communities whose boundaries are amorphous and in the end only interactionally defined. Changing community membership, however, means more than being "in" or "out." Actors rarely join a community with their whole selves; only certain parts of their character are engaged. Here is where Goffman's micro sociology comes into play, for he supplied a transformational grammar, a set of rules for the transformation from individual to group status. Goffman describes the action processes that link the individual to solidary groups. He views strategization as omnipresent (1959). Actors make decisions about the costs of presenting different parts of themselves in open interaction; they also strategize simply about making themselves available as objects for others. Doing some things "backstage" and others "frontstage" makes certain individual actions rather than others available for interpretation and calculation. Rules about face-to-face interaction in public places—for example, understanding that direct eye contact implies (even a fleeting) familiarity (Goffman 1963)—direct typification in a manner that defines group membership. This status, in turn, has enormous strategic consequences.

Finally, one must not forget that the position of human elements in social systems must actually be understood in terms of social roles. Social objects take their position in the division of labor and the authority structure through the roles defined by that system. Roles are defined by complexes of sanctions and normative guidelines. Action orients itself to social system exigencies, then, by relating itself not simply to real objects but to objects as they participate in their social role, to sanction systems and specific norms. Both components of roles—norms and sanctions—alert typification, inspire strategization, and produce invention. Goode (1960) has demonstrated that role performance involves an elaborate micro accounting of social costs, for the complexity of institutional life makes it virtually impossible to fulfill the full complement of the roles in which one participates. The role strain that results from this situation is one of the most important triggers for strategization, and for typification and invention as well. Goode demonstrated that role performance is allocated according to implicit economic calculations about the cost, reward, and price of role compliance and evasion.

Other environments for action are not, however, so "real." Actors do not encounter the objects of social systems simply as external objects, even as objects that are normatively defined. They encounter those objects from within, as the referents of symbol systems, which means, for all practical purposes, as symbols themselves.* Symbols are signs that have a generalized status, that provide categories for understanding the elements of social, individual, and organic life. This understanding is the "meaning of life." Although symbols take as referents the elements of other systems—the interactional objects of society, the cathected objects of unconscious life, the natural objects of the physical/organic world— they define and interrelate these elements in an arbitrary manner (that is, in a manner that cannot be deduced from specific exigencies at other system levels). These symbols, in other words, form a system of their own. This cultural system (Geertz 1973) has an independent internal organization whose principles of functioning have only recently begun to be explored.[1] This cultural functioning inspires and constrains interpretative action and strategization in complex ways.

Cultural systems are continually involved in two fundamental processes: constructing reality and evaluating it. Constructing reality can be understood in structural and semiotic terms. It involves naming, corresponding, and analogizing, each of which rests upon typification and invention (Lévi-Strauss 1966:172–216; Sahlins 1976:170–71; Leach 1976; Barthes 1967). Every object in the world is symbolized through its name.

---

*This notion that all social objects are seen "from within"—indeed, the very phrase itself—is Garfinkel's, from the path-breaking early essay on trust (1963), which introduced a phenomenological lining to Parsons' theory of internalization (see Alexander 1985b). That the same phrase can be used to describe not only action but also one of its environments indicates what I earlier called the "principle of homology," that is, the necessity for the theory of environments and the theory of action to be complementary.

At the some point every name is invented, it is new. Names are chosen because the new object is conceived as corresponding to some previous existing one—it seems "typical." Once a new object is symbolized, moreover, correspondence becomes quite intricate and complex. If I may illustrate this by drawing from some research I am doing on the Watergate crisis in the United States, the break-in to the Watergate Hotel in Washington, D.C., had first to be named (invented as) "Watergate" before "Watergate" could be called a crime (a typifying correspondence). This crime, in turn, was classified as either a third-rate burglary or the crime of the century (secondary correspondence and the beginning of analogy). The intricate web that cultures spin between binary correspondences is powered by analogy, a general term that covers diverse forms of theoretical comparison.* In the course of the Watergate crisis, for example, there developed an analogy between two correspondences: Watergate is to Gordon Liddy as cover-up is to Richard Nixon. Cultural analogies eventually become extraordinarily complex, for their purpose is to relate each different plane of reality—nature, physical world, social world, moral world—to every other so that the actor senses the existence of a meaningful whole. See, for example, the cross-plane analogies implied by the following semantic equation developed during the Watergate crisis: Watergate = river = flood = dirty water = darkness = sin = pollution = Republican party = Nixon presidency. Whether the referent is an extraordinary public event like Watergate or the mundane routines of everyday life, the process of constructing reality through naming, corresponding, and analogizing fundamentally structures typification and invention and, indirectly, strategization. It informs every estimation of the typical and the new and every calculation of cost by providing an "arbitrary" definition of meaning for every encounter with the "reality" of social objects.

Cultural systems do still more than construct reality; they also evaluate it.† Though seamless, reality is not flat. It has centers that hold its mean-

*Again, what I have called the rule of homology is demonstrated by the fact that although this great opponent of historicity and phenomenology, Lévi-Strauss, makes "analogy" basic to the structural analysis of cultural systems, Husserl (1977 [1931]), the great exponent of contingency and individuality, makes "analogizing" fundamental to consciousness. My point is that if either theorist is correct, then both must be. They are identifying different yet interdependent levels of reality.

†Here I am moving back from a structuralist interest in classification to the earlier Durkheimian interest in the emotional charge attached to symbols and their moral meaning.

ingful order in place. These centers (Shils 1975) are the fulcrums of reality's various wholes. They mark its points of sacredness, points that are always strongly positively valued, sometimes awesomely so. In this sense, I believe, modern man is as archaic as Eliade's *homo religioso* (1959); he, too, orients himself to meaning by finding out how he stands in relation to the center of his world, the point that marks the origins of the existential order upon which, he feels, his very being depends. Typifying action often means reproducing one's relation to the sacred center, and invention is often a way of finding either a new relation to it or a new version of the center itself. Every strategic estimation of cost must, of course, take into account the distance between actors and centers.

The names, correspondences, and analogies that create symbolic reality are, then, differentially valued. Alongside the elements that are sacred, moreover, stand not only the world of routine but also the highly charged negative world of the profane (Caillois 1959 [1939]). Symbolic systems are more than cognitive classifications: they are emotional and moral mappings of good and bad.* These fiercely antagonist worlds are privileged sources for analogies in their own right, but they are usually taken one step further than analogy into the realm of myth itself. Myth (Ricoeur 1969) elaborates valued antitheses by putting them into narrative form. This narration allows the central symbols of culture to become persuasive models for social life, for within every human being there is a fundamental commitment to typifying meaningful experience in a chronological, dramatic form. Invention can create new stories and even new genres, but it can never erase the narrative form itself.

What I have described so far refers to symbol systems in themselves. Although signifiers in such systems all have noncultural referents, the meanings that are constructed from their arrangement—the codes they present—remain at one remove from the institutional processes of social life. They tell us the meaning of the elements of social systems, and they provide through their valuation the crucial references upon which economic, political, and integrative processes build. They do not, however, enter into the social system as socially embodied causal forces in their own right. One product of the cultural system does so; this is the element I will call "values." Values are produced (Parsons and Shils 1951) by the

---

*Caillois was the first theorist to notice the ambiguous definition of "profane" in Durkheim's work and to argue, in Durkheimian terms, for a theory of profane as evil. Again, it is necessary to separate such discussions from those of cognitive classification.

mediated encounter of social system relationships with symbolic worlds, the result of which is the differential valuation of specific social processes. By upholding capitalism or socialism, values (by directing typification, inspiring invention, or informing strategization) help to structure specific economic systems. By promoting equality or inequality, they affect stratification. By championing democracy or authority, values refer directly to crucial issues in political systems. By promoting inclusion or exclusion, they help create different societal communities; through asceticism or mysticism, they help effect different religious ones. Parsons' discussion of the "pattern variables" is an abstract, systematic delineation of values relating to the individual choice of, and commitment to, the objects with which one interacts. People may look at objects in terms of their universal or particular qualities and value them for their achieved or ascribed qualities. In defining their commitments to these objects people may value more direct affectivity or more neutral, and they will act toward these objects in a more diffuse or specific manner.

No matter what their proximity to the social system, classification, sacralization, and valuation embody what might be called the "statics" of cultural life. There is also a distinctive class of cultural processes that take a dynamic form. Through them the equilibrium problems of social systems become symbolically reconstructed. Conflicts inside social systems are culturally translated (typified) as threats to the sacred symbols of the center, threats that emanate from the powers of the symbolically profane. Social system threats, in other words, are often seen as polluting (Douglas 1966), for the profane, as cultural disorder or symbols "out of place," soils the purity and cleanliness of the sacred. Social disorder brings tabooed symbols into contact with symbols that are normally protected by the space that surrounds sacred things. This causal sequence can move in the other directions as well, from the threat of cultural pollution to social system disorder.

Pollution and purification, then, are endemically cultural components of social life, and if the threat of pollution is great enough, these purifying processes will take on a ritual form. If social processes threaten to undermine meaningful order, they must be separated from social structure and placed in a marginal or liminal position (Turner 1969). In this liminal form their meaning can be worked through in the simplified, stereotyped, traditionalized manner that is ritual process. Rituals generalize from the specificity of social structure; they shift the conscious attention of actors to the components of meaning itself, to the classifications and valorizations upon which the existence of culture depends. Rituals are not, however, simply typifications of cultural antinomies in a highly charged form; they are inventive processes that create new versions of old forms and sometimes even new forms themselves. This invention is, of course, all in the service of preserving "central" cultural concerns and proceeds under the wary eye of strategic calculations about the costs and benefits of invention and reinstitutionalization.

I have argued that interpretation and strategization are oriented toward external objects representing economic facilities, political authority, and ecological/solidary ties. These social system elements establish constraints and normative guidelines for typification; define the circumstances and allocate the resources for invention; and distribute time, energy, and knowledge in ways that set the costs for strategic behavior. These objects or, more accurately, the exigencies they represent, are encountered from within as symbols, as units in the complex representational systems that define reality, distribute the sacred and profane, and establish the universe of potentially institutionalized social values. This symbolic system introduces the arbitrary into the meaning of social objects: every object is simultaneously cultural form and social fact. Because social objects must be named, not just dominated or deferred to, typification and invention proceed not only within limits established by power and rules but also within the grid of cultural classification. Strategization affects action at both levels. It enters interpretation through the back door, so to speak, by making certain relationships more costly; it enters social interaction through the front by translating system exigencies into considerations of time, energy, and knowledge.

Social forms are not the only objects with which action deals, nor is culture its only reference from within. Actors have personalities. Indeed, more than either of the other two system references, actors "are" personalities, their action proceeding entirely within the confines of this system alone. Yet personalities, in turn, represent a selection of objects introjected from social encounters, a selection dictated by the play of organic and developmental needs. Each acting "I" and his or her personality, moreover, changes decisively at different stages in his or her own life. Personalities supply differential capacities for interpretation and strategization. The actor qua social object rewards and sanctions; the actor qua personality cathects and rejects. The object cathexes, or affective charges, that emanate from the personality are guided by interpretation of and strategizing about the potential responsiveness of the social objects and the meaning they have. "Mother," for a young man, is a complexly defined cultural symbol, a role performer with effective sanctions and rewards, and also a cathected object representing opportunities for security, dependence, sexual fulfillment, and guilt.

Emotional demands and the shifting demands of organic life articulate with changing social objects and cultural grids to produce the complex structures of personality. Not just the superego but also the ego and the id represent unconscious object systems (Weinstein and Platt 1969), distillations from different stages and different modes of social interaction. Together, these objects form the third system with which action must contend. Given the relatively simple unconscious system of a two-year-old child, for example, adult criticism means "bad" and produces tears and conformity. For a four-year-old personality, however, the same criticism—interactionally parallel and symbolically analogous—may mean "unfair" and lead to resistance. At still a later point of development the criticism may not even be heard; the defense mechanisms of the ego allow it to be completely rationalized away.

The active part of the ego responds to the fantasized threats and promises of internalized objects—to the anxieties of object loss and promises of recovery—by constructing defenses (Freud 1936) such as denial, neutralization, projection, and splitting. Because they are systematic distortions of cognition (in the service of unconscious emotional needs), these defenses enter typification as yet another determinant of its specific form. They are one frame of reference for constructing and valorizing reality, but they also provide an affective reference for interpreting symbols that already exist and for calculating the costs and benefits of interaction in society. The cultural need for sacralization and the centering of symbols can valorize reality only if the personality finds gratification in the organization of cathected objects into "good" and "bad." This emotional need develops, according to orthodox theory (Fenichel 1945:279–80, 286), with the anal drive for control and exclusion and, more significantly, with the growth of superego strictures in the first Oedipal phase. It might even be considered to have begun earlier, with the splitting of good and bad breasts that Melanie Klein (1957) believes to be part of the oral stage. Whatever its origins, however, it seems clear that this psychological capacity, which is as necessary for the social system construction of deviance and conformity as it is for cultural classification—must be continued as an "adapting" ego process even if it does not survive in pathological form. Vital social and cultural processes depend on it. Without the psychological inclination for this special kind of organization, action would not have the environmental support to carry it out.

Typification, invention, and strategization, then, are capacities of the personality, not merely modes by which epistemological categories come into play or avenues for social exchange and controla. These capacities change historically. Elias (1978 [1939]) explained how social differentiation creates a "civilizing process" that is at once psychological and social. In the course of modernization, authority becomes more rationalized and specific, whereas the societal community becomes more expansive, impersonal, and inclusive (Alexander 1980). New cultural codes arise that are more ascetic, more universalistic, more committed to world mastery and control. Personalities, too, must change if "civilization" is to occur, however. They must develop the capacity for depersonalization and control, for the repression, neutralization, and splitting upon which modern rationality depends. These affective changes are initiated when traditionally authoritative objects become compromised or withdraw (Weinstein and Platt 1969), but they also occur in more systematic, long-term ways. Childhood becomes elongated (Aries 1962); there is an enormous lengthening of psychosocial training and, with it, a much more jarring transition between the site of early personality development and adult life (Keniston 1960). This simultaneously allows the modern adult personality to be created and the unconscious needs for dependency and immediate fulfillment that remain to be isolated in differentiated, private spheres (Slater 1963).

By a process of affective modernization, then, the personality comes to undergird interpretation and strategization in so-called civilized ways. In this long-term view, equilibrium is assumed. With the uneven development that characterizes real modernization, the independent variable of personality throws a much more problematic element into play. The early emotional experience of German youth immediately following World War I vitally affected the unconscious object systems they brought into the later period of German instability (Loewenberg 1983). As a result, this cohort experienced the same national and international events in more paranoid and unstable ways than Germans in other generations. This emotional experience led them to typify these events in terms of more primordial streams of national culture, to respond to frustration by inventing more aggressive ideologies, to conceive political strategies by a different and more fateful calculation of costs and rewards. Nazism was created by contingent action; it was not the inevitable and determined result of collective forces. The micro arena within which the structures of Nazism were created was not, however, simply an arena of action alone. Action occurs within systemic environments, the organization of unconscious emotional needs not the least among them.

The "Problem of Rationality"

Before concluding I comment on the relevance of the preceding points for the prevailing image of contemporary action as consummately rational and endlessly creative, an image that is vital not only to modern common sense and to important traditions of micro explanation—as typified, for example, by Giddens' (1976) notion of "reflexivity"—but also to various utopian reconstructions of contemporary human capacity. First, I believe that creativity and rationality need not be understood as contravening typifying action or, indeed, the constraints of action's environing systems. Because all action is contingent, typification and strategization make invention continuous. More to the point, social segmentation, which occurs in even the simplest societies, makes invention a fundamental "social need." Segmentation means that institutions are differentiated ecologically. Social objects defined as the same are not physically identical. An individual encounters not "the family," "the father," "the manager" but concrete and segmented versions of the same. This segmentation mediates and makes more inconsistent psychological internalizations, cultural understandings, and the process of sanctioning and rewards. Slightly different objects are constantly thrown up to the acting person. When inconsistency reaches a certain point, strong personalities act to simplify complexity by creative transformations of cultural forms. This "regression in service of the ego" (Krist 1937), however, still does not produce completely new inventions; it appears to the creative person and particularly to his or her appreciative audience in "typical" and strategically possible ways.

What about "rationality" in the modern sense of action carried out according to universalistic, verifiable standards, action that is thereby subject to constant, consciously directed change? This rationality, it seems to me, is not a question of a particular kind of action but of a particular structure of environments. The environments of action can be more or less open, a fact that allows us to conceive a continuum of action stretching from ritual to rationality. Ritual action and rational action both occur within meaningful, experienced worlds, worlds in which typification, cultural order, and "irrational" psychological interests come fully into play.* In ritual, however, the environments of action are relatively closed, structured in ways that are less open to change, whereas in rational action they are relatively open. Rituals are standardized and repeatable sequences of action. They more frequently define action in social situations in which the division of labor is rigid, in which authority for all practical purposes is unchallengeable, in which culture is fused with its social system referents in an anthropomorphic and particularistic way, and in which the personality is cathected to objects through the familial modes of trust, deference, and charismatic domination. In this closed situation standardization follows naturally from interpretation and calculation.

Insofar as the environments of action are less rigid and more complex, depersonalizing capacities develop in the personality and more abstract and generalized classification systems develop in the culture. This separation of the self from its world and the differentiation of the actor's standards of evaluation does not eliminate the noncontingent element of action. Rather, rational action may be conceived as "fixed" above and "open" below. The social objects encountered are more complex and changing; the cultural referents defining them and the personality motivating them are more structured in ways that allow active adaptation and change. Typification is less standardized; strategization is more ramifying; invention is more dramatic. Because action is more rational, specialized institutions of social control are necessary to maintain psychological, social, and interpretative consistency over the life course. New media of exchange, such as money and influence, allow continuous strategic calculation and frequent changes in the direction and lines of action without abandoning the cultural classifications and social role definitions to which typification always returns. The continuum ritual-rationality operates within any given historical system, as I indicated earlier in my analysis of the dynamics of cultural life, but it may also be seen as a

*In what follows I am drawing on the implications of the present chapter to elaborate criticisms I have made of Habermas' recent work (Alexander 1985a).

historical continuum with comparative scope. Medical practice, institutions of mass communications, and political structures and processes, for example, all may be seen as having moved from being embedded in ritual to being more contingent and rational, if we understand this rationality as implying neither utter contingency nor the removal from cultural and emotional controls.

Conclusion

I have argued in this essay against the micro/macro split. There need not be one in sociological theory; there certainly does not seem to be one in empirical reality. Why, then, the great divide in sociological discussion today? Because, I believe, theorists falsely generalize from a single variable to the immediate reconstruction of the whole. They have taken one particular system—the economy, the culture, the personality—as action's total environment; they have taken one action mode—invention, typification, or strategization—as encompassing action in itself. Moreover, by acknowledging only the kind of action presupposed by their conception of collective order, macro theorists have prematurely closed the action-environment circle. Theories of economic systems have reasoned that action is strategic, cultural theorists have stressed typification, social movement theorists the inventive, and so forth. It seems perfectly appropriate that each of these different elements of micro process and macro process can be viewed as the objects of independent scientific disciplines, as they are in the natural and physical sciences. It is unacceptable, however, for any one of these variables and disciplines to be considered privileged in relation to the others. Rather than being thought of as dependent and independent variables, these elements should be conceived as parameters and variables in an interactive system comprising different levels of different "size." This requires, of course, a common conceptual scheme, one the social sciences do not yet possess. The current revival of interest in theorizing about the micro-macro link may make such a conceptual scheme possible, a possibility to which the present, concluding chapter has sought to make a contribution.

NOTES

1. It is precisely for this reason—the underdeveloped state of cultural analysis in the social sciences—that I spend some time analyzing the internal functioning of this environment and do not only consider it in relation to the problem of action, which is the thrust

of my approach with the other environments. Only with a much more nuanced understanding of cultural systems than is currently available can the complex relationship between action and meaningful environment be seen.

This approach to cultural sociology begins, therefore, with the relative autonomy of the cultural system (cf. Alexander 1988a) and asserts that any new understanding of the relation between culture and action must recognize how this system functions in its own right. As the following discussion makes evident, such an assumption leads to an effort to incorporate important elements of extrasociological traditions that focus in a more or less exclusive manner on symbolic logics—e.g., hermeneutics, semiotics, structuralism, symbolic anthropology—rather than simply reject them as idealist. One strand of the recent revival of cultural sociology has supported such a position. Archer, for example, devotes virtually her entire *Culture and Agency* (forthcoming) to establishing the differentiation of culture and social system, and Wuthnow (1984, 1987) insists on the independence of culture as defining the starting point of any cultural sociology. Zelizer (1985) takes the antimony between sacred and profane values as an independent reference point in her discussion of economic life (cf. Buckley 1984, Sewell 1985, and the essays collected in Alexander 1988b).

Others involved in this revival (e.g., Swidler 1986) advocate quite an opposite approach, suggesting that cultural sociology can be revived only if action is given pride of place. Opposing theories that concentrate on the internal relations of symbolic elements and that assume, therefore, the existence of a cultural system, they argue that meaningful *action* should become the focus of analysis. Action is now the principal dynamic force, and culture is reduced to a resource, a "tool kit" whose symbolic supply is so elastic that the limits it imposes become largely irrelevant. The problem with such a position is that it asks us to choose between cultural system and action. I have argued here against the necessity for such a choice. It can be avoided, I have suggested, if an analytic rather than concrete approach to the action-environment relation is taken.

Not surprisingly, the concrete, dichotomizing approach to action and culture is typically justified (again, see Swidler 1986) by constructing a polemic against Parsons' value theory, which, as I have indicated above, overemphasizes the power of values vis-à-vis both material elements and action. As I have demonstrated here, however, recognizing these inadequacies leads neither to a rejection of the analytic, relative autonomy approach nor to the neglect of the control that "values" exert over action. For a detailed empirical study of the significance of values that does not neglect contingent historical activity, see Prager 1985.

REFERENCES

Alexander, Jeffrey C. 1980. "Core Solidarity, Ethnic Outgroup, and Social Differentiation: Towards a Multidimensional Model of Inclusion in Modern Societies." In Jacques Dofny and Akinsola Akiwowo, eds., *National and Ethnic Movements,* pp. 5–28. Beverly Hills and London: Sage.

—— 1982–1983. *Theoretical Logic in Sociology.* Vols. 1–4. Berkeley, Los Angeles, London: University of California Press.

—— 1984. "Structural Analysis in Sociology: Some Notes on Its History and Prospects." *Sociological Quarterly* 25:5–26.

—— 1985a. "Habermas' New Critical Theory: Prospects and Problems." *American Journal of Sociology* 91(2):400–24.

—— 1985b. "The 'Individualist Dilemma' in Phenomenology and Interactionism." In S. N. Eisenstadt and H. J. Helle, eds., *Perspectives on Sociological Theory,* pp. 25–27. Vol. 1. Beverly Hills, Calif.: Sage.

—— 1987. *Twenty Lectures: Sociological Theory Since World War II.* New York: Columbia.

—— 1988a. "Introduction: The Case for the Relative Autonomy of Culture." In Alexander and Seidman, eds., *Culture and Society: Contemporary Debates.* New York: Cambridge University Press.

—— 1988b. *Durkheimian Sociology* (editor). New York: Cambridge University Press.

Archer, Margaret. Forthcoming. *Culture and Agency.* London: Cambridge University Press.

Aries, Phillipe. 1962. *Centuries of Childhood.* New York: Knopf.

Barthes, Roland. 1967. *Elements of Semiology.* New York: Hill and Wang.

Berger, Peter L. and Thomas Luckmann. 1966. *The Social Construction of Reality.* Garden City, N.Y.: Doubleday.

Blau, Peter. 1977. *Inequality and Heterogeneity.* New York: Free Press.

Blumer, Herbert. 1969. *Symbolic Interactionism.* Englewood Cliffs, N.j.: Prentice-Hall.

Bosk, Charles. 1979. *Forgive and Remember: Managing Medical Failure.* Chicago: University of Chicago Press.

Bourdieu, Pierre. 1977. *Outline of a Theory of Practice.* Cambridge: Cambridge University Press.

Buckley, Anthony D. 1984. "Walls Within Walls: Religion and Rough Behaviour in an Ulster Community." *Sociology* 18:19–32.

Caillois, Roger. 1959 (1939). *Man and the Sacred.* New York: Free Press.

Collins, Randall. 1981. "On the Micro-Foundations of Macro-Sociology." *American Journal of Sociology* 86 (March):984–1014.

Dilthey, Wilhelm. 1976. "The Construction of the Historical World in the Human Studies." In H. P. Rickman, ed., *Dilthey: Selected Writings,* pp. 168–245. Cambridge: Cambridge University Press.

Douglas, Mary. 1966. *Purity and Danger.* London: Penguin.

Durkheim, Emile. 1951 (1897). *Suicide.* New York: Free Press.

—— 1965 (1912). *The Elementary Forms of Religious Life.* New York: Free Press.

—— 1974 (1898). "Individual and Collective Representations." In Durkheim, *Sociology and Philosophy.* New York: Free Press.

Eliade, Mircea. 1959. *The Sacred and the Profane.* New York: Harcourt, Brace, and World.

Elias, Norbert. 1978 (1939). *The Civilizing Process.* New York: Urizon Books.

Fenichel, Otto. 1945. *Psychoanalytic Theory of Neurosis.* New York: W. W. Norton.

Freud, Anna. 1936. *The Ego and the Mechanisms of Defense.* Vol. 2. *The Writings of Anna Freud.* New York: International Universities Press.

Garfinkel, Harold. 1963. "A Conception of and Experiments with 'Trust' as a Condition of Concerted Stable Action." In. O. J. Harvey, ed., *Motivation and Social Interaction,* pp. 187–238. New York: Ronald Press.

—— 1967. *Studies in Ethnomethodology*. Englewood Cliffs, N.J.: Prentice-Hall.

Geertz, Clifford. 1973. "Ideology as a Cultural System." In *The Interpretation of Cultures*, pp. 193–233. New York: Basic Books.

Giddens, Anthony. 1976. *New Rules of Sociological Method*. New York: Basic Books.

—— 1979. *Central Problems in Social Theory*. Berkeley and Los Angeles: University of California Press.

Goffman, Erving. 1959. *The Presentation of Self in Everyday Life*. New York: Doubleday.

—— 1963. *Behavior in Public Places*. New York: Free Press.

Goode, William J. 1960. "A Theory of Role Strain." *American Sociological Review* 25:483–96.

Gouldner, Alvin W. 1970. *The Coming Crisis in Western Sociology*. New York: Equinox.

Habermas, Jürgen. 1984. *Reason and the Rationalization of Society*. Vol. I. *Theory of Communicative Action*. Boston: Beacon.

Homans, George C. 1961. *Social Behavior: Its Elementary Forms*. New York: Free Press.

Husserl, Edmund. 1977 (1931). *Cartesian Meditations*. The Hague: Martin Nijhoff.

Keniston, Kenneth. 1960. *The Uncommitted*. New York: Harcourt, Brace, and World.

Keynes, John Maynard. 1965 (1936). *The General Theory of Employment, Interest, and Money*. New York: Harcourt Brace Jovanovich.

—— 1973 (1921). *A Treatise on Probability*. Vol. 8. *The Collected Writings of John Maynard Keynes*. New York: St. Martin's.

Klein, Melanie. 1957. *Envy and Gratitude*. New York: Basic Books.

Krist, Ernst. 1937. "On Inspiration." In *Psychoanalytic Explorations in Art*, pp. 291–302. New York: International Universities Press.

Leach, Edmund. 1976. *Culture and Communication*. Cambridge, England: Cambridge University Press.

Lévi-Strauss, Claude. 1966. *The Savage Mind*. Chicago: University of Chicago Press.

Loewenberg, Peter. 1983. "The Psychohistorical Origins of the Nazi Youth Cohort." In Loewenberg, *Decoding the Past*, pp. 240–83. New York: Alfred A. Knopf.

Luhmann, Niklas. 1980. *Trust and Power*. New York: John Wiley.

Maffesoli, Michel. 1979. *La conquête du présent*. Paris: P.U.F.

Marx, Karl. 1962a (1867). *Capital*. Vol. I. Moscow: International Publishers.

—— 1962b (1852). *The Eighteenth Brumaire of Louis Bonaparte*. In Karl Marx and Frederick Engels, *Selected Works*, pp. 247–344. Vol. 1. Moscow: Internatinal Publishers.

—— 1965 (1845). "Theses on Feuerbach." In Nathan Rotenstreich, ed., *Basic Problems in Marx's Philosophy*. Indianapolis: Bobbs-Merrill.

Parsons, Talcott. 1937. *The Structure of Social Action.* New York: Free Press.
—— 1954. "Certain Primary Sources and Patterns of Aggression in the Social Structure of the Western World." In Parsons, *Essays in Sociological Theory.* New York: Free Press.
Parsons, Talcott and Edward A. Shils. 1951. "Values, Motives, and Systems of Action." In Parson and Shils, eds., *Toward a General Theory of Action.* New York: Harper and Row.
Parsons, Talcott and Gerald N. Platt. 1973. *The American University.* Cambridge, Mass.: Harvard University Press.
Prager, Jeffrey. 1985. *Building Democracy in Ireland: Political Order and Cultural Integration in a New Independent Nation.* New York: Cambridge University Press.
Ricoeur, Paul. 1969. *The Symbolism of Evil.* Boston: Beacon.
Sacks, Harvey, Emmanuel A. Schegloff, and Gail Jefferson. 1974. "A Simplest Systematics for the Organization of Turn-Taking for Conversation." *Language* 50:697–735.
Sahlins, Marshall. 1976. *Culture and Practical Reason.* Chicago: University of Chicago Press.
Sartre, Jean-Paul. 1956. *Being and Nothingness.* New York: Philosophical Library.
—— 1963. *Search for a Method.* New York: Alfred A. Knopf.
—— 1976. *Critique of a Dialectical Reason.* London: New Left Books.
Schutz, Alfred. 1967. *The Phenomenology of the Social World.* Evanson, Ill.: Northwestern University Press.
—— 1978a (1940). "Phenomenology and Sociology." In Thomas Luckmann, ed., *Phenomenology and the Social Sciences.* London: Penguin.
—— 1978b. "Parsons' Theory of Action: A Critical Review by Schutz." In Richard Grathoff, ed., *The Theory of Action: The Correspondence of Alfred Schutz and Talcott Parsons,* pp. 8–70. Bloomington: Indiana University Press.
Sewell, William H., Jr. 1985. "Ideologies and Social Revolutions: Reflections on the French Case." *Journal of Modern History* 57:57–85.
Shils, Edward A. 1975. *Center and Periphery: Essays on Macrosociology.* Chicago: University of Chicago Press.
Simmel, Georg. 1955. *Conflict and the Web of Group Affiliations.* New York: Free Press.
Slater, Philip. 1963. "On Social Regression." *American Sociological Review* 28:339–64.
Swidler, Ann. 1986. "Culture in Action." *American Sociological Review* 5:273–86.
Touraine, Alain. 1977. *The Self-Reproduction of Society.* Chicago: University of Chicago.
Turner, Victor. 1969. *The Ritual Process.* Chicago: Aldine Publishing.
Weber, Max. 1946 (1916). "The Social Psychology of World Religions." In Hans Gerth and C. Wright Mills, eds., *From Max Weber: Essays in Sociology.* New York: Oxford University Press.

—— 1978. *Economy and Society*. Berkeley and Los Angeles: University of California Press.
Weinstein, Fred and Gerald N. Platt. 1969. *The Wish To Be Free*. Berkeley and Los Angeles: University of California Press.
Wuthnow, Robert. 1984. "Introduction." In Wuthnow, James Hunter, Albert Bergesen, and Edith Kurzweil. *Cultural Analysis*. London: Routledge and Kegan Paul.
—— 1987. *Meaning and the Moral Order: Explorations in Cultural Analysis*. Berkeley and Los Angeles: University of California Press.
Zelizer, Viviana. 1985. *Pricing the Priceless Child*. New York: Basic Books.

Index of Names

Subject Index

Action: in Alexander's early work, 290; and consciousness, in Marx, 260–64, 306; in exchange theory, 309; in interactionism, 309; interpretation in, 312; invention in, 314; motivation for, 13; nature of, 223; Parsons' frame of reference for, 308; in phenomenology and ethnomethodology, 309; social system as environment of, 317; strategization in, 314–16; and structure, Parsons on, 2; typification in, 312–14

Ad hocing: and maintenance of culture, 238; and signification, in Garfinkel, 240

Affirmative action: and ethnically conscious inclusion, 96; university commitment to, 185

Alienation, as empirical fact, in Marx, 261–62

Assimilation: defined, 95; and equal opportunity, 95

"Backlash": and Nixon, 166; and reaction against universalism, 163

Behaviorism, as rational action approach, 267

Bentham, Jeremy, utilitarianism of, 18

Bureaucracy: and differentiation, 49–50; as coercive structure, in Weber, 19–20

Capitalism: debates about: by critical theorists, 21–22; by Marxists, 21; by structuralists, 21–22; democratic participation in, 22; as external environment, in Marx, 19

Center-periphery theory, of Shils, in Eisenstadt, 198

Civic Republican tradition, American concensus on, 170–71

Civic ritualization, and affirmation of solidary bonds, 82*

Civil solidarity: in America, 87–88; and Christian Church, 81; and differentiation, 82; and economic development, 81; and inclusion, 80–85; uneven development of, 83

Civil ties, and inclusion, 80

Class analysis, problems with, 35–36

Cleavage, between subsystems, 139

Codes, Eisenstadt's study of, 204, 217

Cognitive rationality, in technological specialization, 177

Collective behavior: contingency in, 206; and natural history, 205; and public dialogue, 211; relation to neofunctionalism, 206

Collective order: instrumental-objective form of, 270; interpretive subjective form of, 270; as "uniformities of action," in Weber, 272

Colonialism: of England, 92–93; as polar opposite of inclusion, 92; of South Africa, 93–94

Conflation: definition of, 154*; of the term specification, 154

Consciousness: "constitutive techniques" of, in Husserl, 230–32; "transcendental features" of, in Husserl, 310

Contingency: absence of, in Parsons, 281; lack of, in structuralism, 37; in phenomenology and interactionism, 254; in Sartre, 304